HANAKO 花子
AND THE TERROR OF ALLEGORY

VOLUME 2

BY SAKAE ESUNO

TOKYOPOP®

HAMBURG // LONDON // LOS ANGELES // TOKYO

Hanako and the Terror of Allegory 2
Created by Sakae Esuno

Translation - Satsuki Yamashita
English Adaptation - Bryce P. Coleman
Copy Editor - Sarah Kniss
Retouch and Lettering - Star Print Brokers
Production Artist - Rui Kyo
Graphic Designer - Al-Insan Lashley

Editor - Cindy Suzuki
Print Production Manager - Lucas Rivera
Managing Editor - Vy Nguyen
Senior Designer - Louis Csontos
Art Director - Al-Insan Lashley
Director of Sales and Manufacturing - Allyson De Simone
Associate Publisher - Marco F. Pavia
President and C.O.O. - John Parker
C.E.O. and Chief Creative Officer - Stu Levy

A  Manga

TOKYOPOP Inc.
5900 Wilshire Blvd. Suite 2000
Los Angeles, CA 90036

E-mail: info@TOKYOPOP.com
Come visit us online at www.TOKYOPOP.com

HANAKO TO GUUWA NO TELLER Volume 2
© Sakae ESUNO 2005
First published in Japan in 2005 by KADOKAWA
SHOTEN PUBLISHING CO., LTD., Tokyo.
English translation rights arranged with KADOKAWA
SHOTEN PUBLISHING CO., LTD., Tokyo
through TUTTLE–MORI AGENCY, INC., Tokyo.
English text copyright © 2010 TOKYOPOP Inc.

ISBN: 978-1-4278-1609-2

First TOKYOPOP printing: August 2010
10 9 8 7 6 5 4 3 2 1
Printed in the USA

Folklore; The Demon in the Mirror

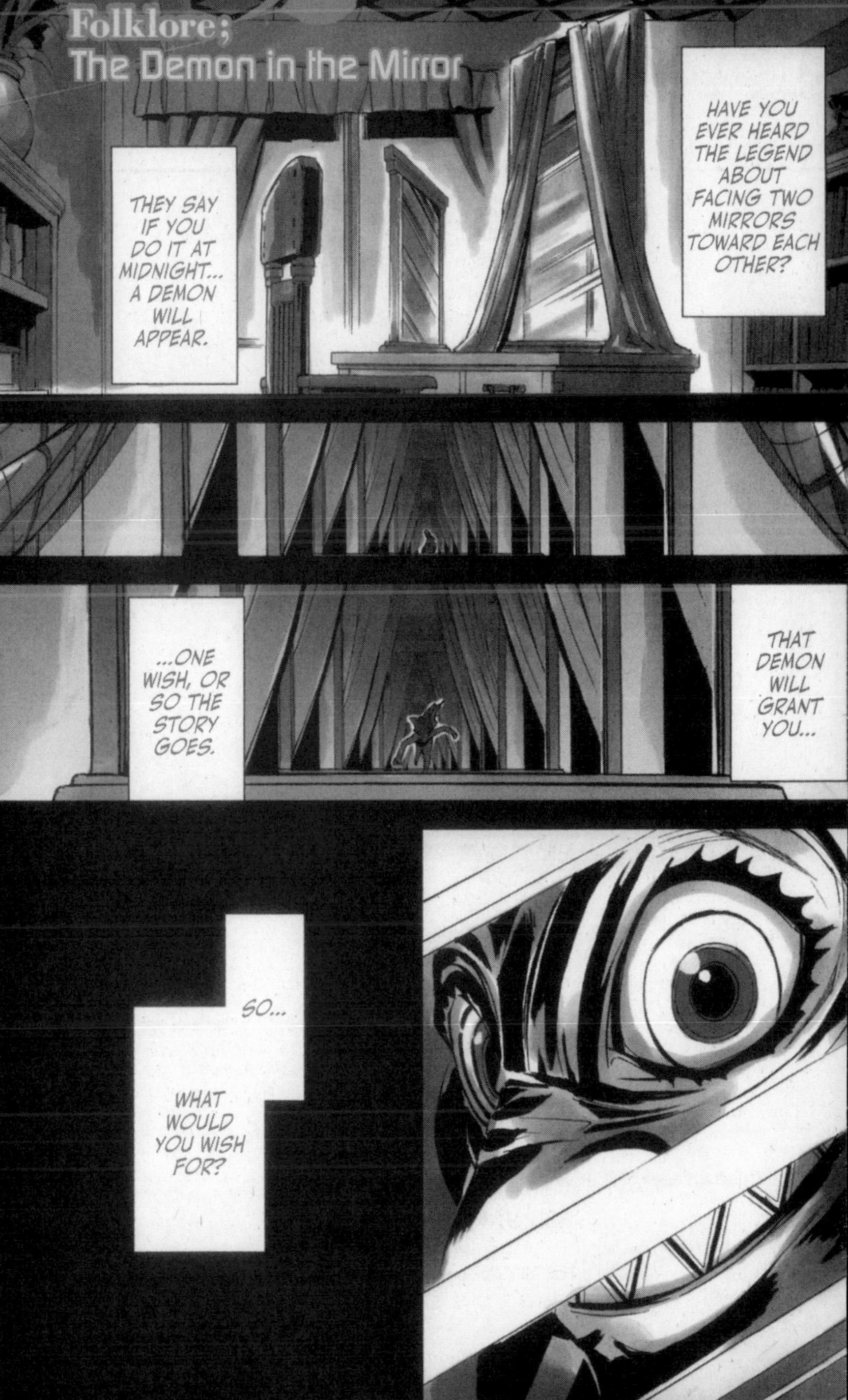
HAVE YOU EVER HEARD THE LEGEND ABOUT FACING TWO MIRRORS TOWARD EACH OTHER?
THEY SAY IF YOU DO IT AT MIDNIGHT... A DEMON WILL APPEAR.
THAT DEMON WILL GRANT YOU...
...ONE WISH, OR SO THE STORY GOES.
SO...
WHAT WOULD YOU WISH FOR?

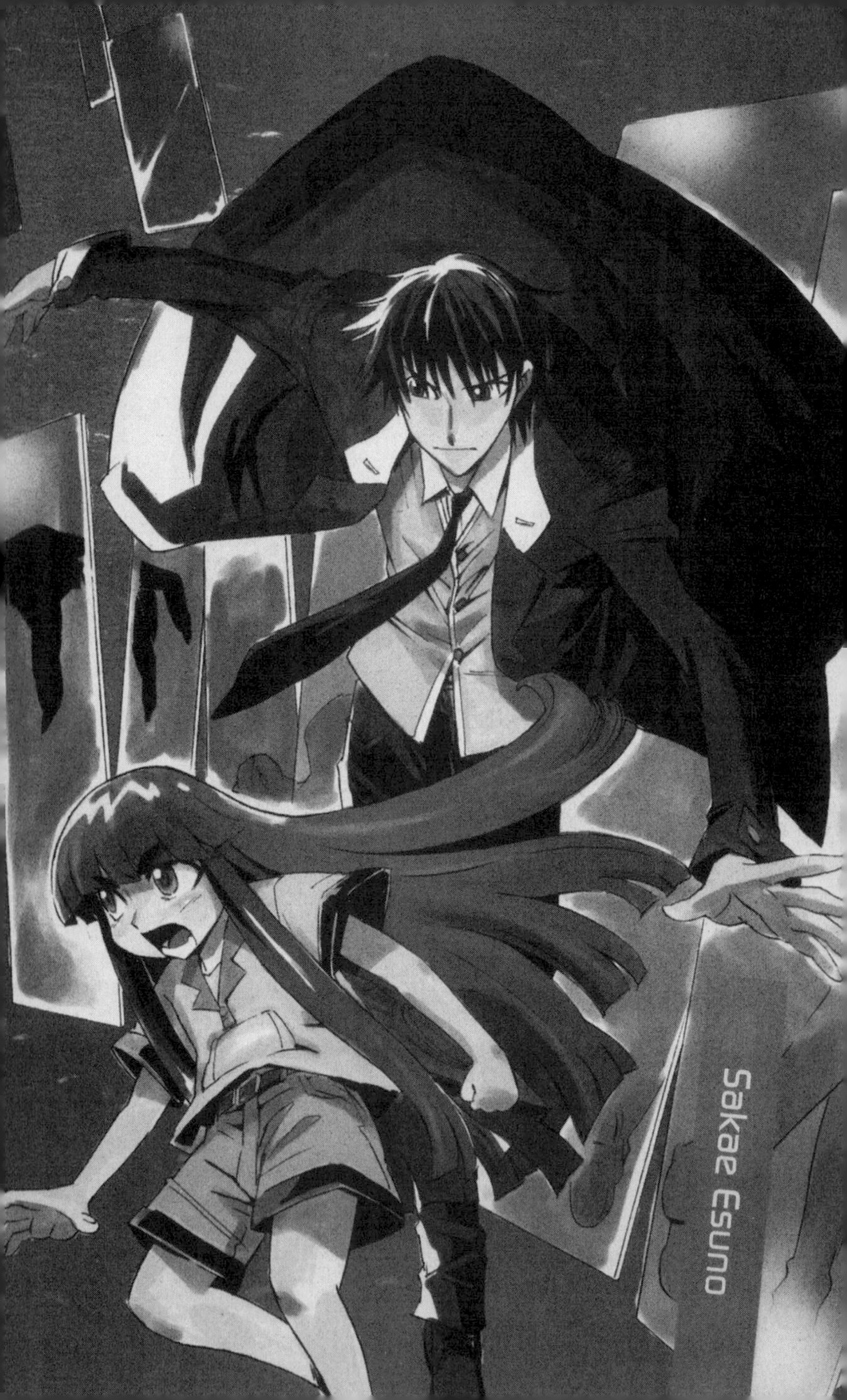
Sakae Esuno

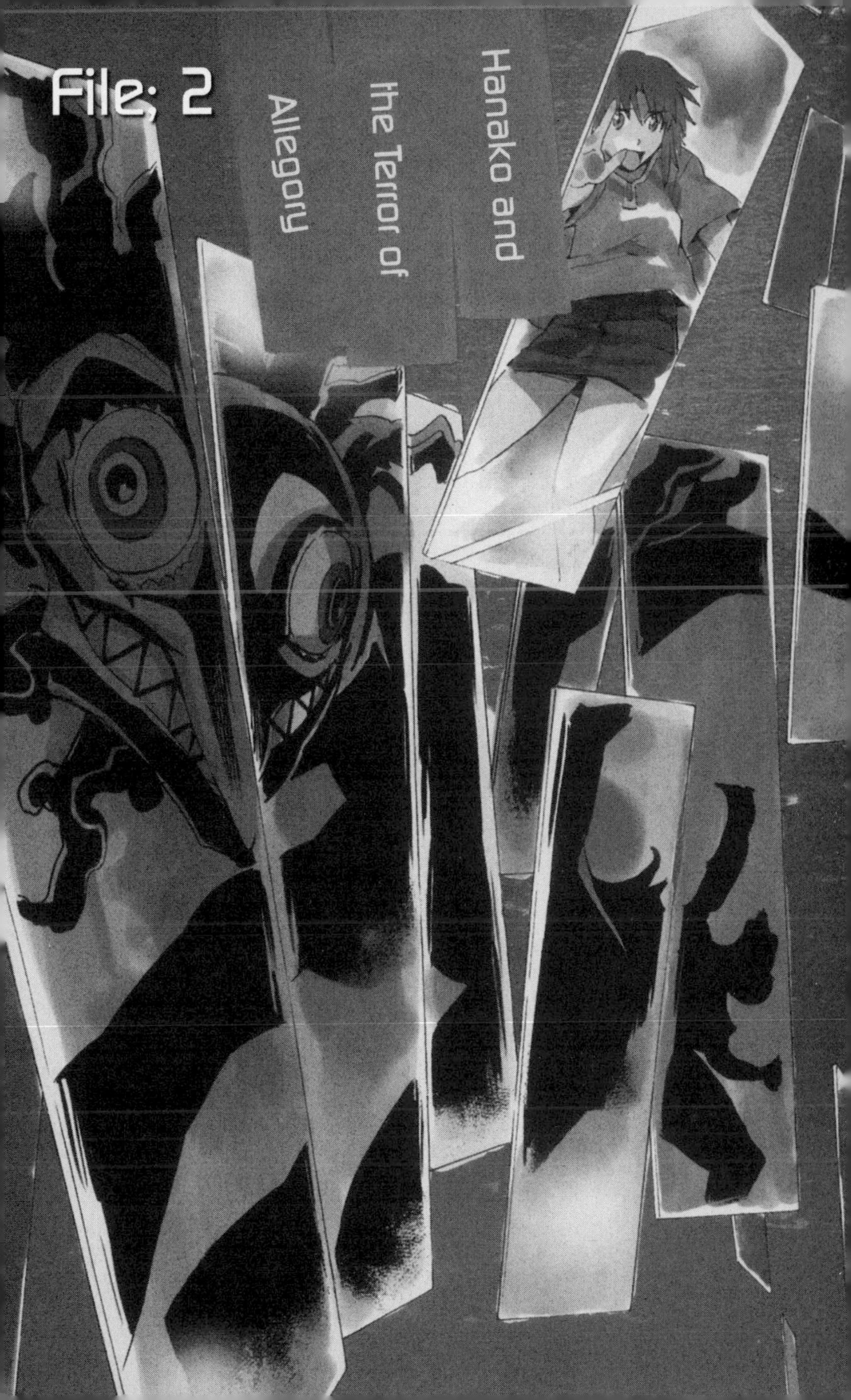
File; 2
Hanako and the Terror of Allegory

Hanako and the Terror of Allegory

File; 2

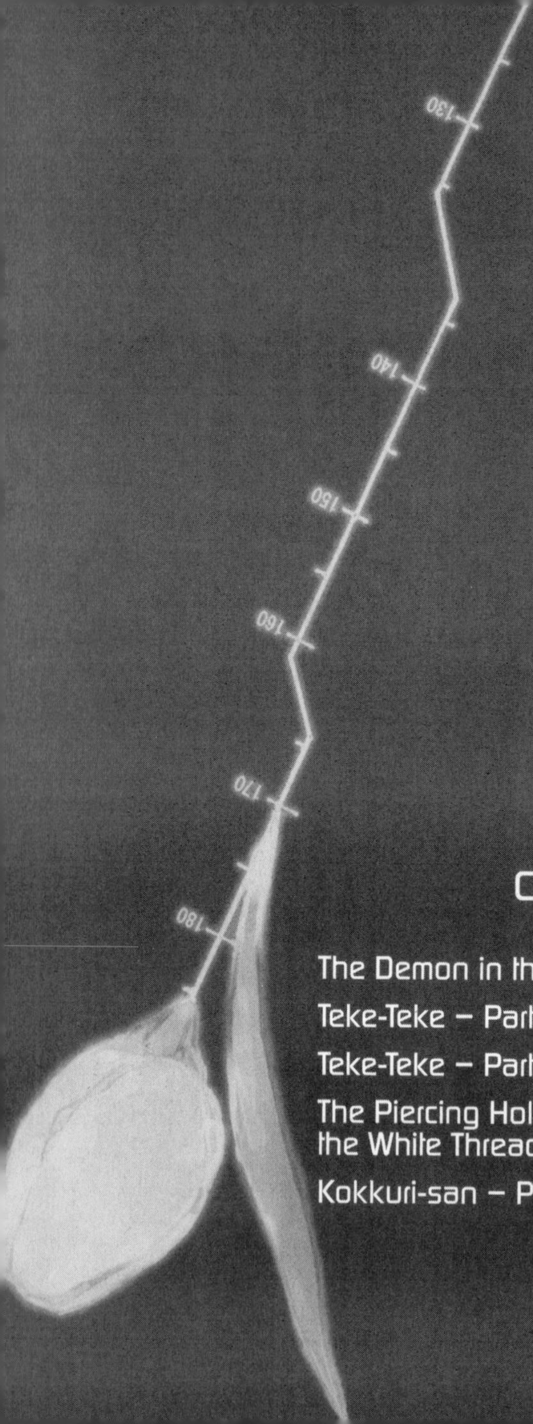
130
140
150
160
170
180

Contents

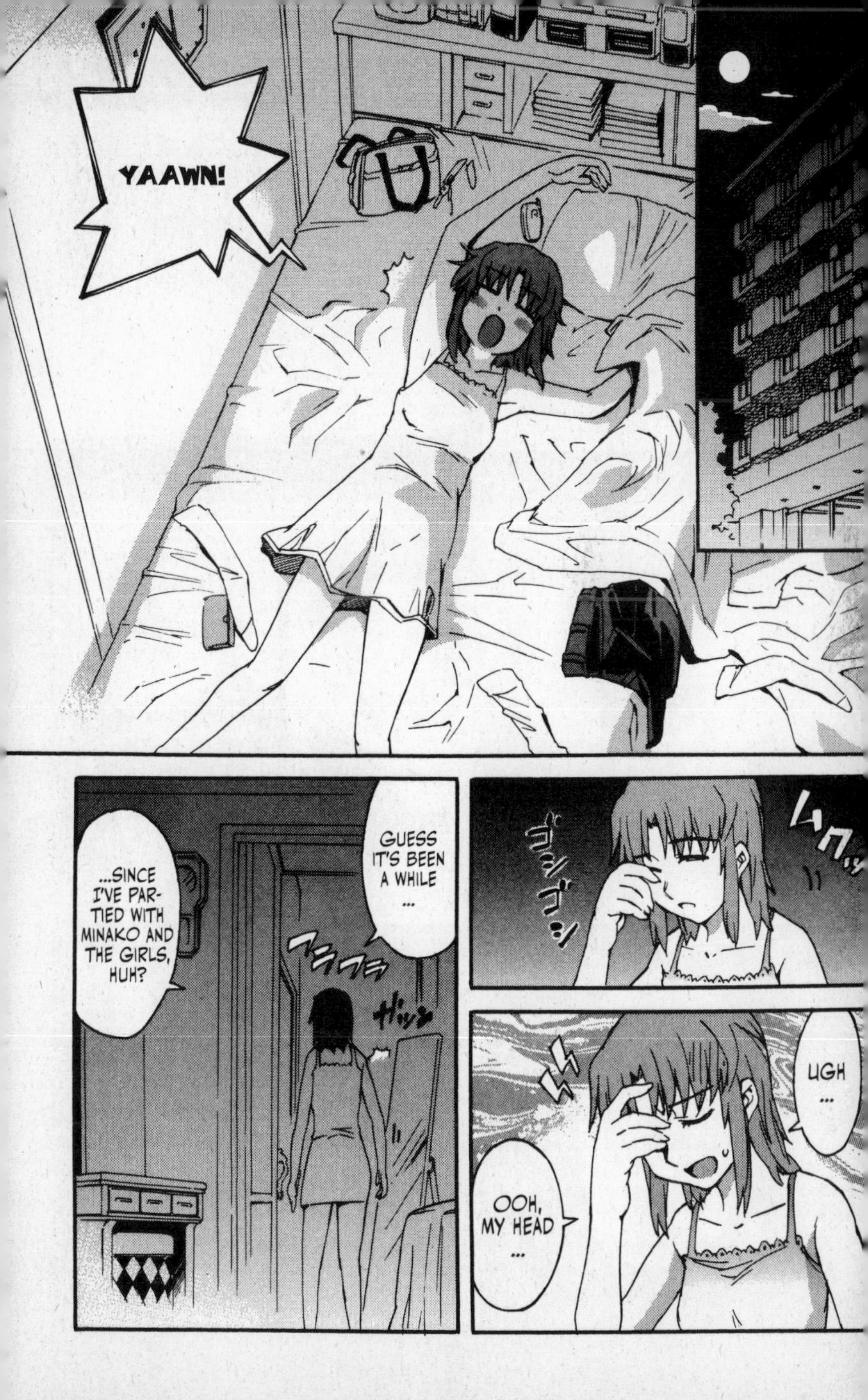
YAAWN!
UGH ...
OOH, MY HEAD ...
GUESS IT'S BEEN A WHILE ...
...SINCE I'VE PARTIED WITH MINAKO AND THE GIRLS, HUH?

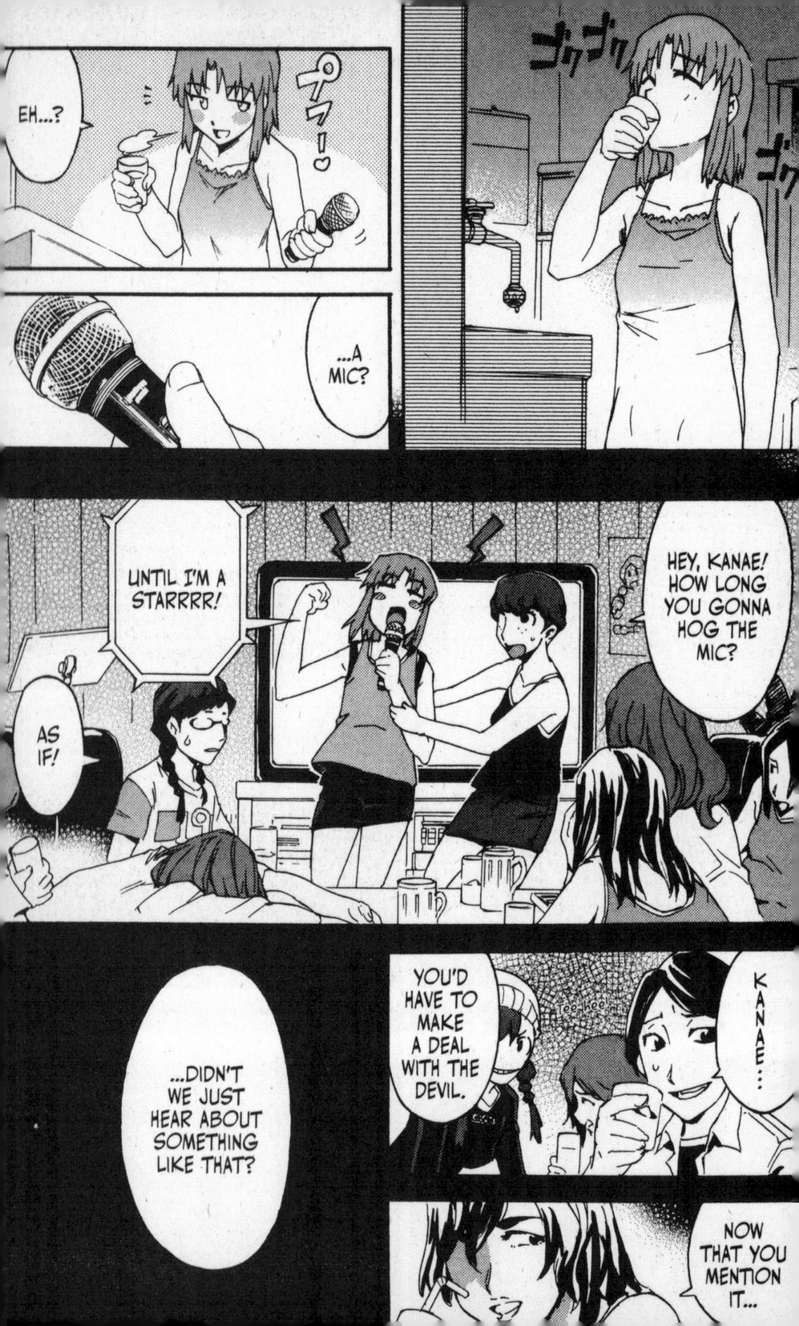
ゴクゴク
ゴク
EH...?
...A MIC?
HEY, KANAE! HOW LONG YOU GONNA HOG THE MIC?
UNTIL I'M A STARRRR!
AS IF!
KANAE...
Tee-hee
YOU'D HAVE TO MAKE A DEAL WITH THE DEVIL.
NOW THAT YOU MENTION IT...
...DIDN'T WE JUST HEAR ABOUT SOMETHING LIKE THAT?

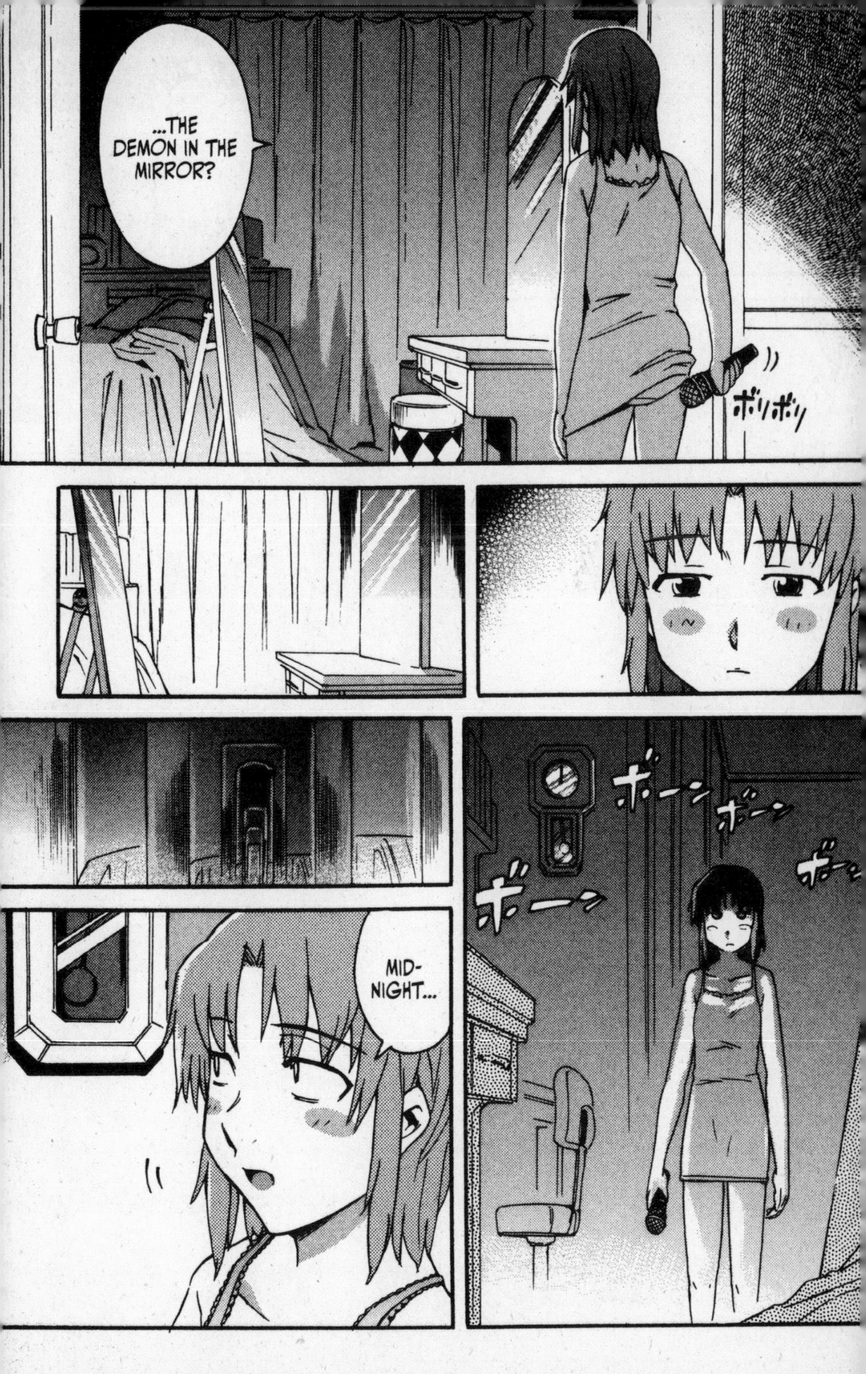
...THE DEMON IN THE MIRROR?
ボリボリ
ボーン
ボーン
ボーン
ボーン
MID-NIGHT...

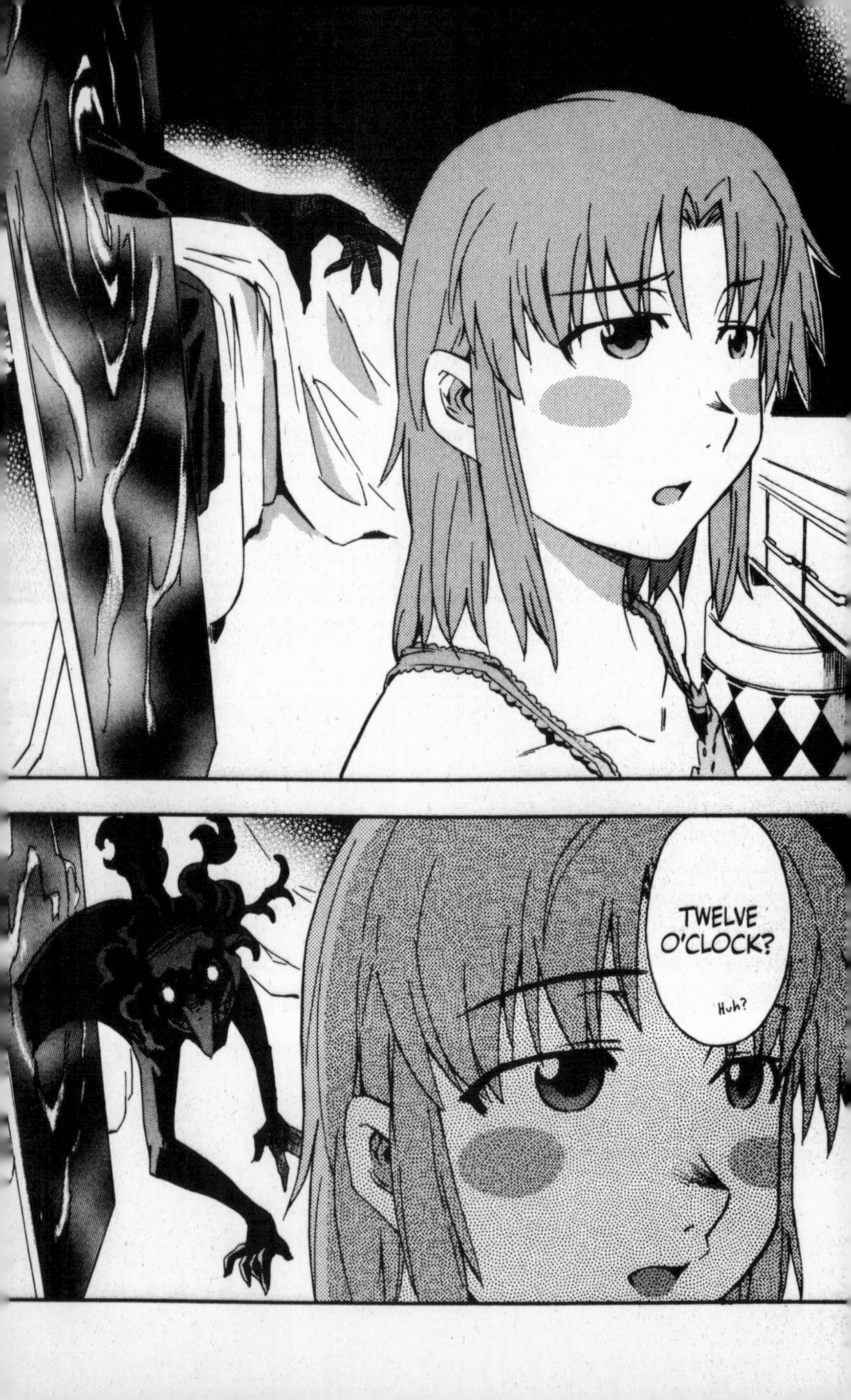
TWELVE O'CLOCK?
Huh?

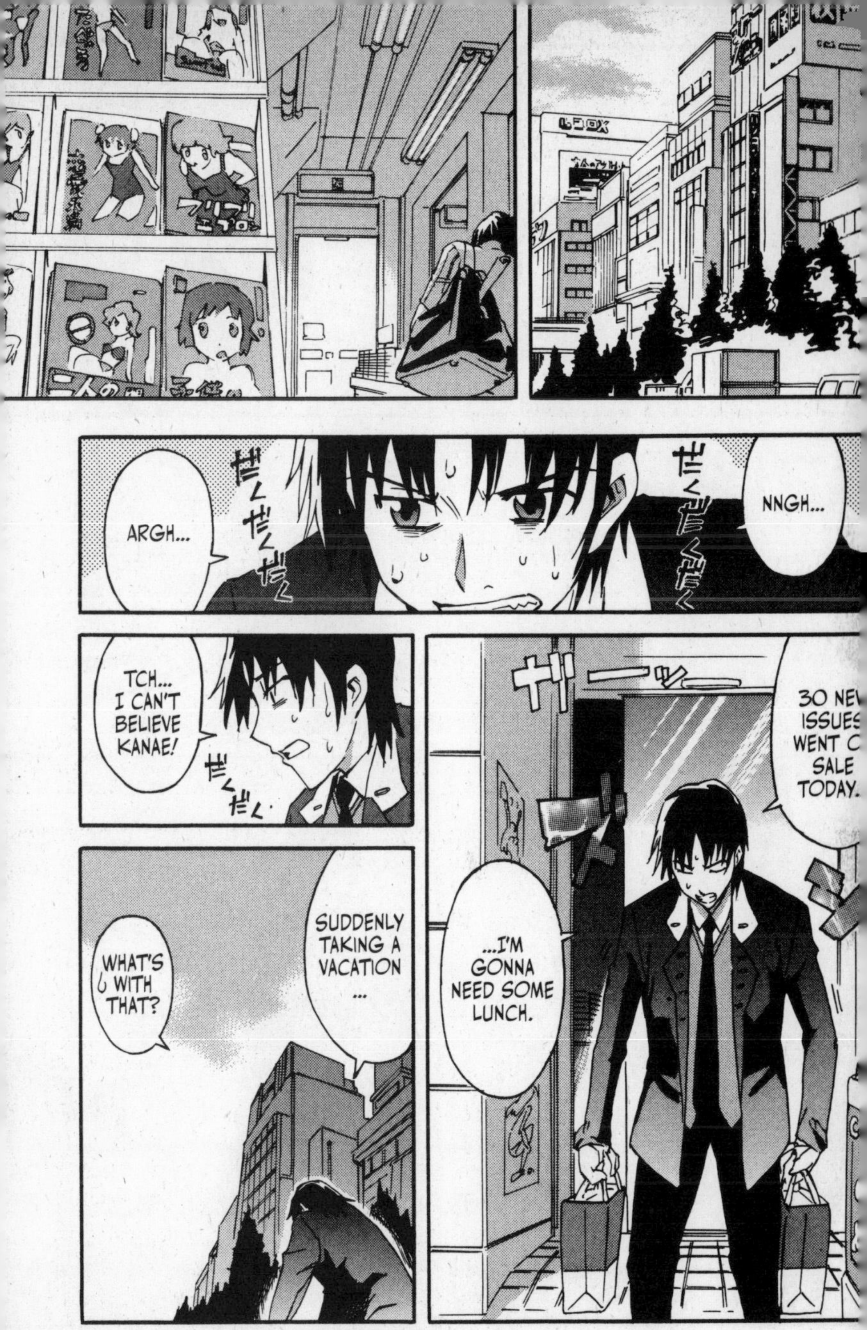
だくだくだく
NNGH...
ARGH...
だくだくだく
30 NEW ISSUES WENT O SALE TODAY.
...I'M GONNA NEED SOME LUNCH.
TCH... I CAN'T BELIEVE KANAE!
だくだく
SUDDENLY TAKING A VACATION ...
WHAT'S WITH THAT?

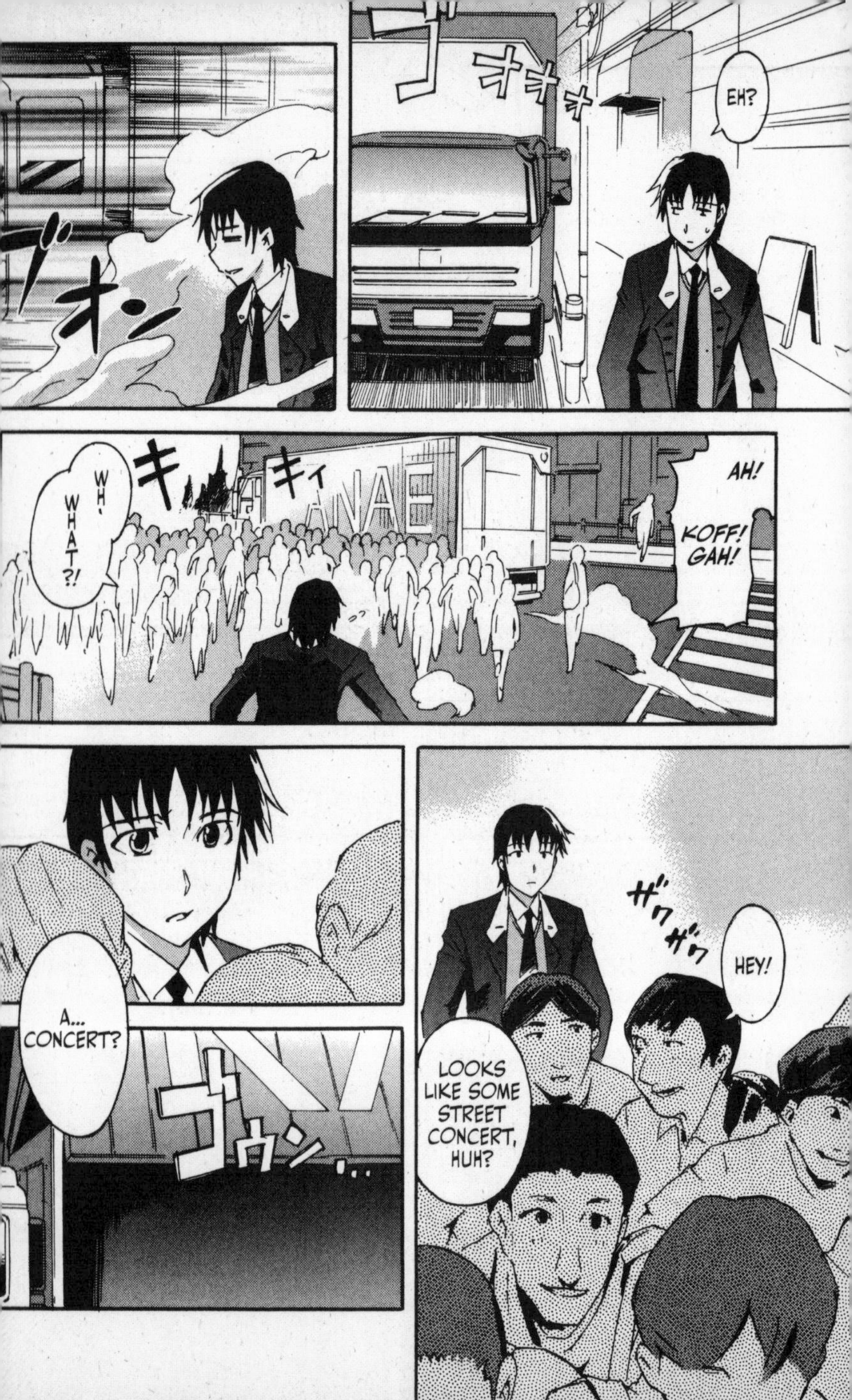
ゴオォォ
EH?
ブォン
AH!
KOFF! GAH!
キキィ
WH- WHAT?!
ザワザワ
HEY!
LOOKS LIKE SOME STREET CONCERT, HUH?
A... CONCERT?
ゴウン...

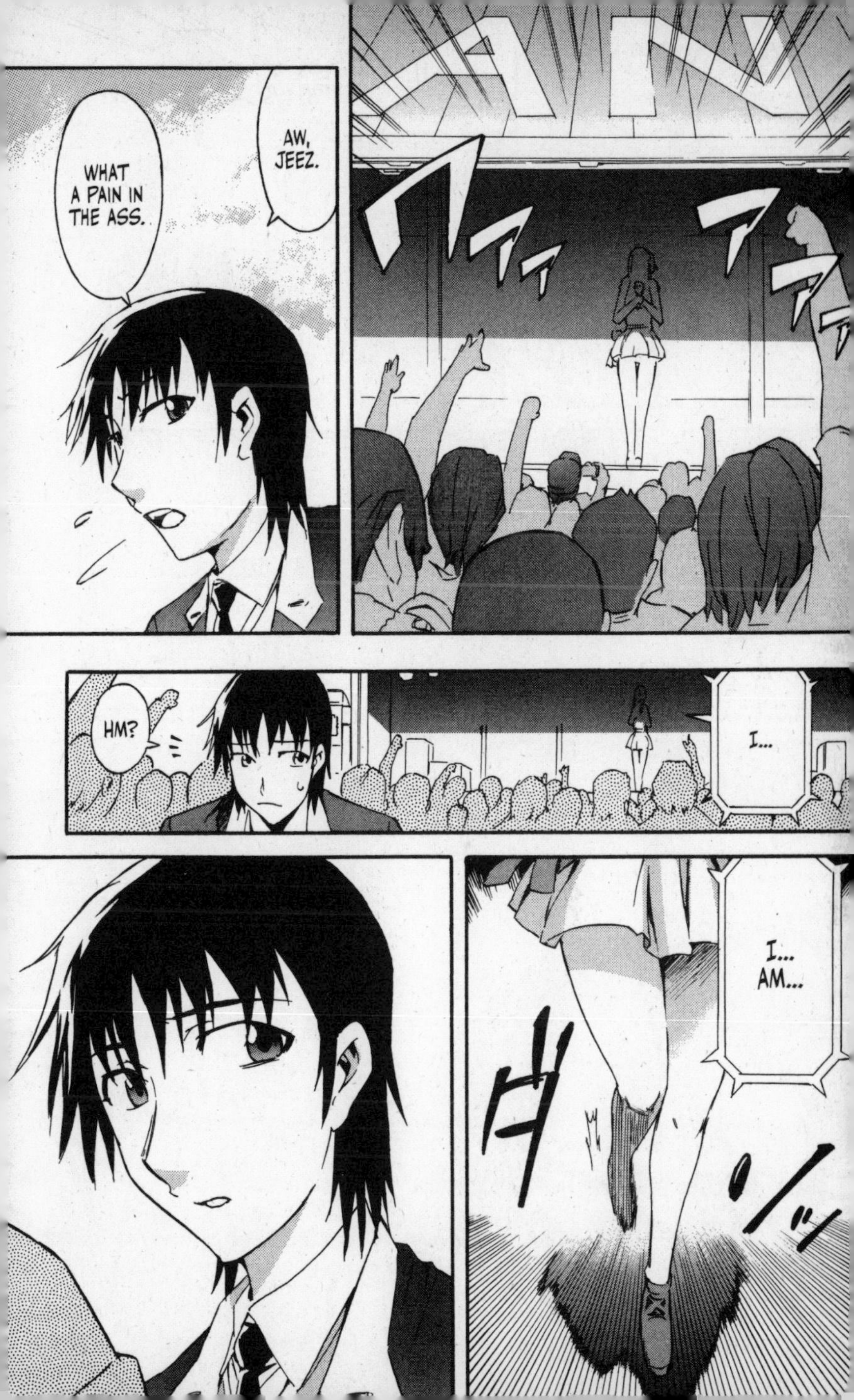
AW, JEEZ.
WHAT A PAIN IN THE ASS.
I...
HM?
I... AM...

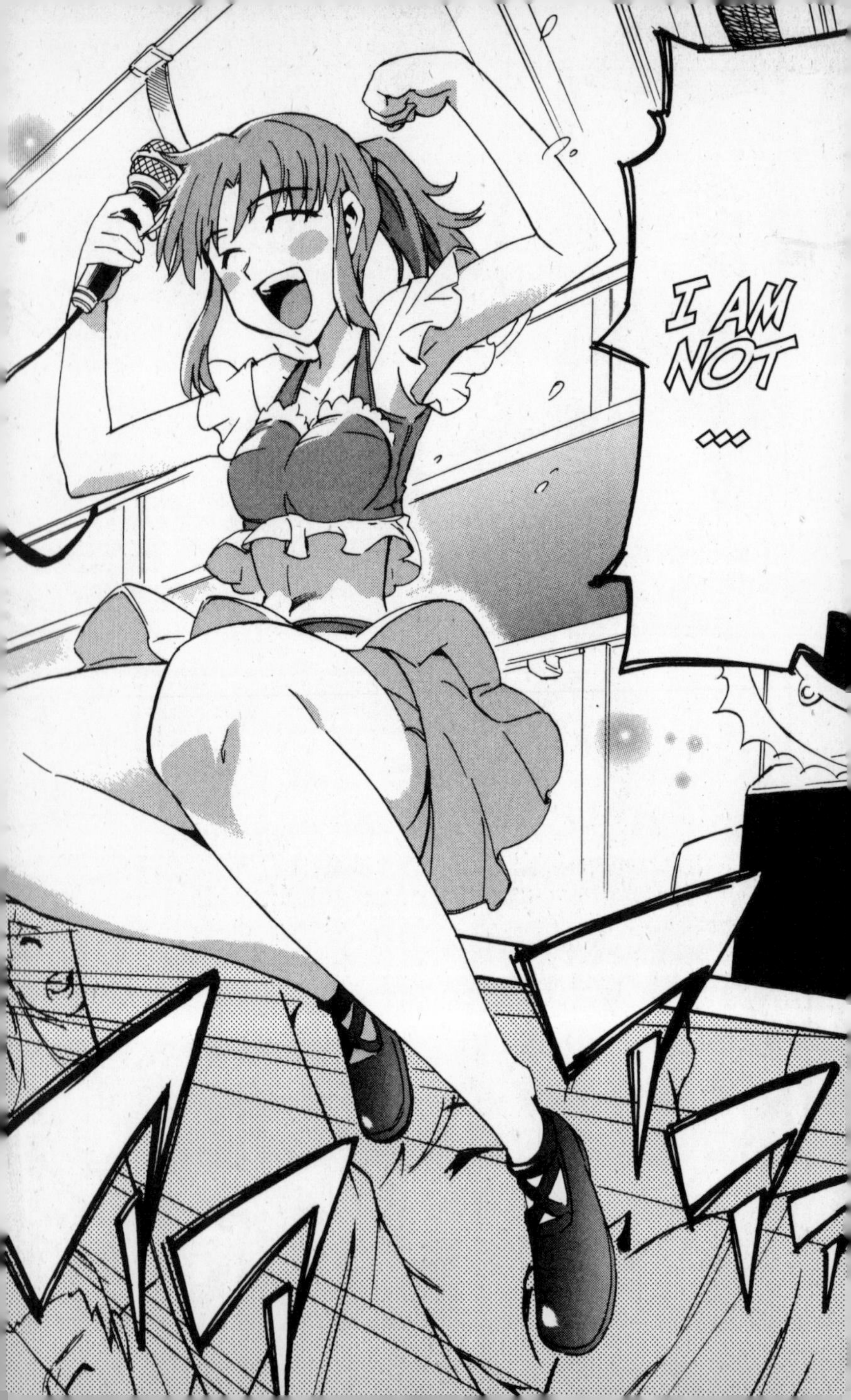
I AM NOT
...

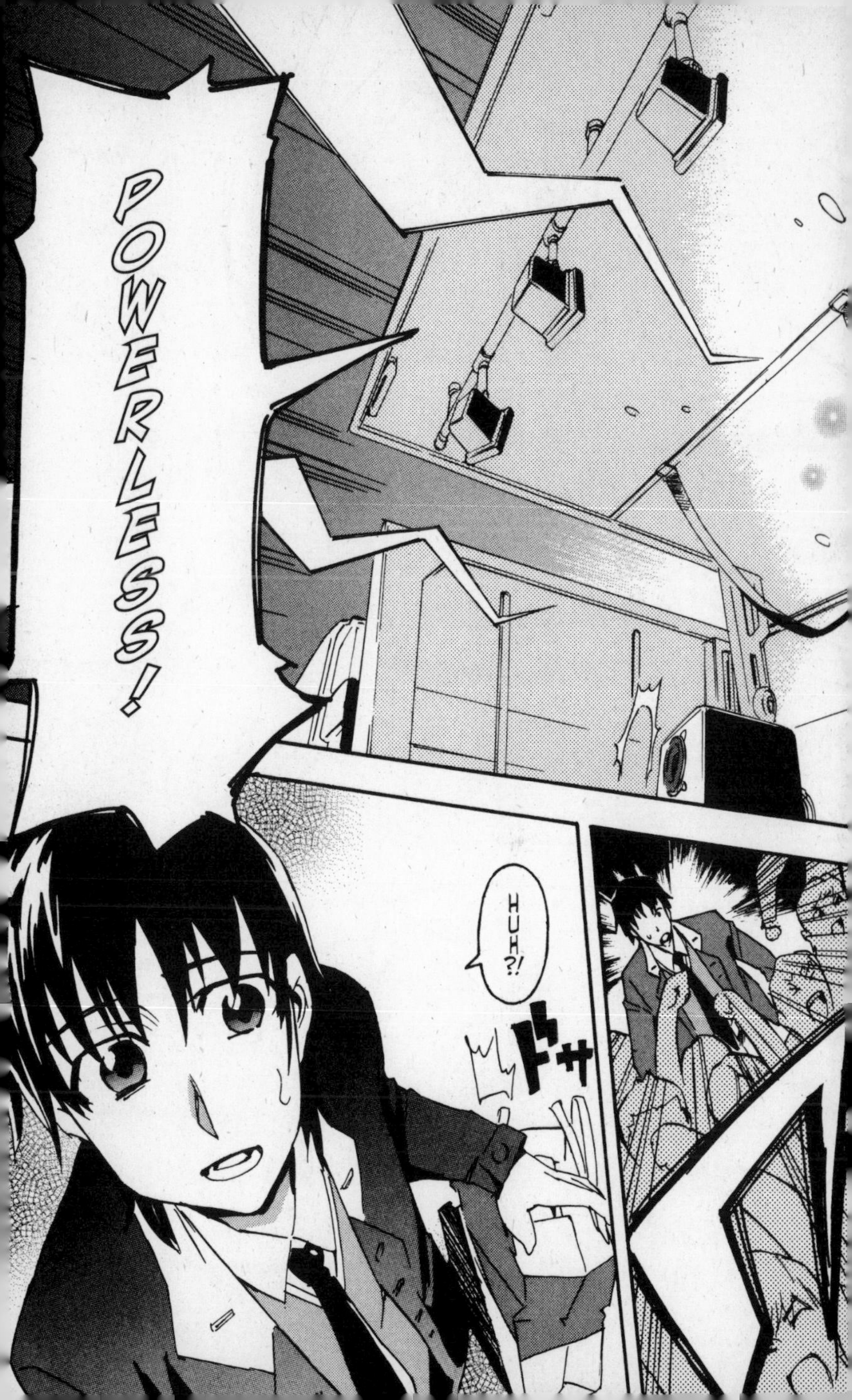
POWERLESS!
HUH?!
ドサ

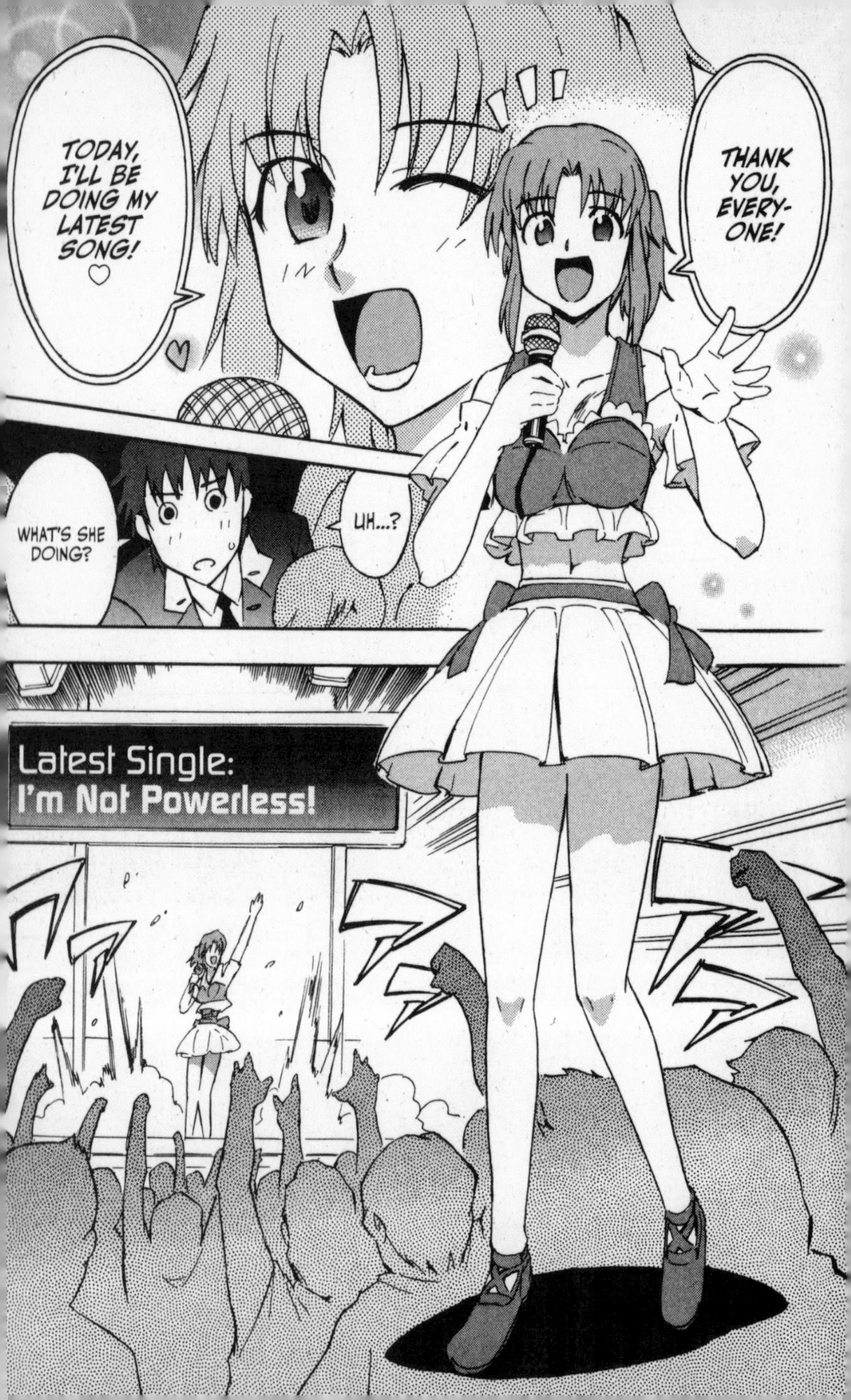
THANK YOU, EVERYONE!
TODAY, I'LL BE DOING MY LATEST SONG! ♡
UH...?
WHAT'S SHE DOING?
Latest Single: I'm Not Powerless!

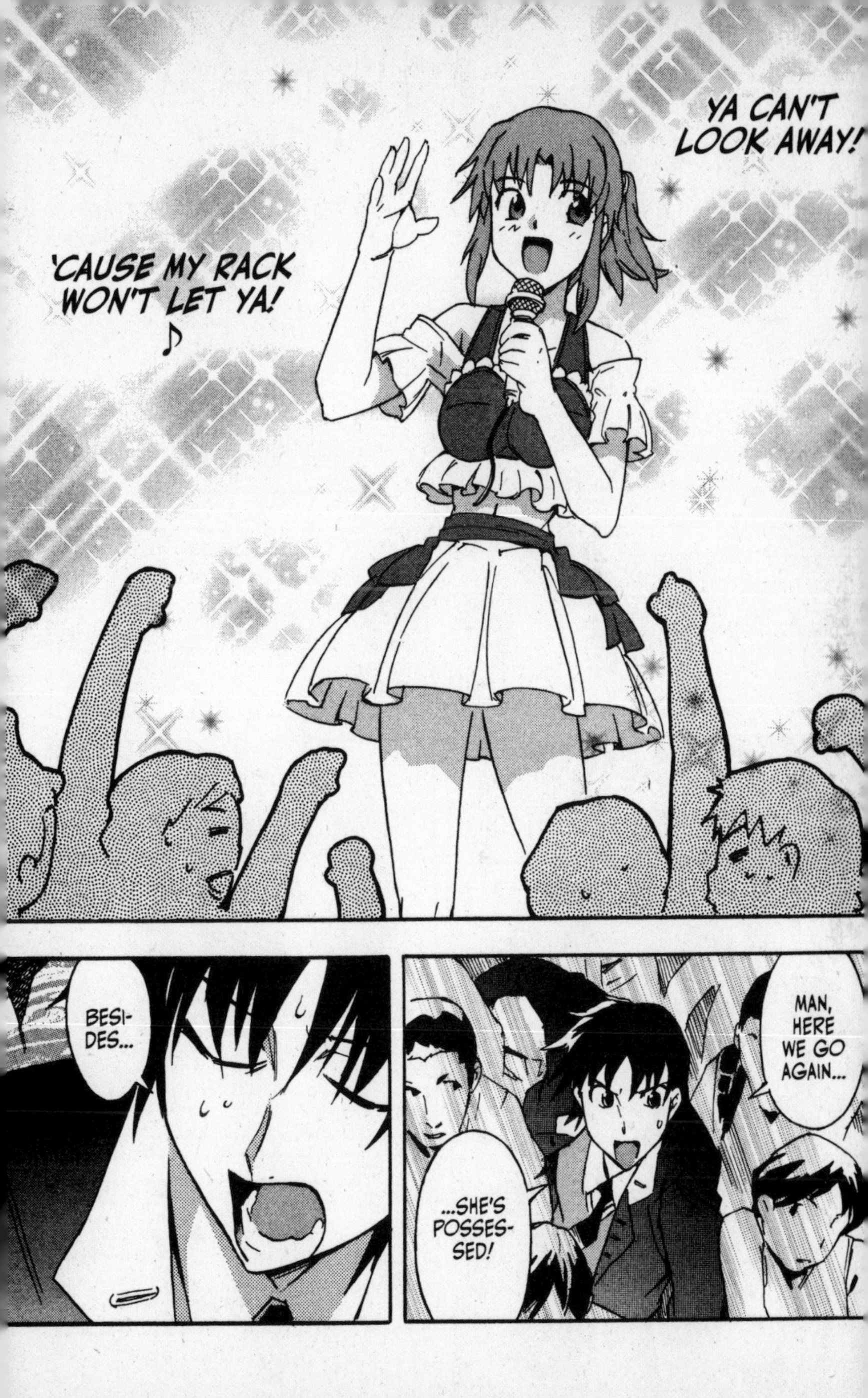
YA CAN'T LOOK AWAY!
'CAUSE MY RACK WON'T LET YA! ♪
MAN, HERE WE GO AGAIN...
...SHE'S POSSES-SED!
BESI-DES...

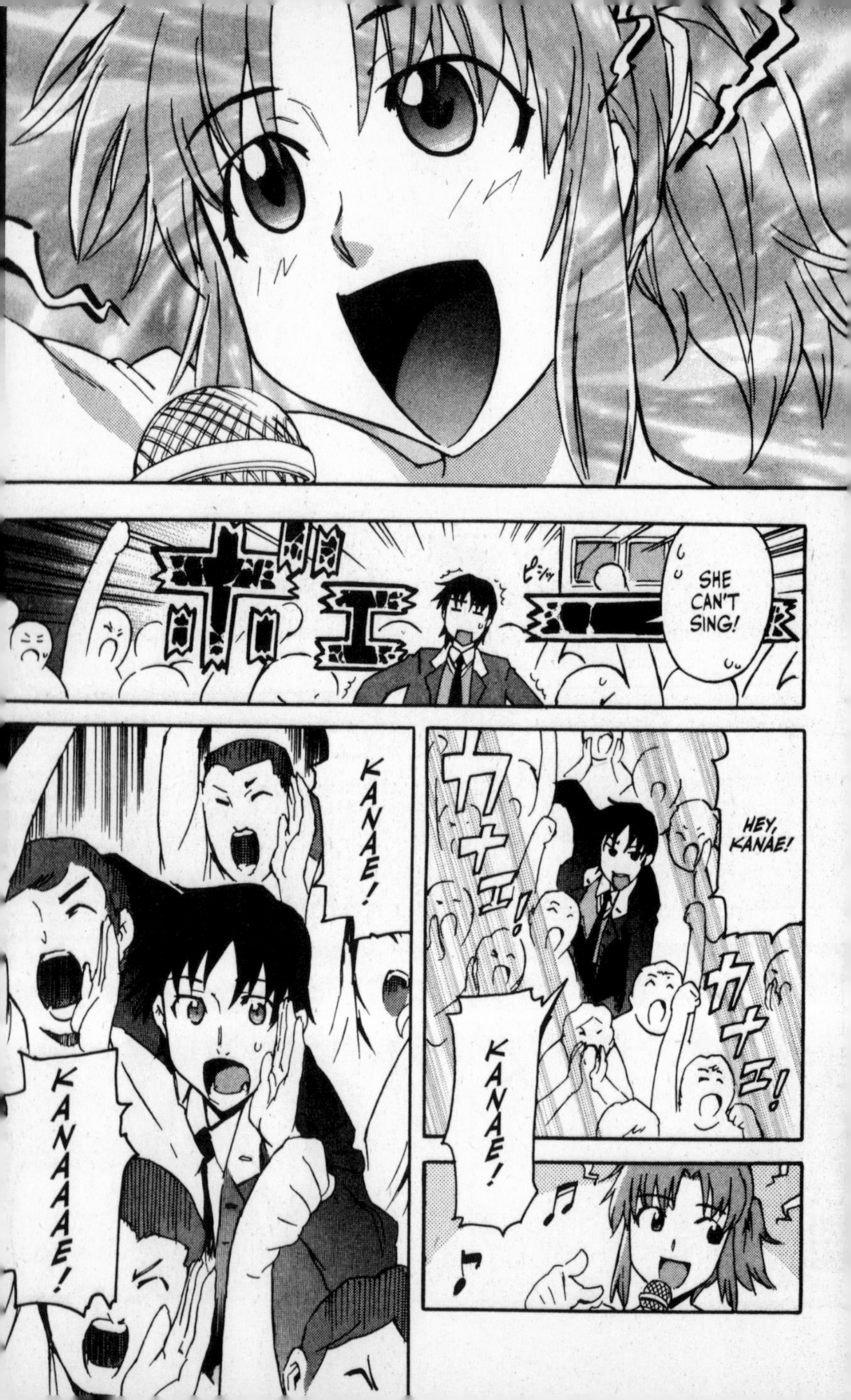
SHE CAN'T SING!
HEY, KANAE!
カナエ!
カナエ!
KANAE!
KANAE!
KANAAAAE!

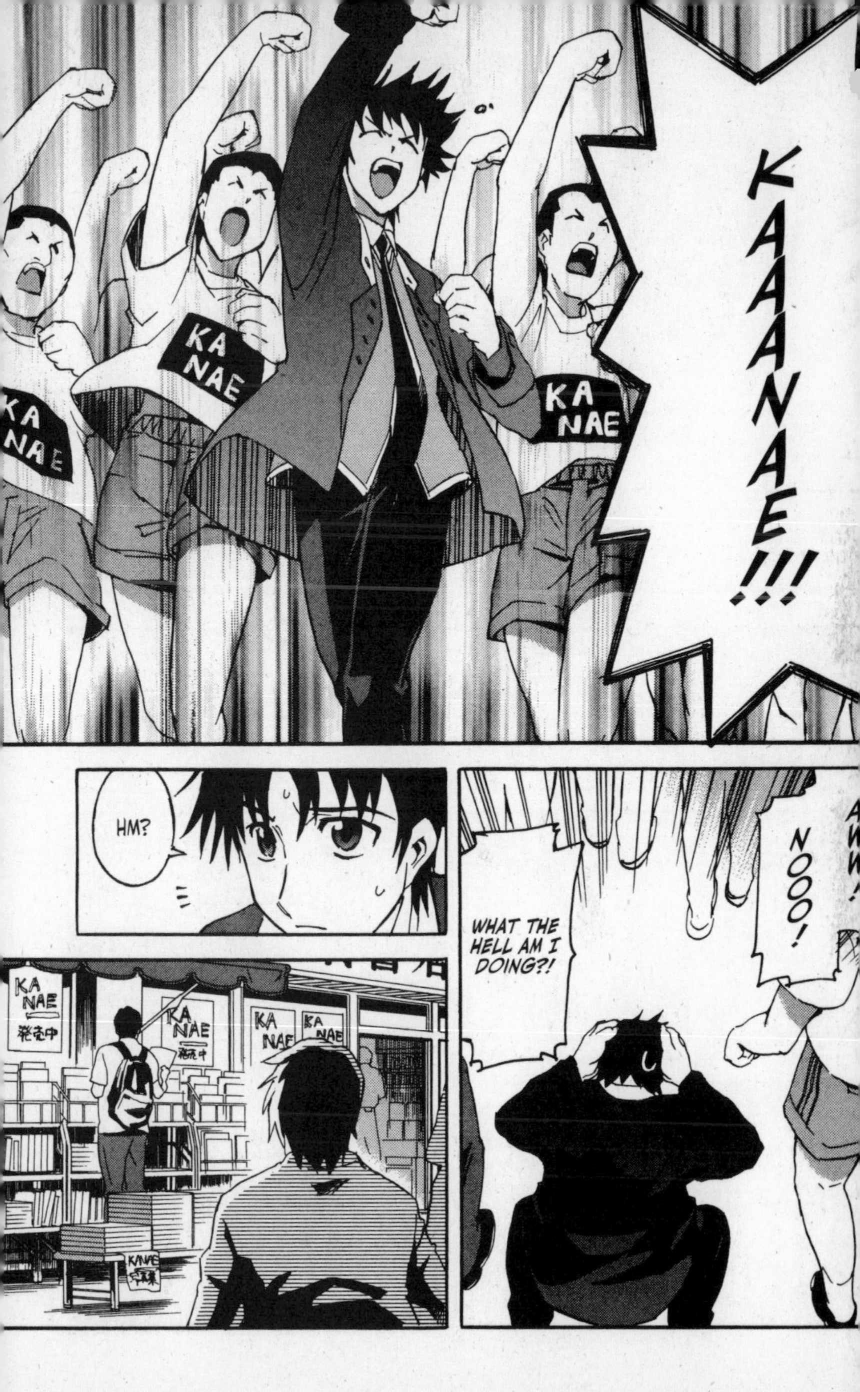
KAAANAE!!!
KA NAE
KA NAE
KA NAE
AWW!
NOOO!
WHAT THE HELL AM I DOING?!
HM?
KA NAE 発売中
KA NAE 発売中
KA NAE
KA NAE
KA NAE

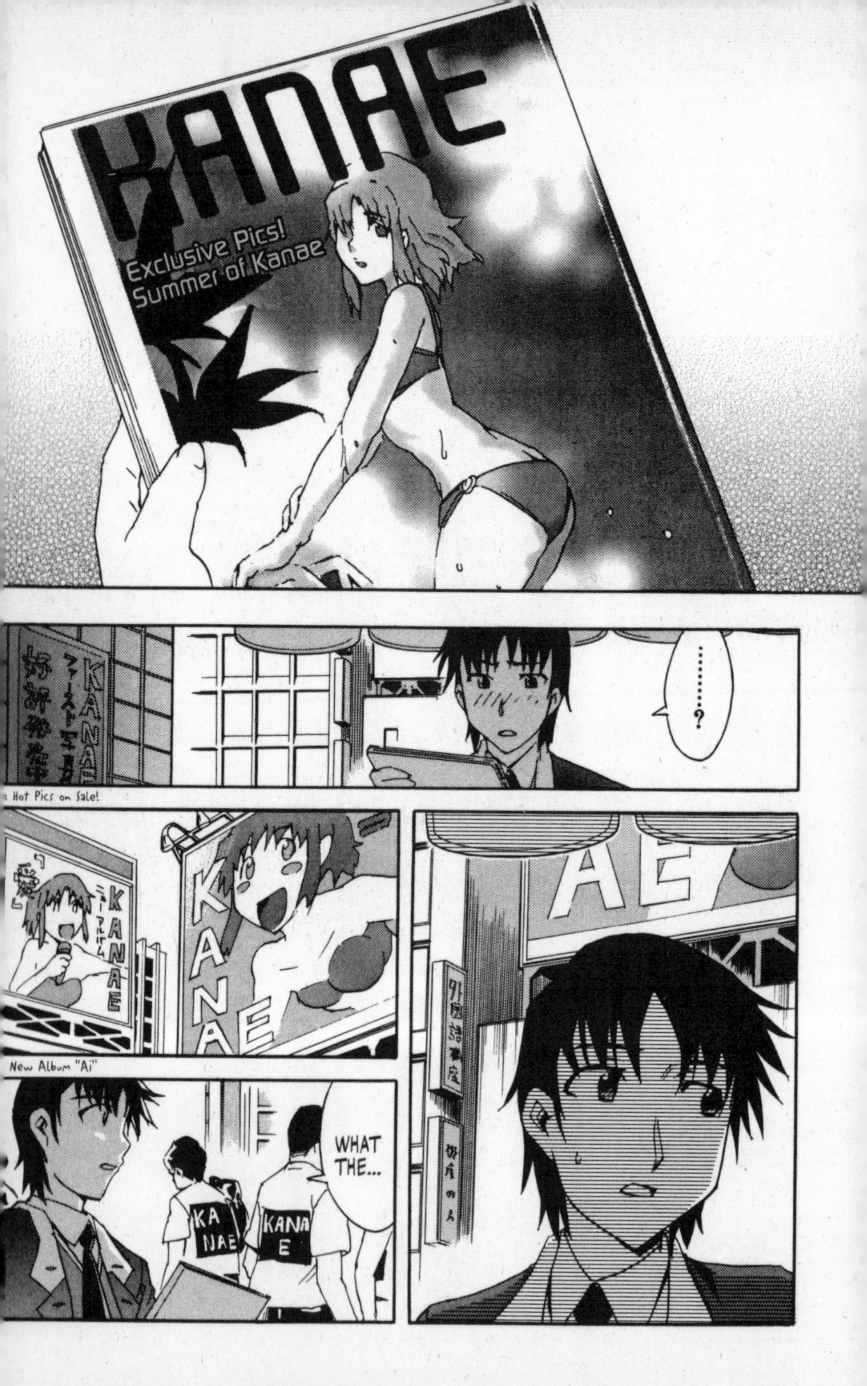
KANAE
Exclusive Pics! Summer of Kanae
KANAE
......?
Hot Pics on Sale!
AE
KANAE
KANAE
New Album "Ai"
WHAT THE...
KA NAE
KANA E

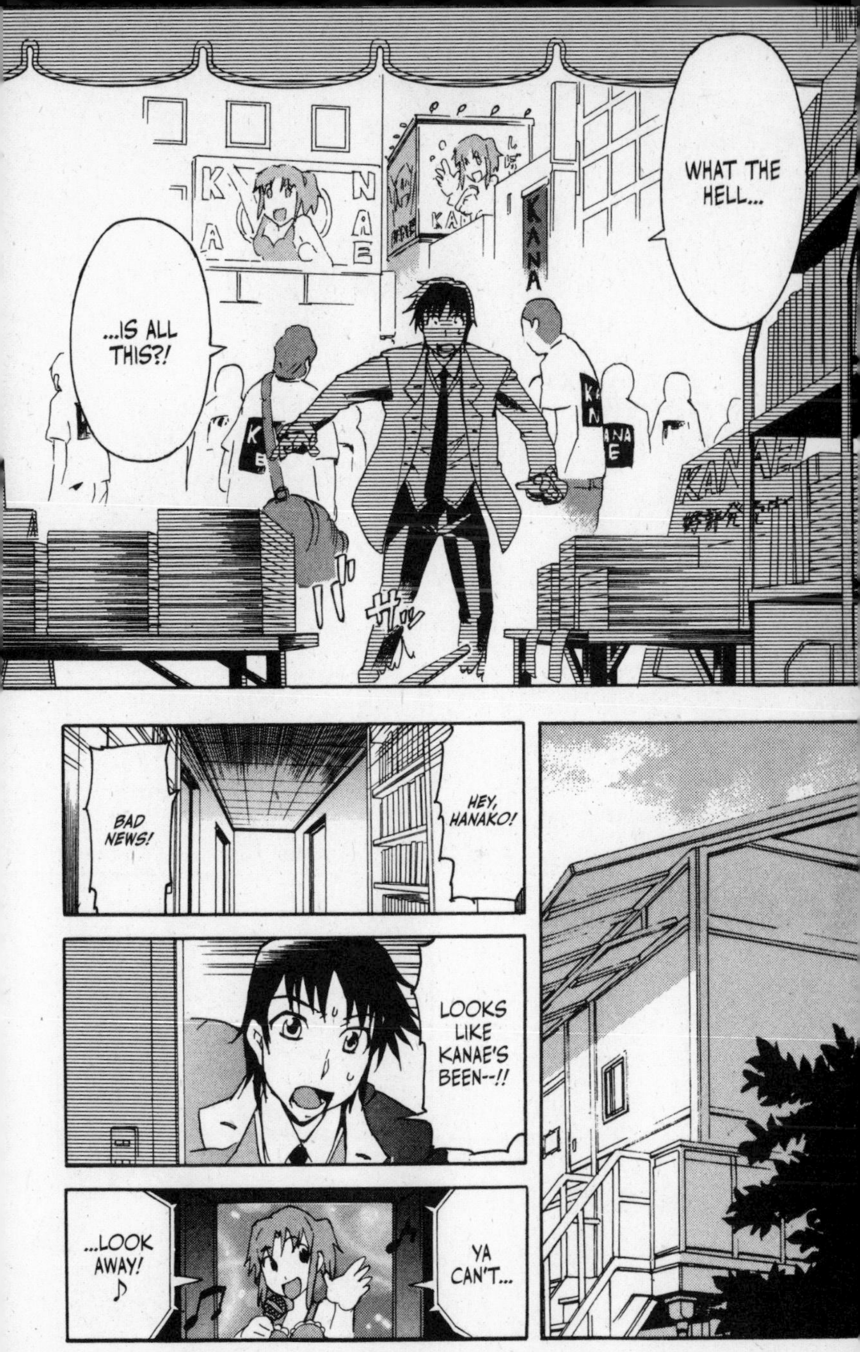
WHAT THE HELL...
...IS ALL THIS?!
HEY, HANAKO!
BAD NEWS!
LOOKS LIKE KANAE'S BEEN--!!
YA CAN'T...
...LOOK AWAY! ♪

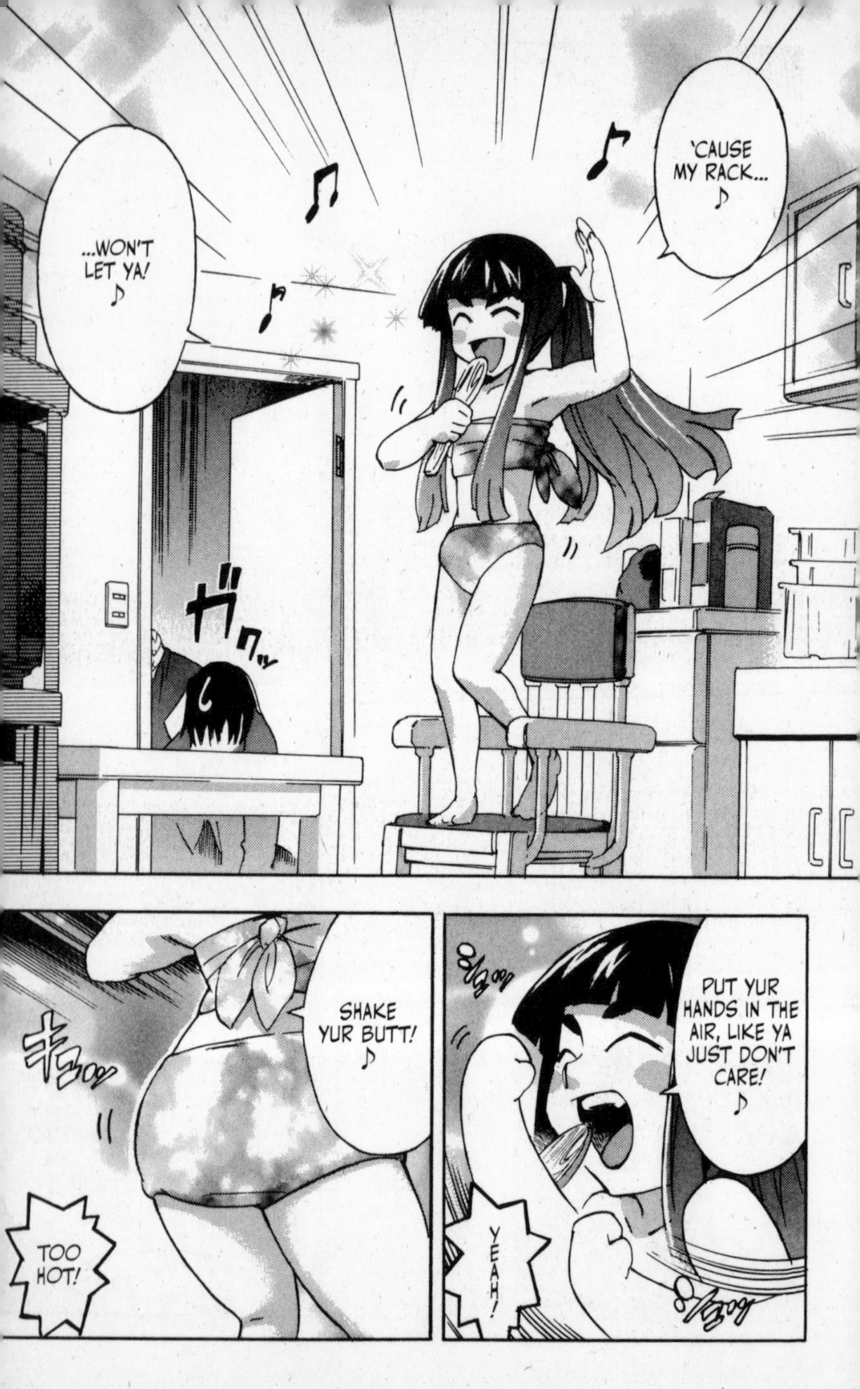
'CAUSE MY RACK... ♪
...WON'T LET YA! ♪
PUT YUR HANDS IN THE AIR, LIKE YA JUST DON'T CARE! ♪
YEAH!
SHAKE YUR BUTT! ♪
TOO HOT!

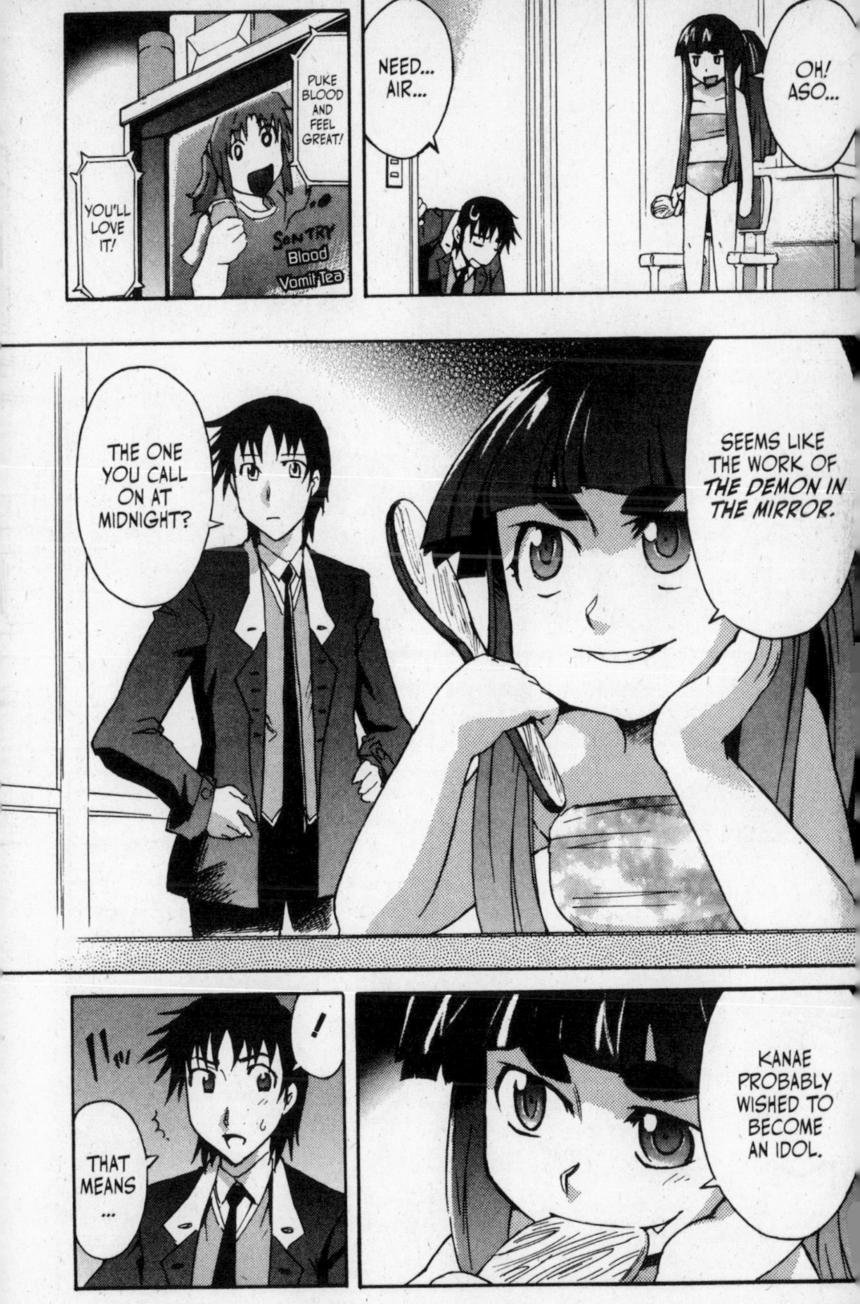
OH! ASO...
NEED... AIR...
PUKE BLOOD AND FEEL GREAT!
YOU'LL LOVE IT!
SONTRY
Blood
Vomit Tea
SEEMS LIKE THE WORK OF *THE DEMON IN THE MIRROR.*
THE ONE YOU CALL ON AT MIDNIGHT?
KANAE PROBABLY WISHED TO BECOME AN IDOL.
!
THAT MEANS ...

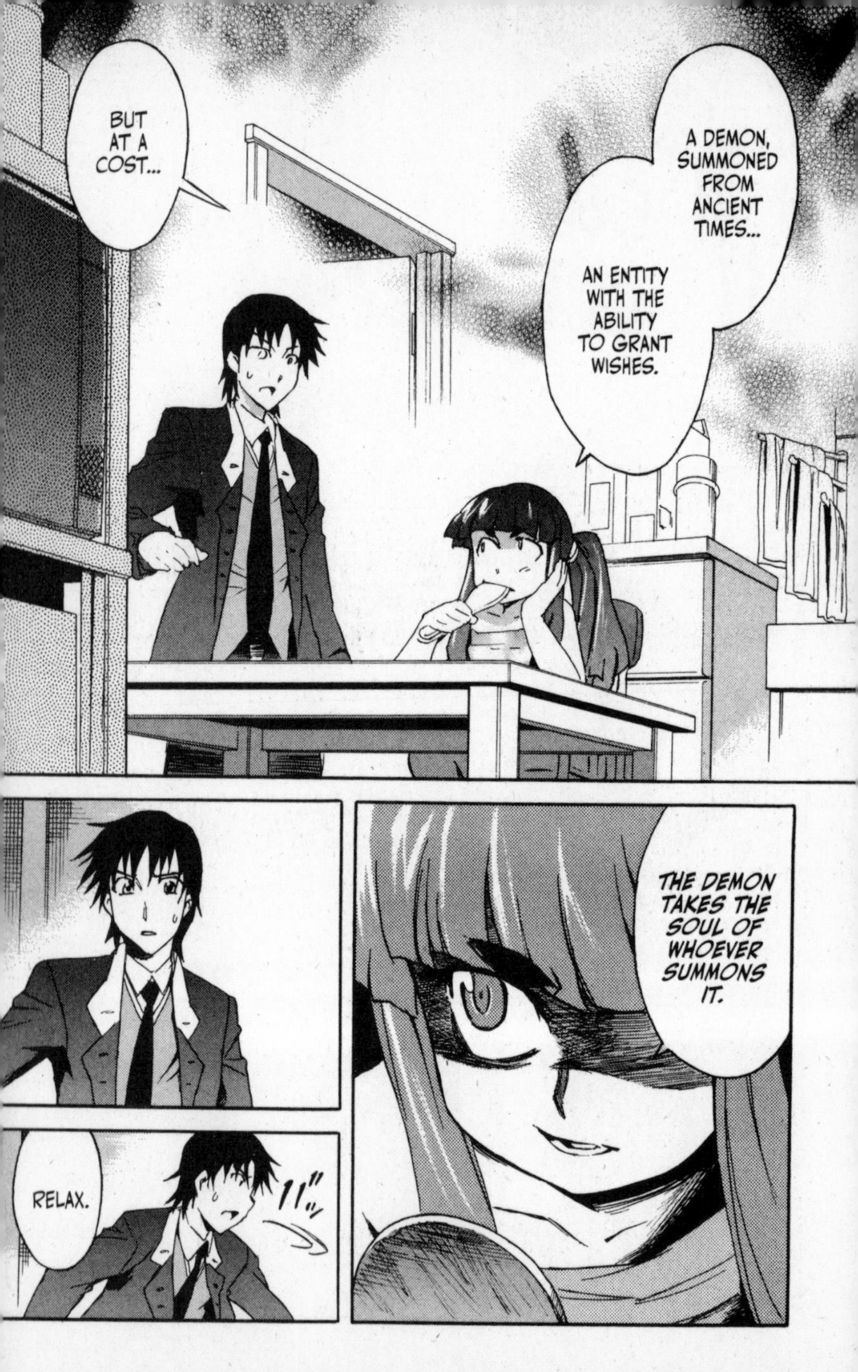
A DEMON, SUMMONED FROM ANCIENT TIMES...
AN ENTITY WITH THE ABILITY TO GRANT WISHES.
BUT AT A COST...
THE DEMON TAKES THE SOUL OF WHOEVER SUMMONS IT.
RELAX.

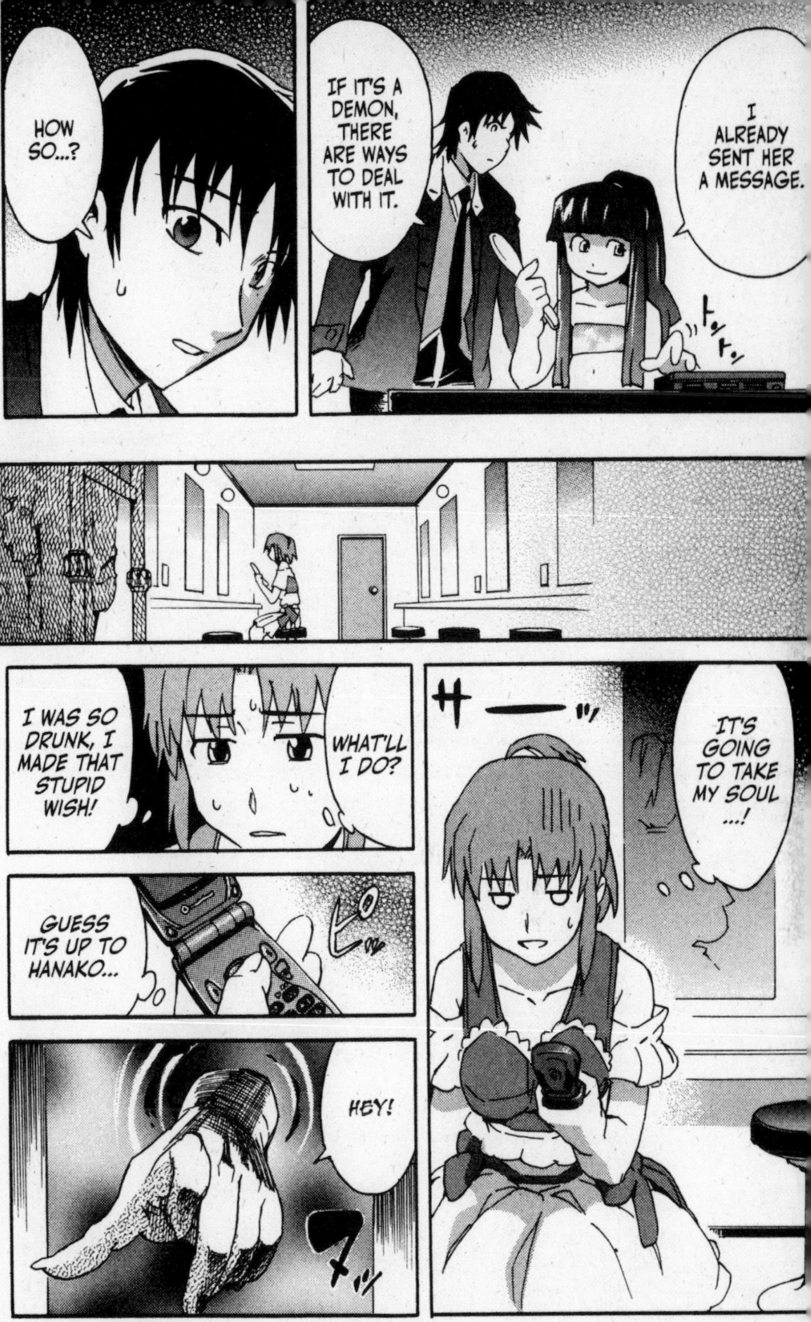
I ALREADY SENT HER A MESSAGE.
IF IT'S A DEMON, THERE ARE WAYS TO DEAL WITH IT.
HOW SO...?
IT'S GOING TO TAKE MY SOUL ...!
WHAT'LL I DO?
I WAS SO DRUNK, I MADE THAT STUPID WISH!
GUESS IT'S UP TO HANAKO...
HEY!

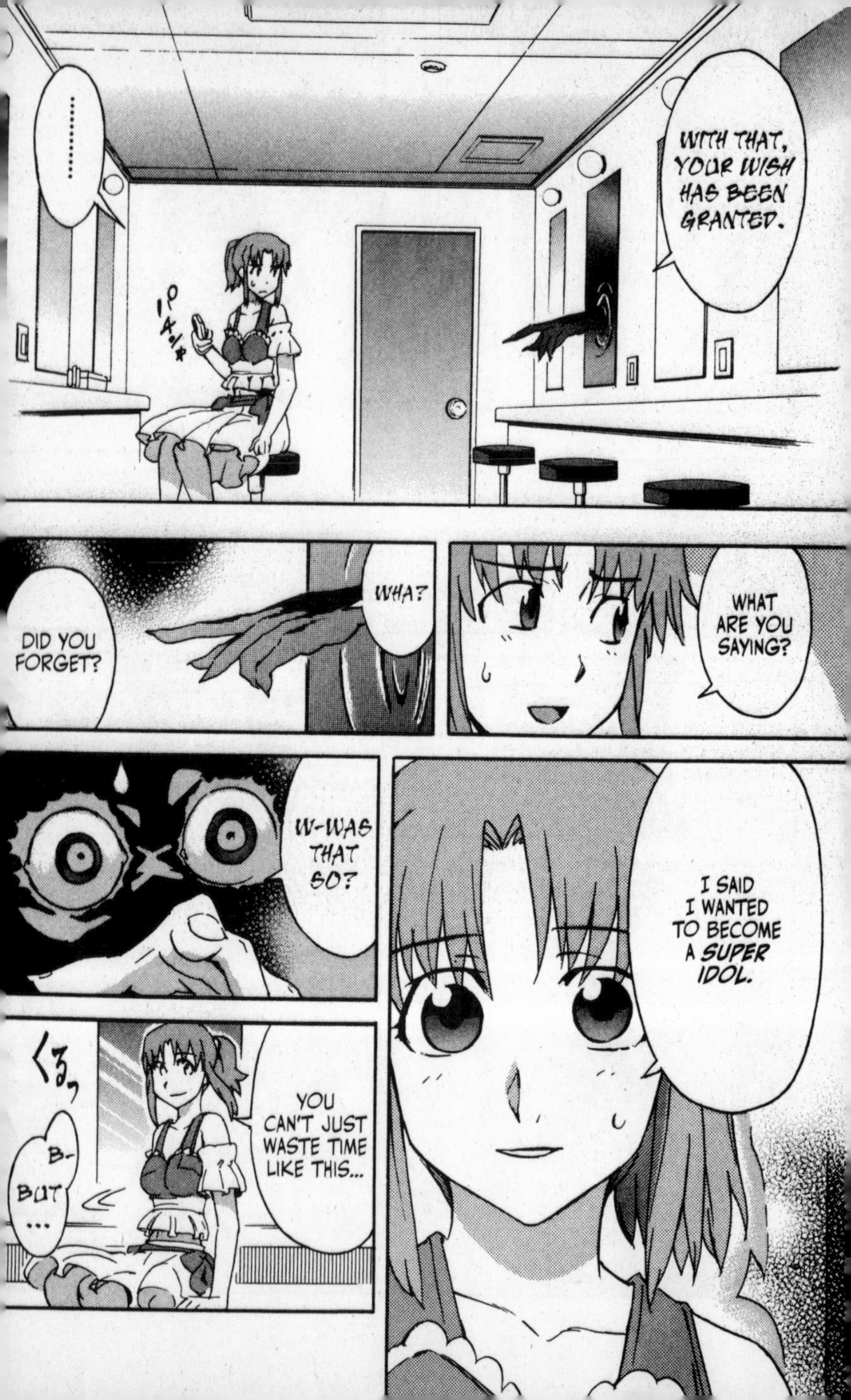
WITH THAT, YOUR WISH HAS BEEN GRANTED.
......
WHAT ARE YOU SAYING?
WHA?
DID YOU FORGET?
I SAID I WANTED TO BECOME A SUPER IDOL.
W-WAS THAT SO?
YOU CAN'T JUST WASTE TIME LIKE THIS...
くるっ
B-BUT...

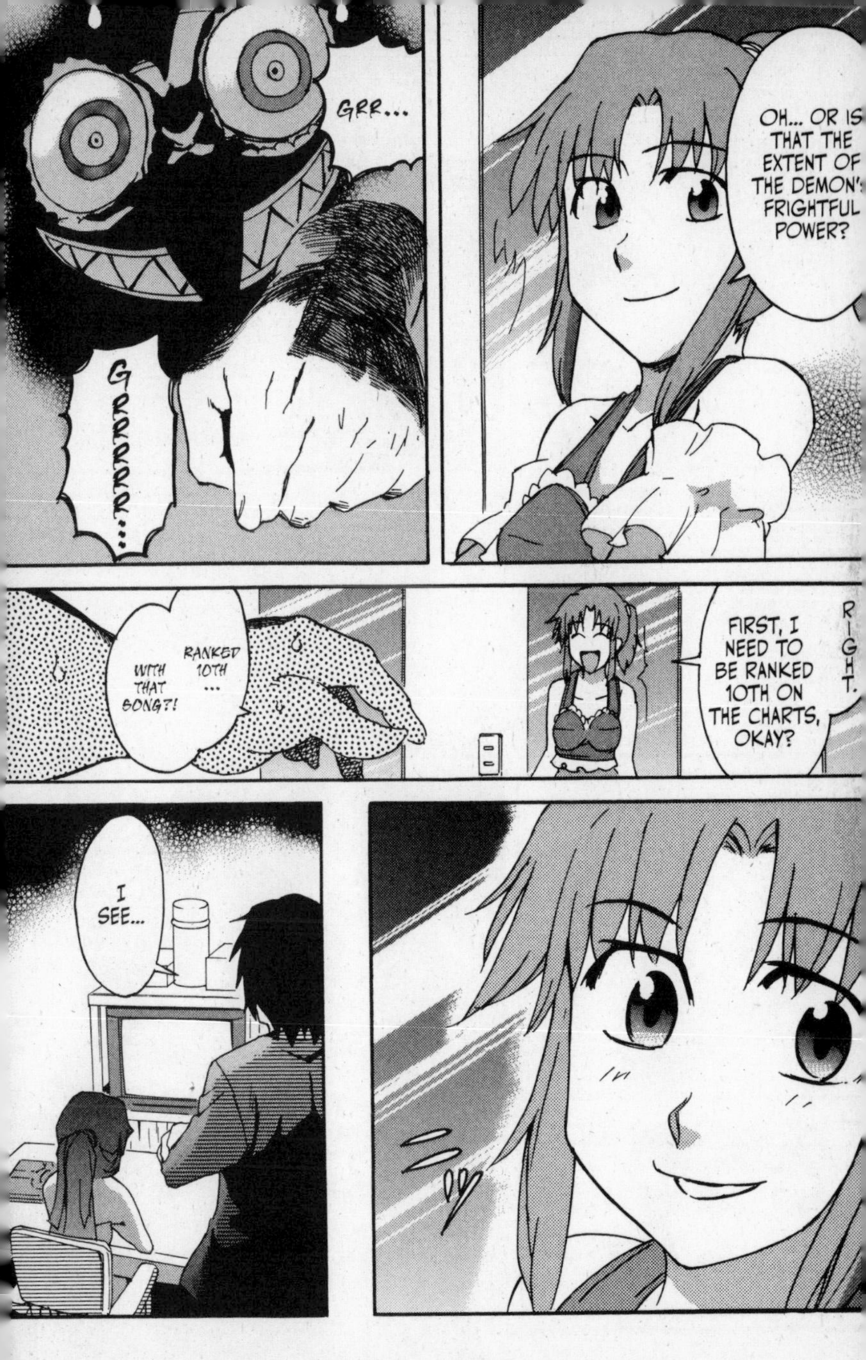
OH... OR IS THAT THE EXTENT OF THE DEMON'S FRIGHTFUL POWER?
GRR...
GRRRRRR...
RIGHT.
FIRST, I NEED TO BE RANKED 10TH ON THE CHARTS, OKAY?
RANKED 10TH...
WITH THAT SONG?!
I SEE...

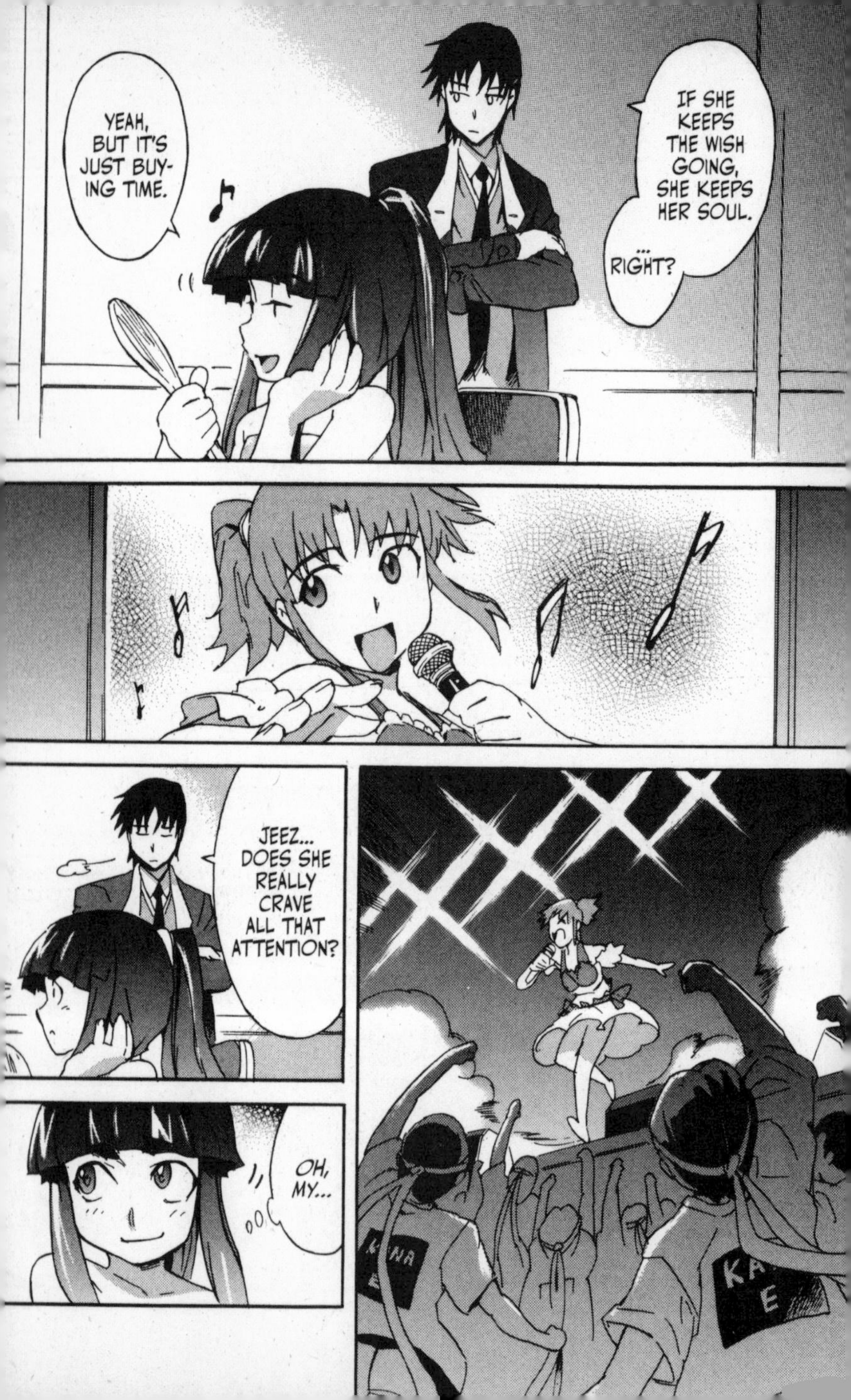
IF SHE KEEPS THE WISH GOING, SHE KEEPS HER SOUL.
... RIGHT?
YEAH, BUT IT'S JUST BUYING TIME.
JEEZ... DOES SHE REALLY CRAVE ALL THAT ATTENTION?
OH, MY...

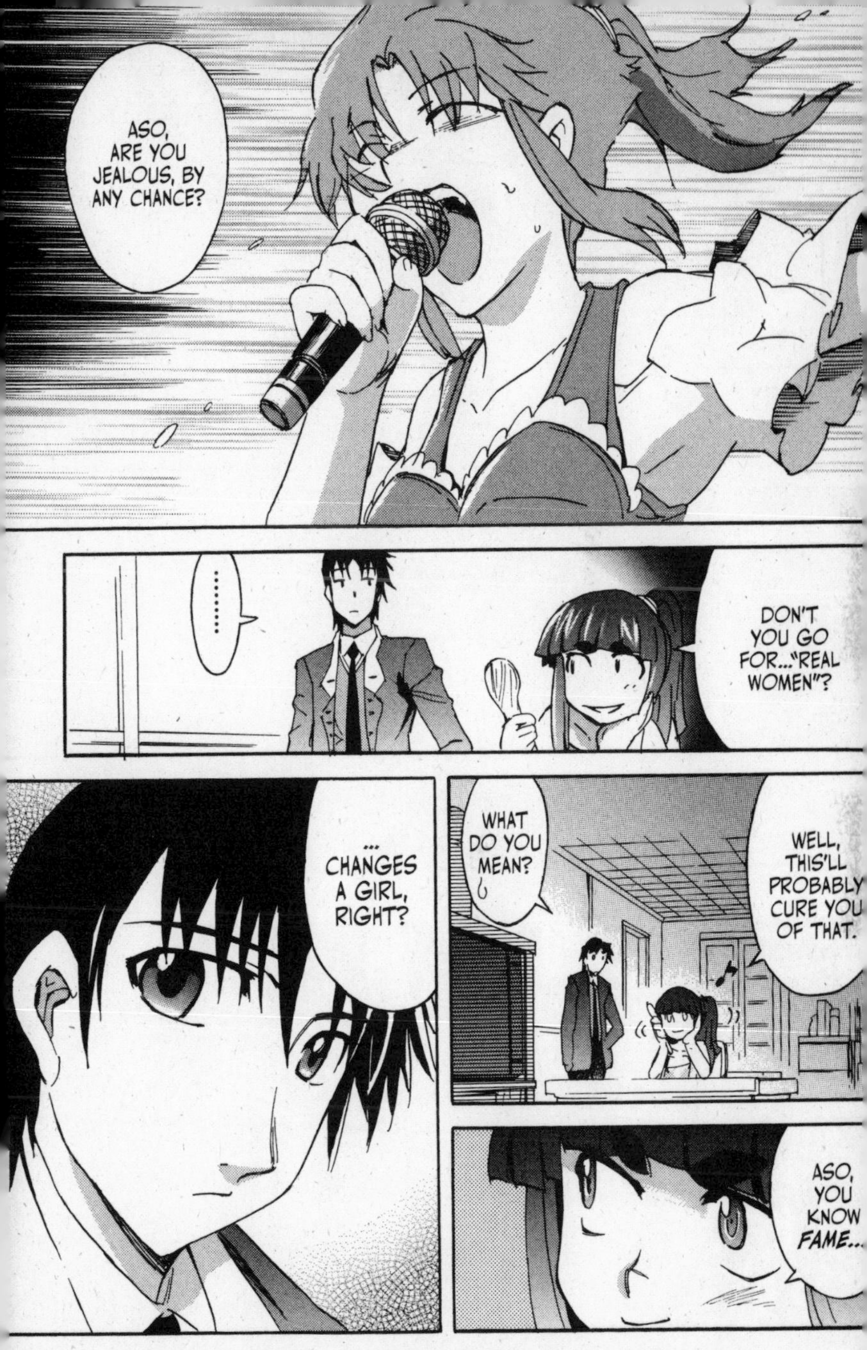
ASO, ARE YOU JEALOUS, BY ANY CHANCE?
DON'T YOU GO FOR..."REAL WOMEN"?
......
WELL, THIS'LL PROBABLY CURE YOU OF THAT.
WHAT DO YOU MEAN?
ASO, YOU KNOW *FAME*...
...CHANGES A GIRL, RIGHT?

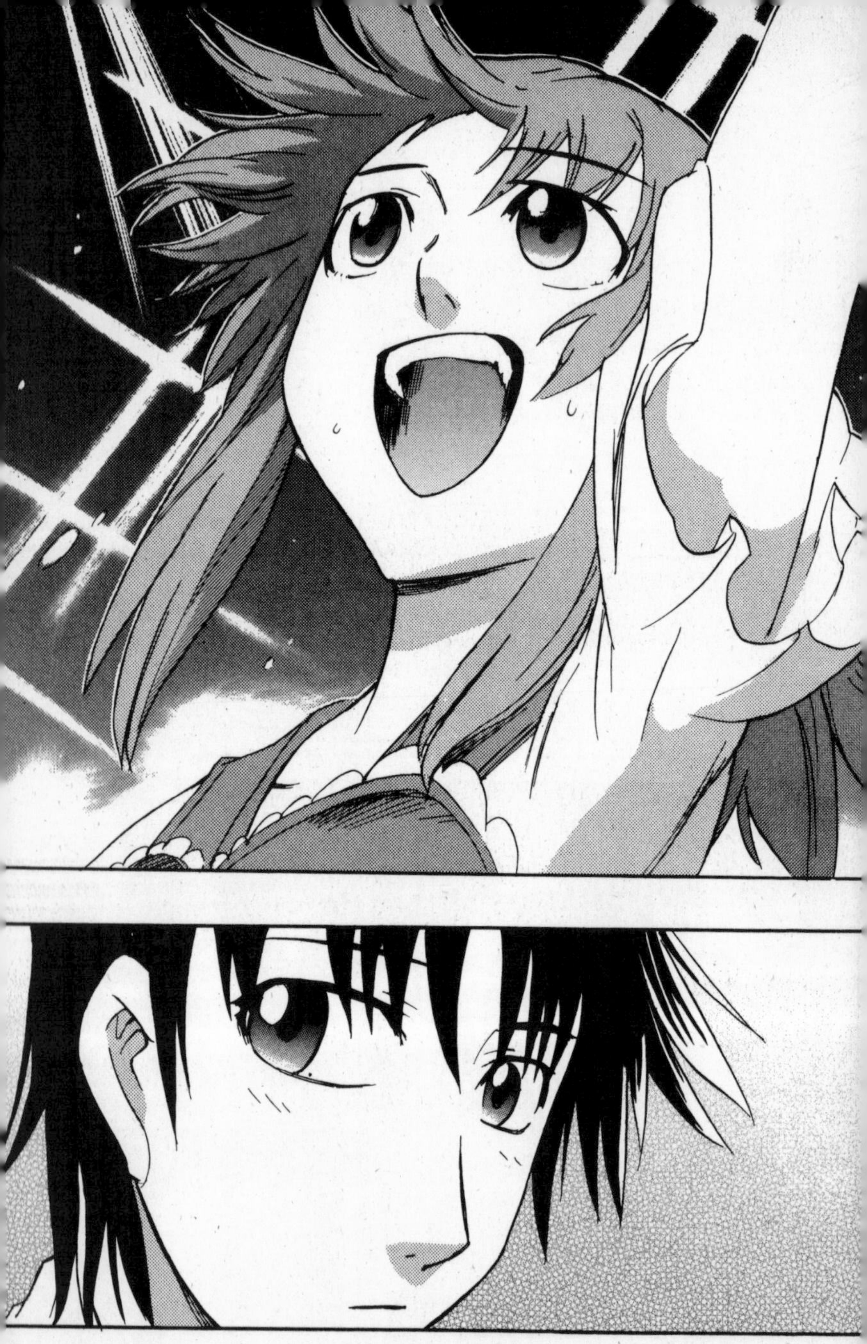

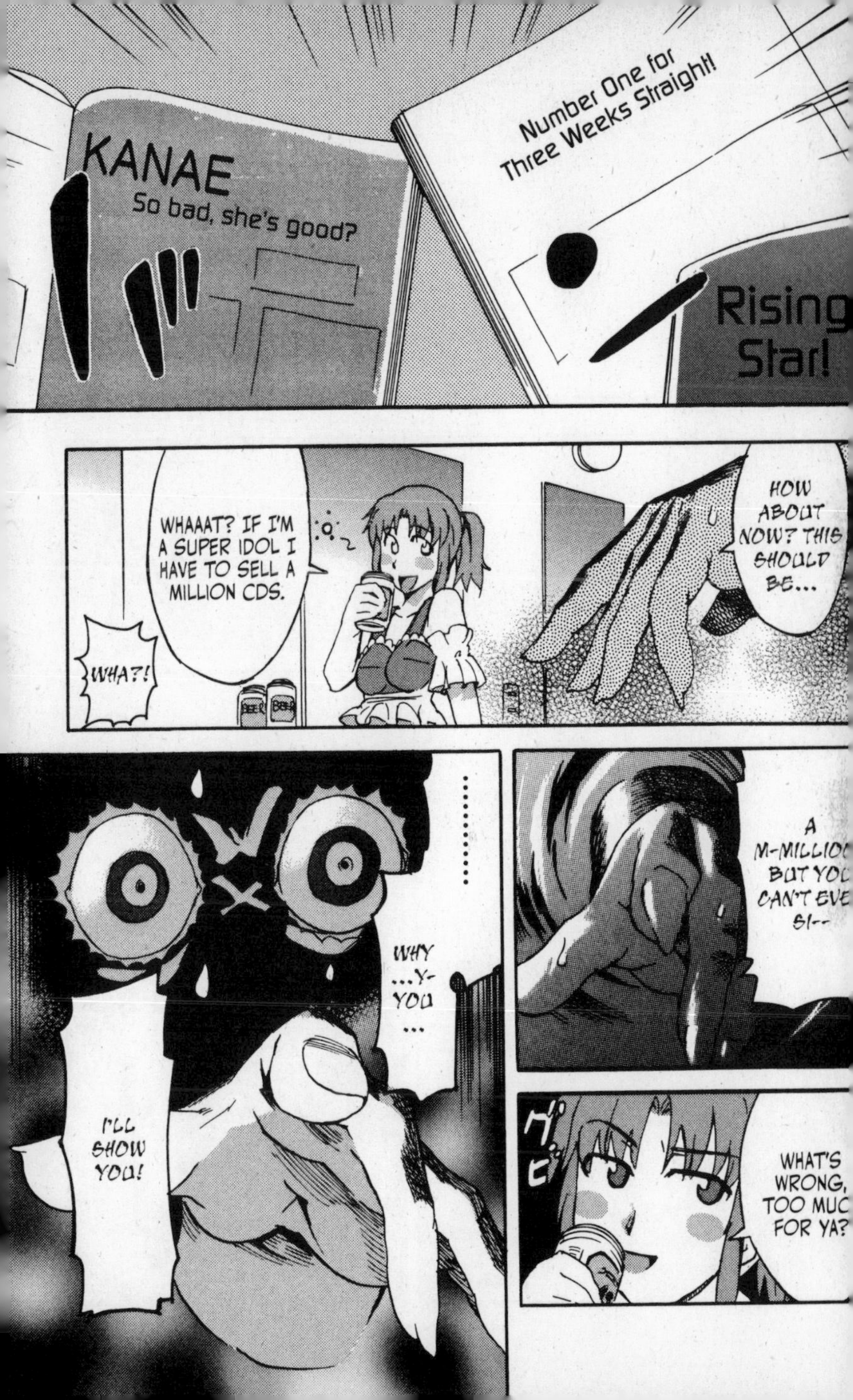
Number One for Three Weeks Straight!
KANAE
So bad, she's good?
Rising Star!
HOW ABOUT NOW? THIS SHOULD BE...
WHAAAT? IF I'M A SUPER IDOL I HAVE TO SELL A MILLION CDS.
WHA?!
A M-MILLIO BUT YO CAN'T EVE SI--
WHAT'S WRONG, TOO MUC FOR YA?
....
WHY ...Y-YOU ...
I'LL SHOW YOU!

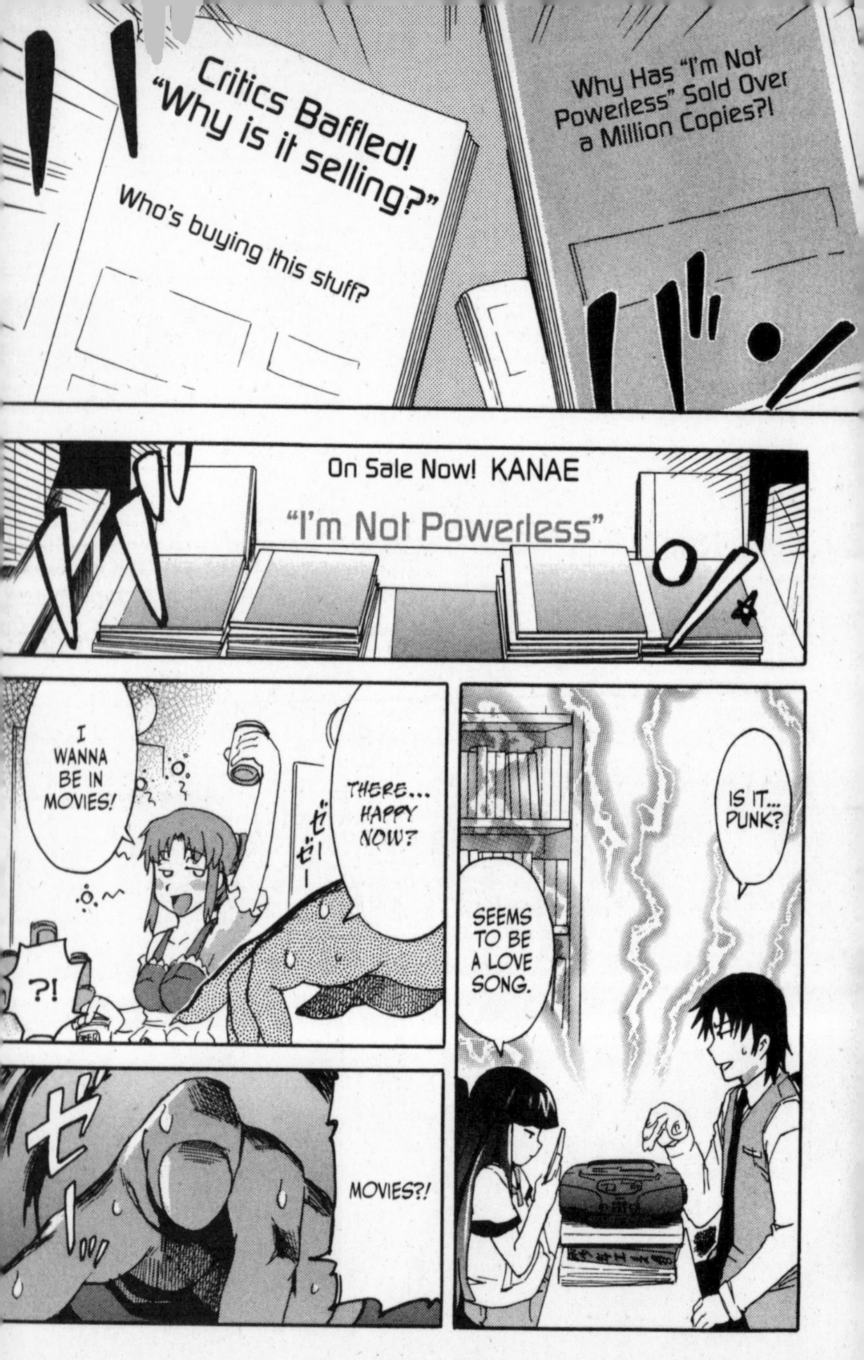
Why Has "I'm Not Powerless" Sold Over a Million Copies?!
Critics Baffled! "Why is it selling?"
Who's buying this stuff?
On Sale Now! KANAE
"I'm Not Powerless"
IS IT... PUNK?
SEEMS TO BE A LOVE SONG.
THERE... HAPPY NOW?
I WANNA BE IN MOVIES!
?!
MOVIES?!

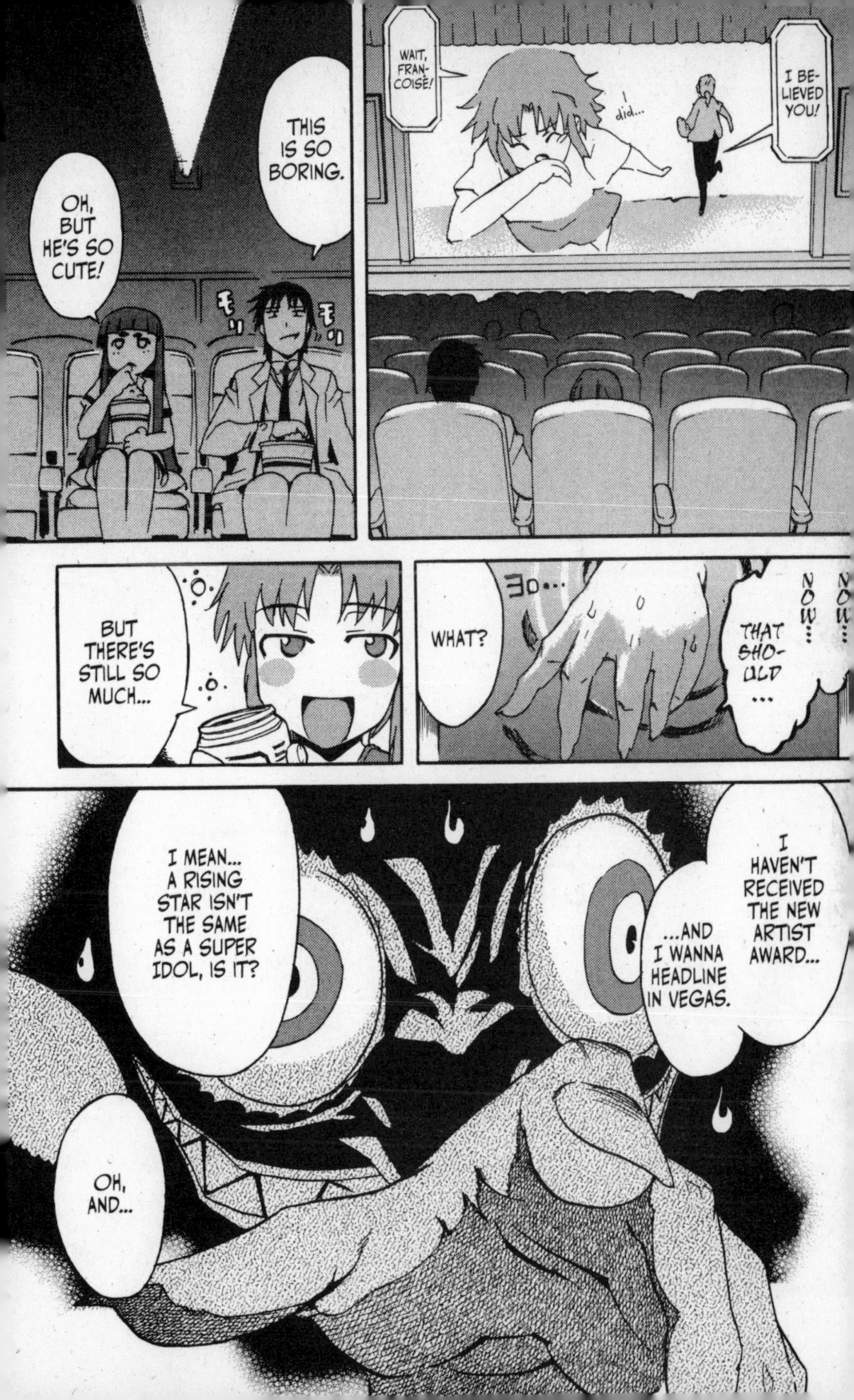
I BE-LIEVED YOU!
I did...
WAIT, FRAN-COISÉ!
THIS IS SO BORING.
OH, BUT HE'S SO CUTE!
NOW...
NOW...
THAT SHO-ULD ...
WHAT?
BUT THERE'S STILL SO MUCH...
I HAVEN'T RECEIVED THE NEW ARTIST AWARD...
...AND I WANNA HEADLINE IN VEGAS.
I MEAN... A RISING STAR ISN'T THE SAME AS A SUPER IDOL, IS IT?
OH, AND...

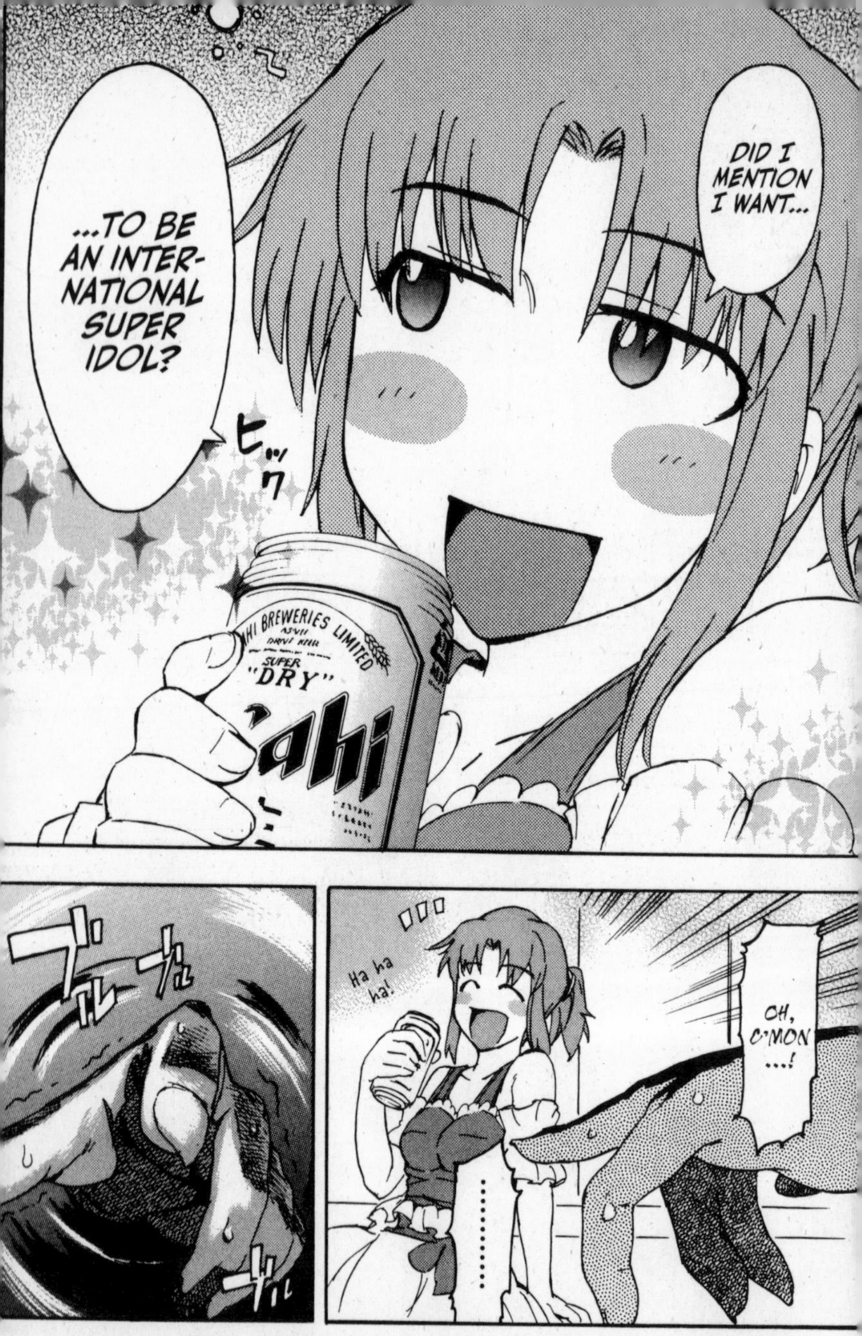
DID I MENTION I WANT...
...TO BE AN INTER-NATIONAL SUPER IDOL?
ヒック
SUPER "DRY"
OH, C'MON ...!
Ha ha ha!

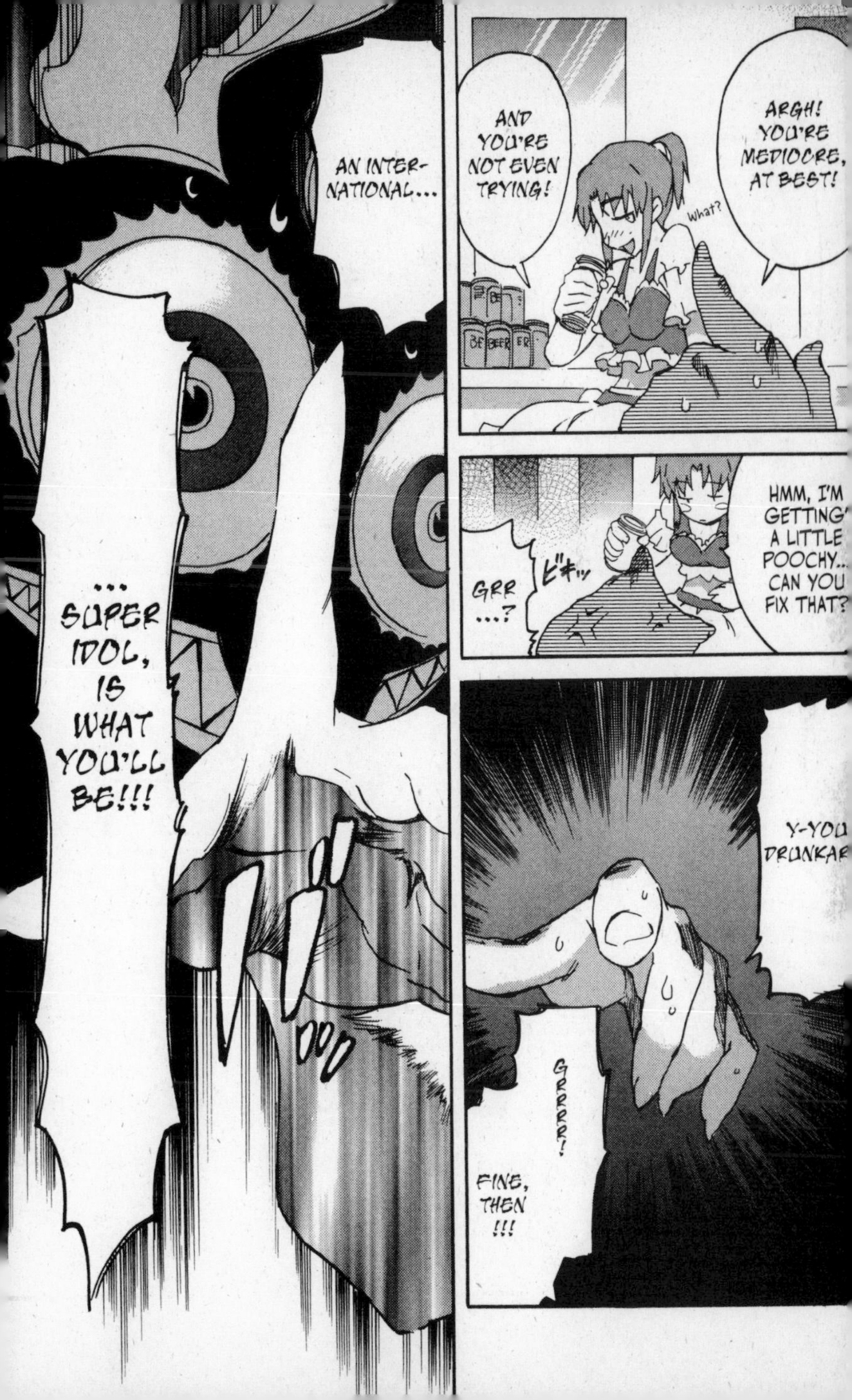
ARGH! YOU'RE MEDIOCRE, AT BEST!
What?
AND YOU'RE NOT EVEN TRYING!
HMM, I'M GETTING A LITTLE POOCHY... CAN YOU FIX THAT?
ビキッ
GRR ...?
Y-YOU DRUNKAR
GRRRRR!
FINE, THEN !!!
AN INTER-NATIONAL...
... SUPER IDOL, IS WHAT YOU'LL BE!!!

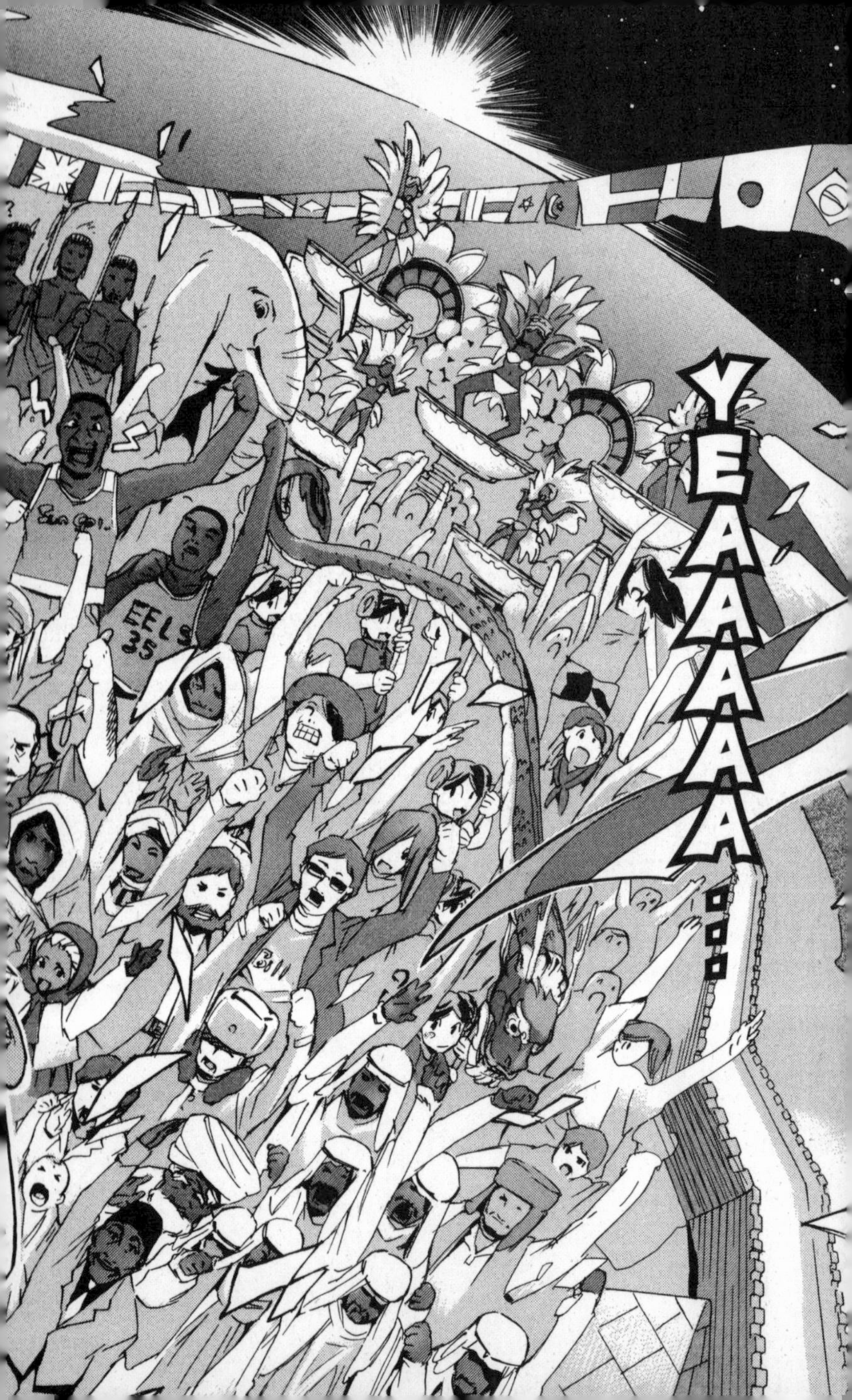
YEAAAAA...
EELS
35

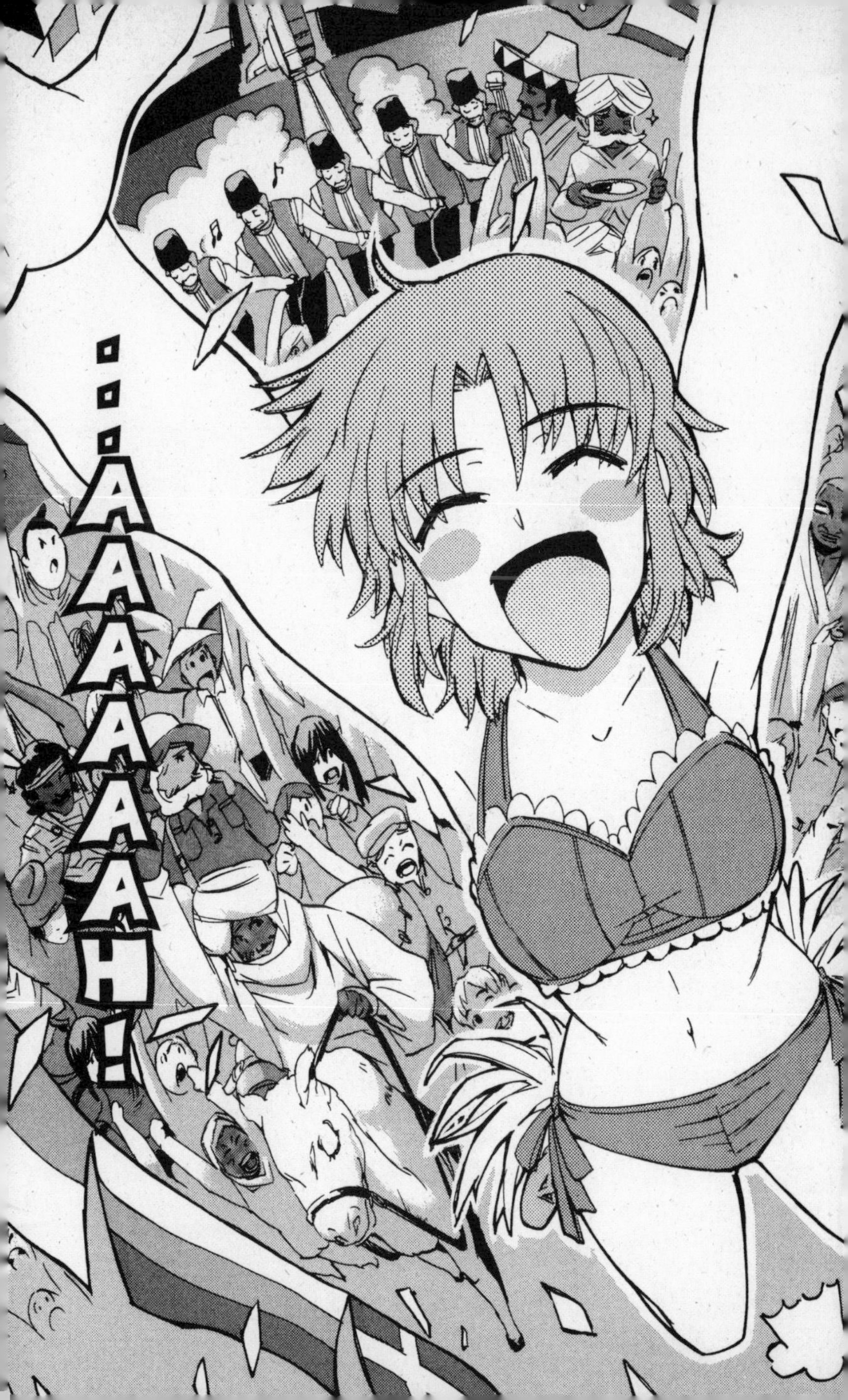
...AAAAAAH!

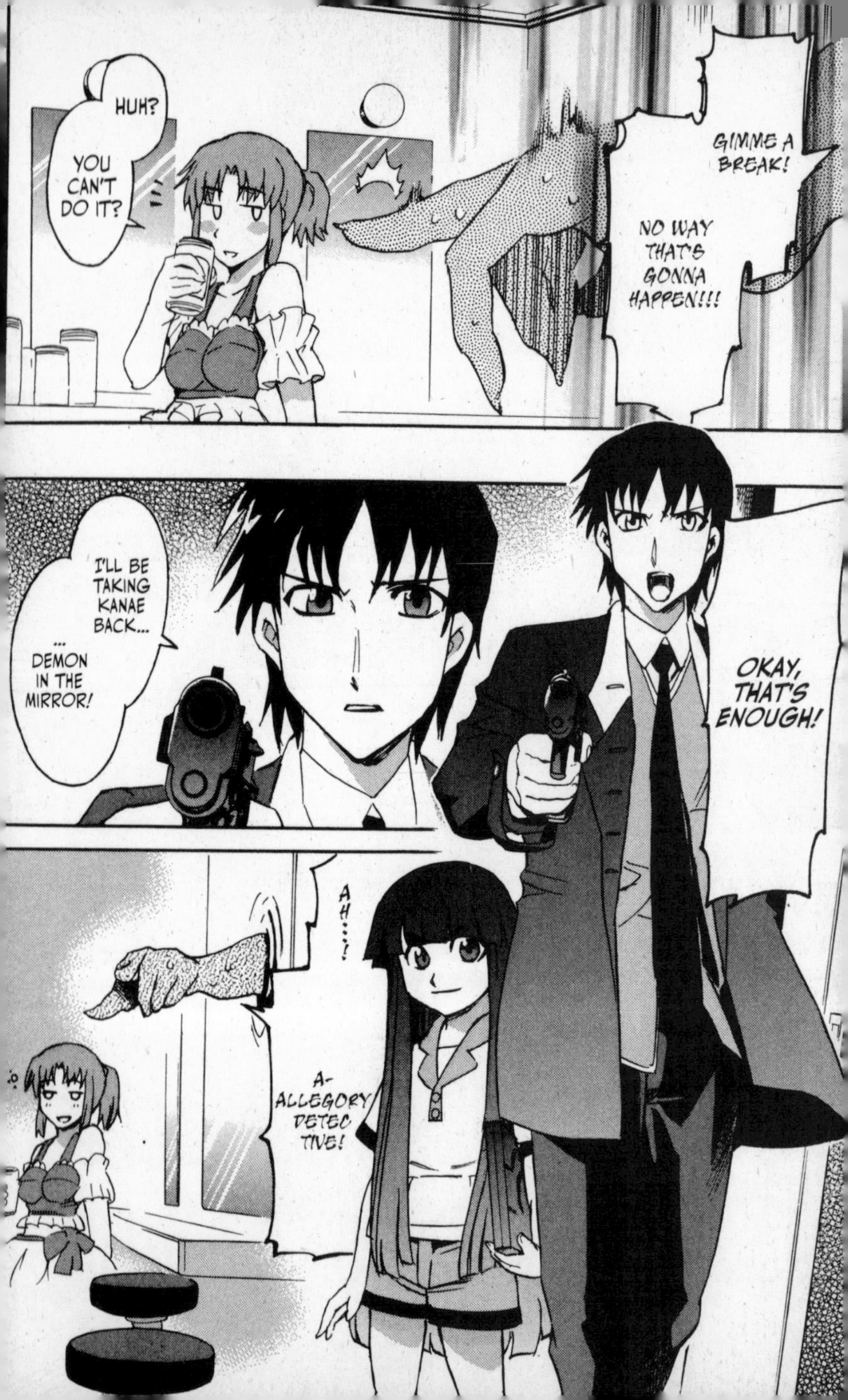
GIMME A BREAK!
NO WAY THAT'S GONNA HAPPEN!!!
HUH?
YOU CAN'T DO IT?
OKAY, THAT'S ENOUGH!
I'LL BE TAKING KANAE BACK...
... DEMON IN THE MIRROR!
AH...!
A-ALLEGORY DETEC TIVE!

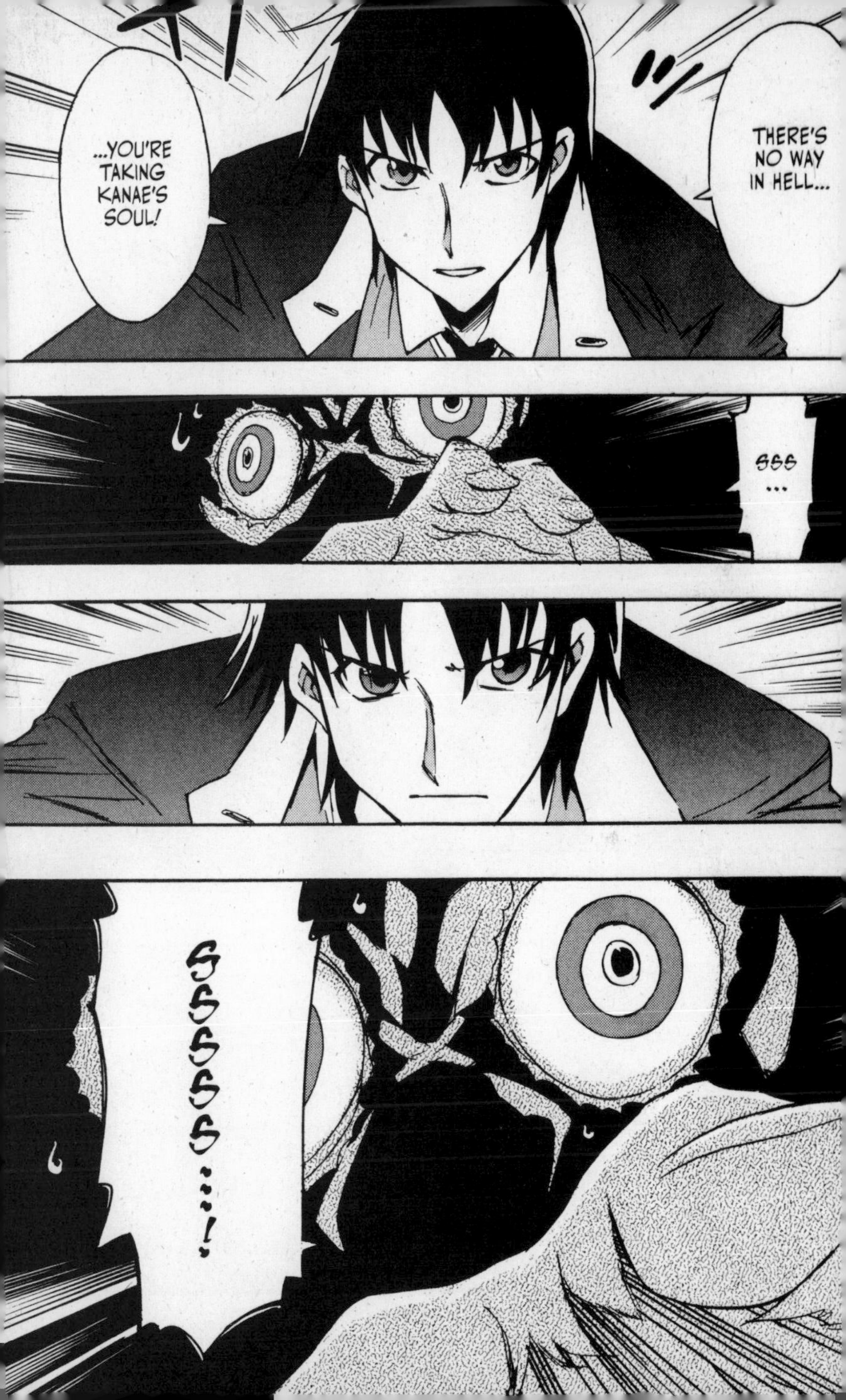
THERE'S NO WAY IN HELL...
...YOU'RE TAKING KANAE'S SOUL!
SSS...
SSSSS...!

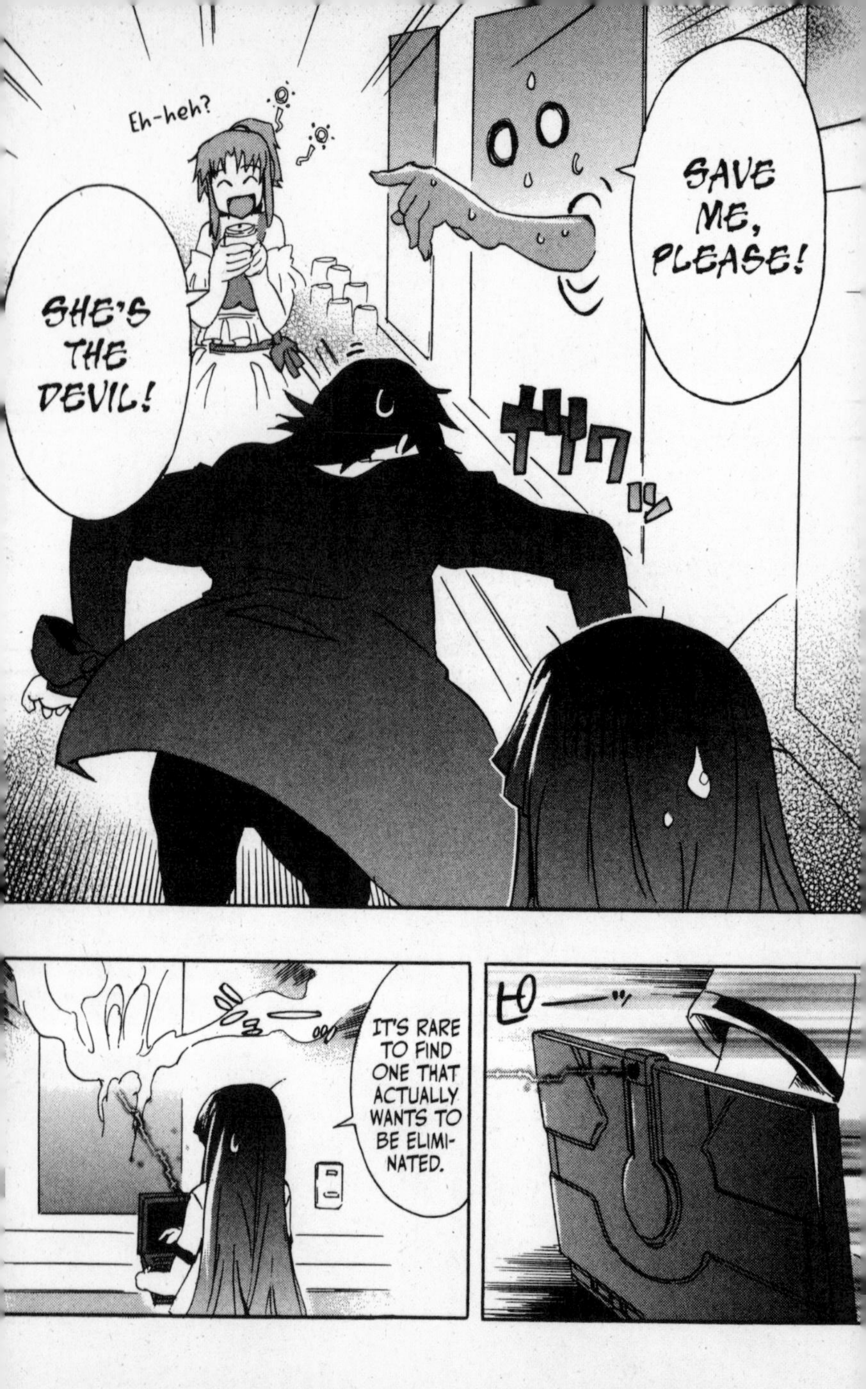
SAVE ME, PLEASE!
Eh-heh?
SHE'S THE DEVIL!
IT'S RARE TO FIND ONE THAT ACTUALLY WANTS TO BE ELIMINATED.

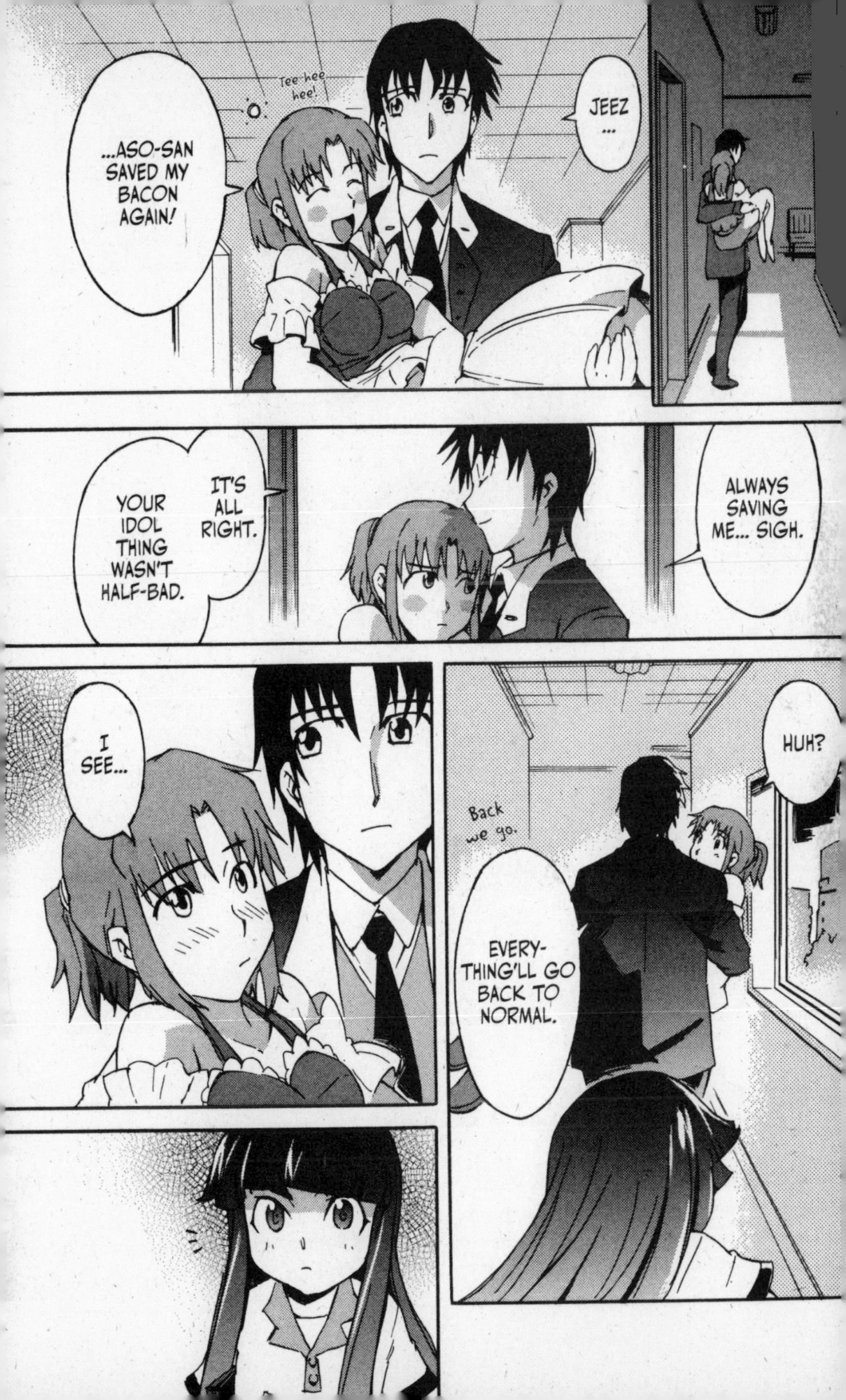
JEEZ ...
Tee hee hee!
...ASO-SAN SAVED MY BACON AGAIN!
ALWAYS SAVING ME... SIGH.
IT'S ALL RIGHT.
YOUR IDOL THING WASN'T HALF-BAD.
HUH?
Back we go.
EVERY-THING'LL GO BACK TO NORMAL.
I SEE...

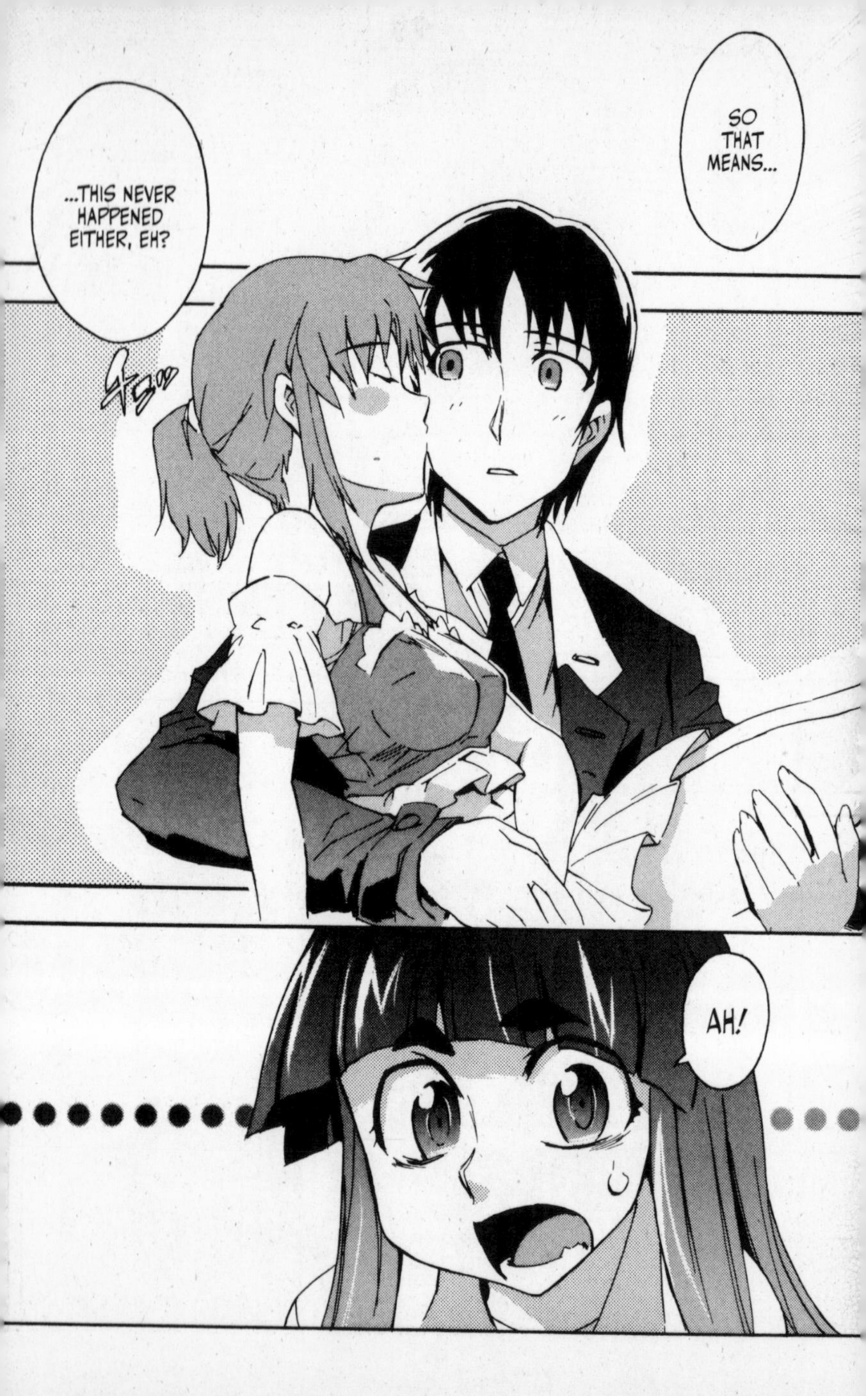
SO THAT MEANS...
...THIS NEVER HAPPENED EITHER, EH?
AH!

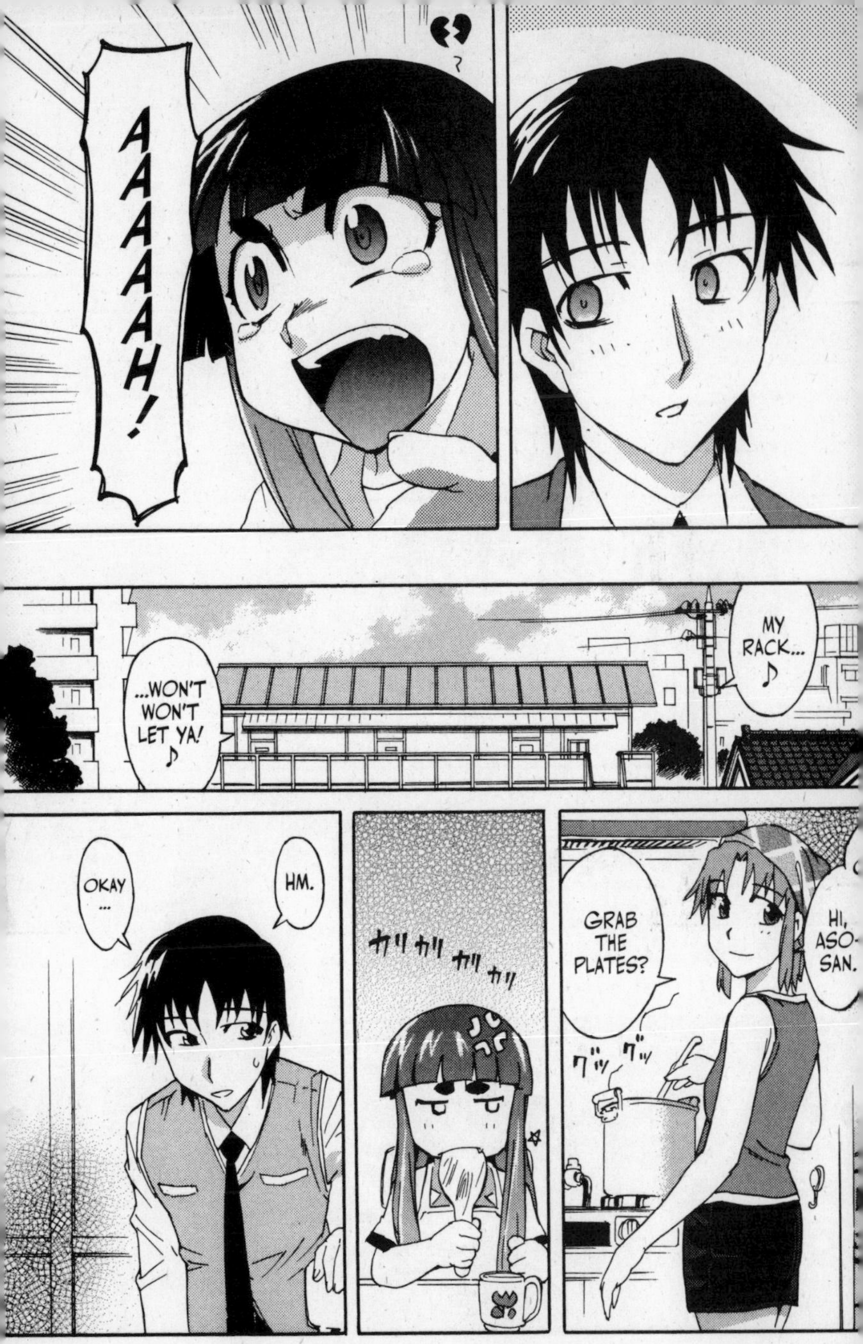
AAAAAAH!
MY RACK... ♪
...WON'T WON'T LET YA! ♪
HI, ASO-SAN.
GRAB THE PLATES?
HM.
OKAY ...

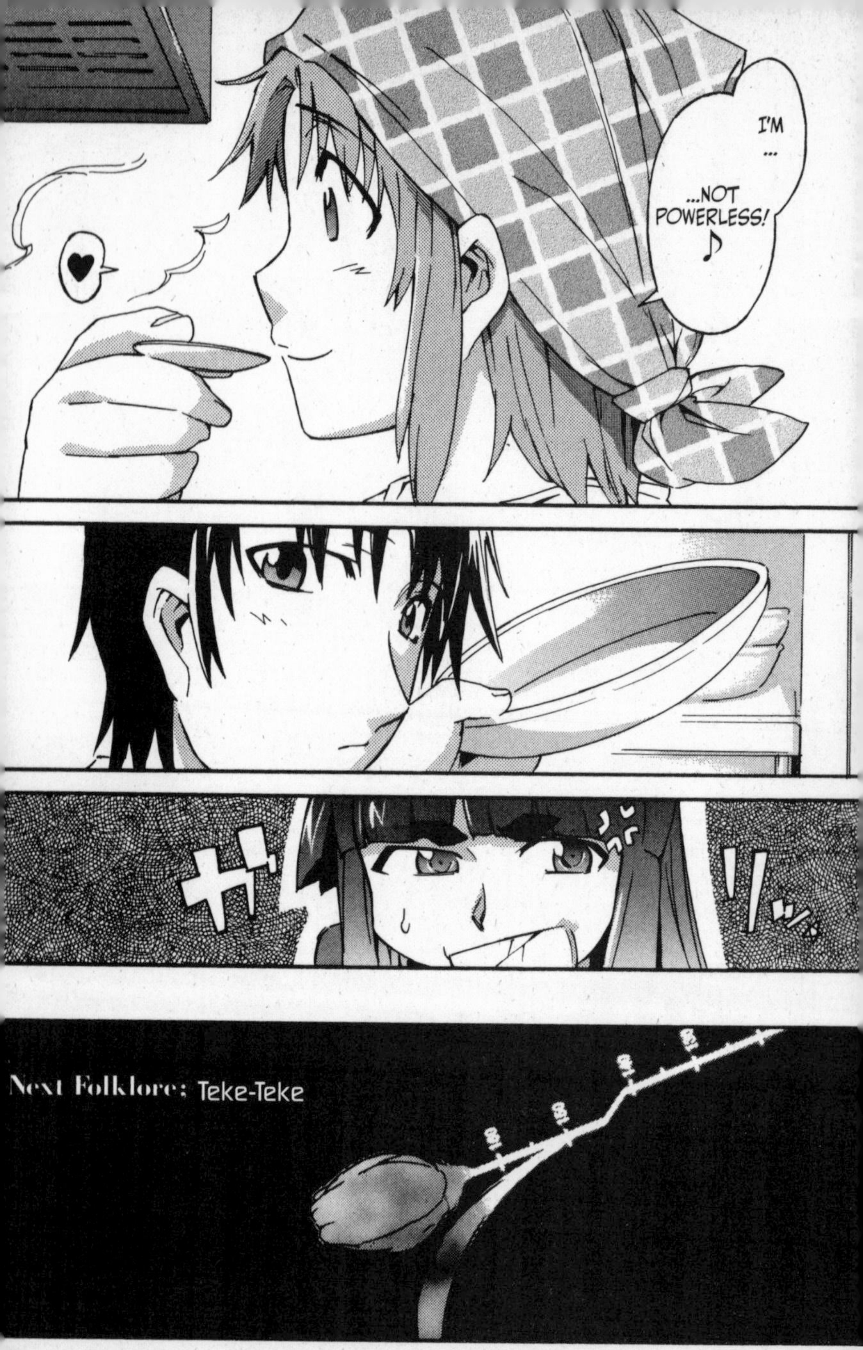
I'M ... ...NOT POWERLESS! ♪
Next Folklore: Teke-Teke

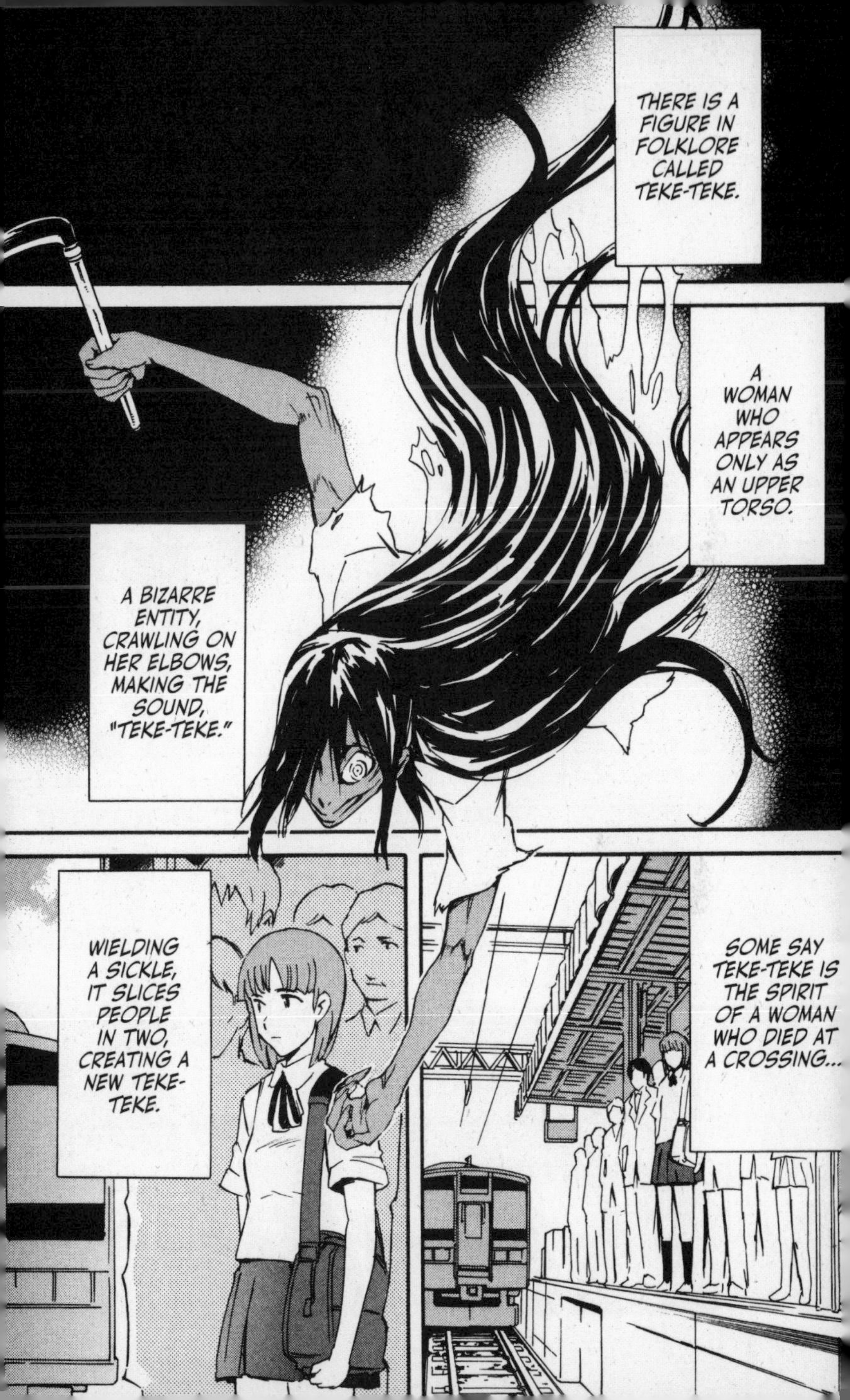
THERE IS A FIGURE IN FOLKLORE CALLED TEKE-TEKE.
A WOMAN WHO APPEARS ONLY AS AN UPPER TORSO.
A BIZARRE ENTITY, CRAWLING ON HER ELBOWS, MAKING THE SOUND, "TEKE-TEKE."
SOME SAY TEKE-TEKE IS THE SPIRIT OF A WOMAN WHO DIED AT A CROSSING...
WIELDING A SICKLE, IT SLICES PEOPLE IN TWO, CREATING A NEW TEKE-TEKE.

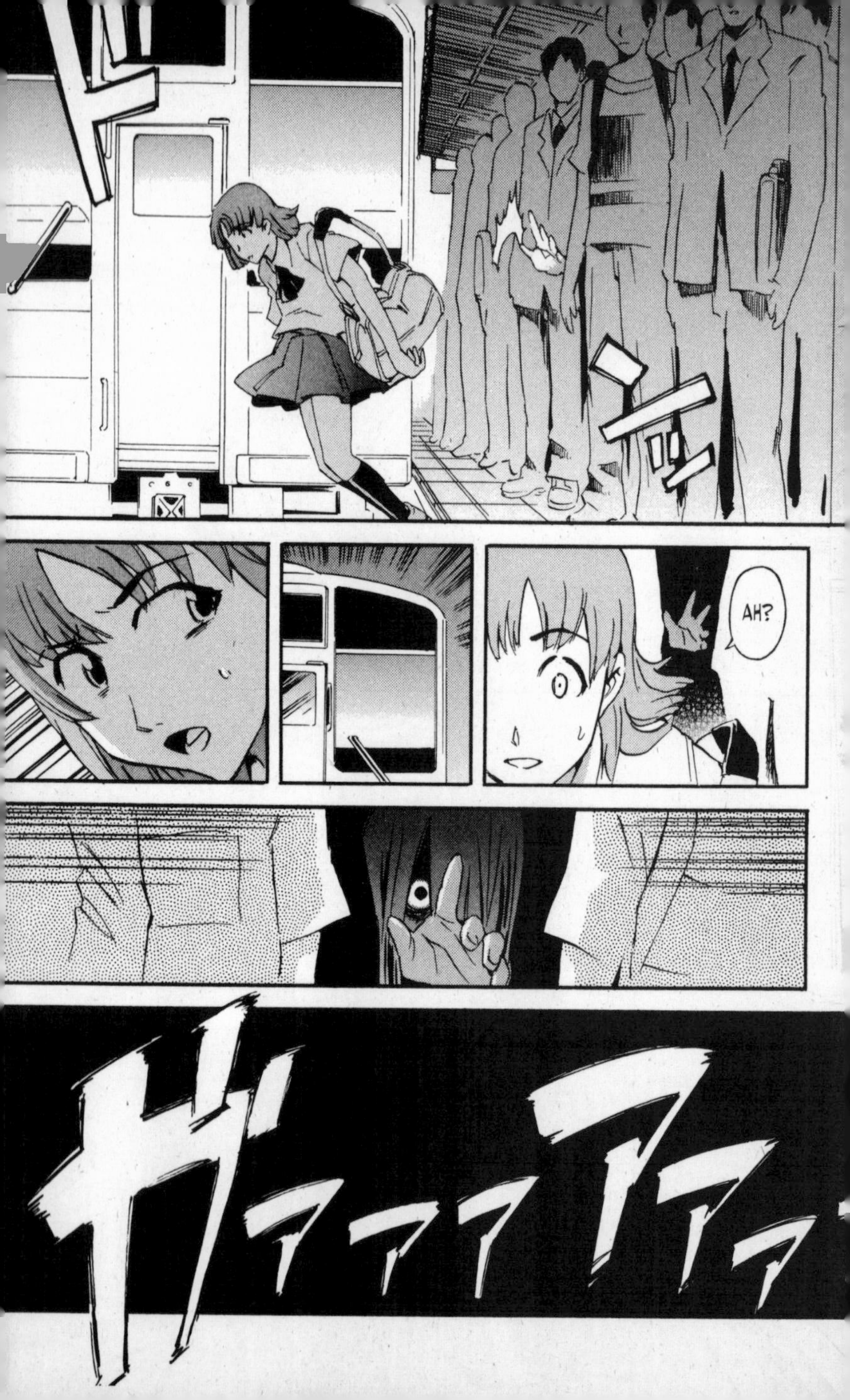
AH?
ザァァァアァァ

Folklore;
Teke-Teke – Part 1 –

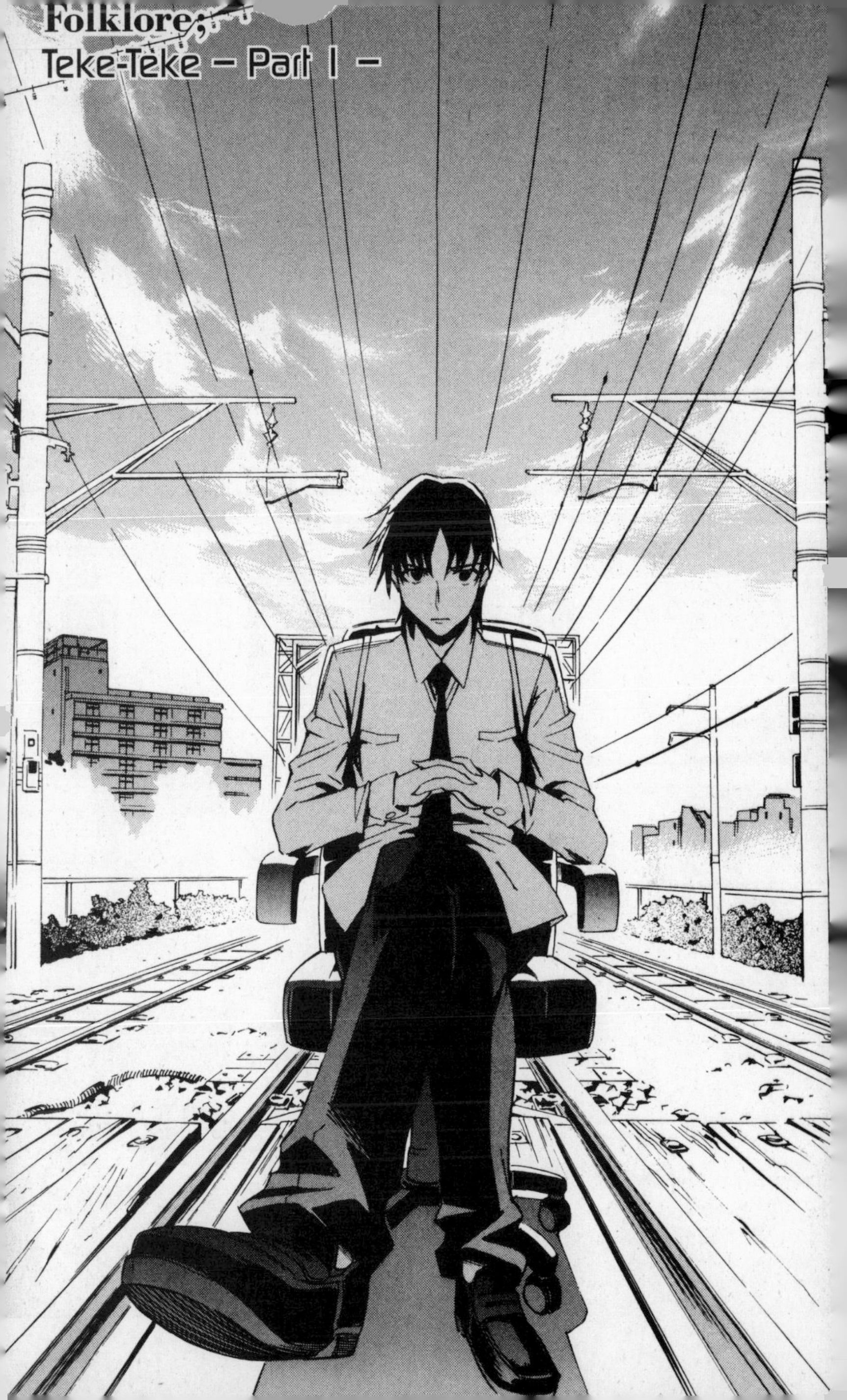

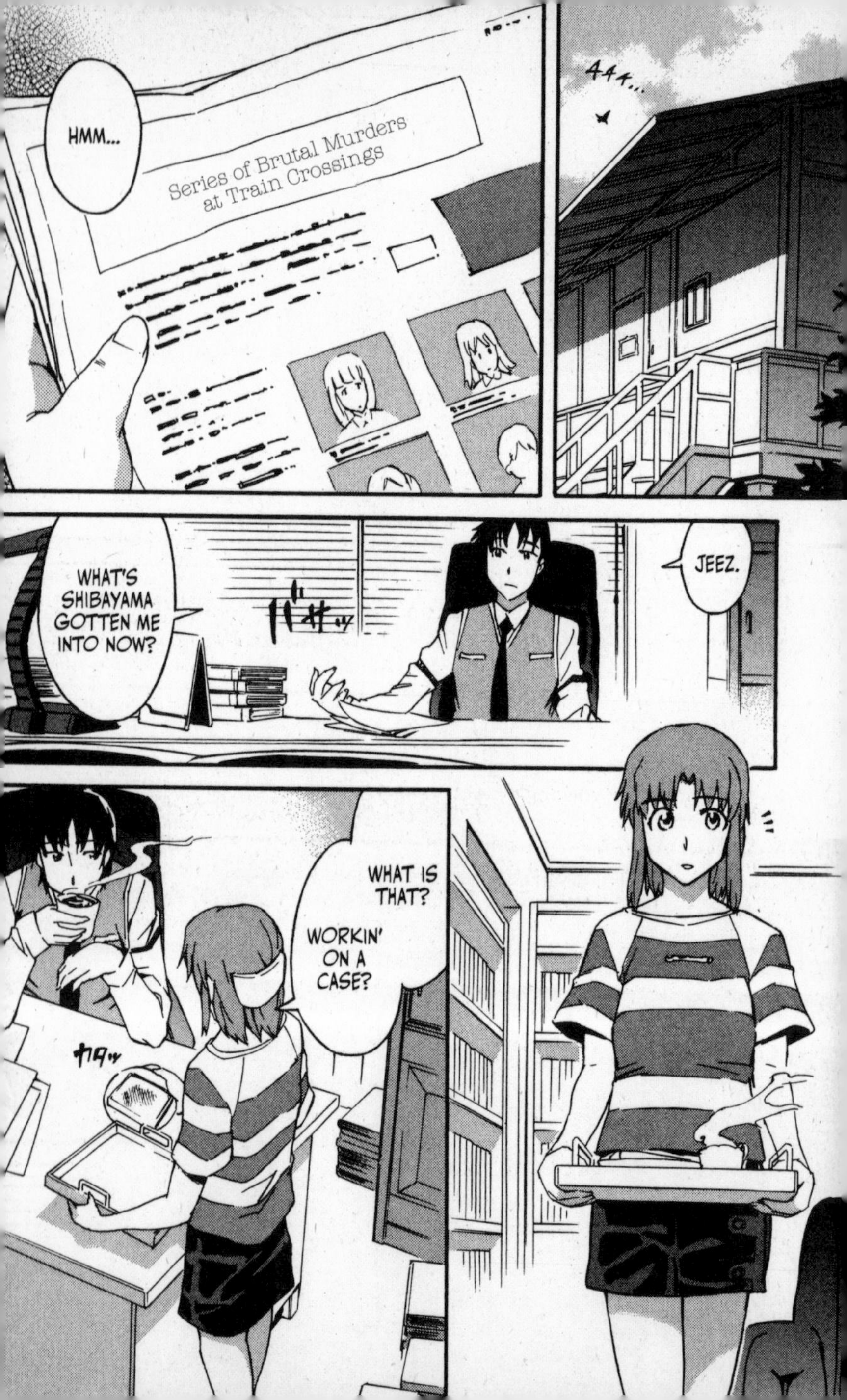
Series of Brutal Murders at Train Crossings
HMM...
JEEZ.
WHAT'S SHIBAYAMA GOTTEN ME INTO NOW?
WHAT IS THAT?
WORKIN' ON A CASE?

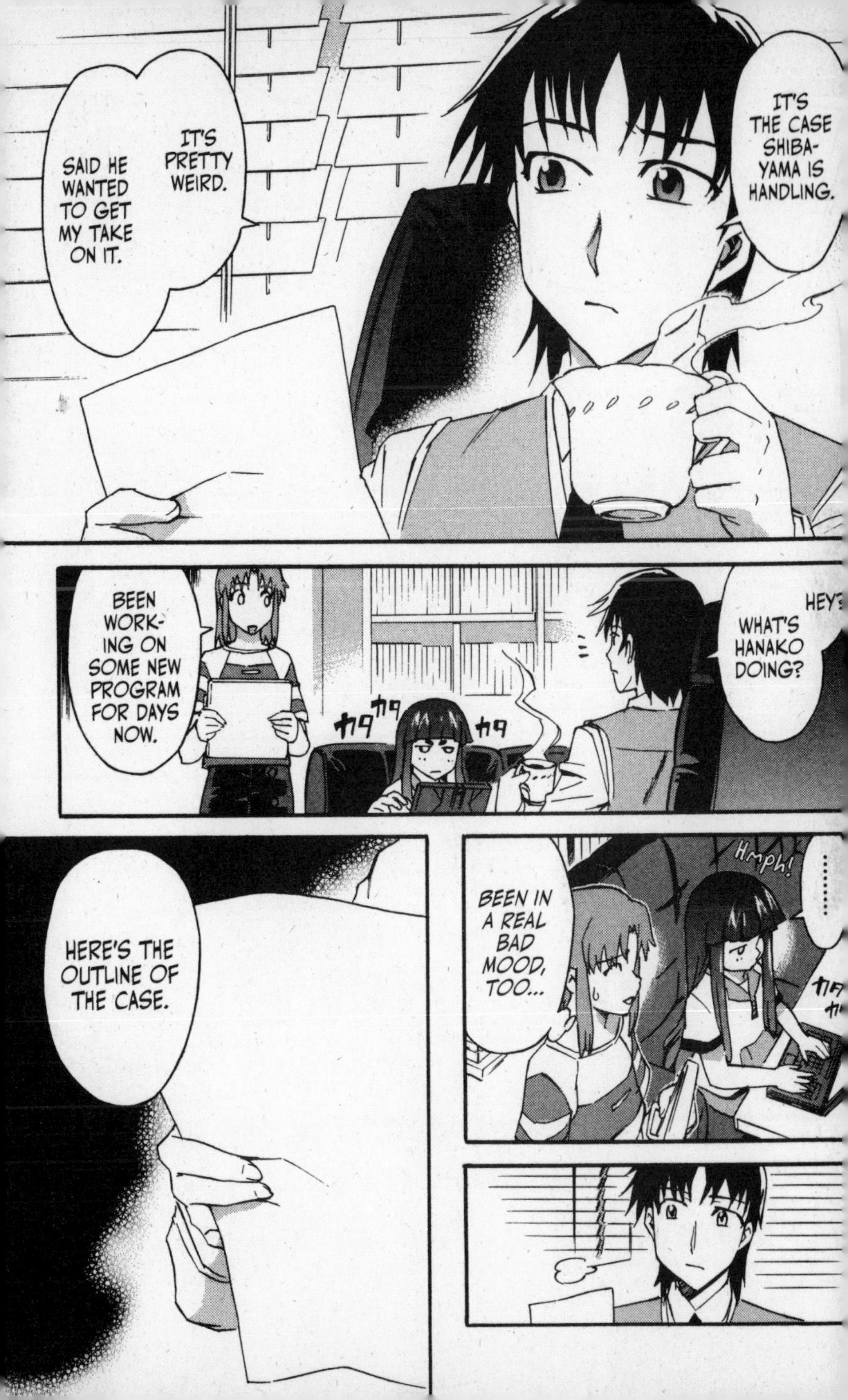
IT'S THE CASE SHIBA-YAMA IS HANDLING.
IT'S PRETTY WEIRD.
SAID HE WANTED TO GET MY TAKE ON IT.
HEY?
WHAT'S HANAKO DOING?
カタ カタ カタ
BEEN WORK-ING ON SOME NEW PROGRAM FOR DAYS NOW.
......
Hmph!
BEEN IN A REAL BAD MOOD, TOO...
HERE'S THE OUTLINE OF THE CASE.

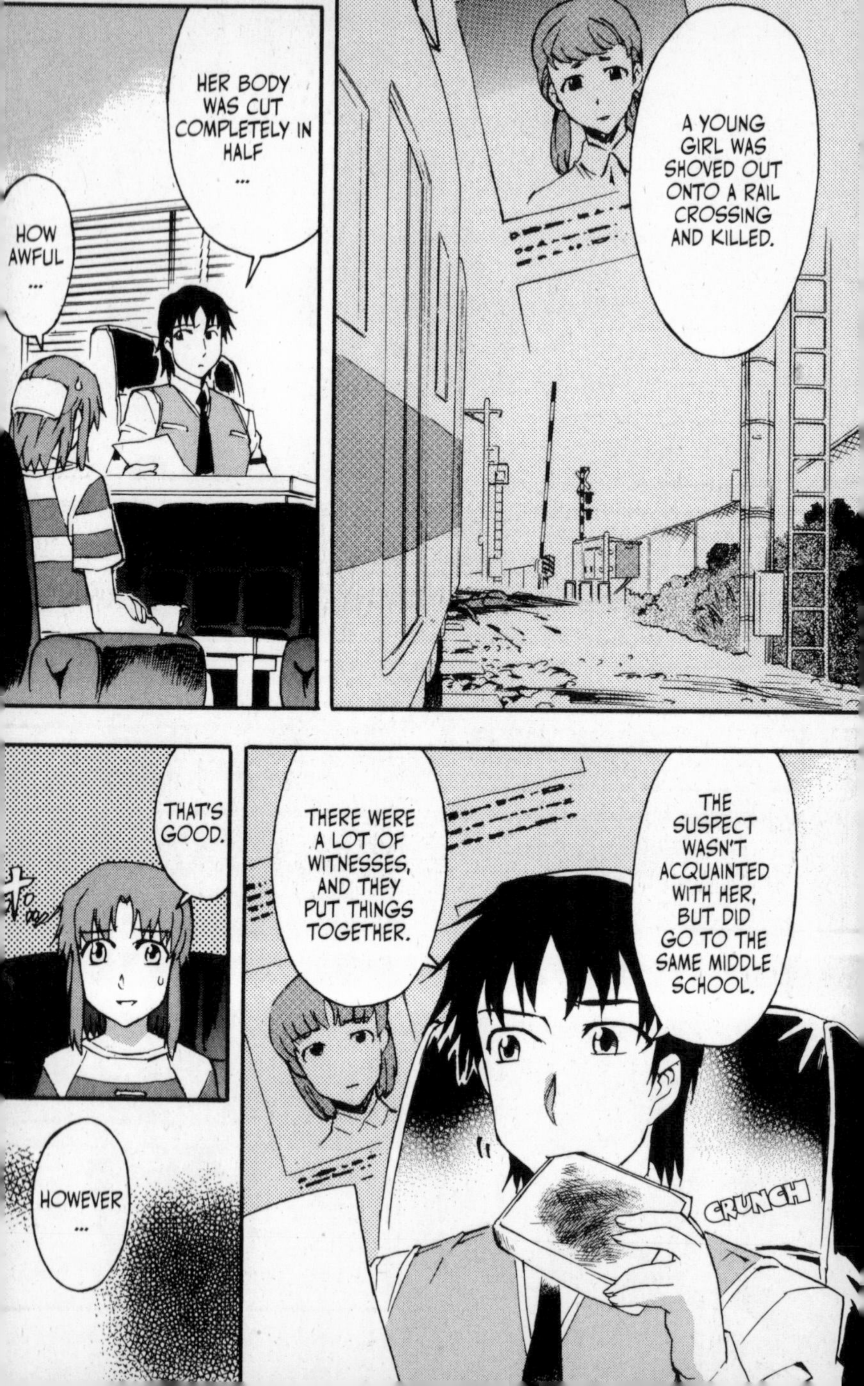
A YOUNG GIRL WAS SHOVED OUT ONTO A RAIL CROSSING AND KILLED.
HER BODY WAS CUT COMPLETELY IN HALF ...
HOW AWFUL ...
THE SUSPECT WASN'T ACQUAINTED WITH HER, BUT DID GO TO THE SAME MIDDLE SCHOOL.
THERE WERE A LOT OF WITNESSES, AND THEY PUT THINGS TOGETHER.
CRUNCH
THAT'S GOOD.
HOWEVER ...

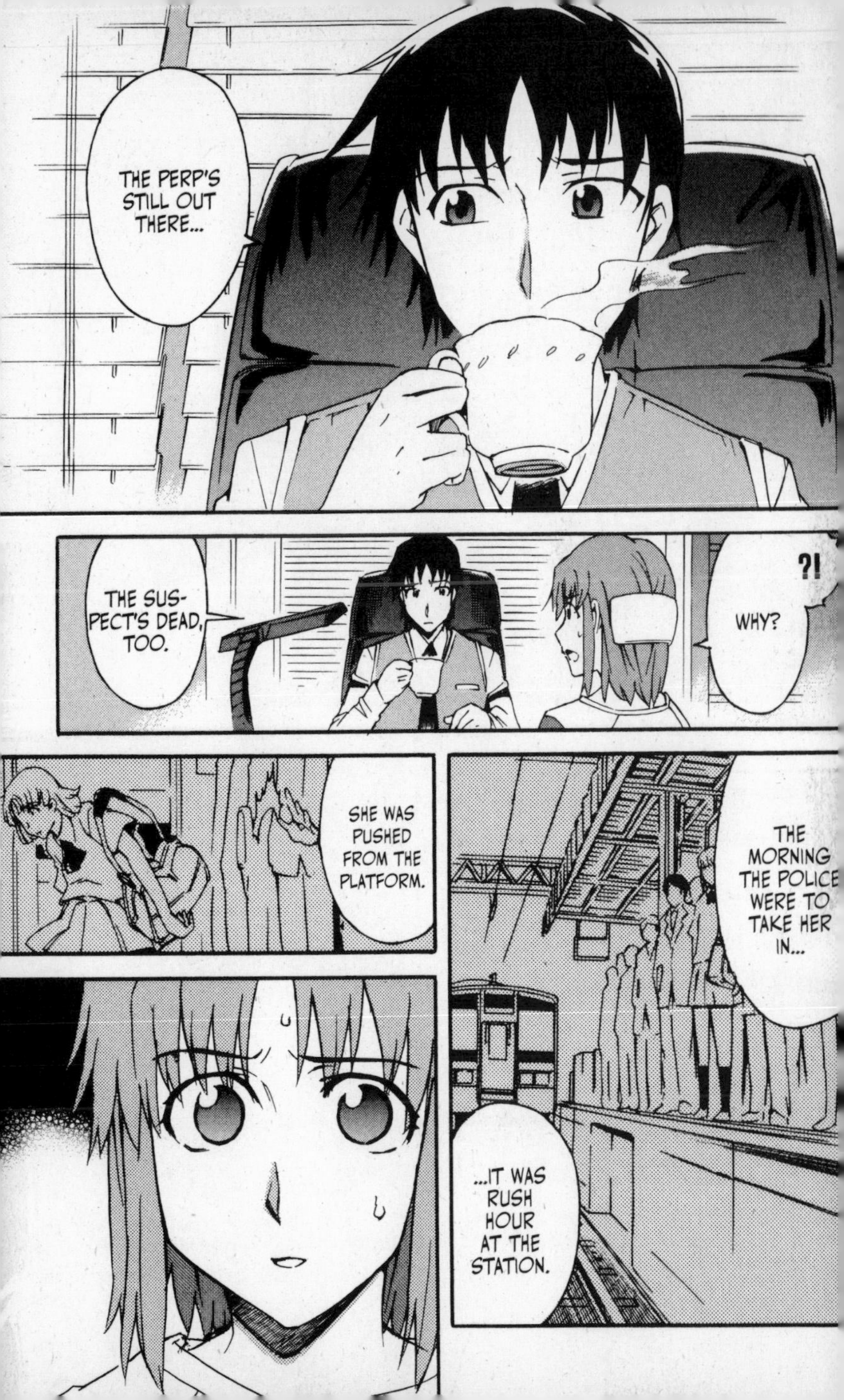
THE PERP'S STILL OUT THERE...
?!
WHY?
THE SUS-PECT'S DEAD, TOO.
THE MORNING THE POLICE WERE TO TAKE HER IN...
...IT WAS RUSH HOUR AT THE STATION.
SHE WAS PUSHED FROM THE PLATFORM.

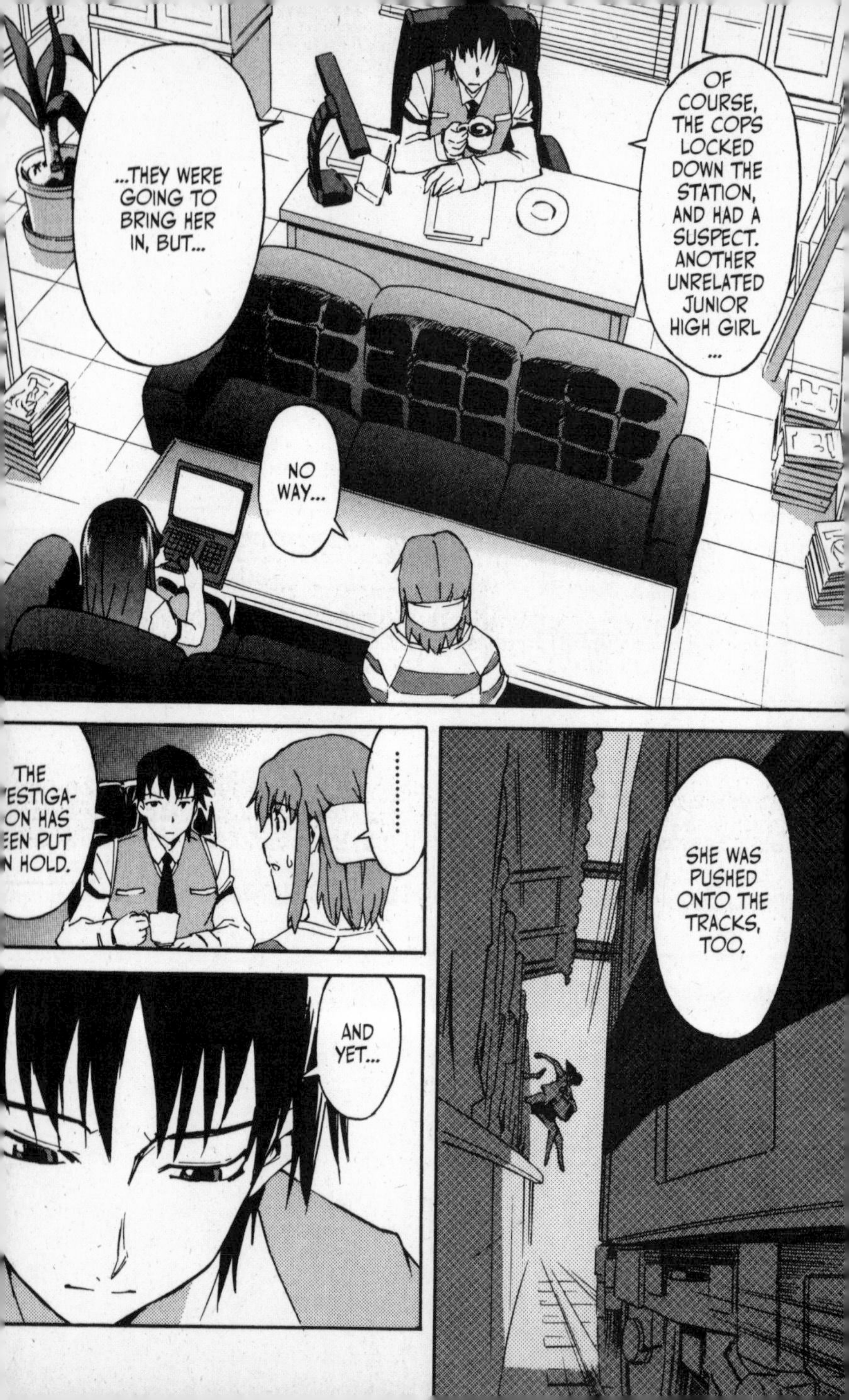
OF COURSE, THE COPS LOCKED DOWN THE STATION, AND HAD A SUSPECT. ANOTHER UNRELATED JUNIOR HIGH GIRL ...
...THEY WERE GOING TO BRING HER IN, BUT...
NO WAY...
SHE WAS PUSHED ONTO THE TRACKS, TOO.
....
THE ESTIGA- ON HAS EEN PUT N HOLD.
AND YET...

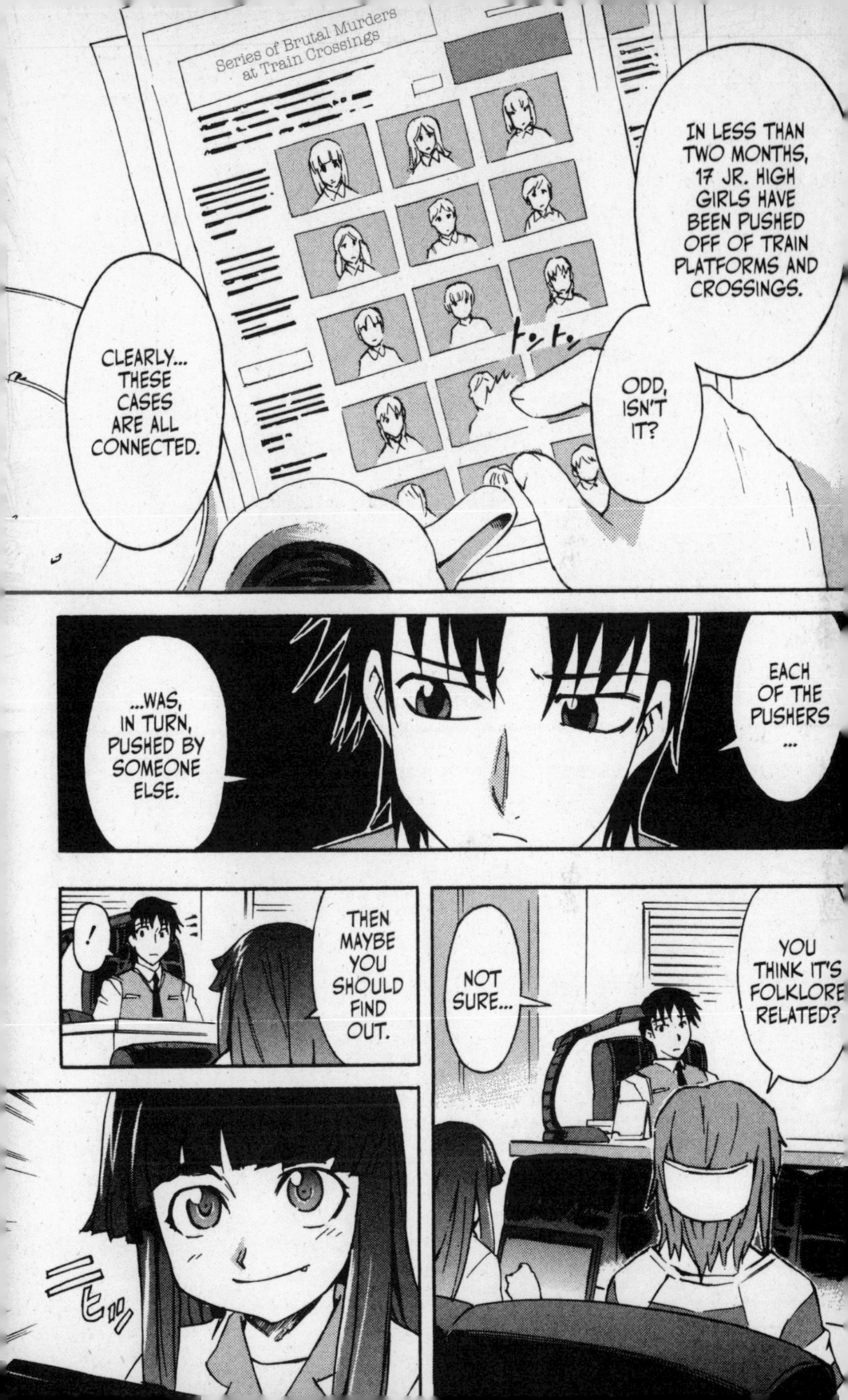
Series of Brutal Murders at Train Crossings
IN LESS THAN TWO MONTHS, 17 JR. HIGH GIRLS HAVE BEEN PUSHED OFF OF TRAIN PLATFORMS AND CROSSINGS.
ODD, ISN'T IT?
トントン
CLEARLY... THESE CASES ARE ALL CONNECTED.
EACH OF THE PUSHERS ...
...WAS, IN TURN, PUSHED BY SOMEONE ELSE.
YOU THINK IT'S FOLKLORE RELATED?
NOT SURE...
!
THEN MAYBE YOU SHOULD FIND OUT.
ニヒッ

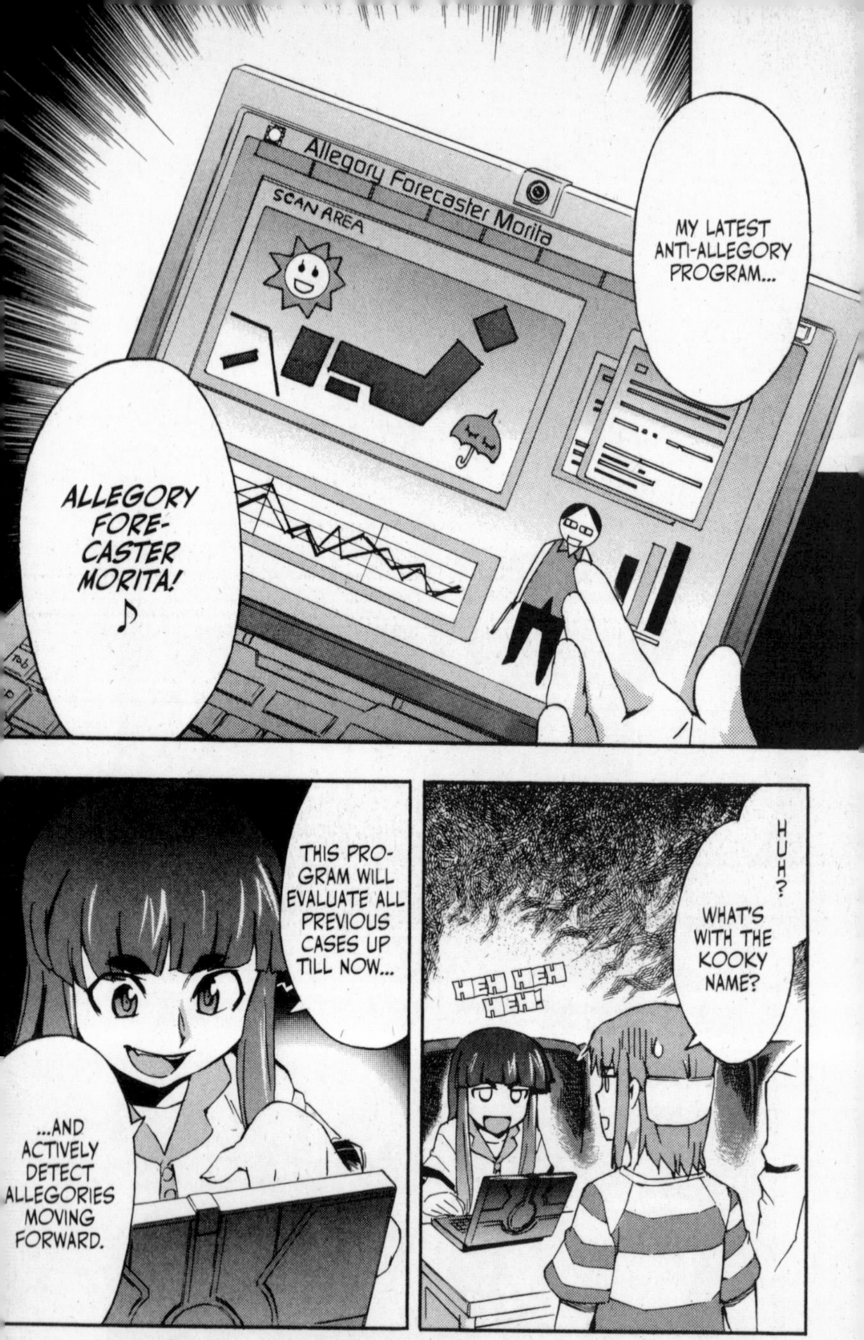
MY LATEST ANTI-ALLEGORY PROGRAM...
Allegory Forecaster Morita
SCAN AREA
ALLEGORY FORE-CASTER MORITA! ♪
HUH? WHAT'S WITH THE KOOKY NAME?
HEH HEH HEH!
THIS PRO-GRAM WILL EVALUATE ALL PREVIOUS CASES UP TILL NOW...
...AND ACTIVELY DETECT ALLEGORIES MOVING FORWARD.

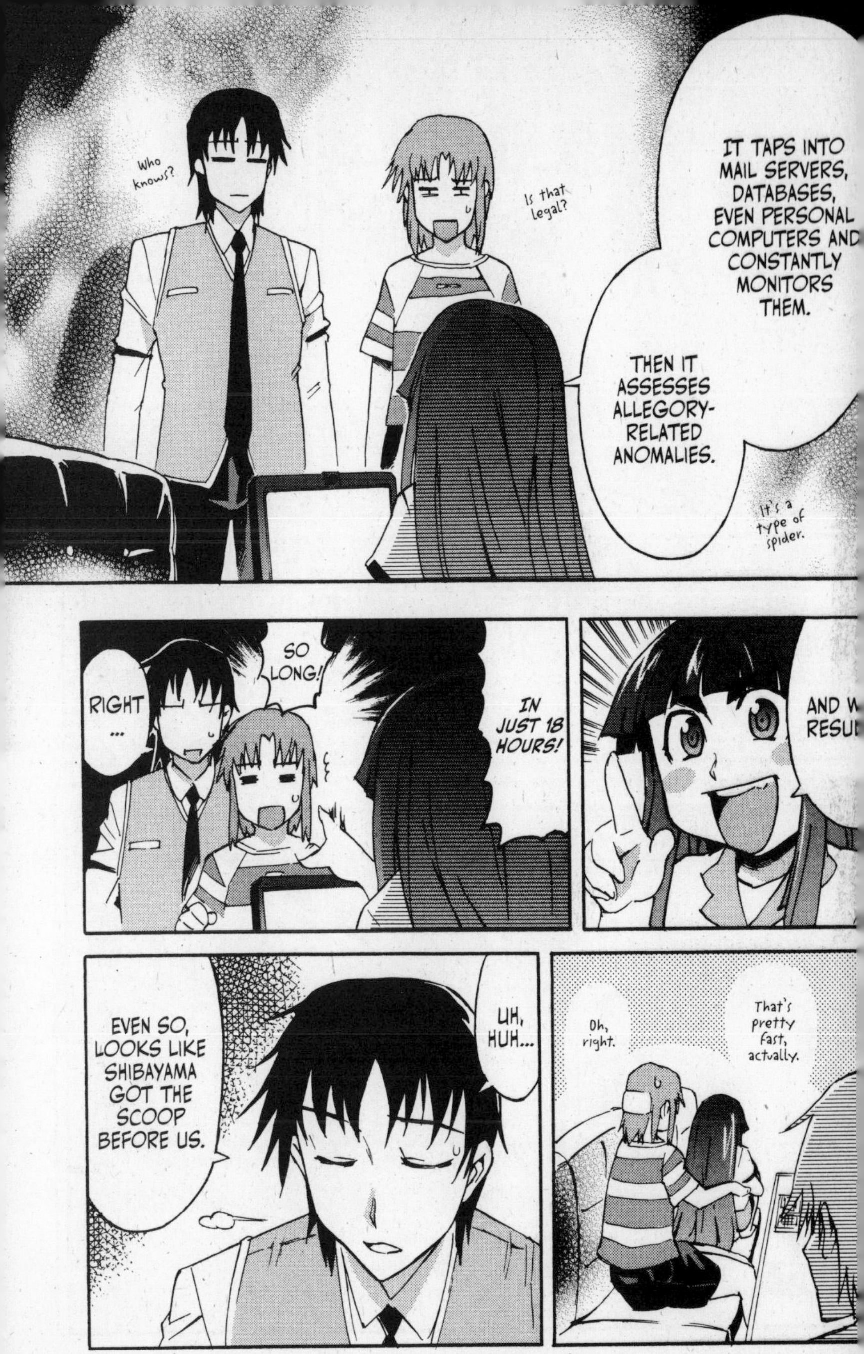
IT TAPS INTO MAIL SERVERS, DATABASES, EVEN PERSONAL COMPUTERS AND CONSTANTLY MONITORS THEM.
THEN IT ASSESSES ALLEGORY-RELATED ANOMALIES.
It's a type of spider.
Is that legal?
Who knows?
IN JUST 18 HOURS!
SO LONG!
RIGHT ...
That's pretty fast, actually.
Oh, right.
UH, HUH...
EVEN SO, LOOKS LIKE SHIBAYAMA GOT THE SCOOP BEFORE US.

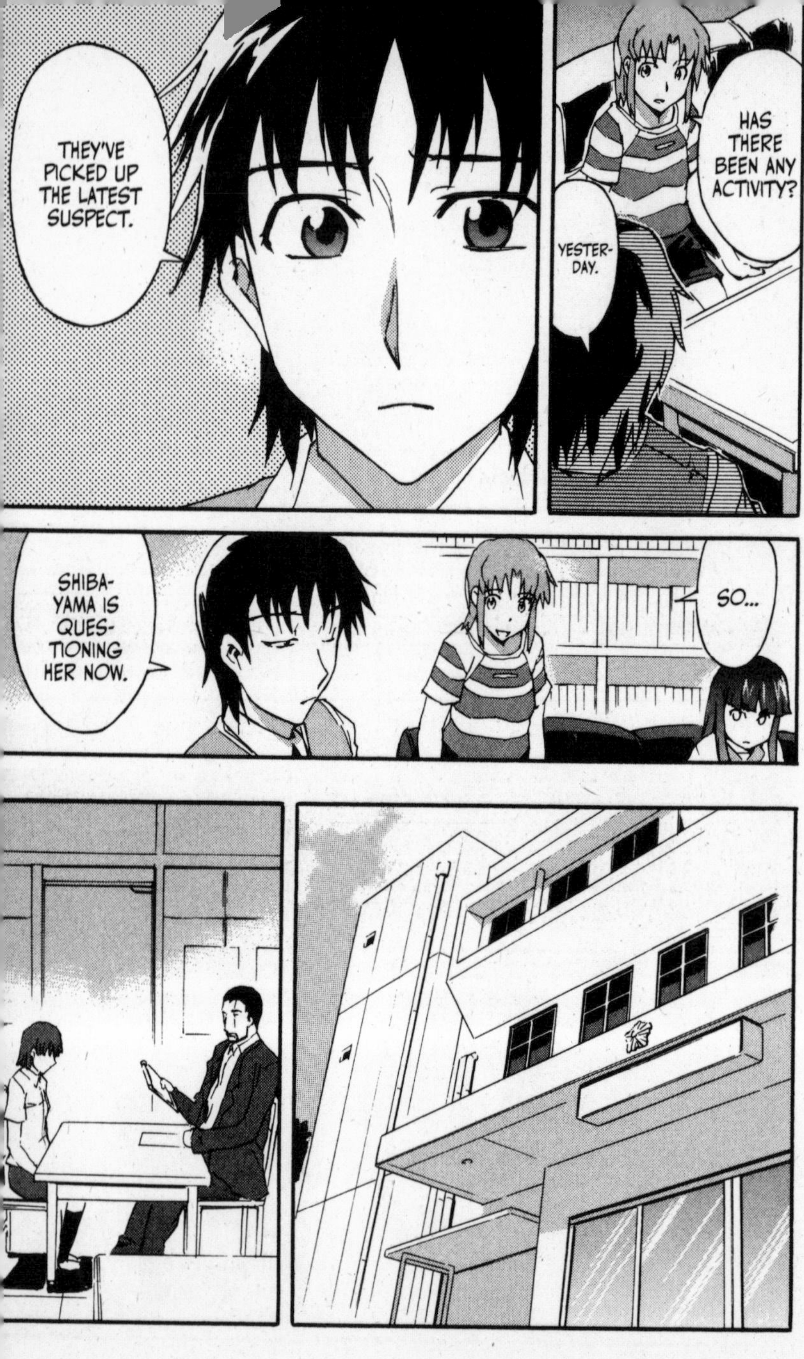
HAS THERE BEEN ANY ACTIVITY?
YESTER-DAY.
THEY'VE PICKED UP THE LATEST SUSPECT.
SO...
SHIBA-YAMA IS QUES-TIONING HER NOW.

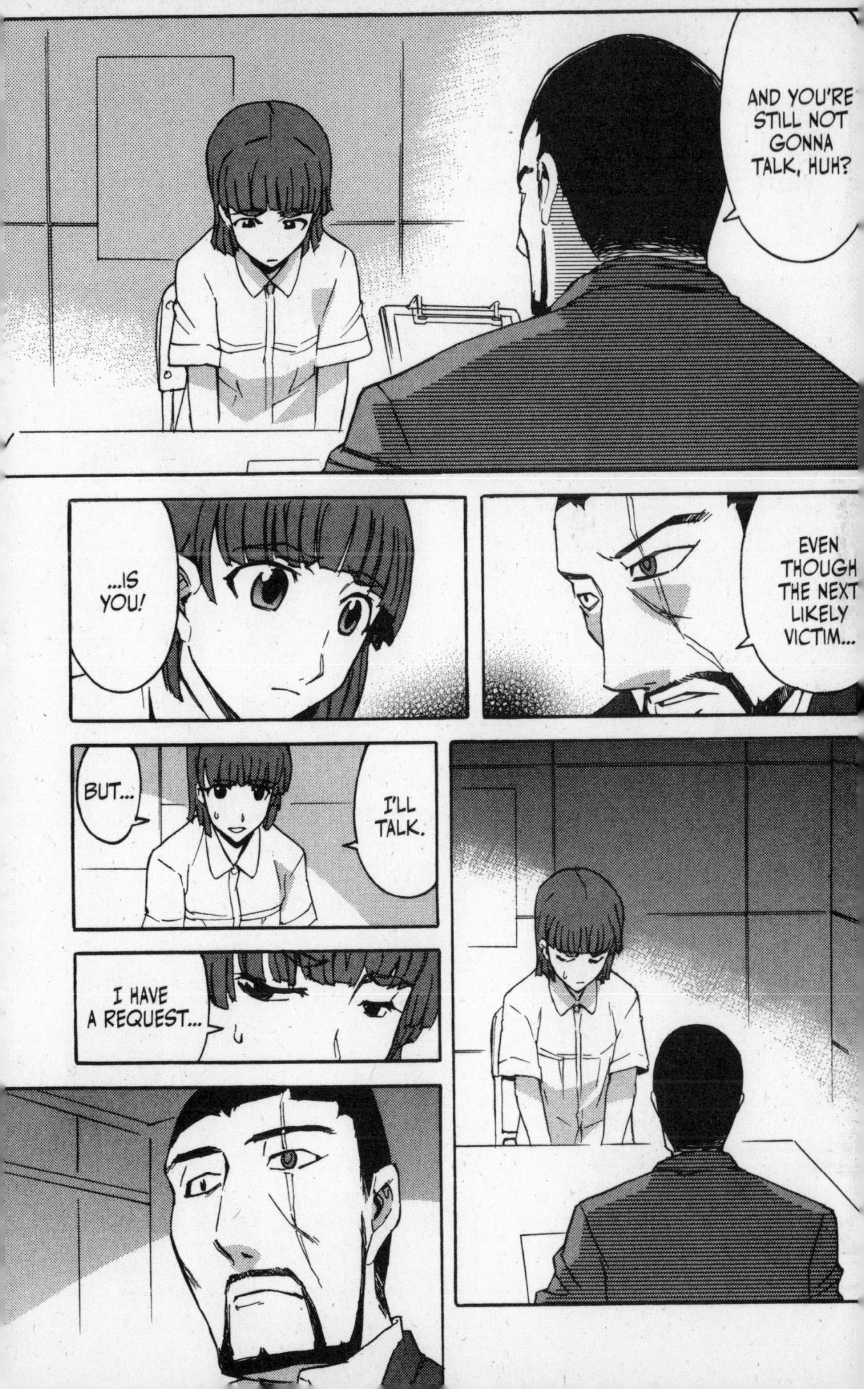
AND YOU'RE STILL NOT GONNA TALK, HUH?
EVEN THOUGH THE NEXT LIKELY VICTIM...
...IS YOU!
I'LL TALK.
BUT...
I HAVE A REQUEST...

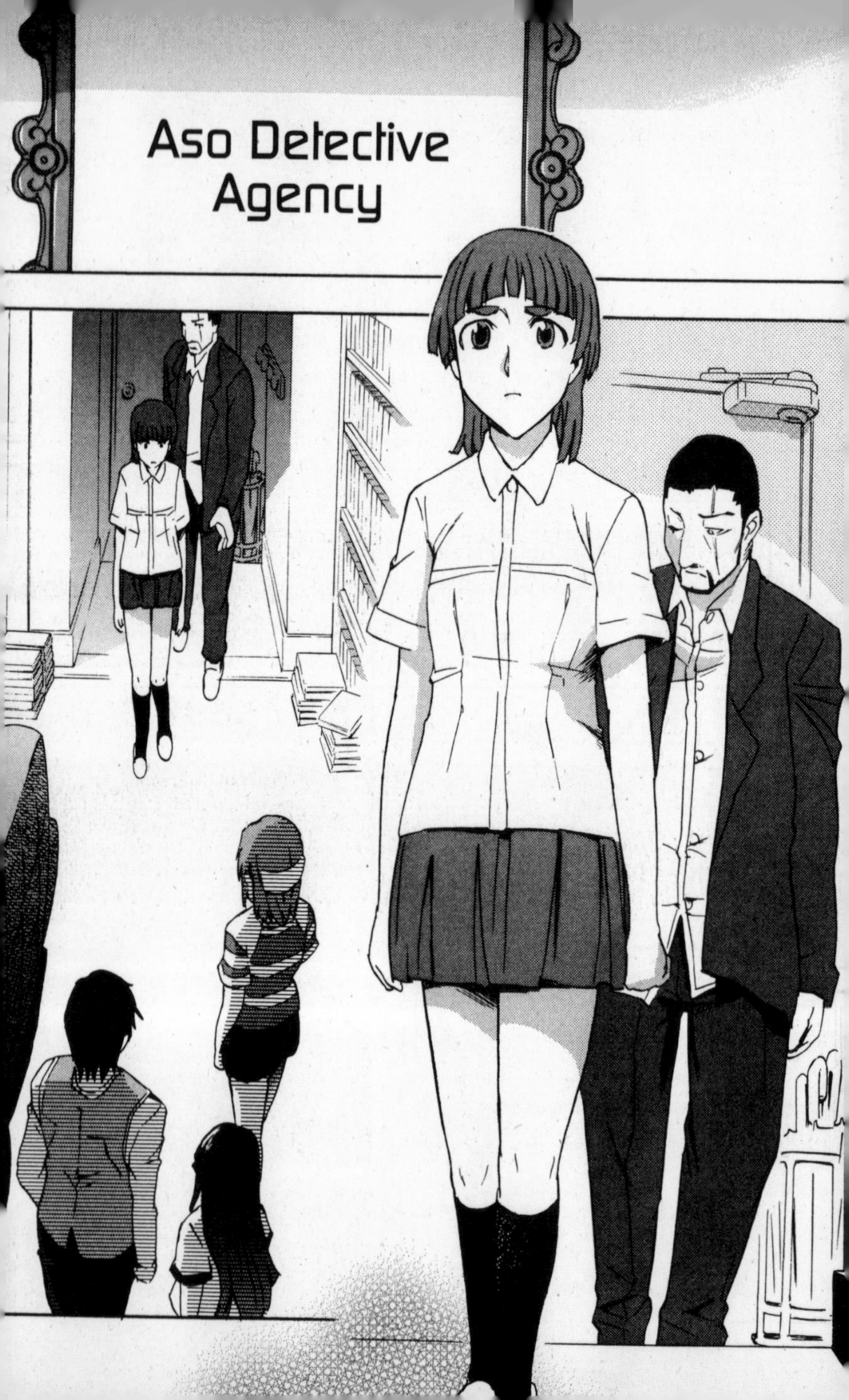
Aso Detective Agency

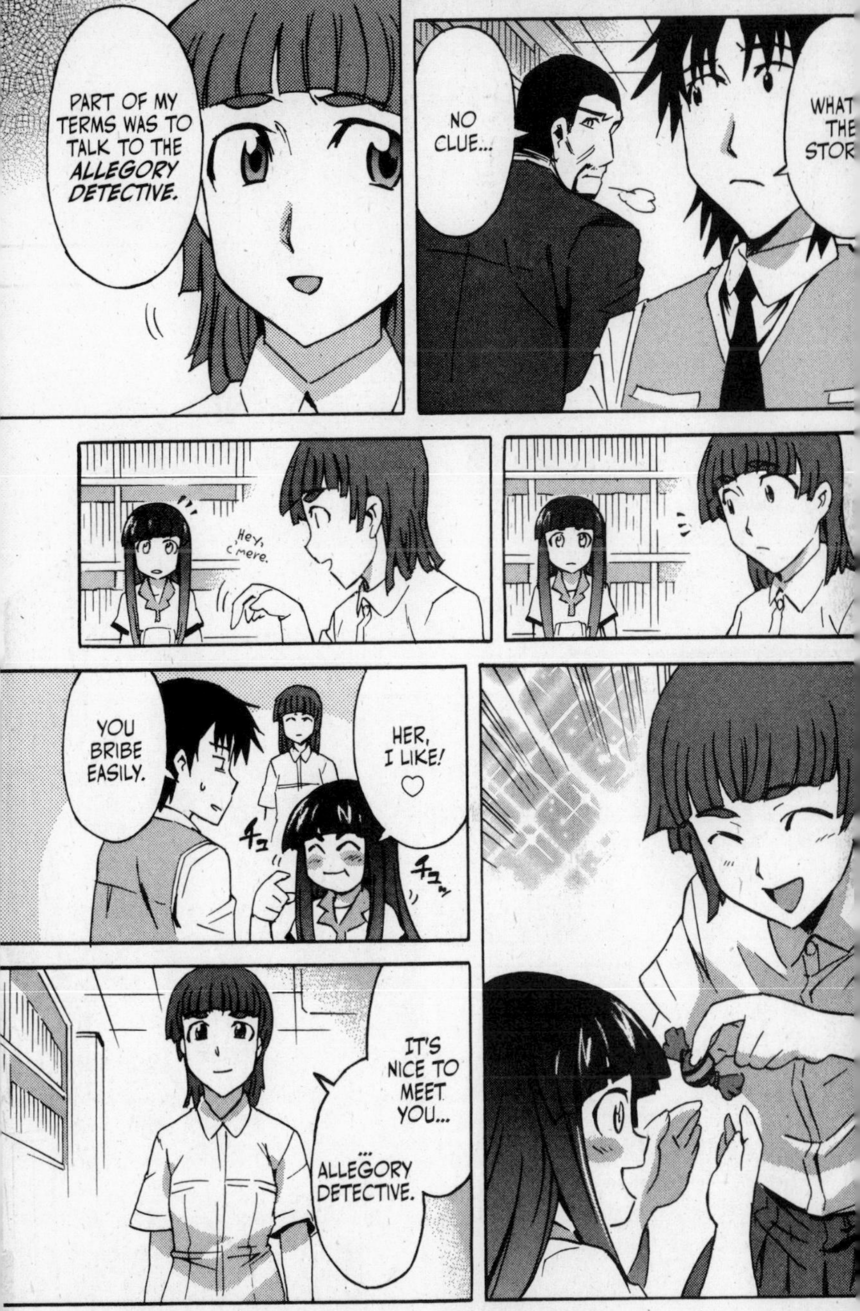
WHAT THE STOR
NO CLUE...
PART OF MY TERMS WAS TO TALK TO THE *ALLEGORY DETECTIVE.*
Hey, c'mere.
HER, I LIKE! ♡
YOU BRIBE EASILY.
チュ
チュッ
IT'S NICE TO MEET YOU...
...ALLEGORY DETECTIVE.

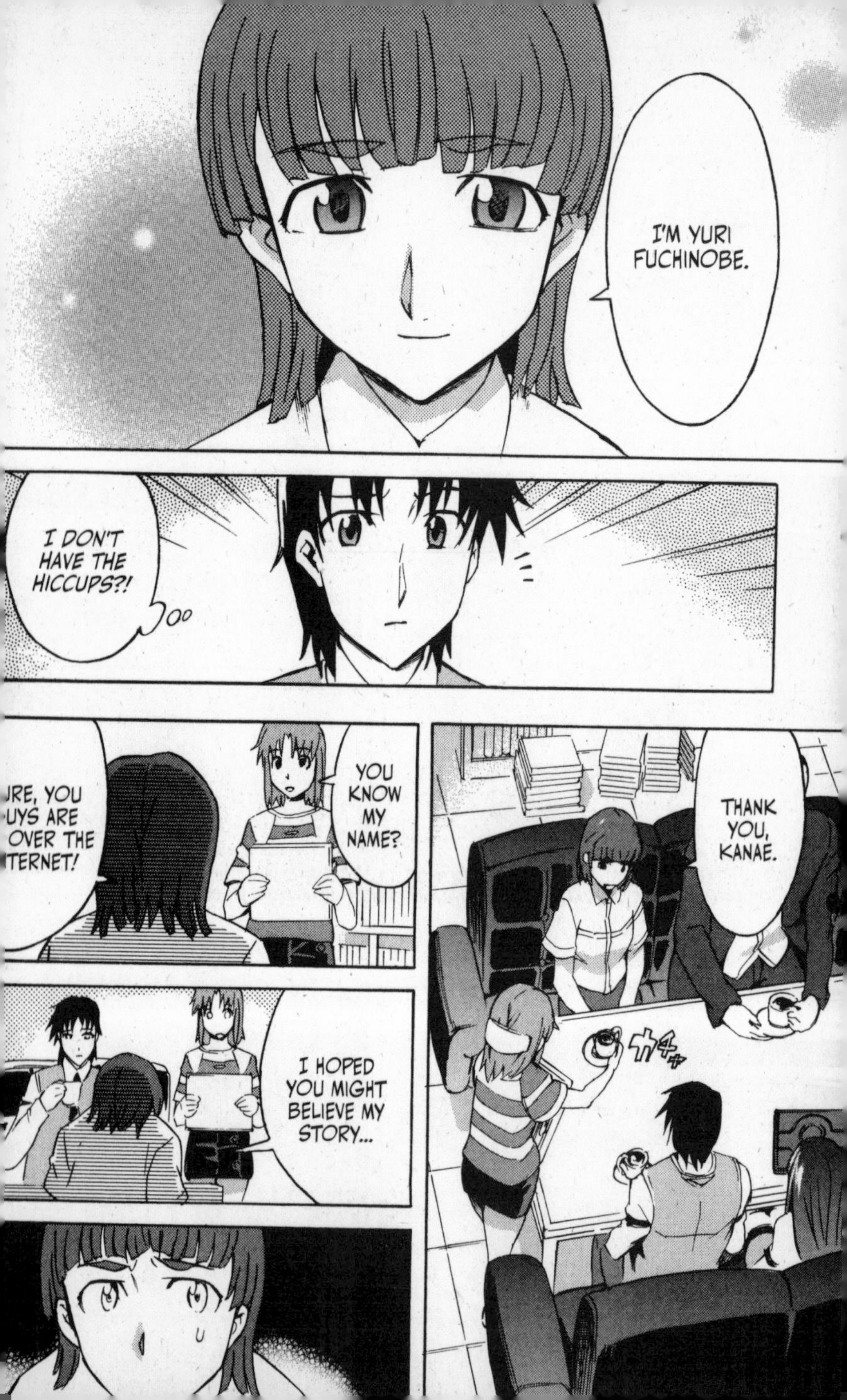
I'M YURI FUCHINOBE.
I DON'T HAVE THE HICCUPS?!
THANK YOU, KANAE.
カチャ
YOU KNOW MY NAME?
RE, YOU UYS ARE OVER THE TERNET!
I HOPED YOU MIGHT BELIEVE MY STORY...

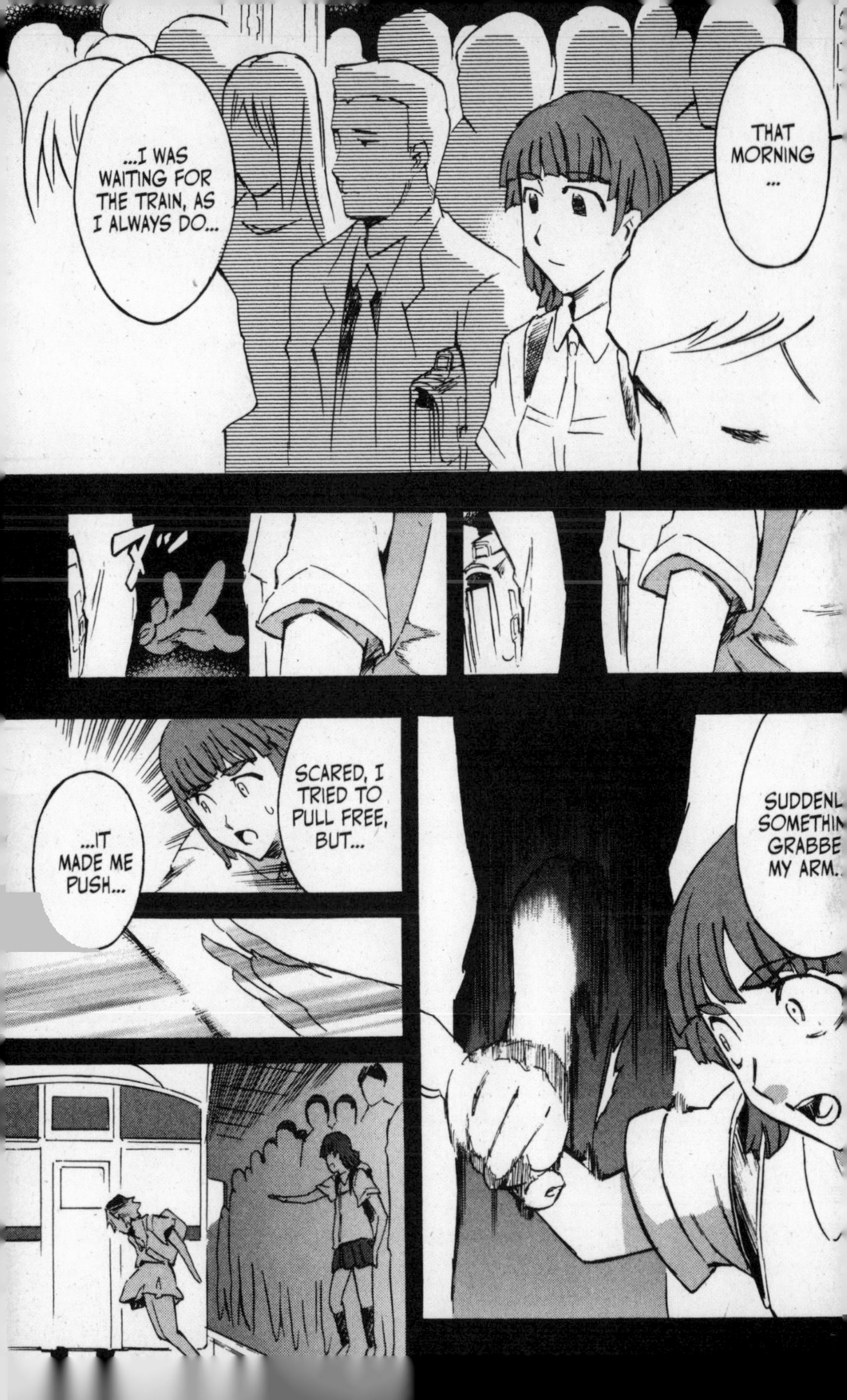
THAT MORNING ...
...I WAS WAITING FOR THE TRAIN, AS I ALWAYS DO...
SUDDENL SOMETHIN GRABBE MY ARM..
SCARED, I TRIED TO PULL FREE, BUT...
...IT MADE ME PUSH...

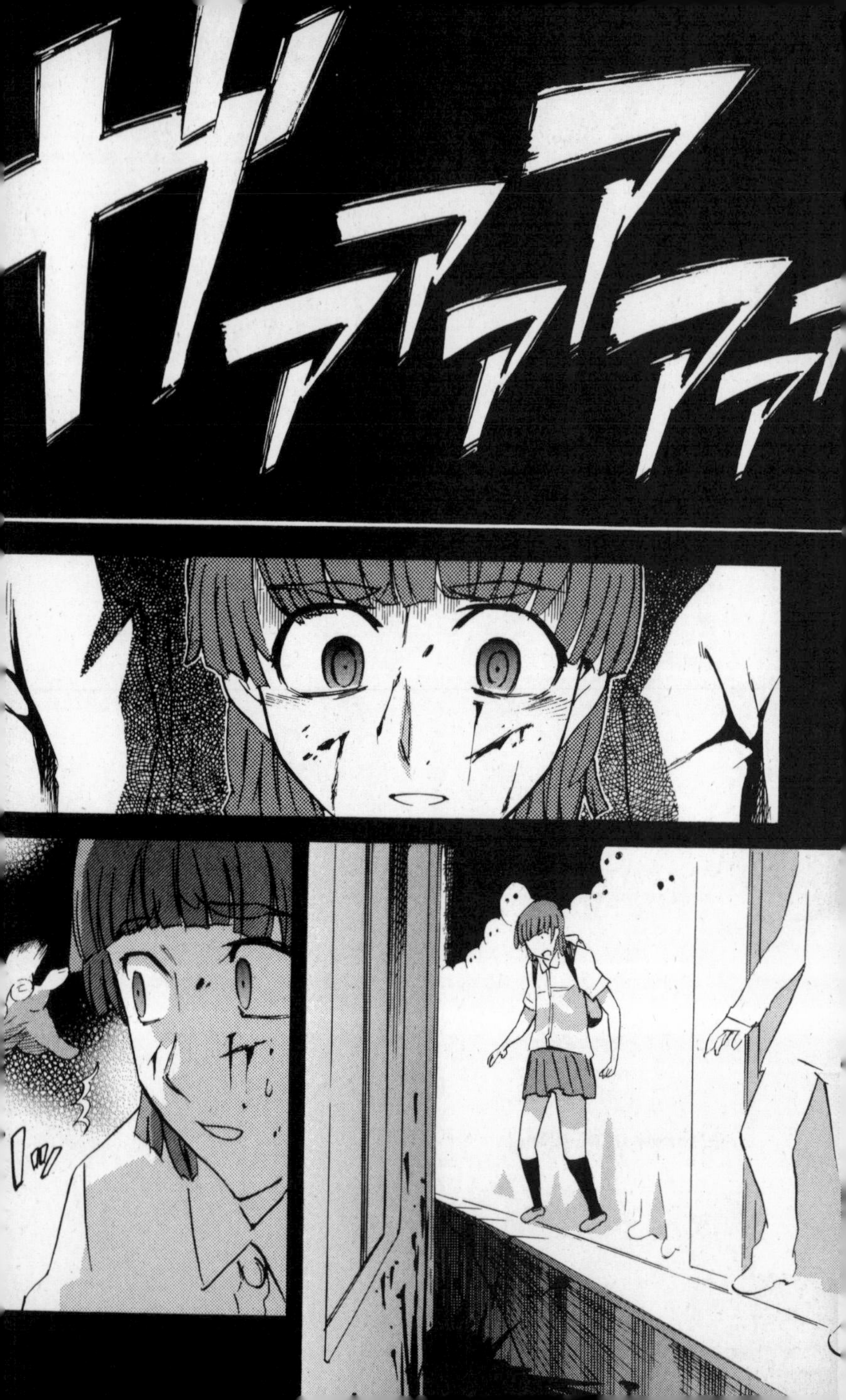
ザァァァァ

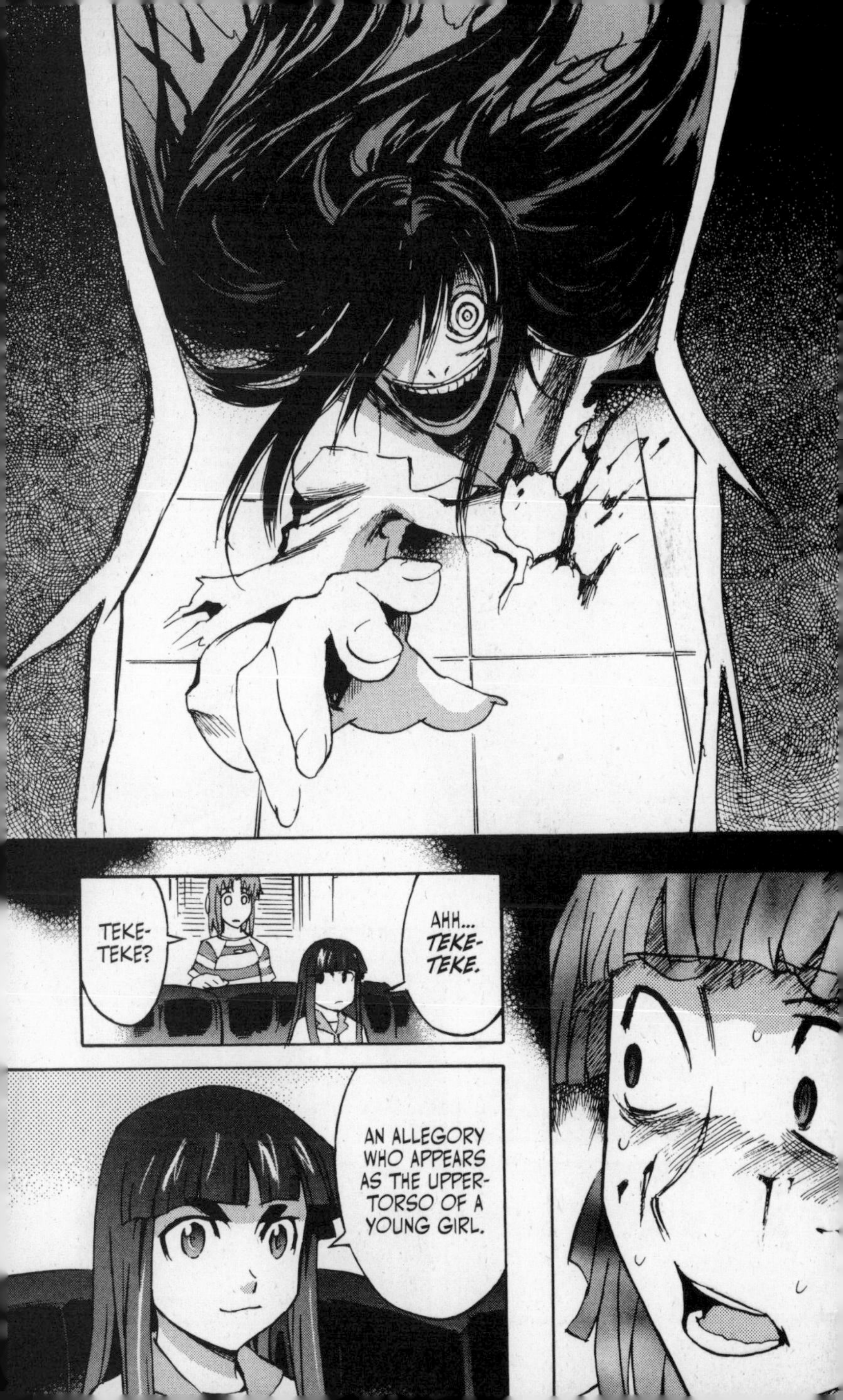
AHH... TEKE-TEKE.
TEKE-TEKE?
AN ALLEGORY WHO APPEARS AS THE UPPER-TORSO OF A YOUNG GIRL.

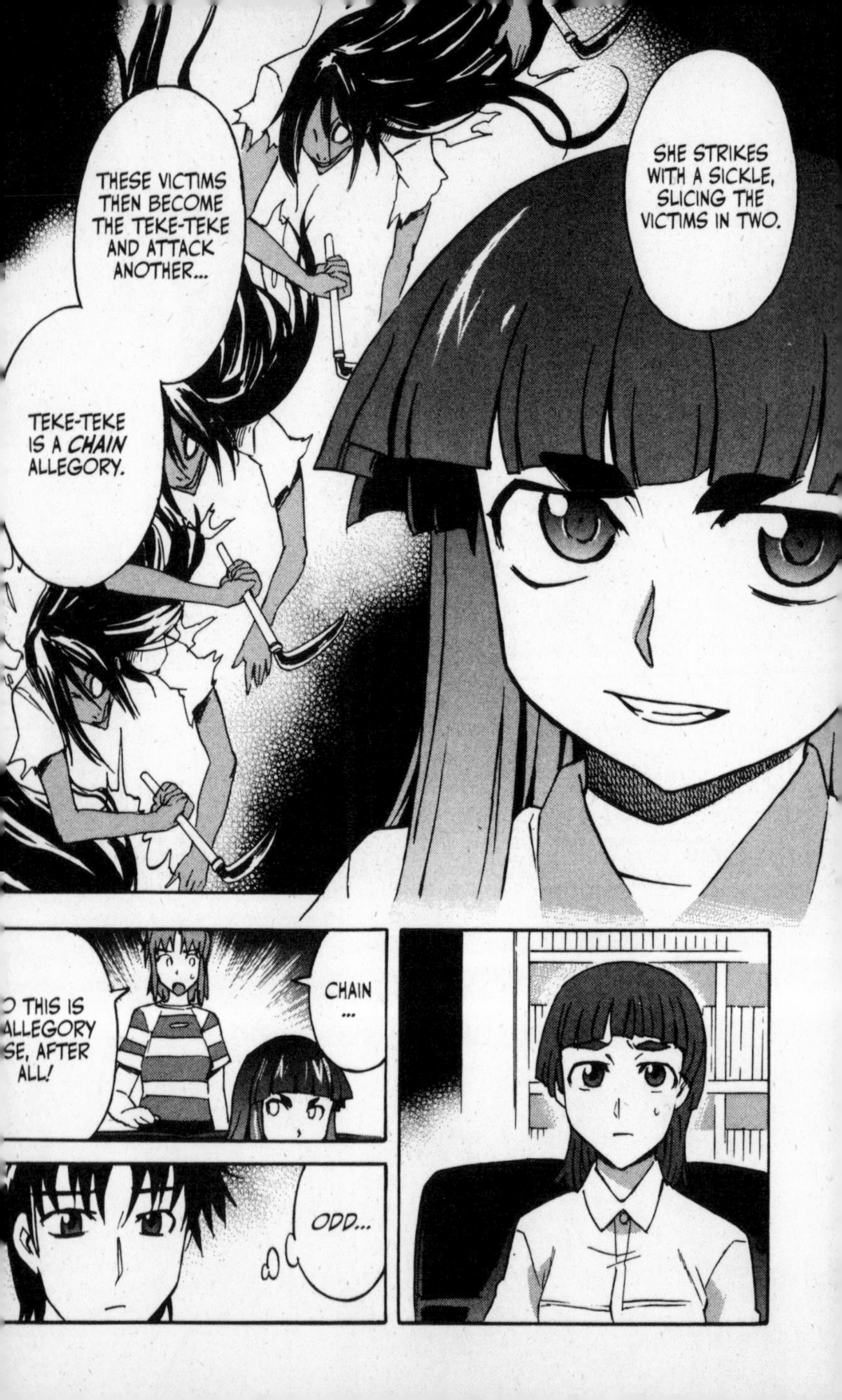
SHE STRIKES WITH A SICKLE, SLICING THE VICTIMS IN TWO.
THESE VICTIMS THEN BECOME THE TEKE-TEKE AND ATTACK ANOTHER...
TEKE-TEKE IS A *CHAIN* ALLEGORY.
CHAIN ...
THIS IS ALLEGORY SE, AFTER ALL!
ODD...

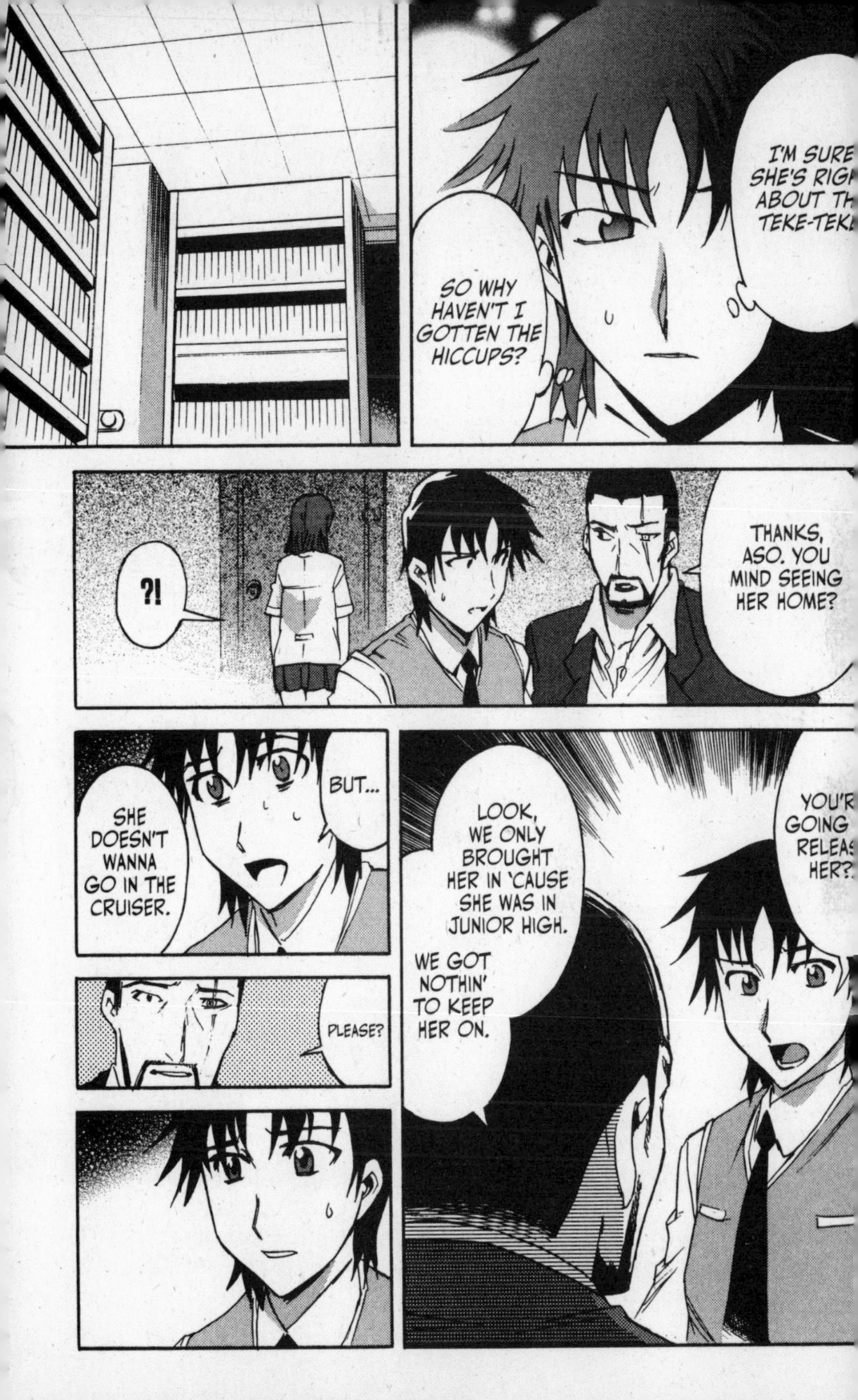
I'M SURE SHE'S RIG ABOUT TH TEKE-TEK
SO WHY HAVEN'T I GOTTEN THE HICCUPS?
THANKS, ASO. YOU MIND SEEING HER HOME?
?!
YOU'R GOING RELEAS HER?
LOOK, WE ONLY BROUGHT HER IN 'CAUSE SHE WAS IN JUNIOR HIGH.
WE GOT NOTHIN' TO KEEP HER ON.
BUT...
SHE DOESN'T WANNA GO IN THE CRUISER.
PLEASE?

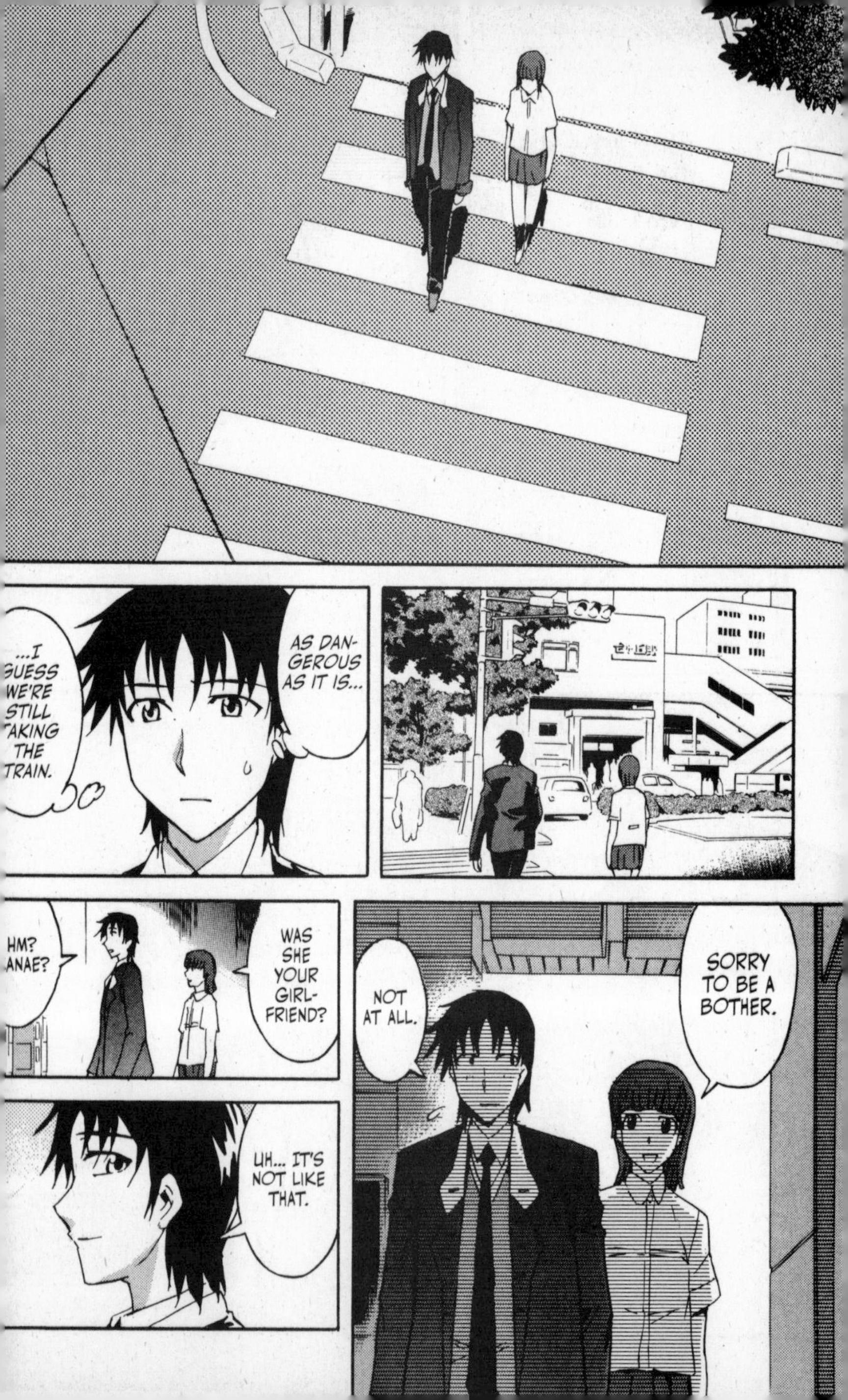
AS DANGEROUS AS IT IS...
...I GUESS WE'RE STILL TAKING THE TRAIN.
SORRY TO BE A BOTHER.
NOT AT ALL.
WAS SHE YOUR GIRLFRIEND?
HM? ANAE?
UH... IT'S NOT LIKE THAT.

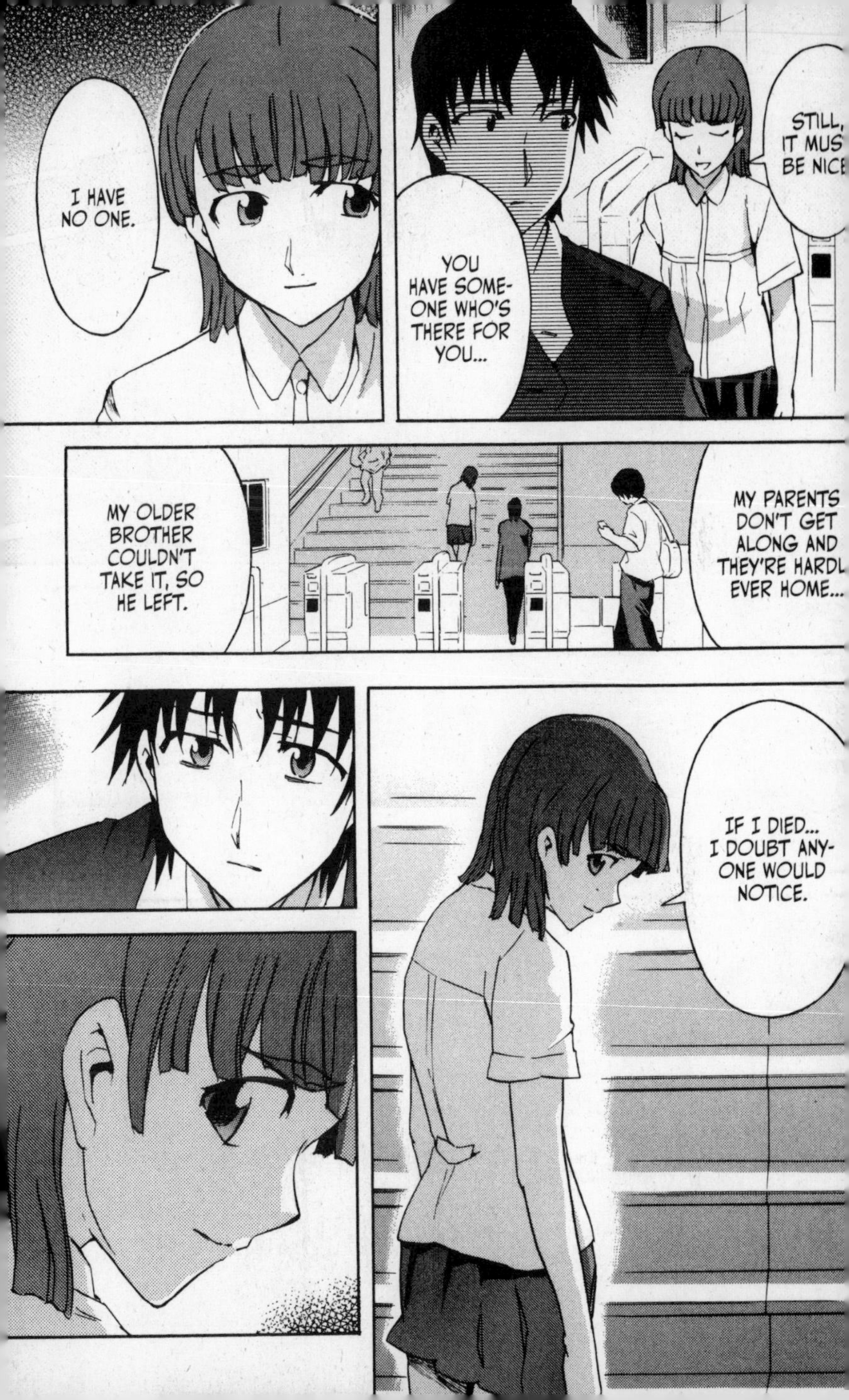
STILL, IT MUS BE NICE
YOU HAVE SOME-ONE WHO'S THERE FOR YOU...
I HAVE NO ONE.
MY PARENTS DON'T GET ALONG AND THEY'RE HARDL EVER HOME...
MY OLDER BROTHER COULDN'T TAKE IT, SO HE LEFT.
IF I DIED... I DOUBT ANY-ONE WOULD NOTICE.

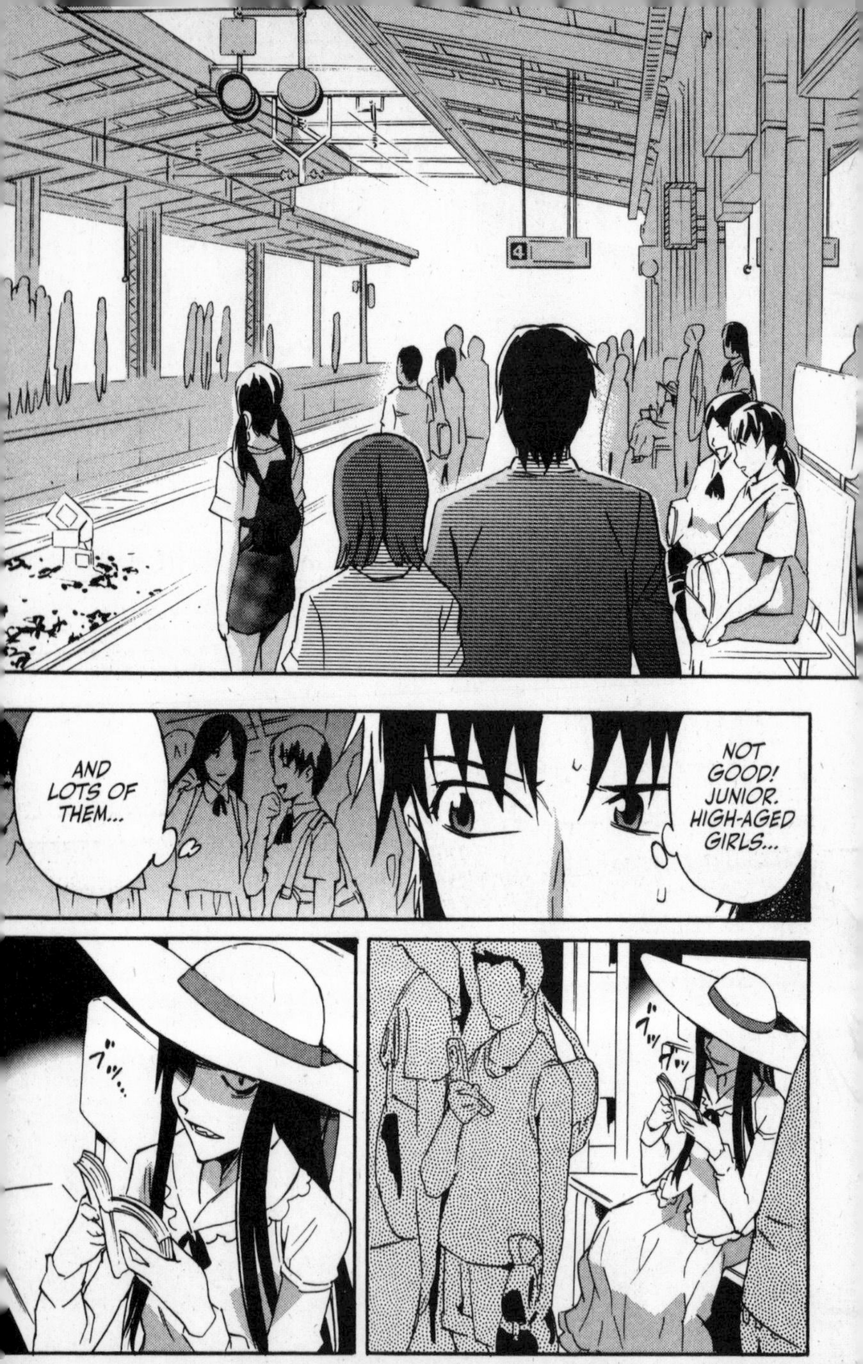
NOT GOOD! JUNIOR. HIGH-AGED GIRLS...
AND LOTS OF THEM...
ブツ ブツ
ブツ…

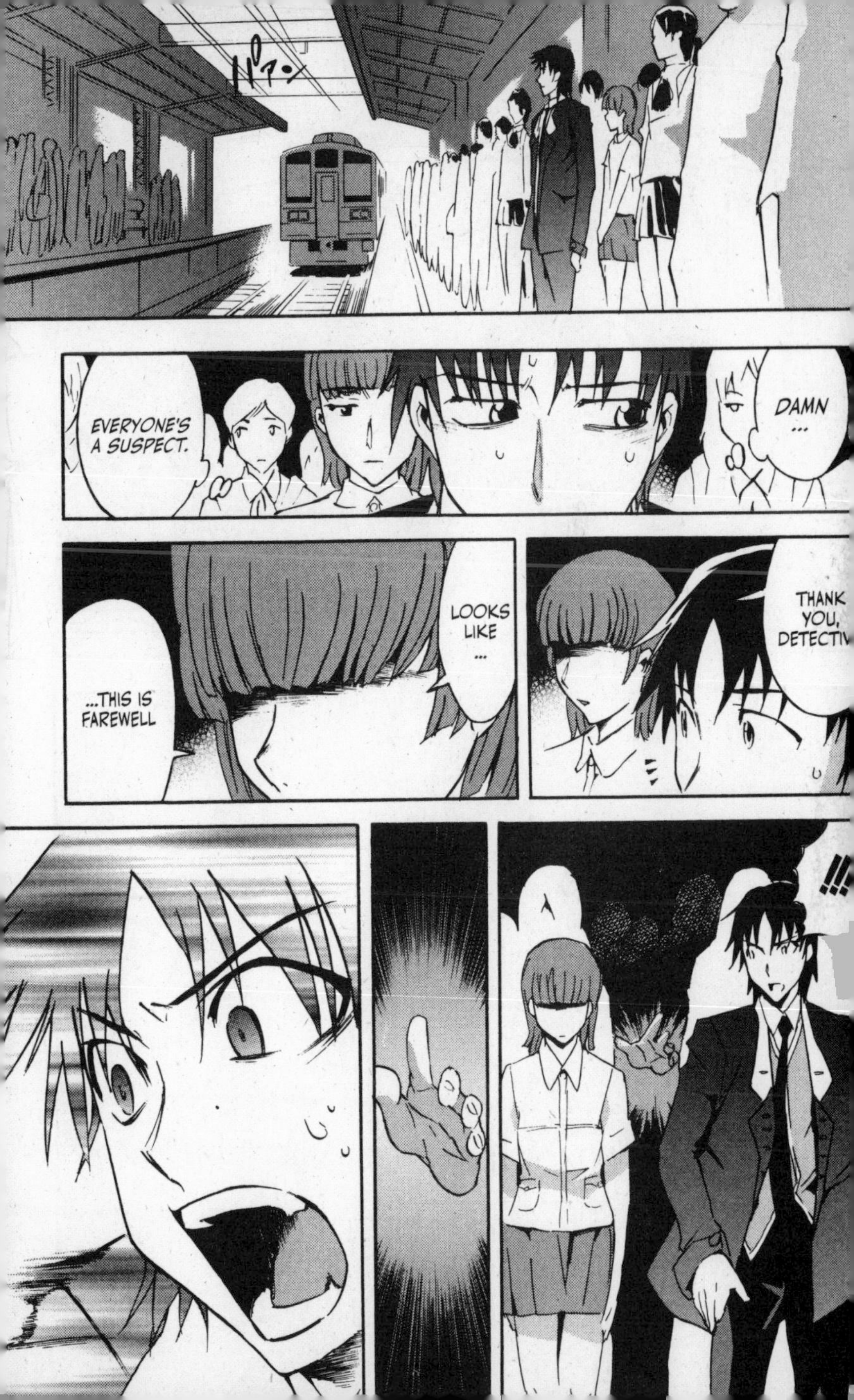
パァン
DAMN ...
EVERYONE'S A SUSPECT.
THANK YOU, DETECTIV
LOOKS LIKE ...
...THIS IS FAREWELL
!!!

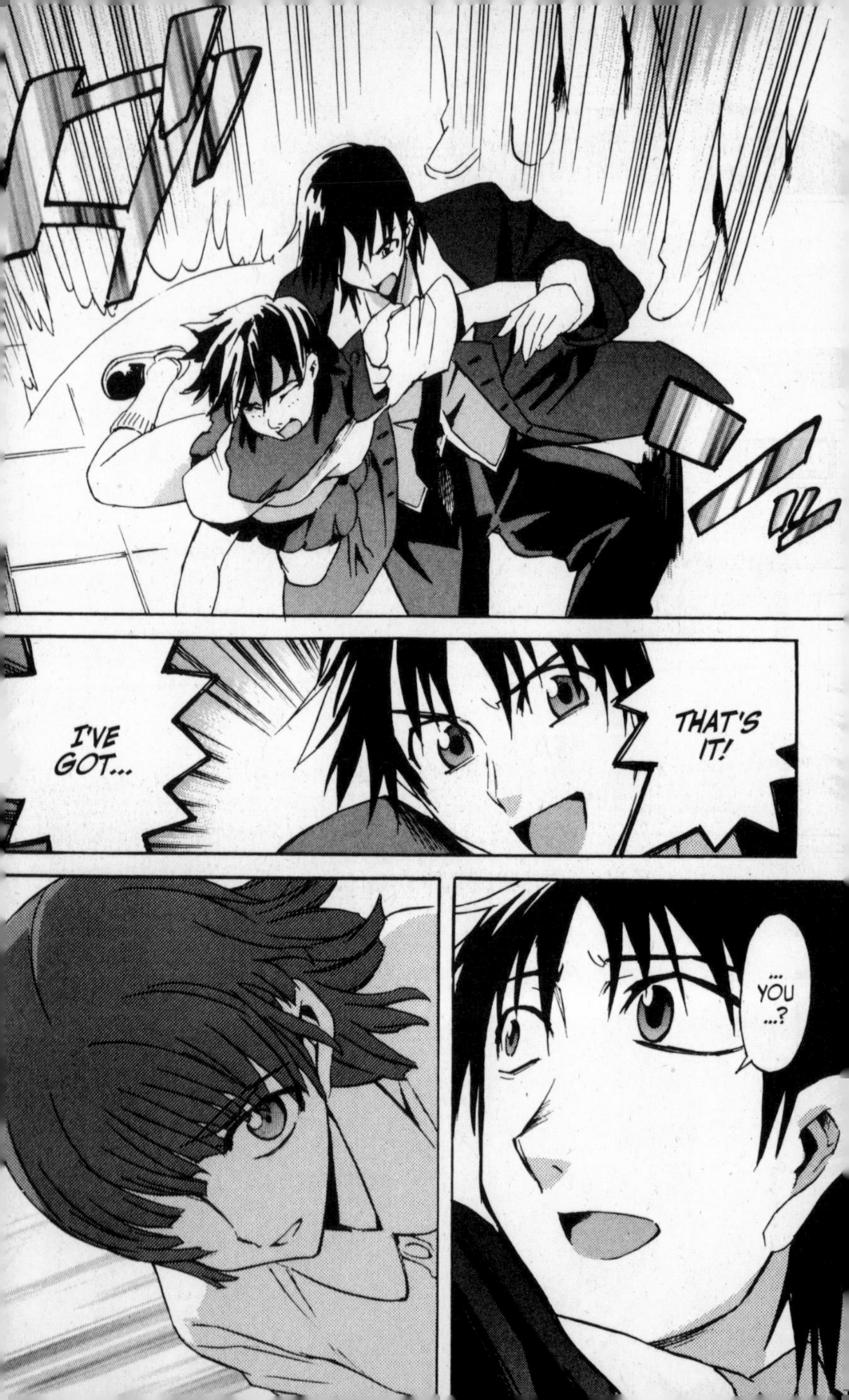
THAT'S IT!
I'VE GOT...
...YOU...?

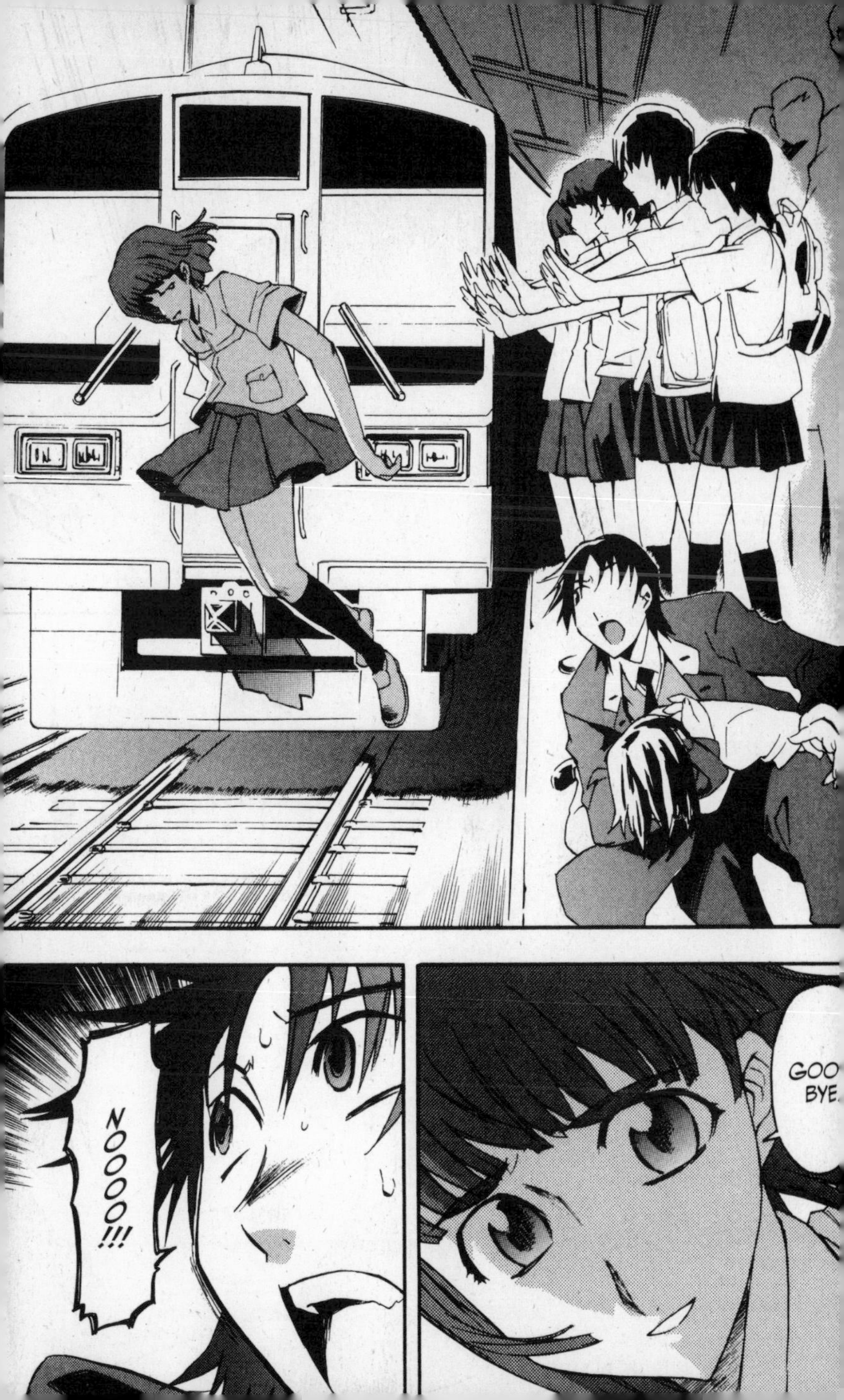
GOO
BYE.
NOOOOO!!!

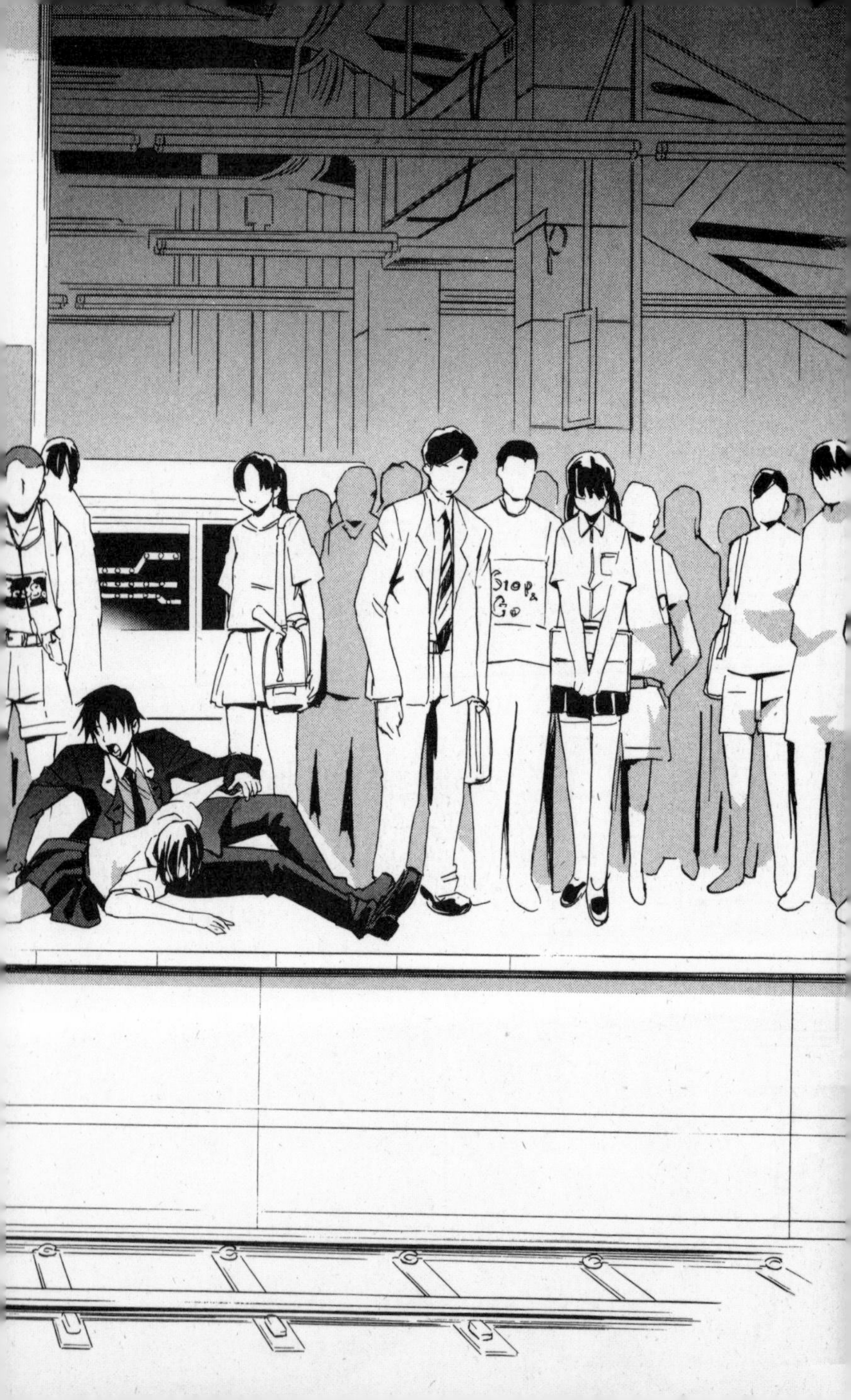
Stop & Go

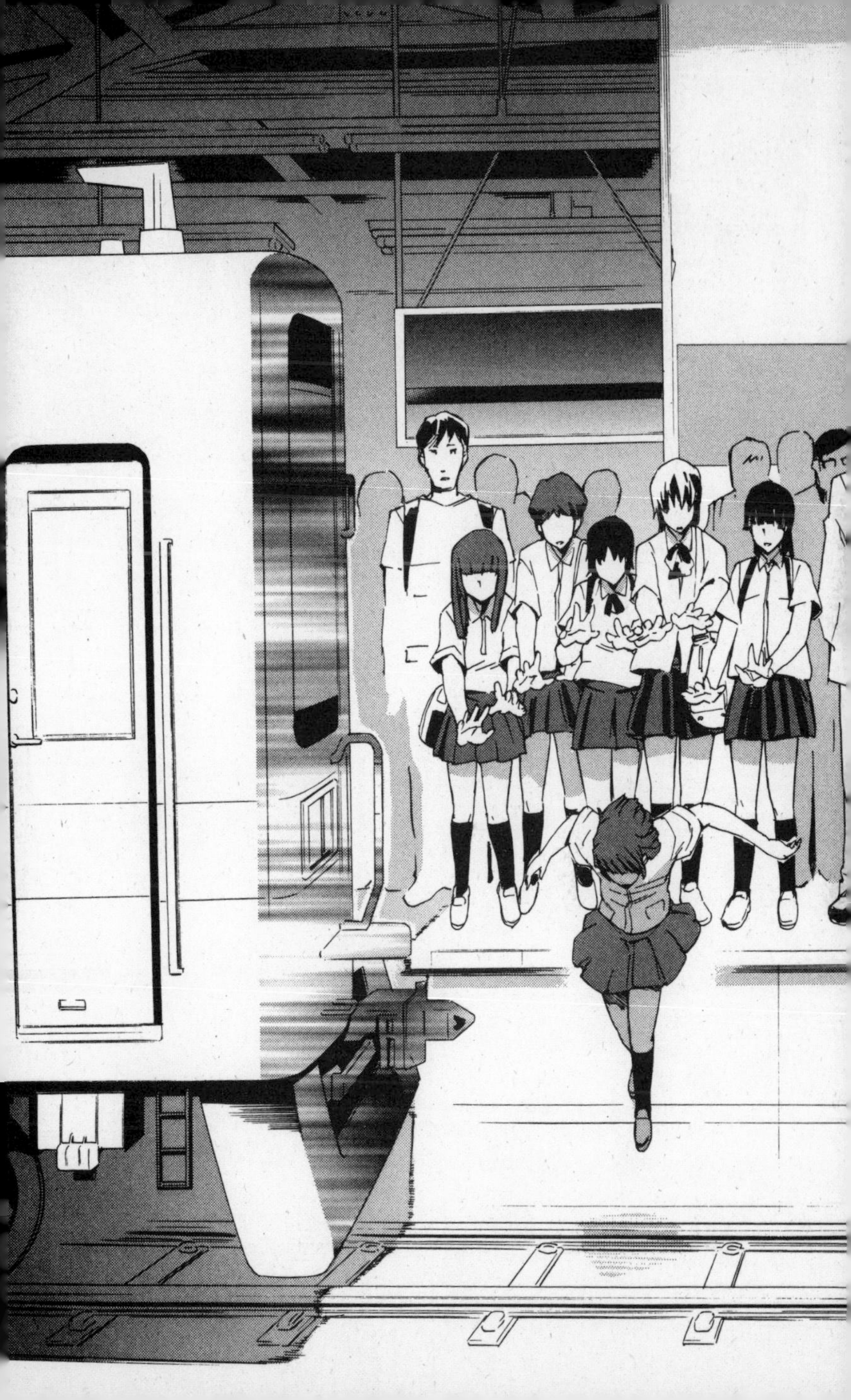

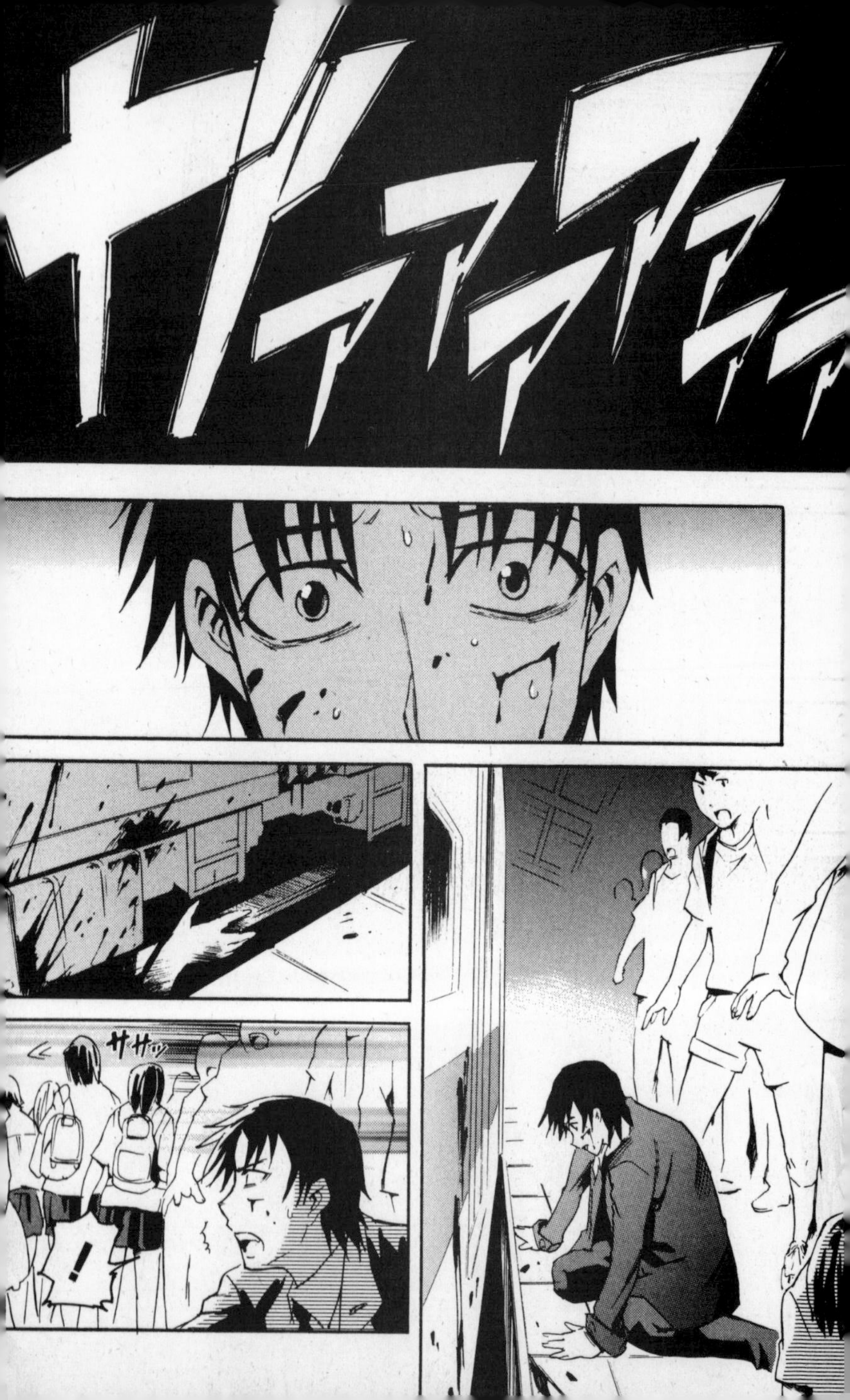
ササッ
!

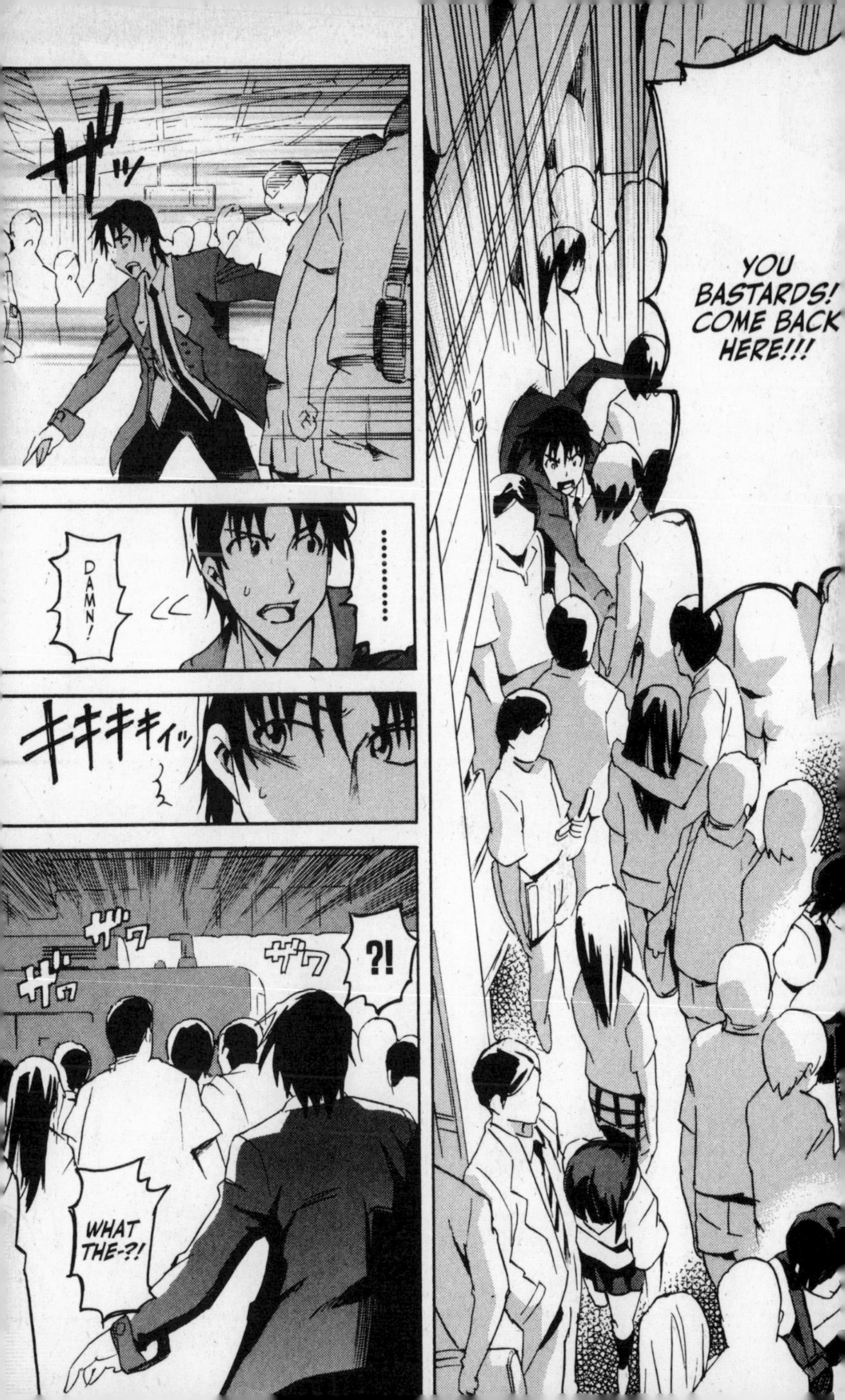
YOU BASTARDS! COME BACK HERE!!!
ザッ
......
DAMN!
キキキキィッ
?!
ザワ
ザワ
ザワ
WHAT THE-?!

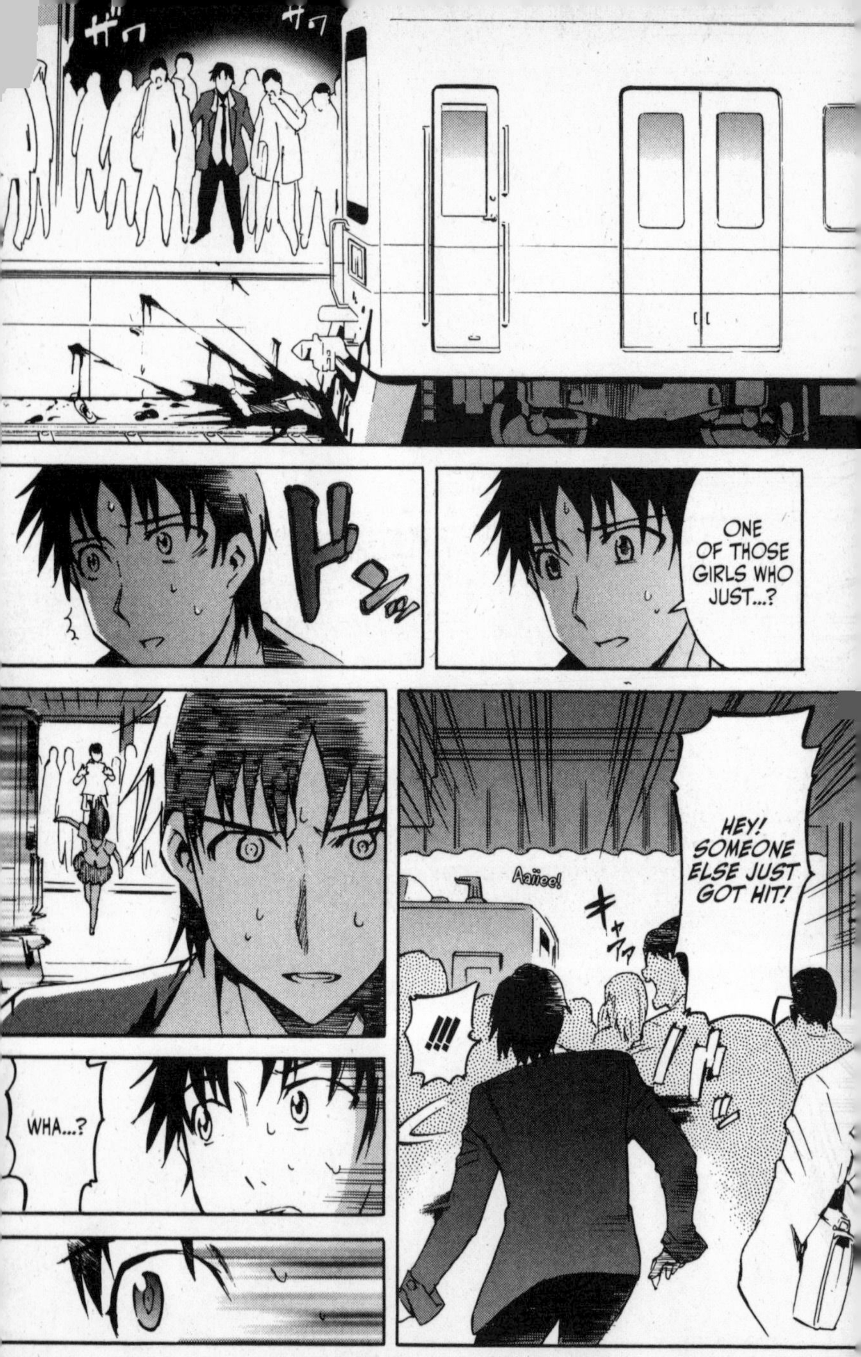
ザワ
ザワ
ONE OF THOSE GIRLS WHO JUST...?
HEY! SOMEONE ELSE JUST GOT HIT!
Aaiiee!
キャァァ
!!!
WHA...?

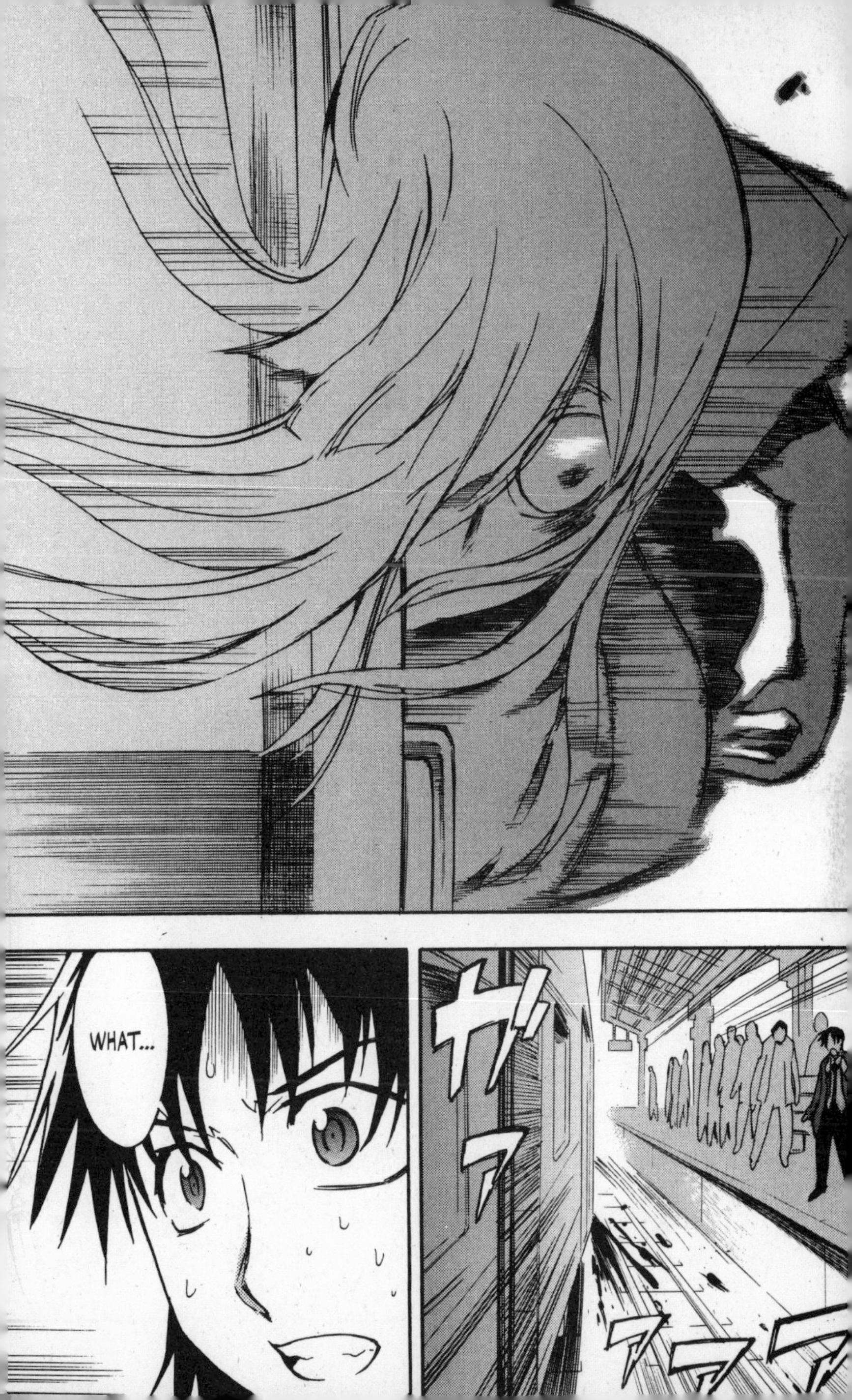
WHAT...

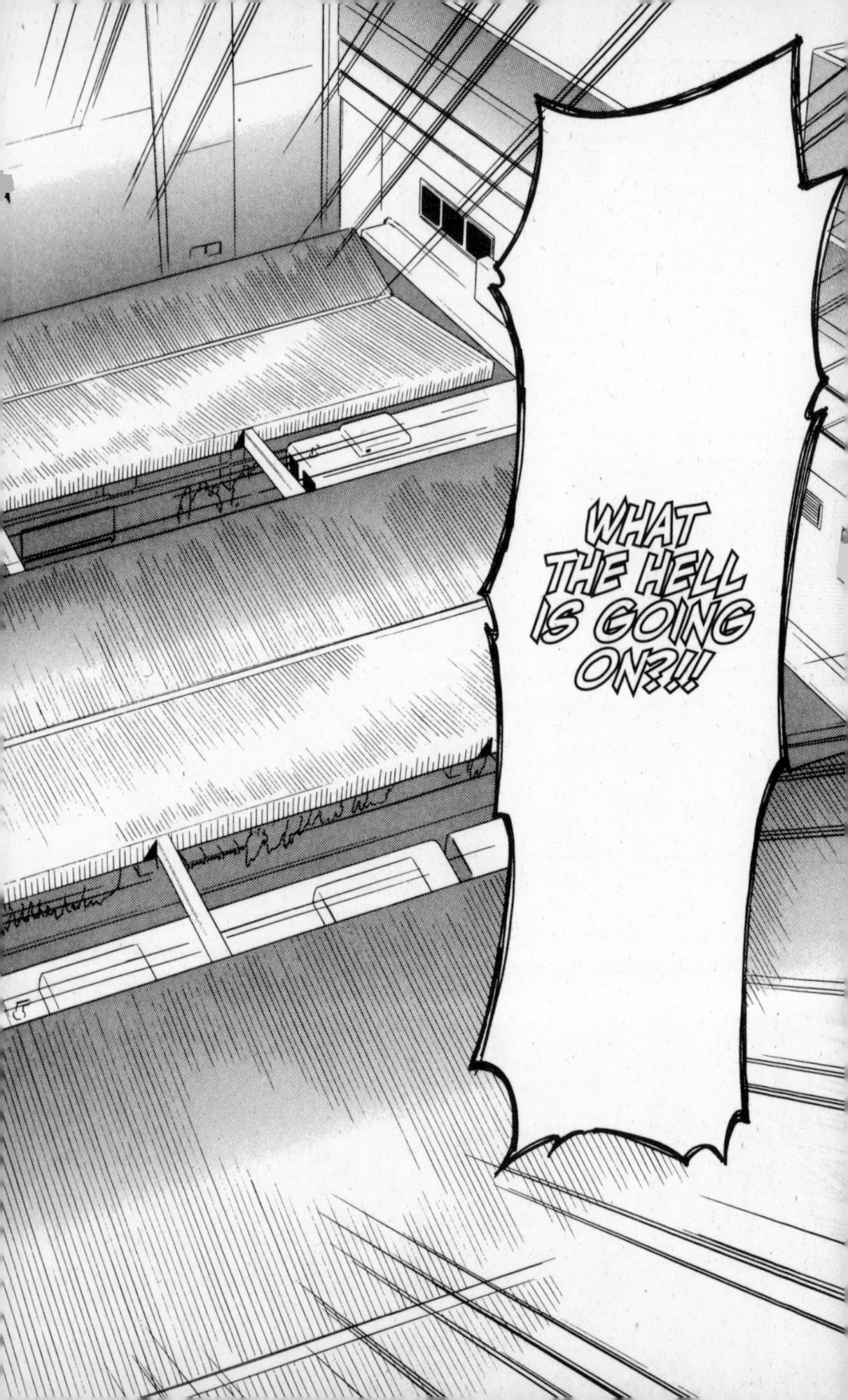
WHAT THE HELL IS GOING ON?!!

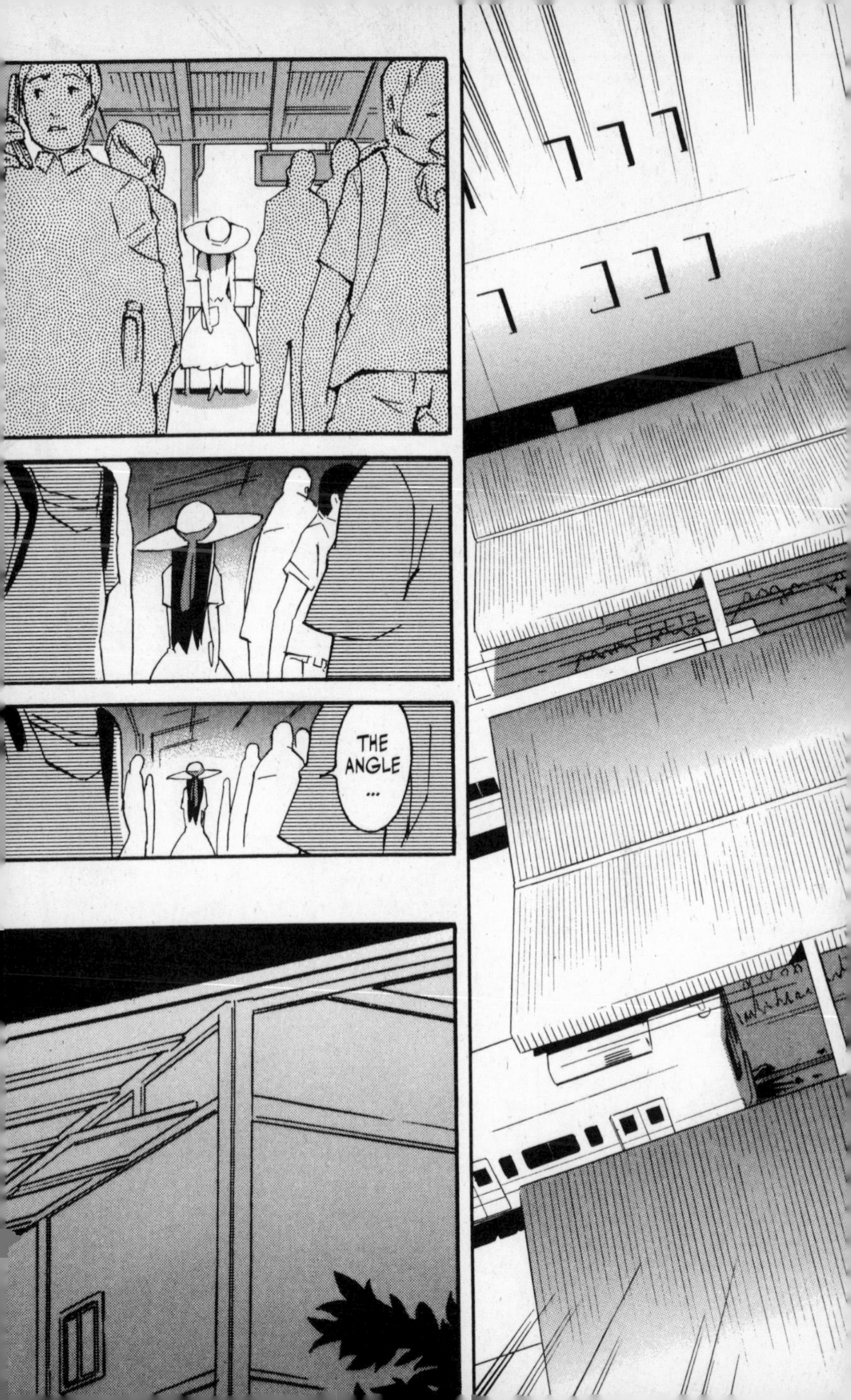
THE ANGLE ...

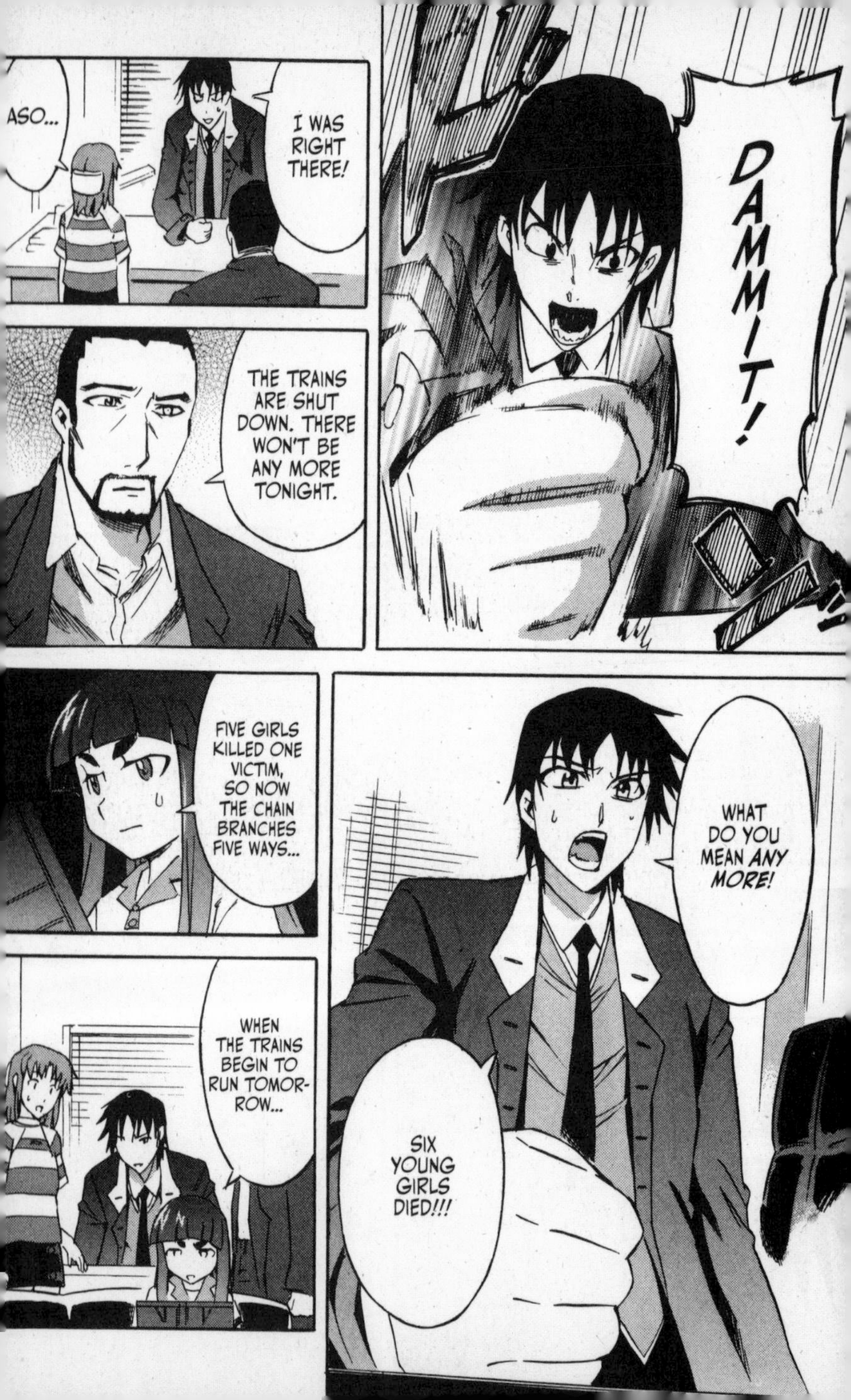
DAMMIT!
I WAS RIGHT THERE!
ASO...
THE TRAINS ARE SHUT DOWN. THERE WON'T BE ANY MORE TONIGHT.
WHAT DO YOU MEAN *ANY MORE*!
SIX YOUNG GIRLS DIED!!!
FIVE GIRLS KILLED ONE VICTIM, SO NOW THE CHAIN BRANCHES FIVE WAYS...
WHEN THE TRAINS BEGIN TO RUN TOMORROW...

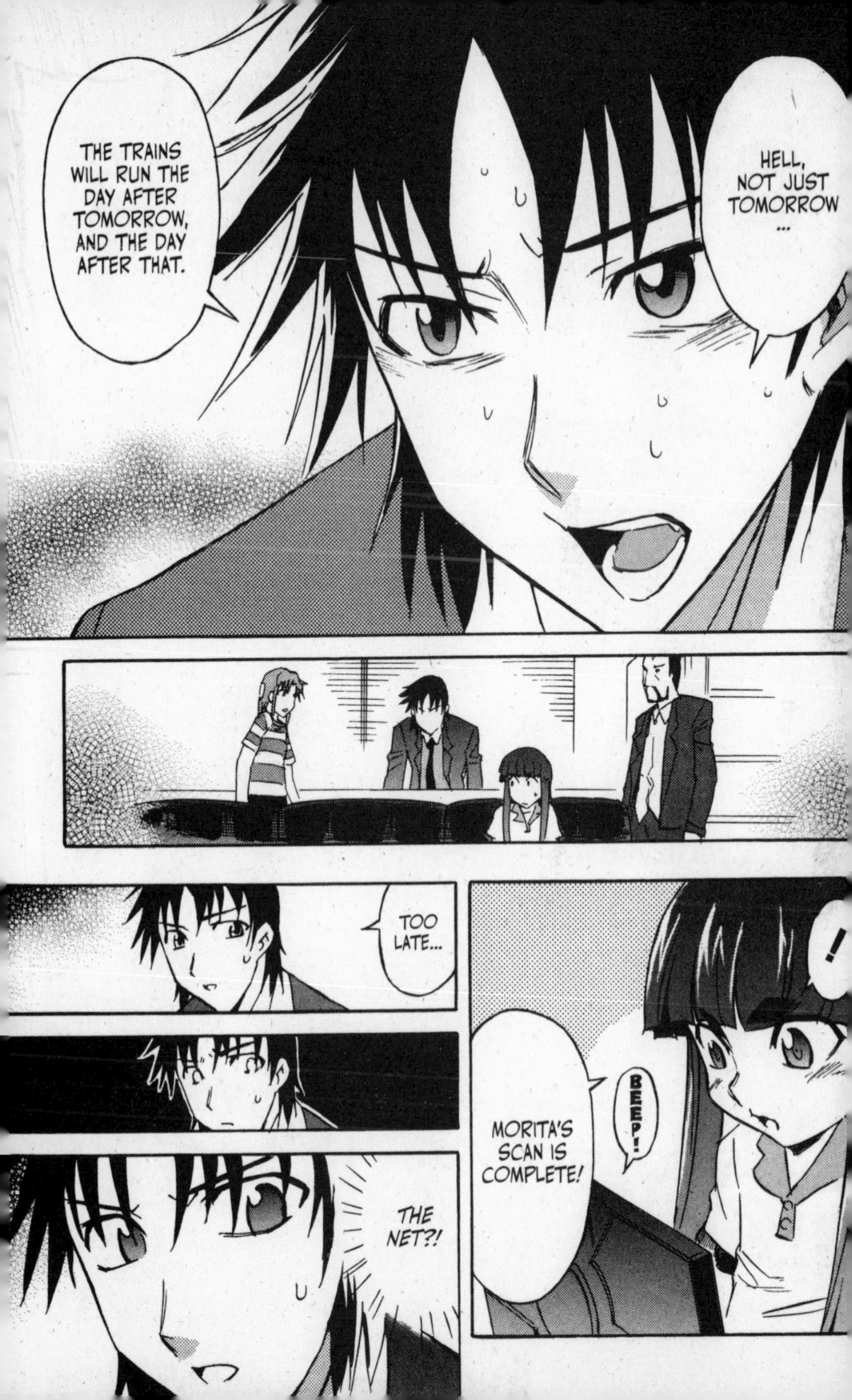
HELL, NOT JUST TOMORROW ...
THE TRAINS WILL RUN THE DAY AFTER TOMORROW, AND THE DAY AFTER THAT.
!
BEEP!
MORITA'S SCAN IS COMPLETE!
TOO LATE...
THE NET?!

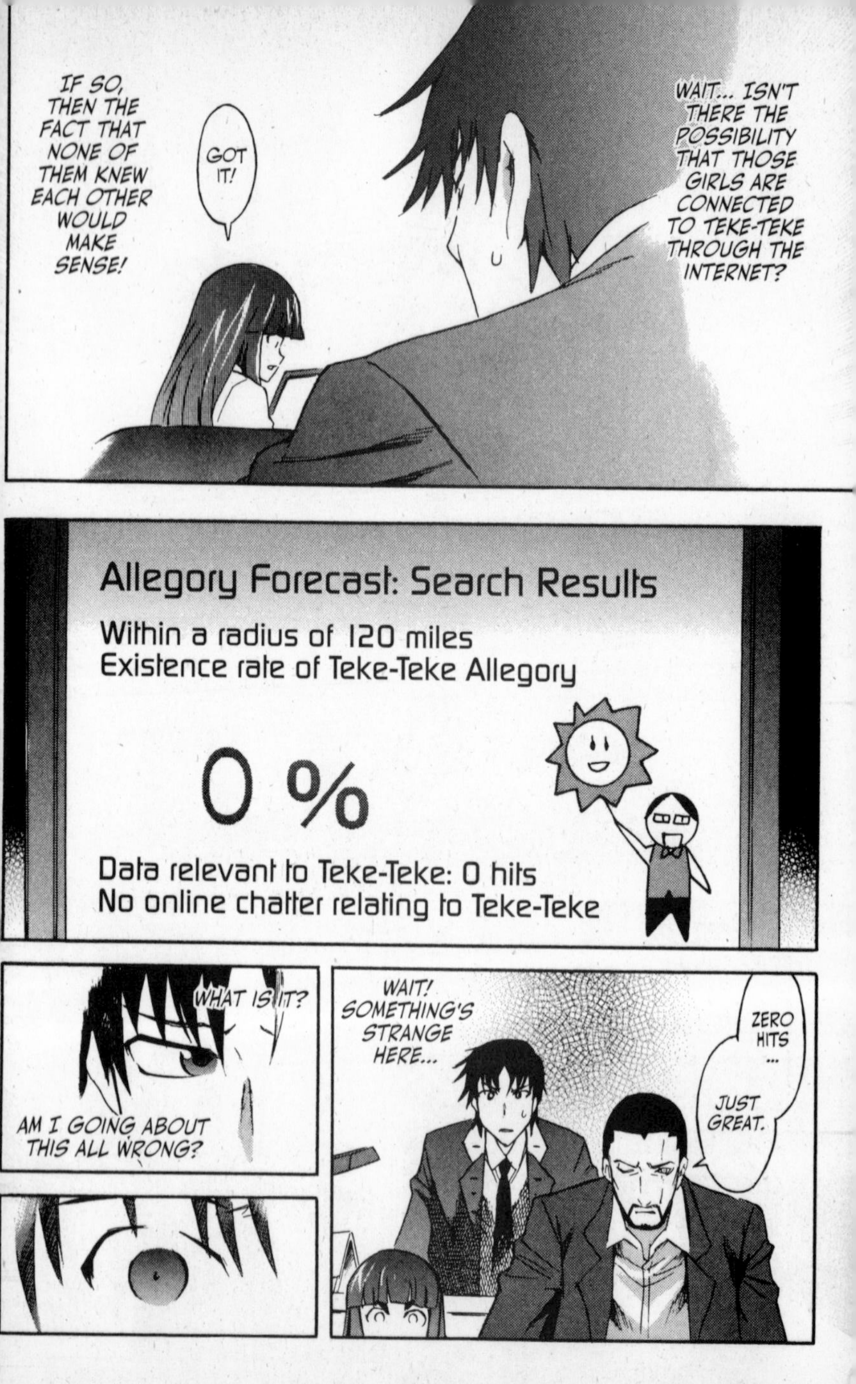
WAIT... ISN'T THERE THE POSSIBILITY THAT THOSE GIRLS ARE CONNECTED TO TEKE-TEKE THROUGH THE INTERNET?
GOT IT!
IF SO, THEN THE FACT THAT NONE OF THEM KNEW EACH OTHER WOULD MAKE SENSE!
Allegory Forecast: Search Results
Within a radius of 120 miles
Existence rate of Teke-Teke Allegory
0 %
Data relevant to Teke-Teke: 0 hits
No online chatter relating to Teke-Teke
ZERO HITS...
JUST GREAT.
WAIT! SOMETHING'S STRANGE HERE...
WHAT IS IT?
AM I GOING ABOUT THIS ALL WRONG?

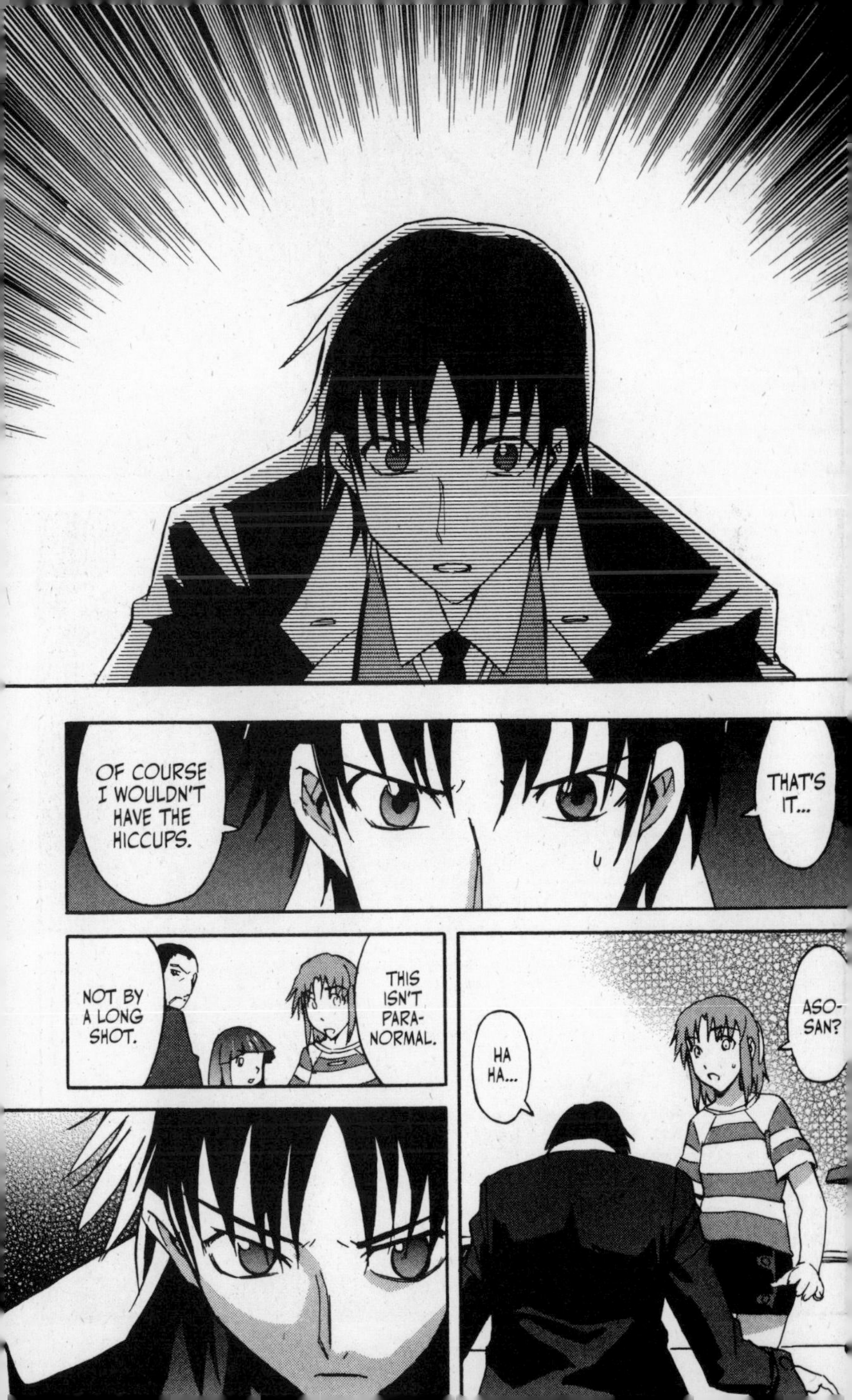
THAT'S IT...
OF COURSE I WOULDN'T HAVE THE HICCUPS.
ASO-SAN?
HA HA...
THIS ISN'T PARA-NORMAL.
NOT BY A LONG SHOT.

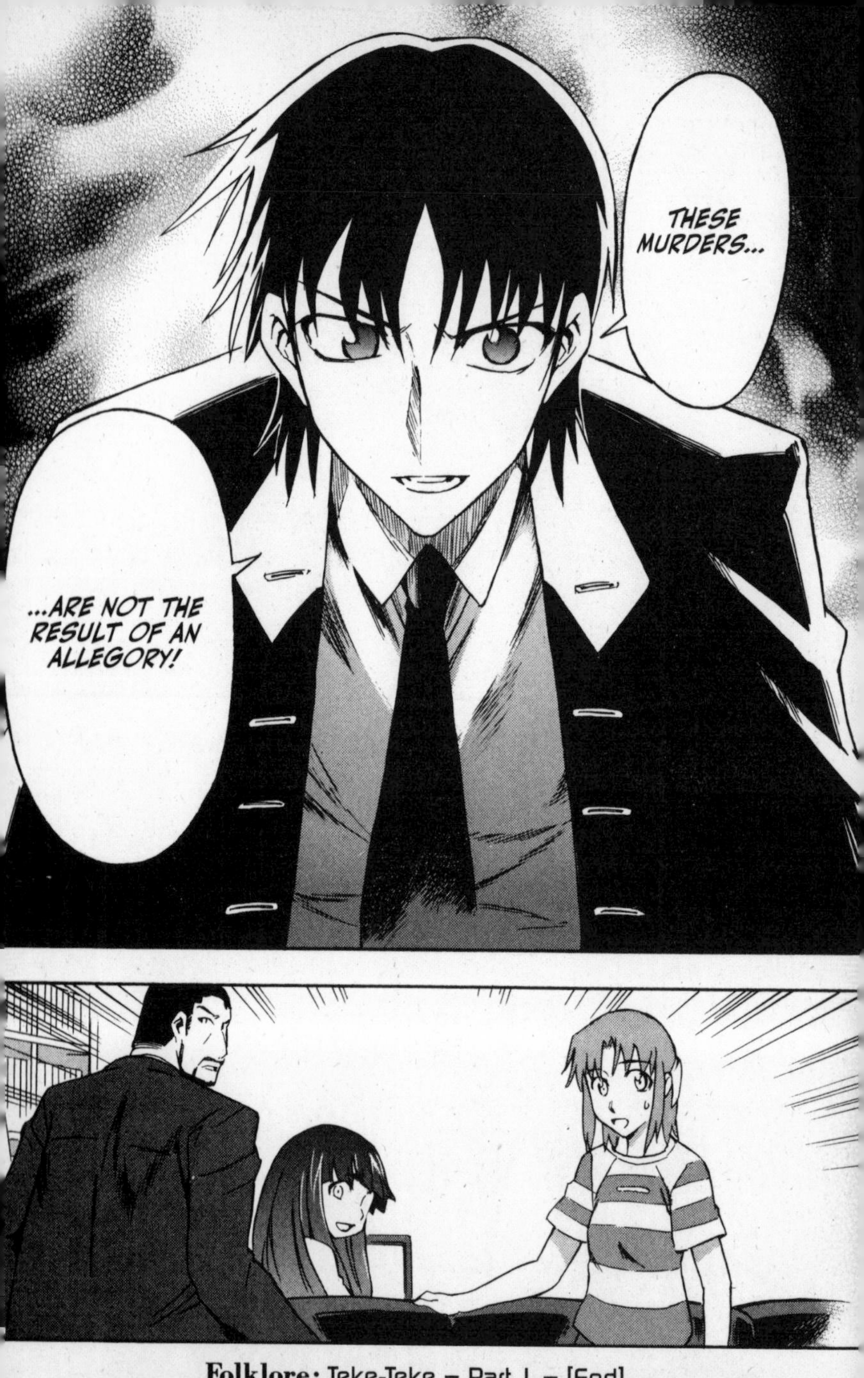
THESE MURDERS...
...ARE NOT THE RESULT OF AN ALLEGORY!

Folklore; Teke-Teke – Part 1 – [End]

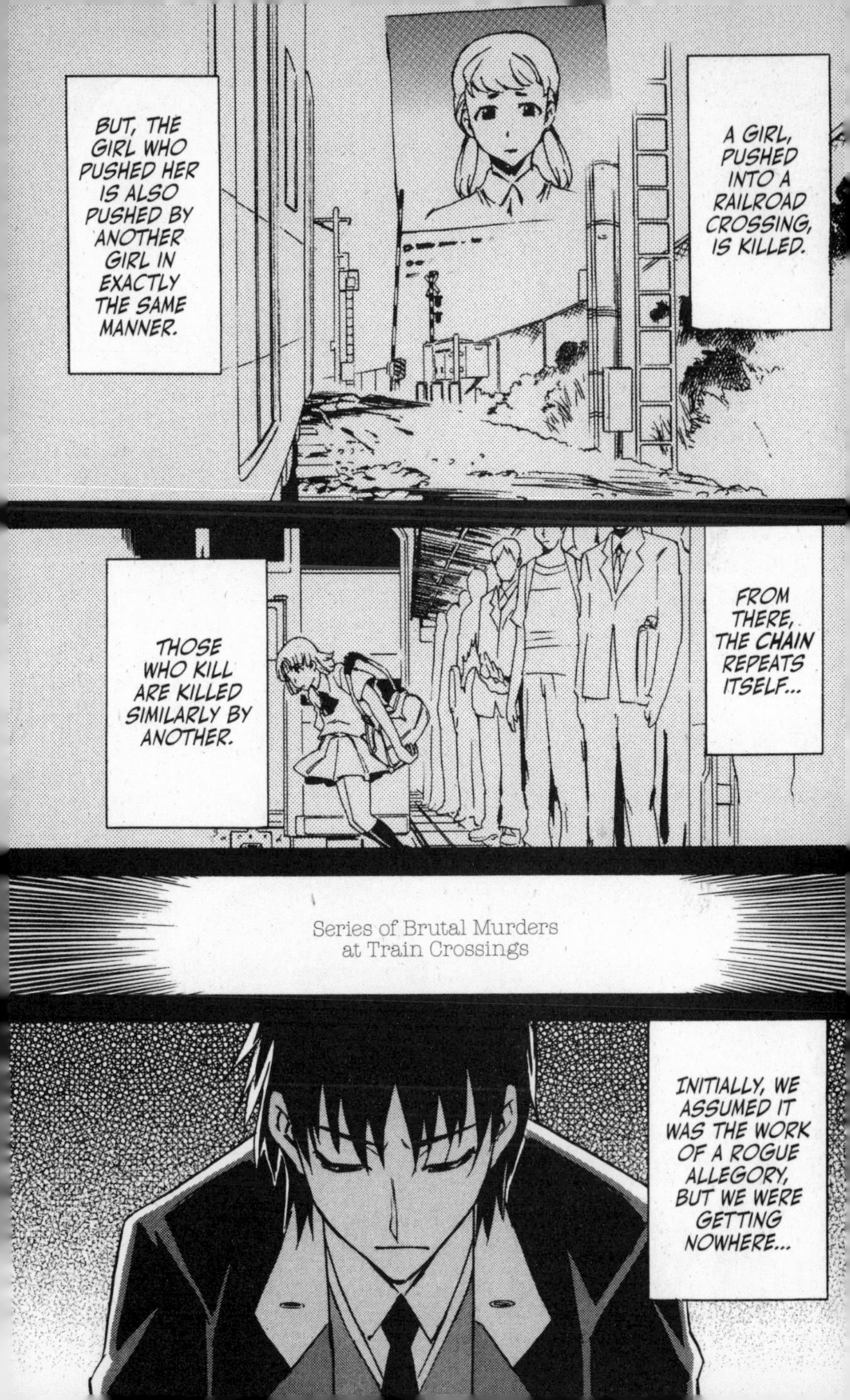
A GIRL, PUSHED INTO A RAILROAD CROSSING, IS KILLED.
BUT, THE GIRL WHO PUSHED HER IS ALSO PUSHED BY ANOTHER GIRL IN EXACTLY THE SAME MANNER.
FROM THERE, THE CHAIN REPEATS ITSELF...
THOSE WHO KILL ARE KILLED SIMILARLY BY ANOTHER.
Series of Brutal Murders at Train Crossings
INITIALLY, WE ASSUMED IT WAS THE WORK OF A ROGUE ALLEGORY, BUT WE WERE GETTING NOWHERE...

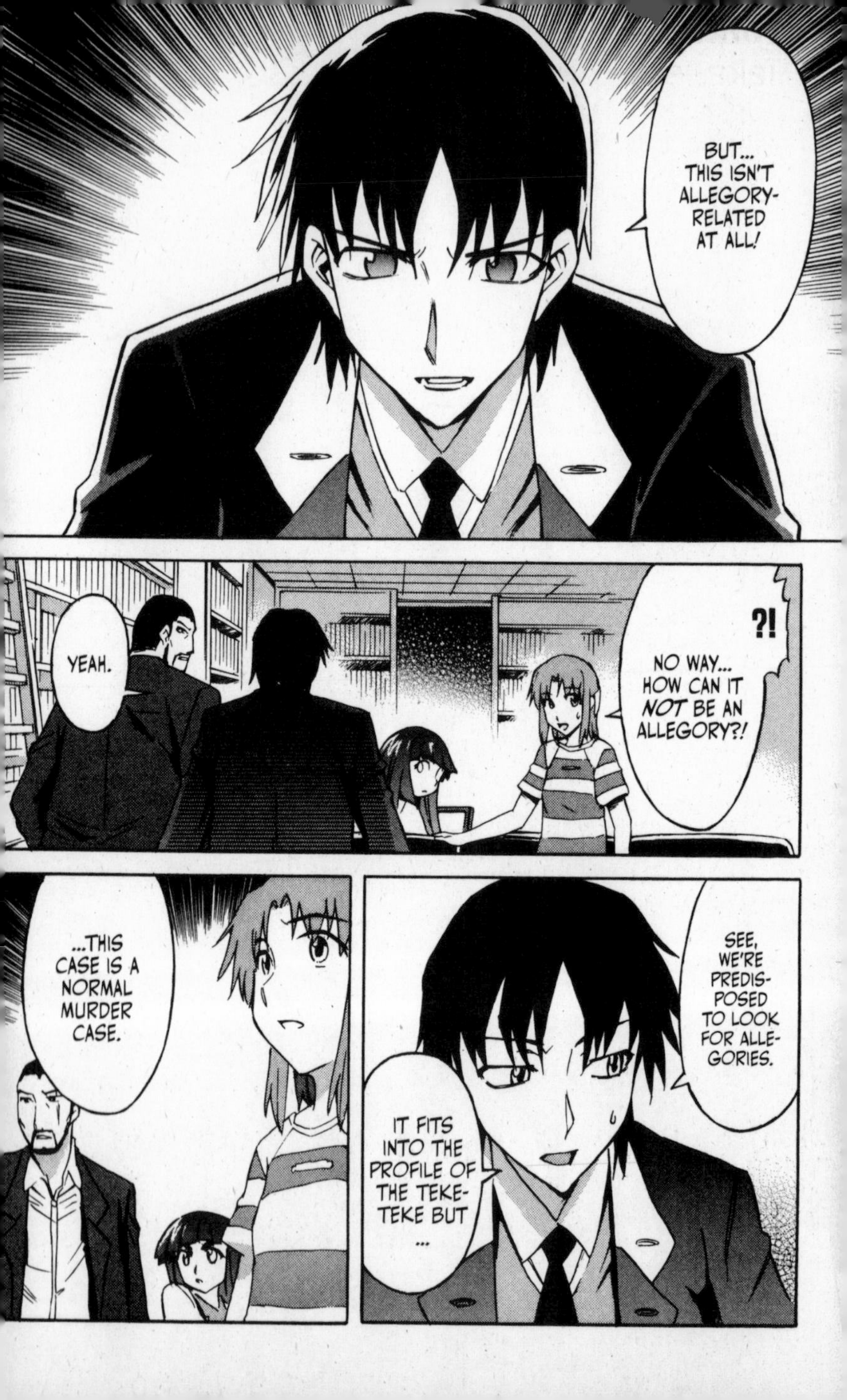
BUT... THIS ISN'T ALLEGORY-RELATED AT ALL!
?!
NO WAY... HOW CAN IT *NOT* BE AN ALLEGORY?!
YEAH.
SEE, WE'RE PREDIS-POSED TO LOOK FOR ALLE-GORIES.
IT FITS INTO THE PROFILE OF THE TEKE-TEKE BUT ...
...THIS CASE IS A NORMAL MURDER CASE.

Folklore; Teke-Teke – Part 2 –

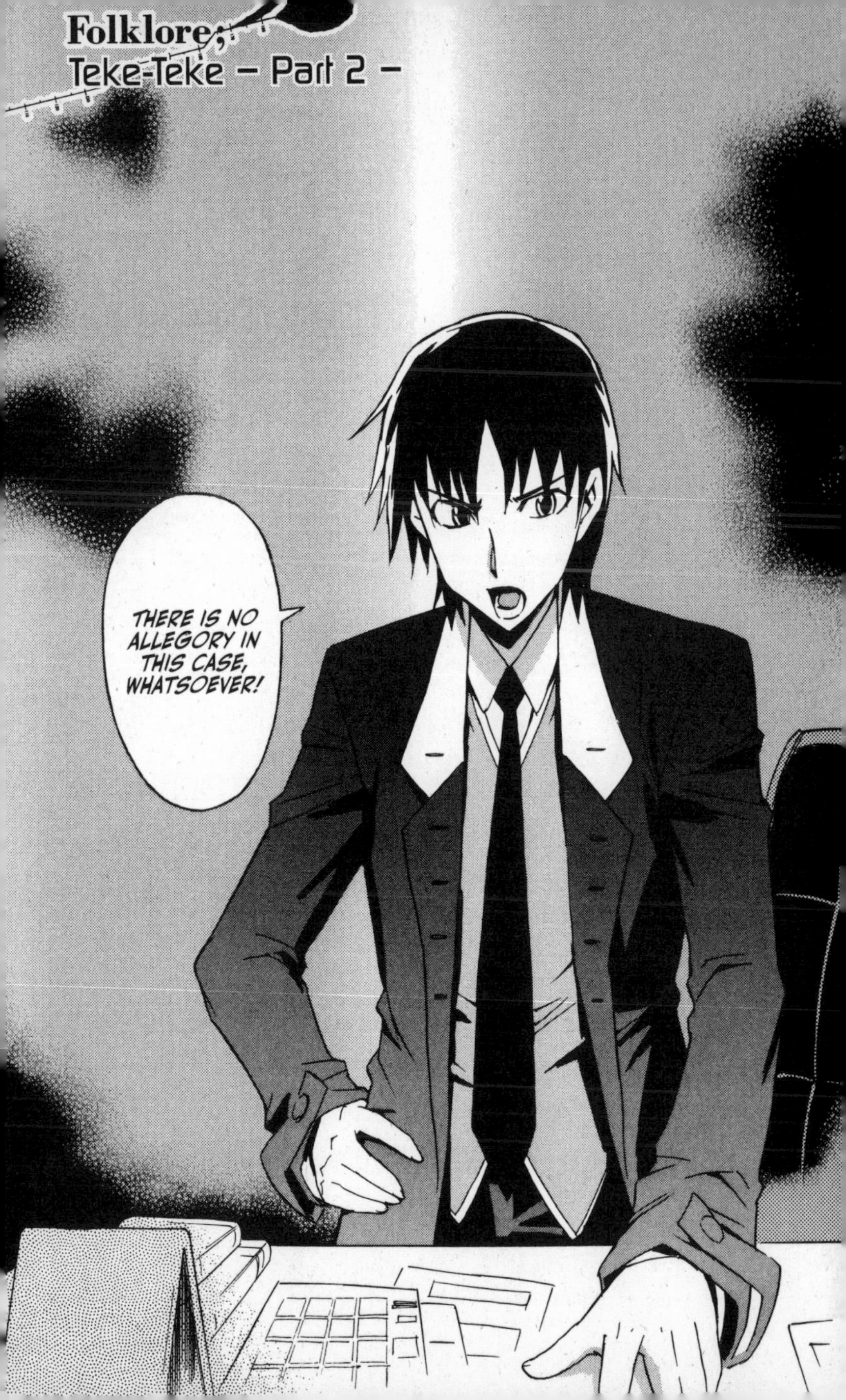
THERE IS NO ALLEGORY IN THIS CASE, WHATSOEVER!

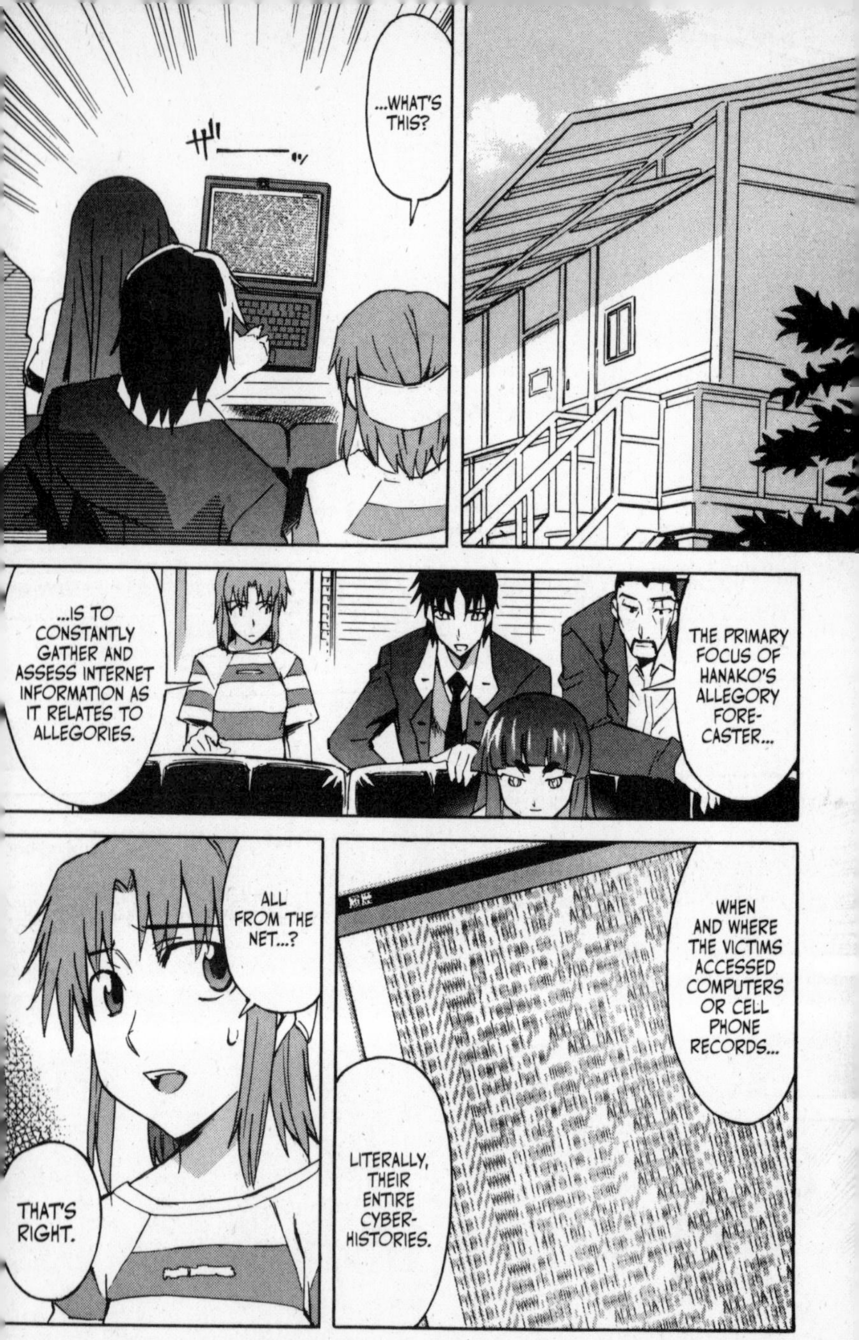
...WHAT'S THIS?
THE PRIMARY FOCUS OF HANAKO'S ALLEGORY FORE-CASTER...
...IS TO CONSTANTLY GATHER AND ASSESS INTERNET INFORMATION AS IT RELATES TO ALLEGORIES.
WHEN AND WHERE THE VICTIMS ACCESSED COMPUTERS OR CELL PHONE RECORDS...
LITERALLY, THEIR ENTIRE CYBER-HISTORIES.
ALL FROM THE NET...?
THAT'S RIGHT.

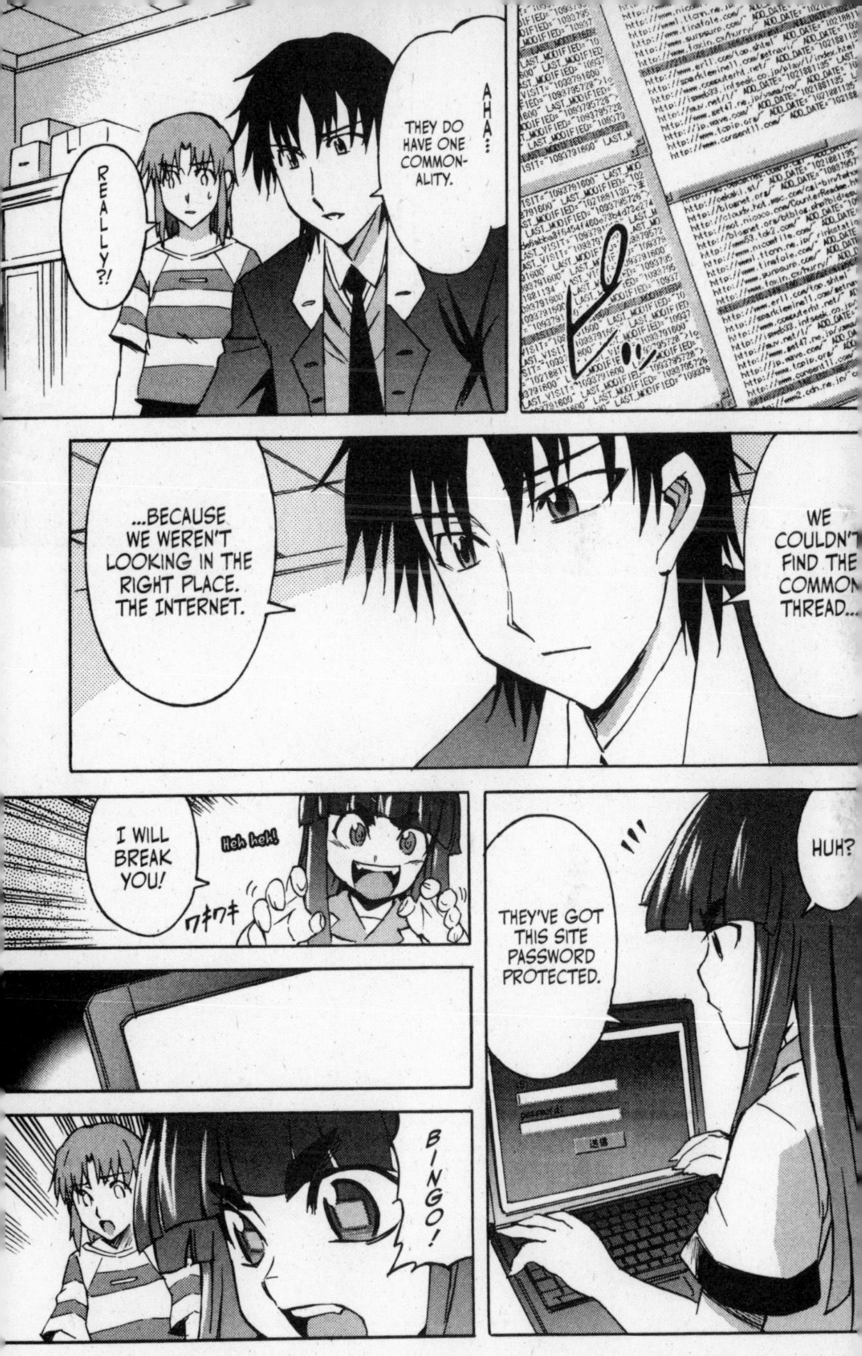
AHA... THEY DO HAVE ONE COMMON-ALITY.
REALLY?!
WE COULDN'T FIND THE COMMON THREAD...
...BECAUSE WE WEREN'T LOOKING IN THE RIGHT PLACE. THE INTERNET.
HUH?
THEY'VE GOT THIS SITE PASSWORD PROTECTED.
I WILL BREAK YOU!
Heh heh!
ワキワキ
BINGO!

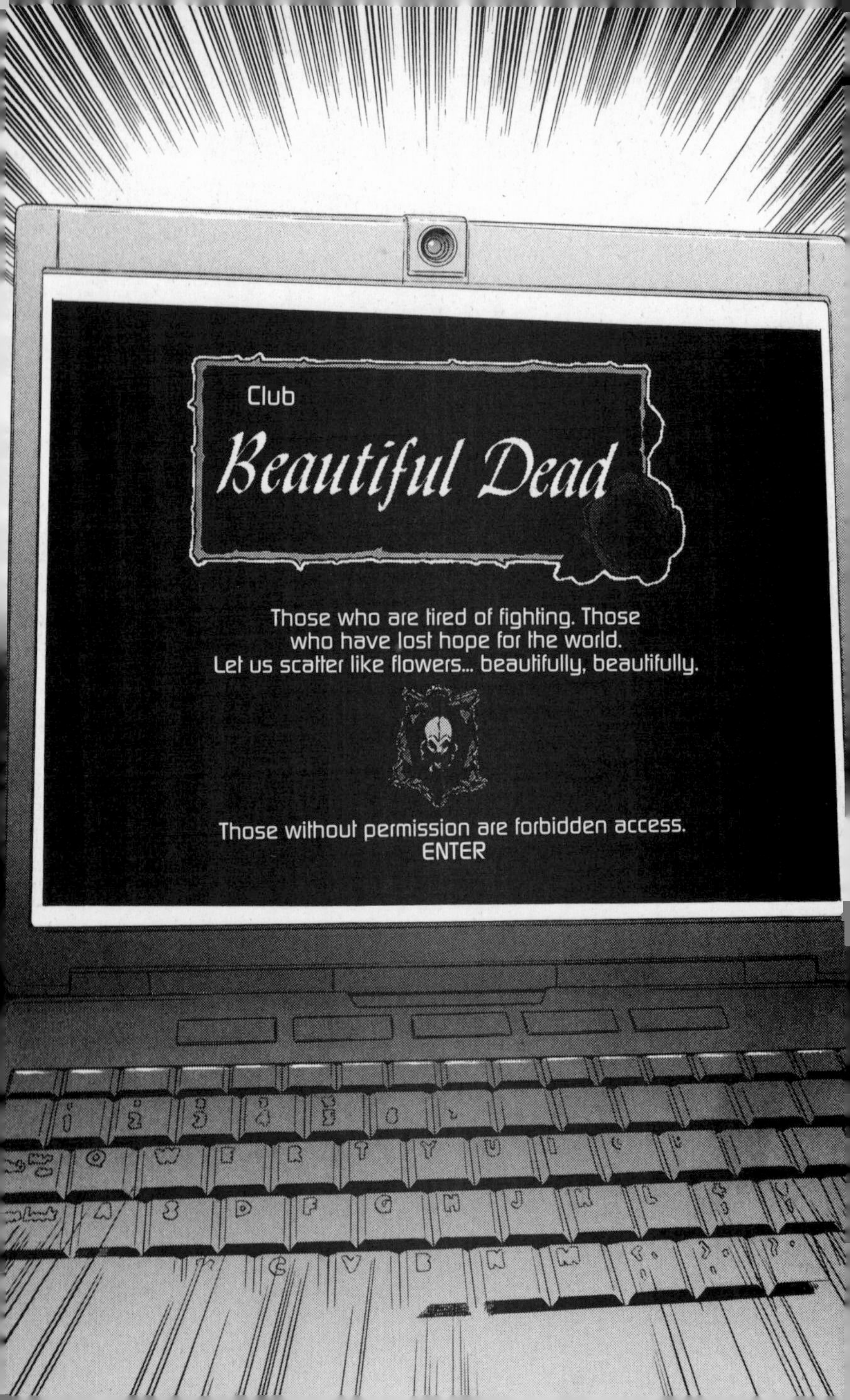
Club
Beautiful Dead
Those who are tired of fighting. Those who have lost hope for the world. Let us scatter like flowers... beautifully, beautifully.
Those without permission are forbidden access.
ENTER

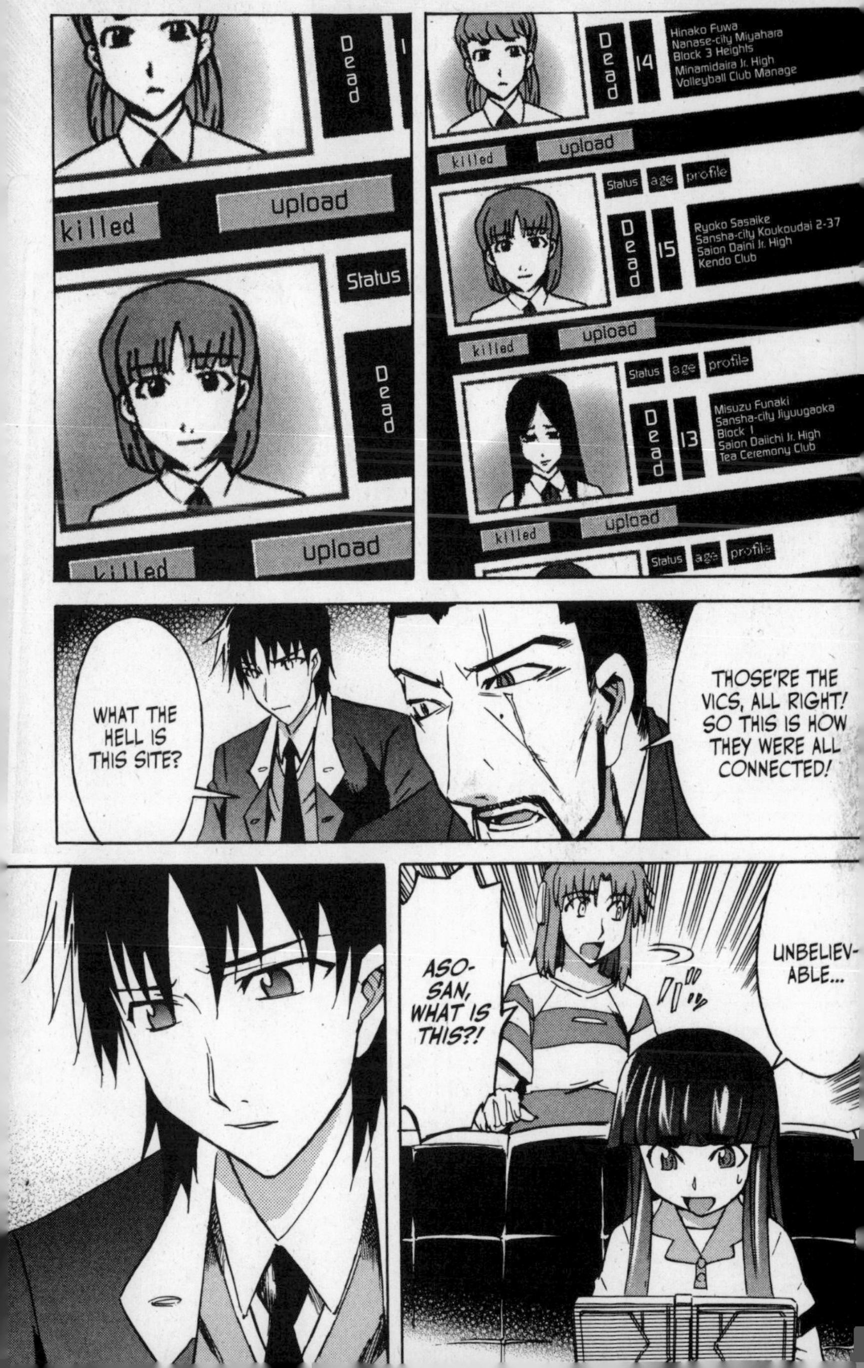
Dead
14
Hinako Fuwa
Nanase-city Miyahara
Block 3 Heights
Minamidaira Jr. High
Volleyball Club Manage
killed
upload
Status
age
profile
Dead
15
Ryoko Sasaike
Sansha-city Koukoudai 2-37
Saion Daini Jr. High
Kendo Club
killed
upload
Status
age
profile
Dead
13
Misuzu Funaki
Sansha-city Jiyuugaoka
Block 1
Saion Daiichi Jr. High
Tea Ceremony Club
killed
upload
Status
age
profile
Dead
killed
upload
Status
Dead
upload
THOSE'RE THE VICS, ALL RIGHT! SO THIS IS HOW THEY WERE ALL CONNECTED!
WHAT THE HELL IS THIS SITE?
UNBELIEV-ABLE...
ASO-SAN, WHAT IS THIS?!

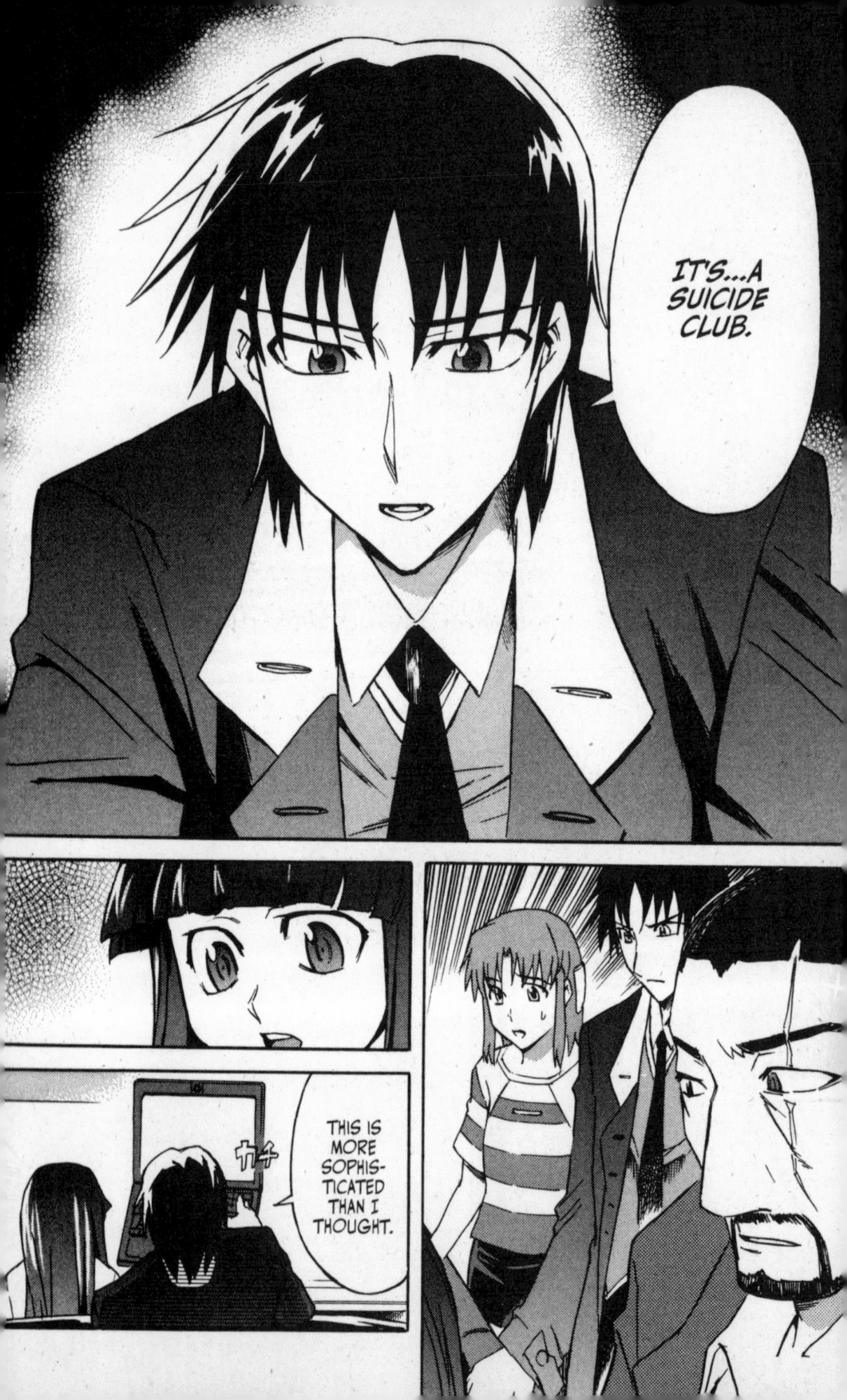
IT'S...A SUICIDE CLUB.
THIS IS MORE SOPHISTICATED THAN I THOUGHT.
カチ

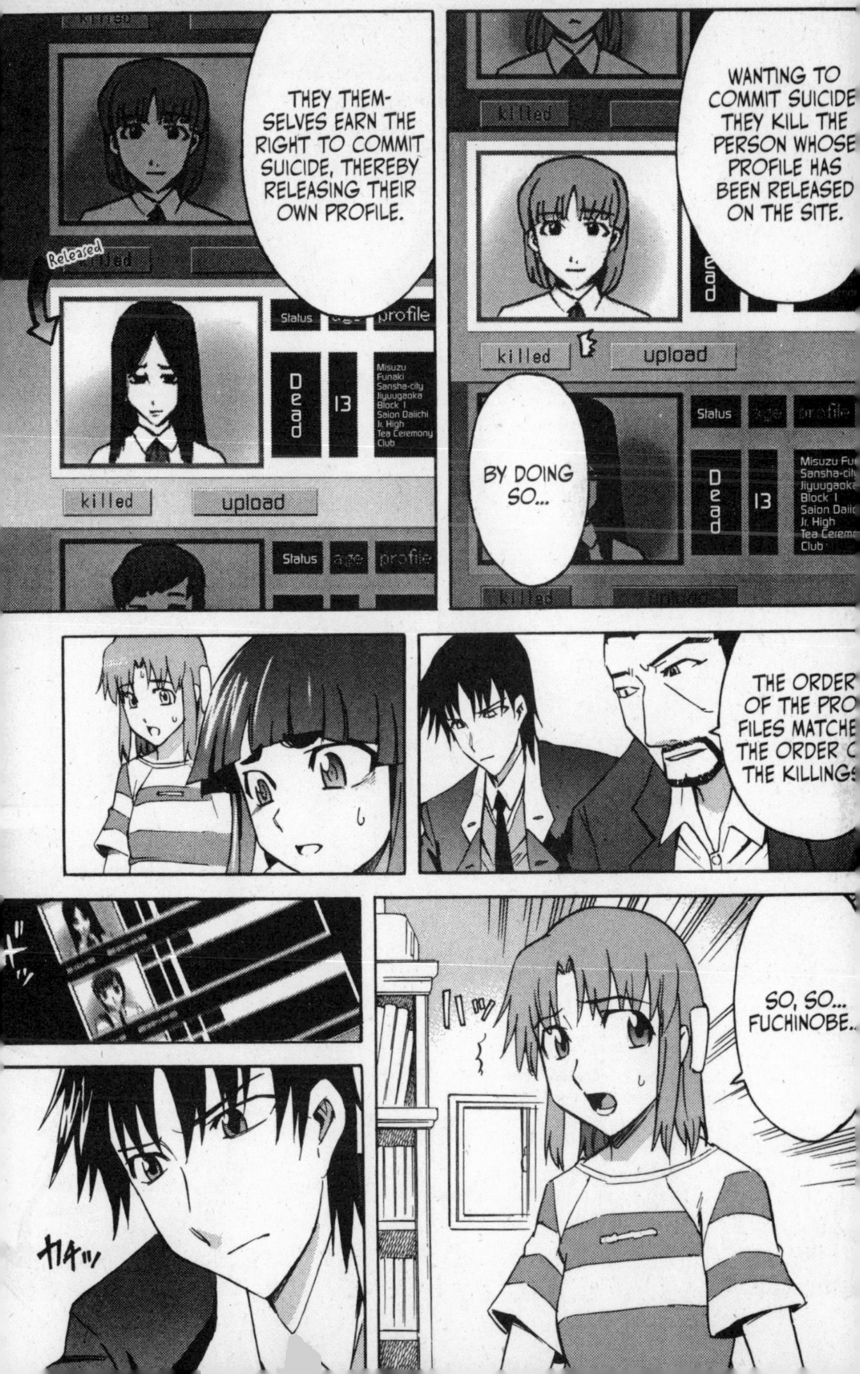
WANTING TO COMMIT SUICIDE THEY KILL THE PERSON WHOSE PROFILE HAS BEEN RELEASED ON THE SITE.
killed
upload
BY DOING SO...
Status
Dead
13
THEY THEM-SELVES EARN THE RIGHT TO COMMIT SUICIDE, THEREBY RELEASING THEIR OWN PROFILE.
Released
Status
profile
Dead
13
Misuzu Funaki Sansha-city Jiyuugaoka Block 1 Saion Daiichi Jr. High Tea Ceremony Club
killed
upload
Status
THE ORDER OF THE PRO FILES MATCHE THE ORDER THE KILLINGS
SO, SO... FUCHINOBE..

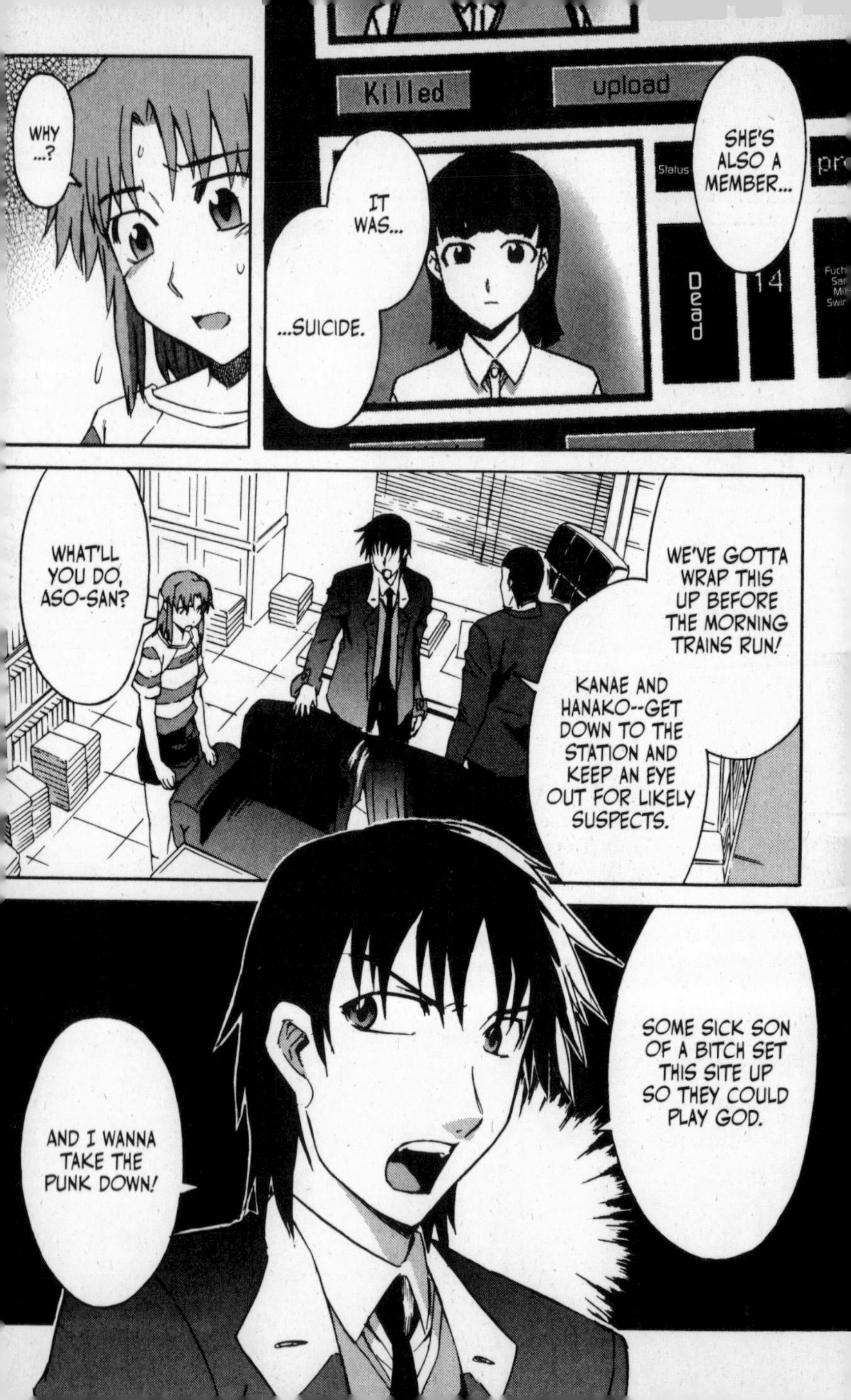
Killed
upload
Status
SHE'S ALSO A MEMBER...
IT WAS...
...SUICIDE.
Dead
14
WHY ...?
WHAT'LL YOU DO, ASO-SAN?
WE'VE GOTTA WRAP THIS UP BEFORE THE MORNING TRAINS RUN!
KANAE AND HANAKO--GET DOWN TO THE STATION AND KEEP AN EYE OUT FOR LIKELY SUSPECTS.
SOME SICK SON OF A BITCH SET THIS SITE UP SO THEY COULD PLAY GOD.
AND I WANNA TAKE THE PUNK DOWN!

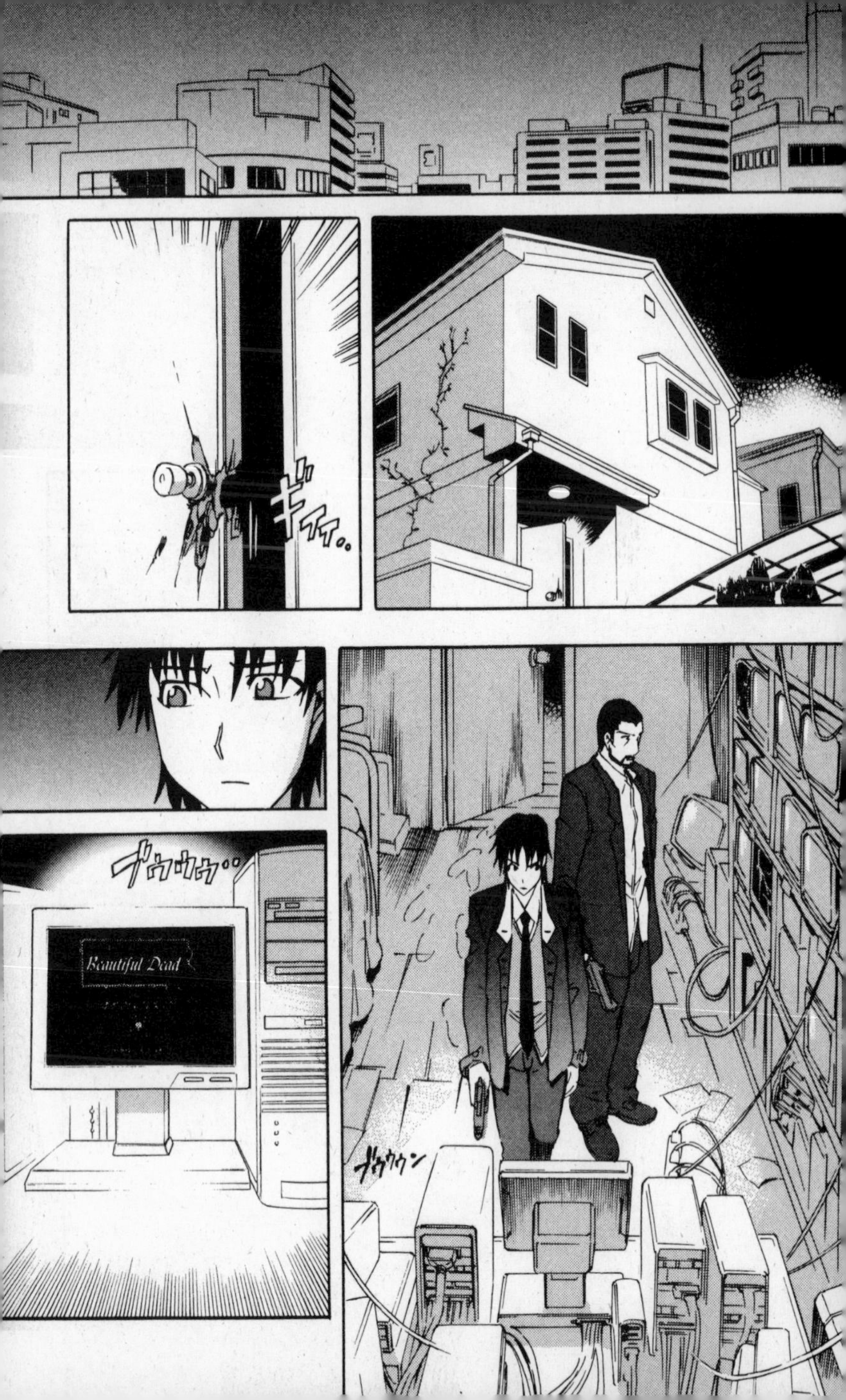
ギィィ。。
ブゥウン
ブウウウ゛
Beautiful Dead

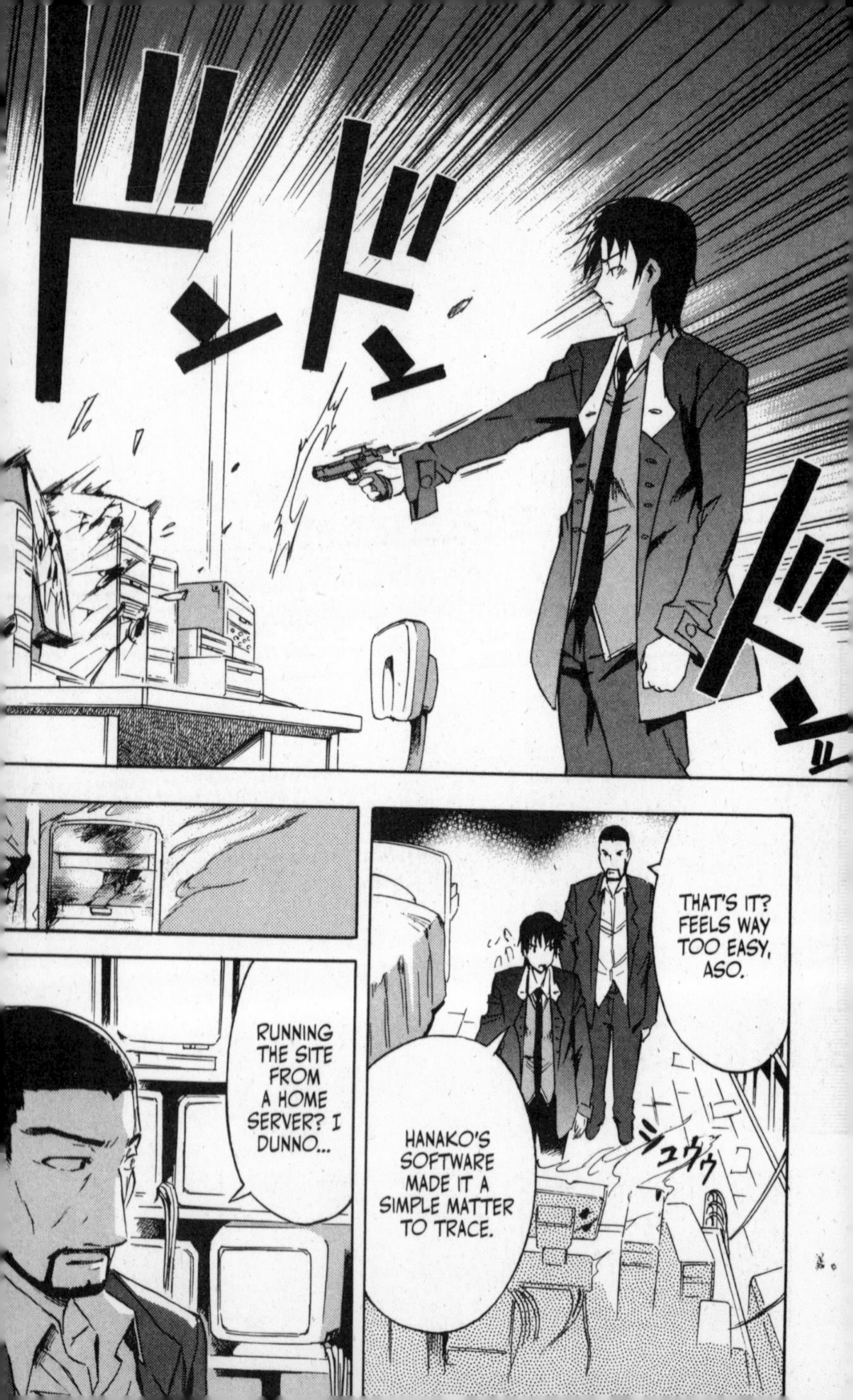
ドュ
ドュ
ドュッ
THAT'S IT? FEELS WAY TOO EASY, ASO.
HANAKO'S SOFTWARE MADE IT A SIMPLE MATTER TO TRACE.
シュウゥ
RUNNING THE SITE FROM A HOME SERVER? I DUNNO...

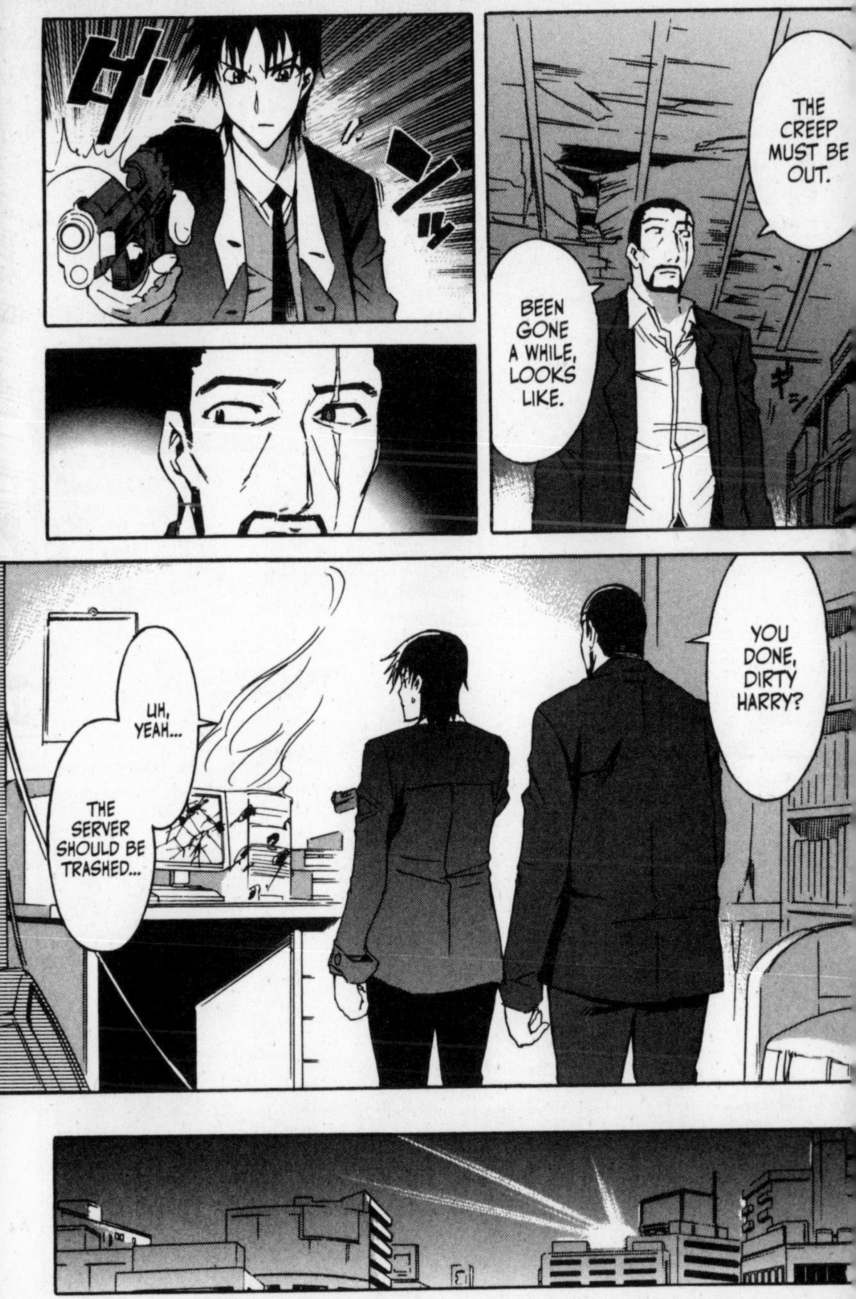
THE CREEP MUST BE OUT.
BEEN GONE A WHILE, LOOKS LIKE.
YOU DONE, DIRTY HARRY?
UH, YEAH...
THE SERVER SHOULD BE TRASHED...

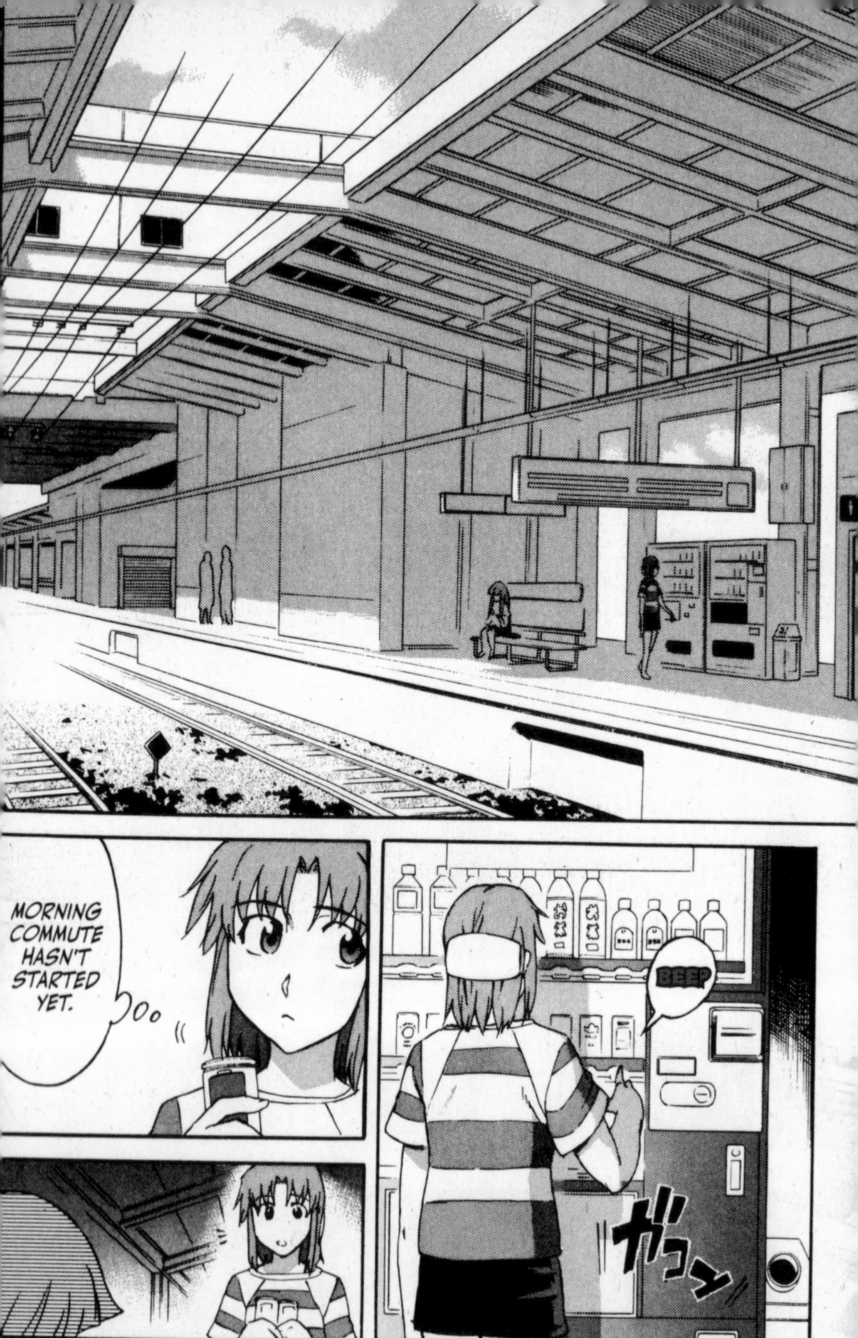
BEEP
ガコン
MORNING COMMUTE HASN'T STARTED YET.

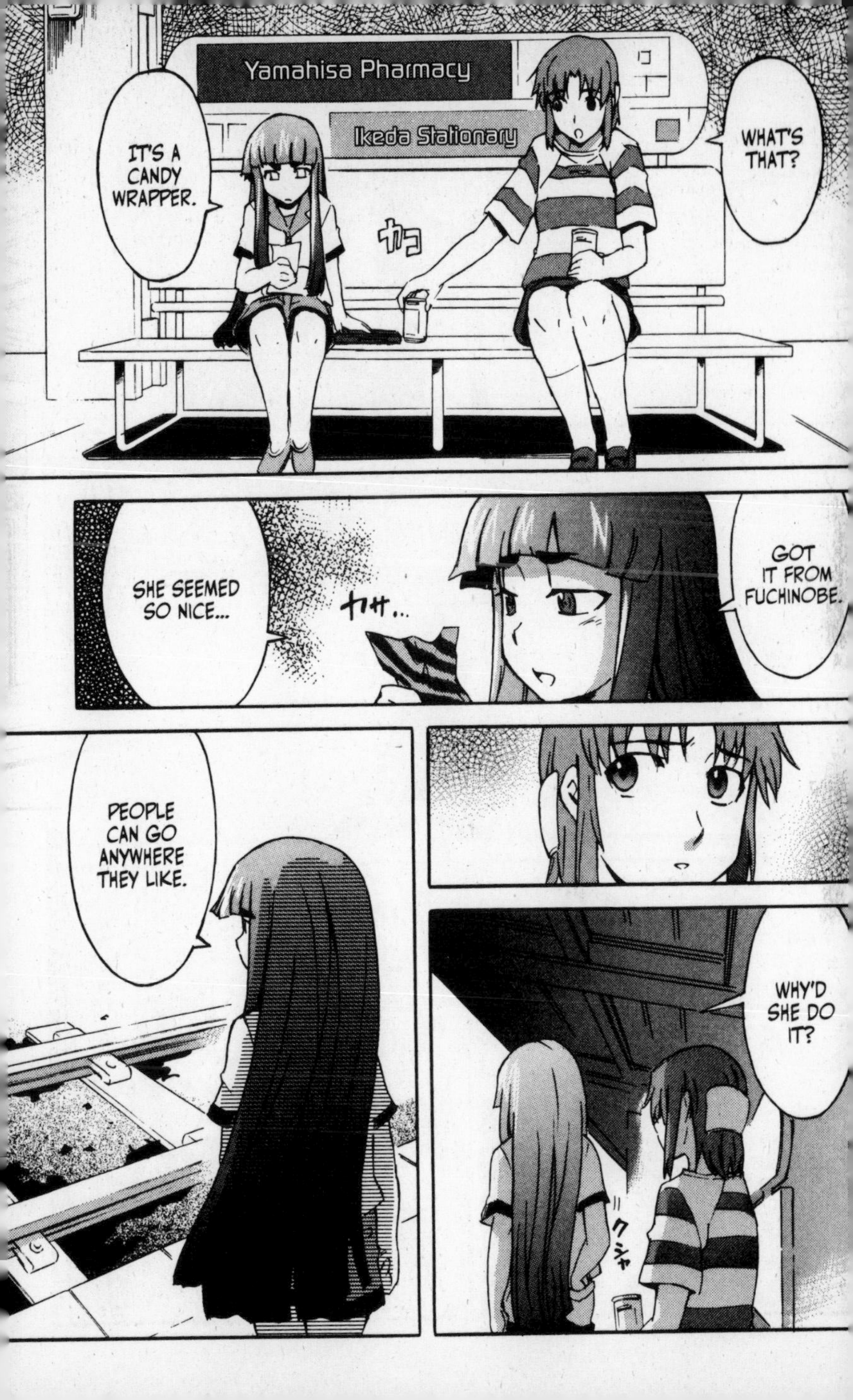
WHAT'S THAT?
Yamahisa Pharmacy
Ikeda Stationary
IT'S A CANDY WRAPPER.
カコ
GOT IT FROM FUCHINOBE.
カサ...
SHE SEEMED SO NICE...
WHY'D SHE DO IT?
クシャ
PEOPLE CAN GO ANYWHERE THEY LIKE.

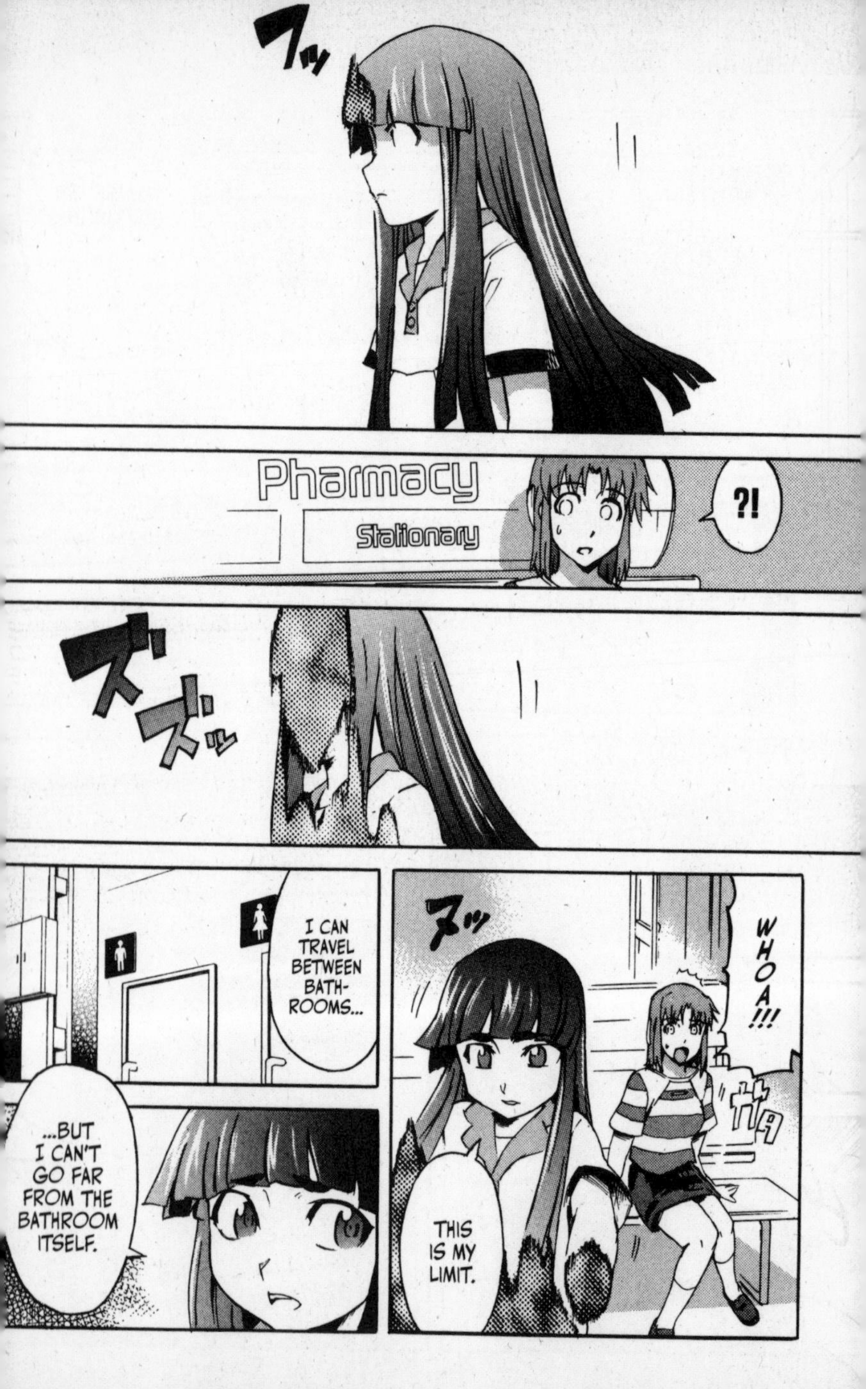
フッ
Pharmacy
Stationary
?!
ズズッ
スッ
WHOA!!!
ガタ
THIS IS MY LIMIT.
I CAN TRAVEL BETWEEN BATH-ROOMS...
...BUT I CAN'T GO FAR FROM THE BATHROOM ITSELF.

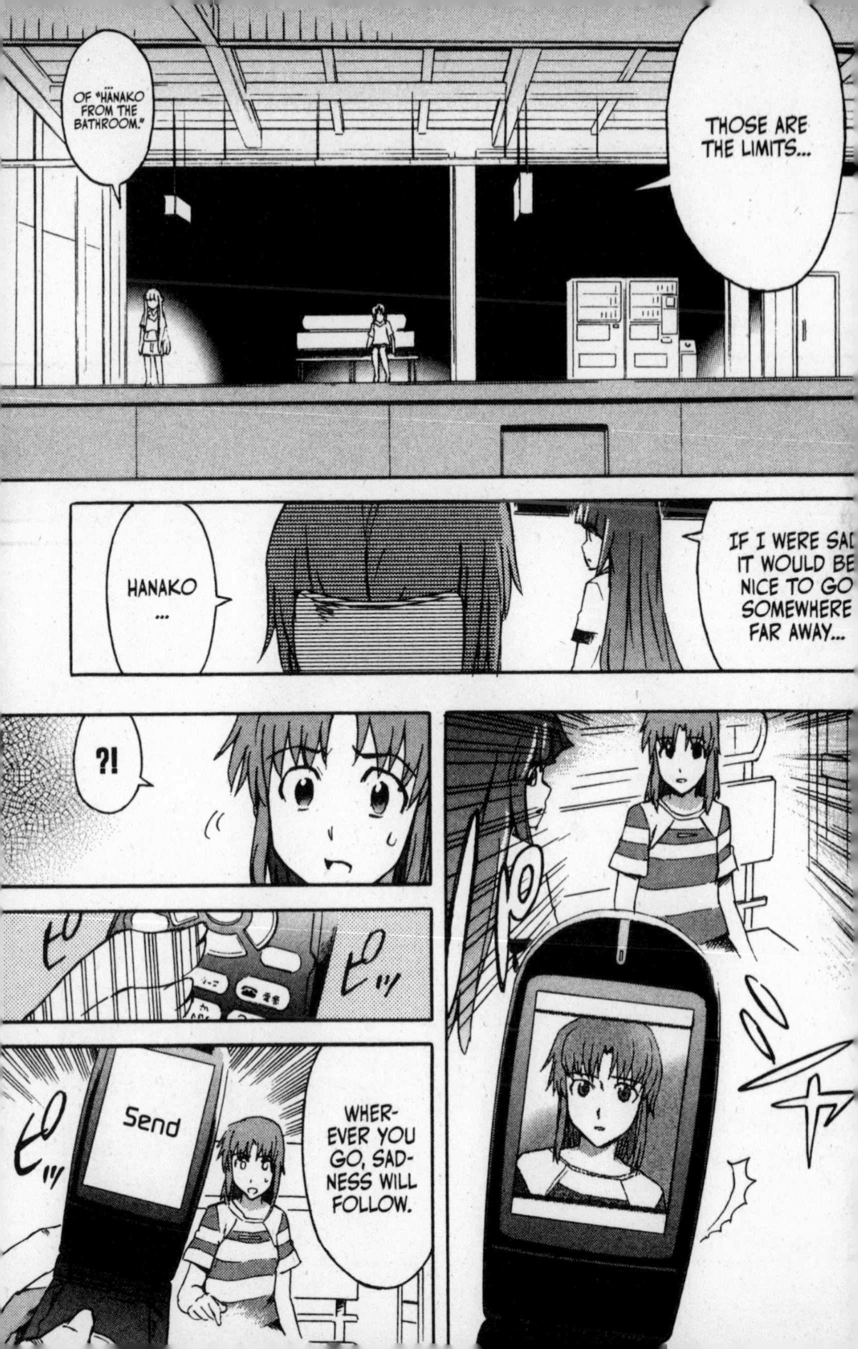
THOSE ARE THE LIMITS...
... OF "HANAKO FROM THE BATHROOM."
IF I WERE SAD IT WOULD BE NICE TO GO SOMEWHERE FAR AWAY...
HANAKO ...
?!
ピッ
ピッ
Send
ピッ
WHER-EVER YOU GO, SAD-NESS WILL FOLLOW.

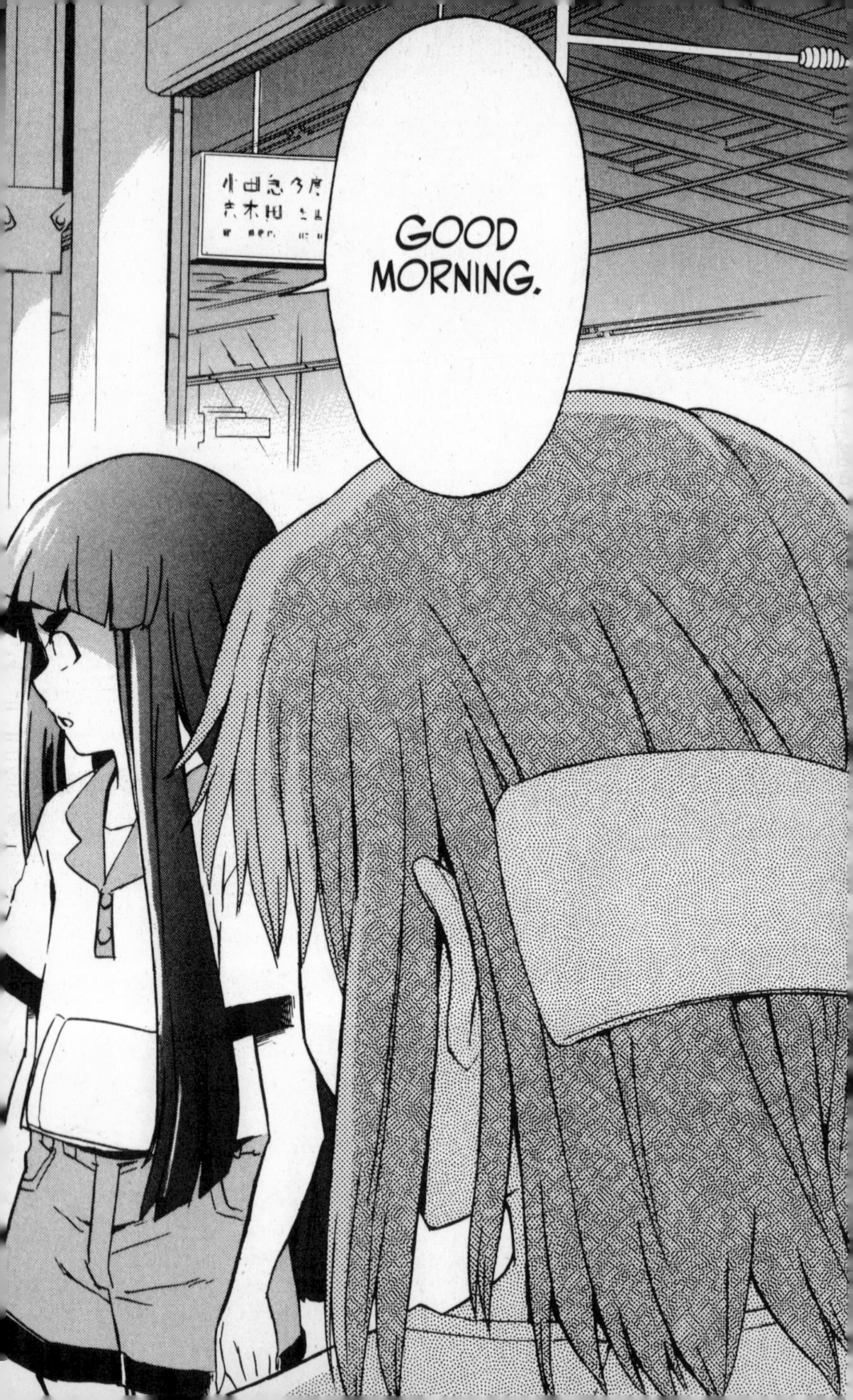
GOOD MORNING.

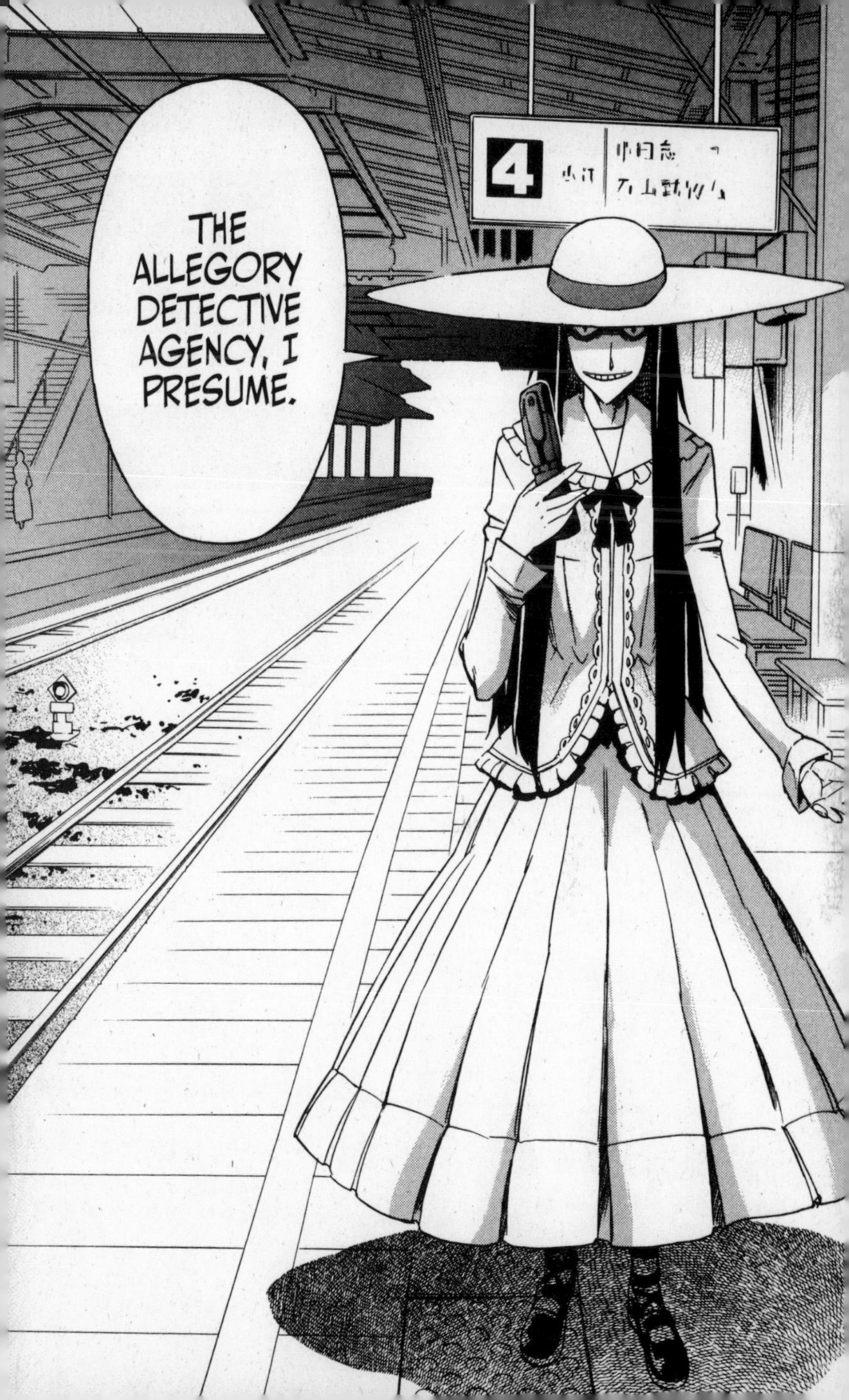
THE ALLEGORY DETECTIVE AGENCY, I PRESUME.

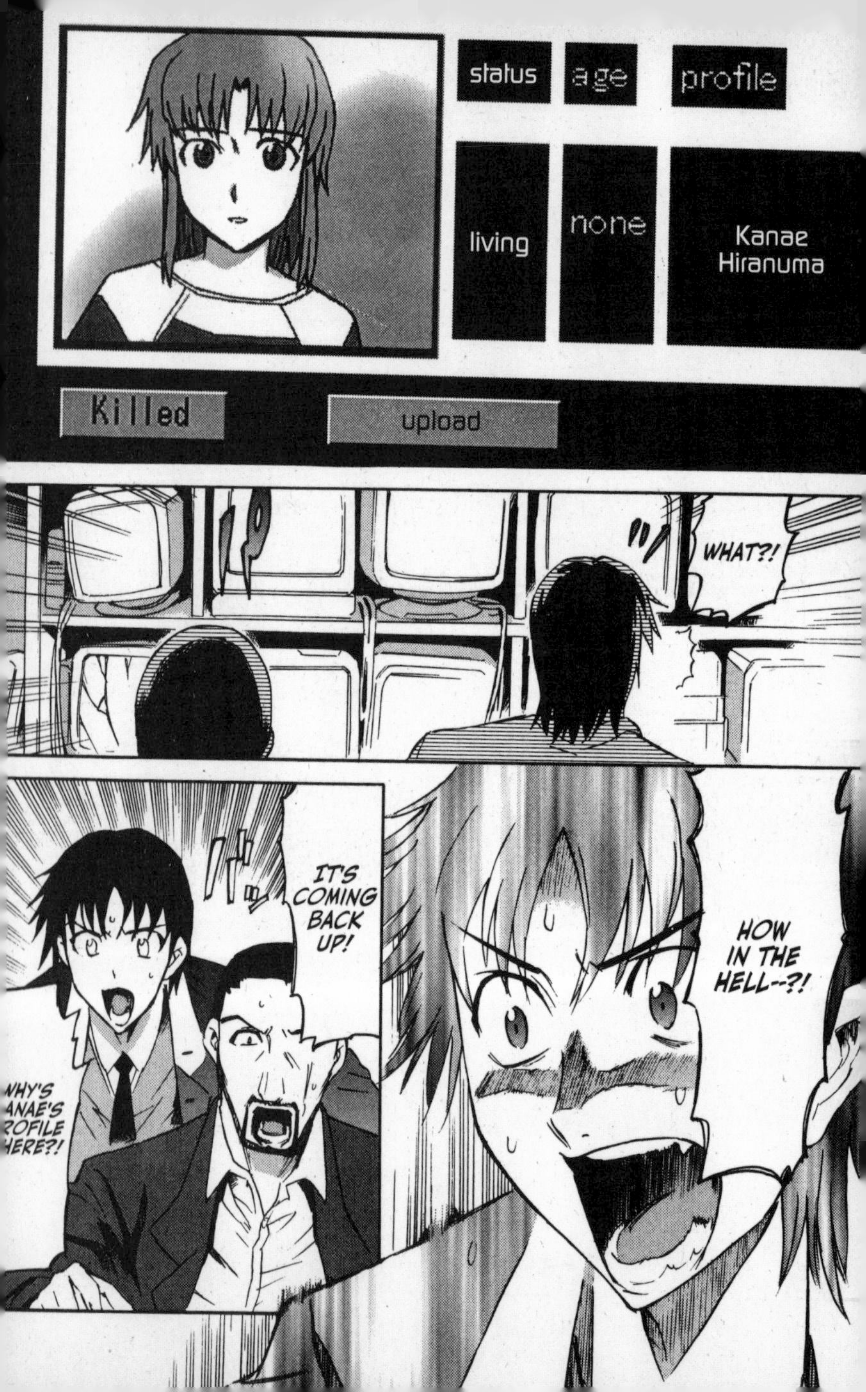
status
age
profile
living
none
Kanae Hiranuma
Killed
upload
WHAT?!
HOW IN THE HELL--?!
IT'S COMING BACK UP!
WHY'S ANAE'S ROFILE HERE?!

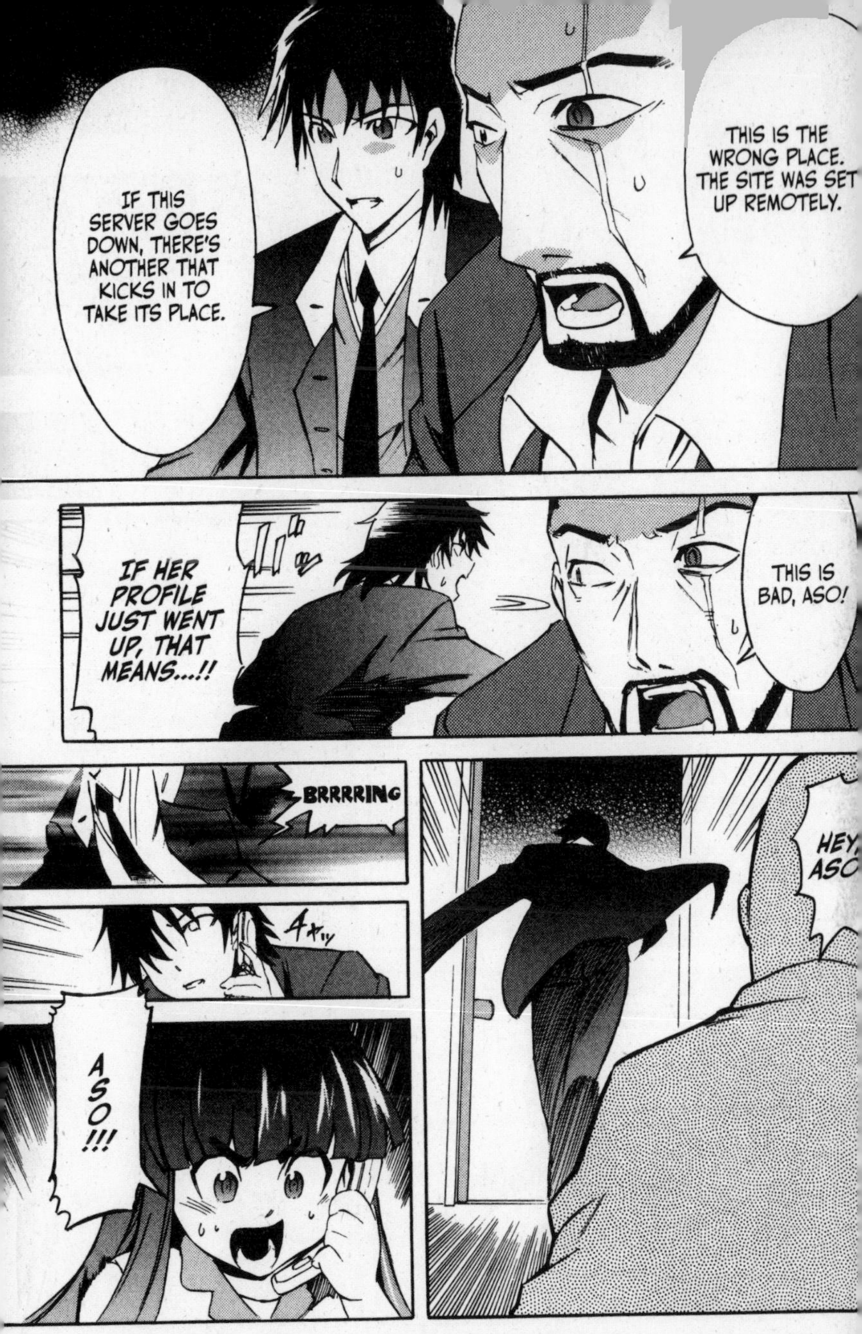
THIS IS THE WRONG PLACE. THE SITE WAS SET UP REMOTELY.
IF THIS SERVER GOES DOWN, THERE'S ANOTHER THAT KICKS IN TO TAKE ITS PLACE.
THIS IS BAD, ASO!
IF HER PROFILE JUST WENT UP, THAT MEANS...!!
HEY, ASO
BRRRRING
ASO!!!

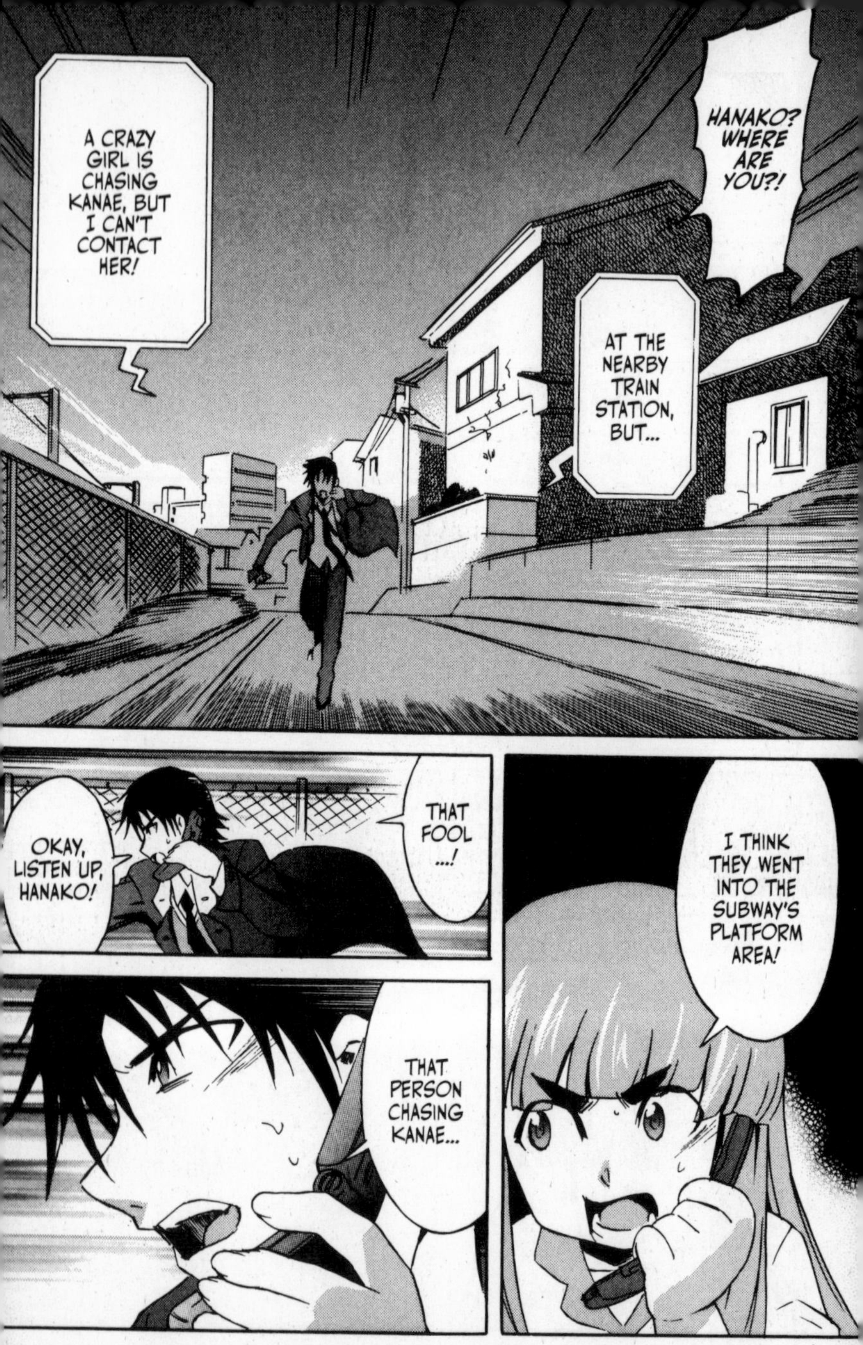
HANAKO? WHERE ARE YOU?!
AT THE NEARBY TRAIN STATION, BUT...
A CRAZY GIRL IS CHASING KANAE, BUT I CAN'T CONTACT HER!
I THINK THEY WENT INTO THE SUBWAY'S PLATFORM AREA!
THAT FOOL ...!
OKAY, LISTEN UP, HANAKO!
THAT PERSON CHASING KANAE...

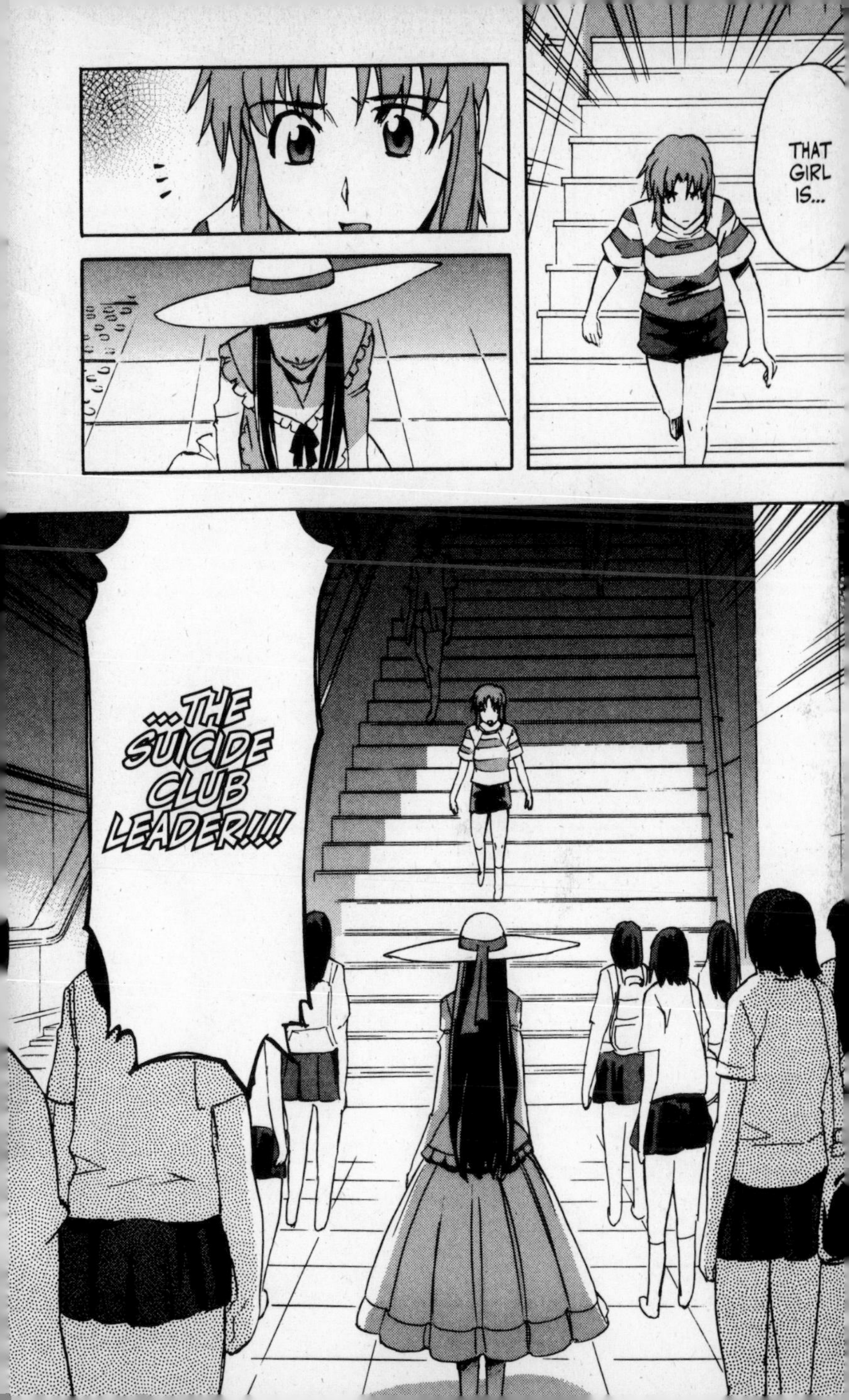
THAT GIRL IS...
...THE SUICIDE CLUB LEADER!!!!

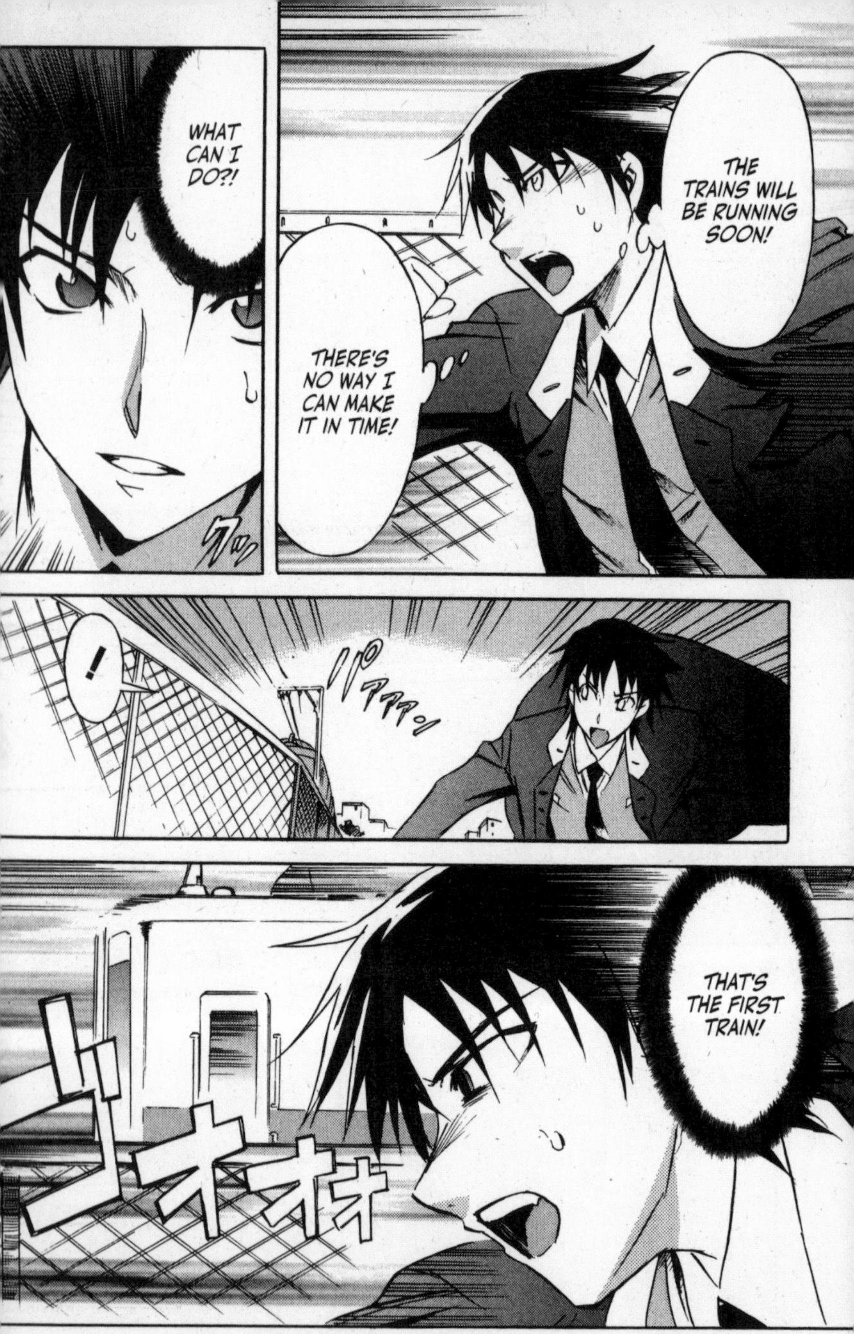
THE TRAINS WILL BE RUNNING SOON!
THERE'S NO WAY I CAN MAKE IT IN TIME!
WHAT CAN I DO?!
!
THAT'S THE FIRST TRAIN!

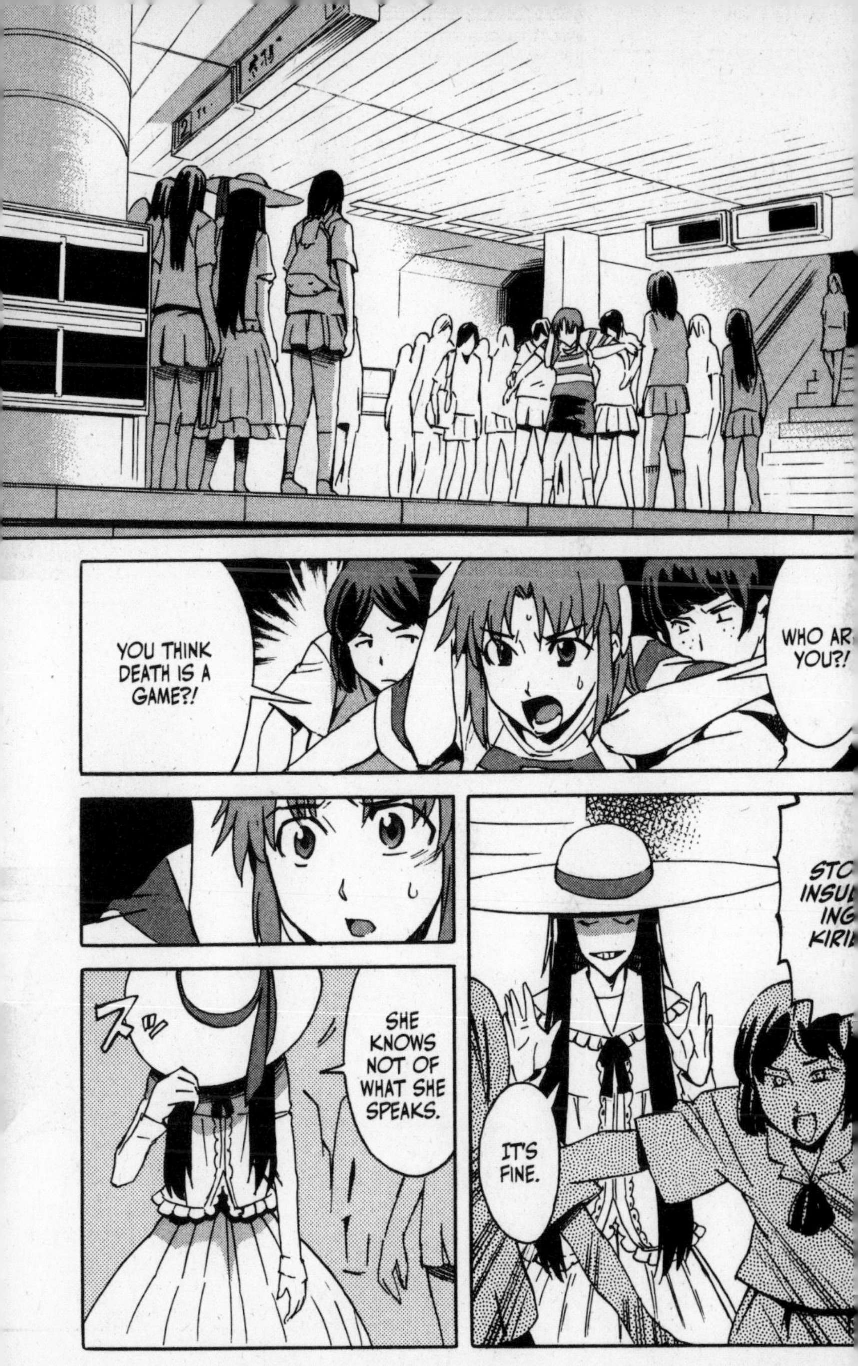
WHO AR YOU?!
YOU THINK DEATH IS A GAME?!
STO INSUL ING KIRI
IT'S FINE.
SHE KNOWS NOT OF WHAT SHE SPEAKS.

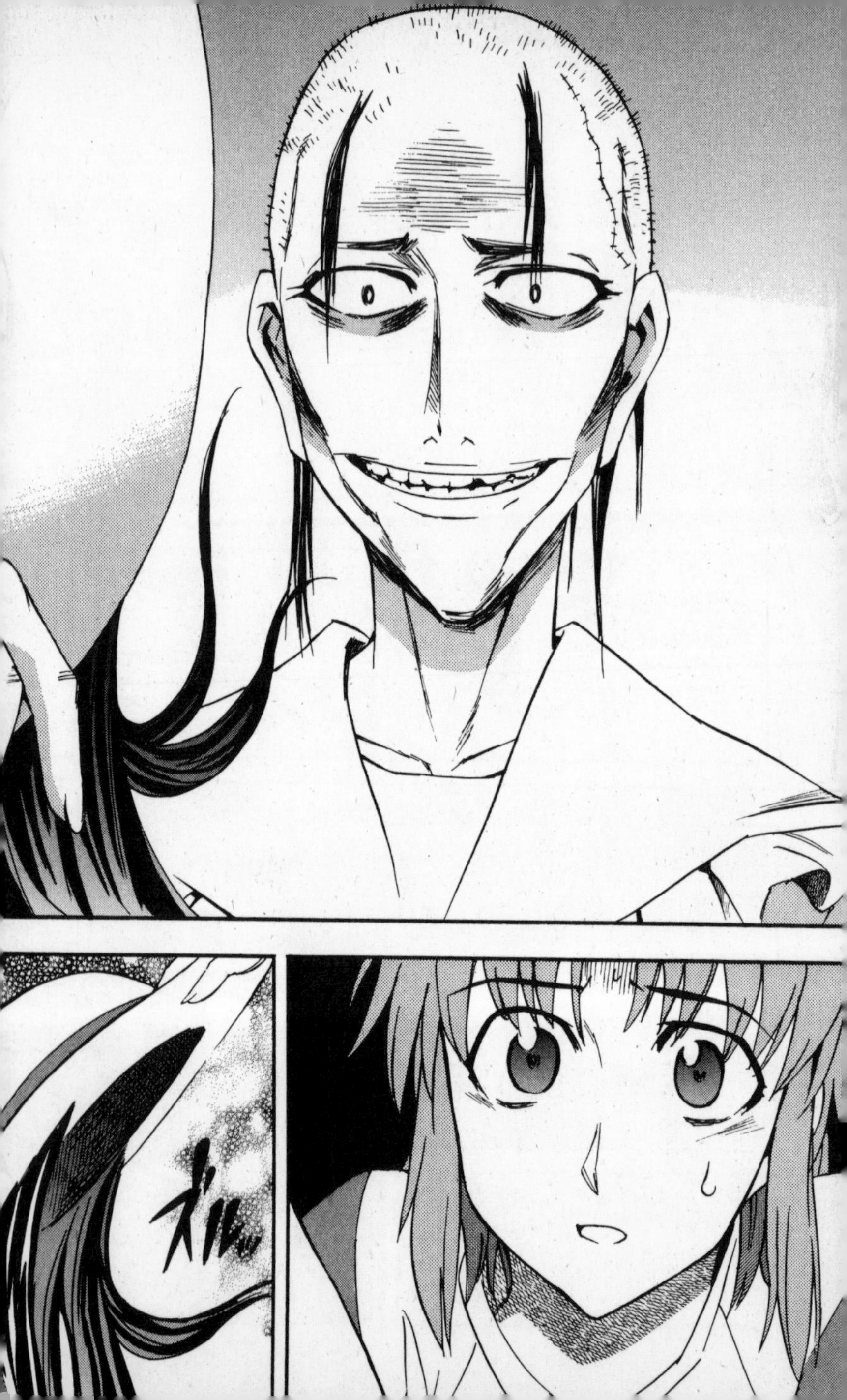
ズル…

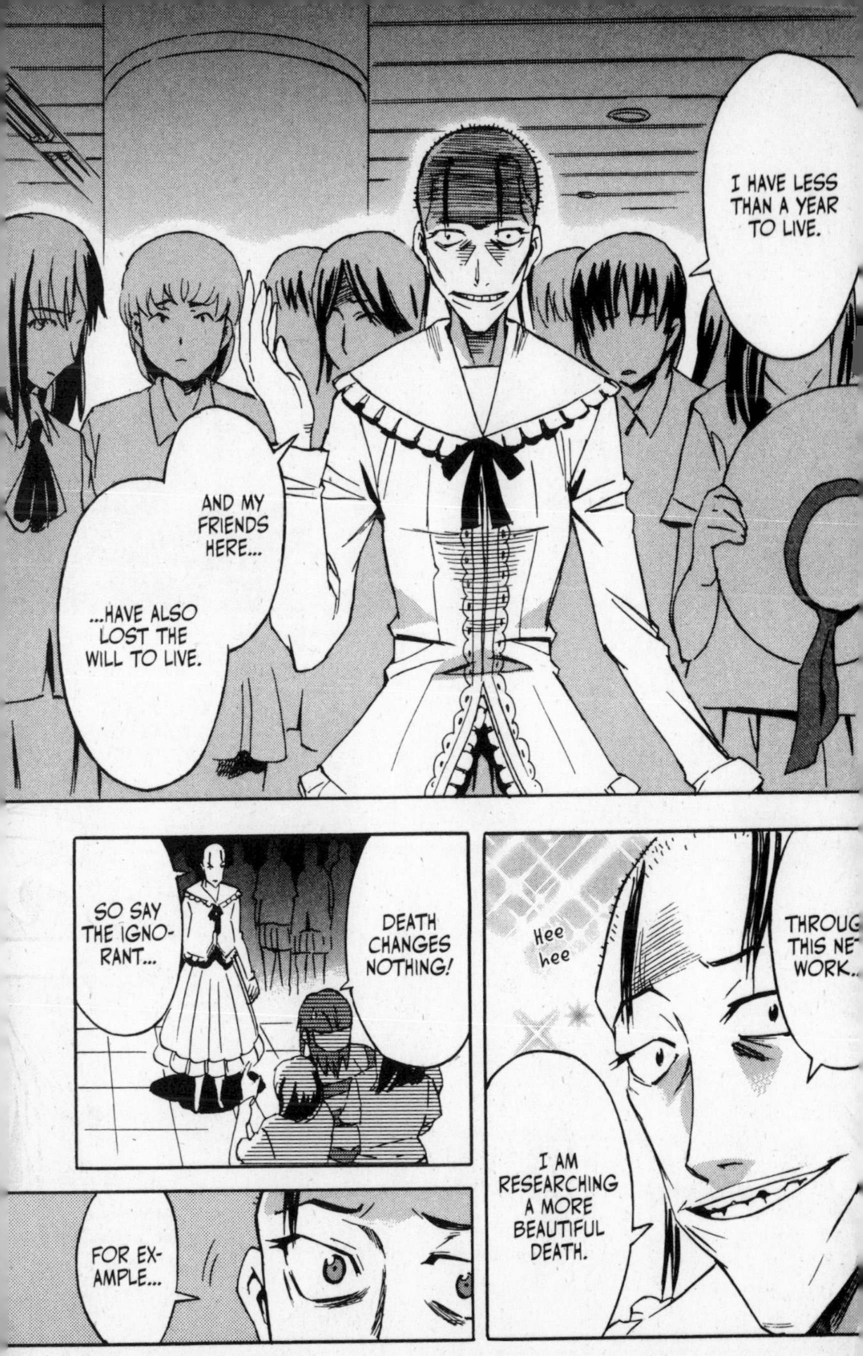
I HAVE LESS THAN A YEAR TO LIVE.
AND MY FRIENDS HERE...
...HAVE ALSO LOST THE WILL TO LIVE.
THROUG THIS NE WORK..
Hee hee
I AM RESEARCHING A MORE BEAUTIFUL DEATH.
DEATH CHANGES NOTHING!
SO SAY THE IGNO-RANT...
FOR EX-AMPLE...

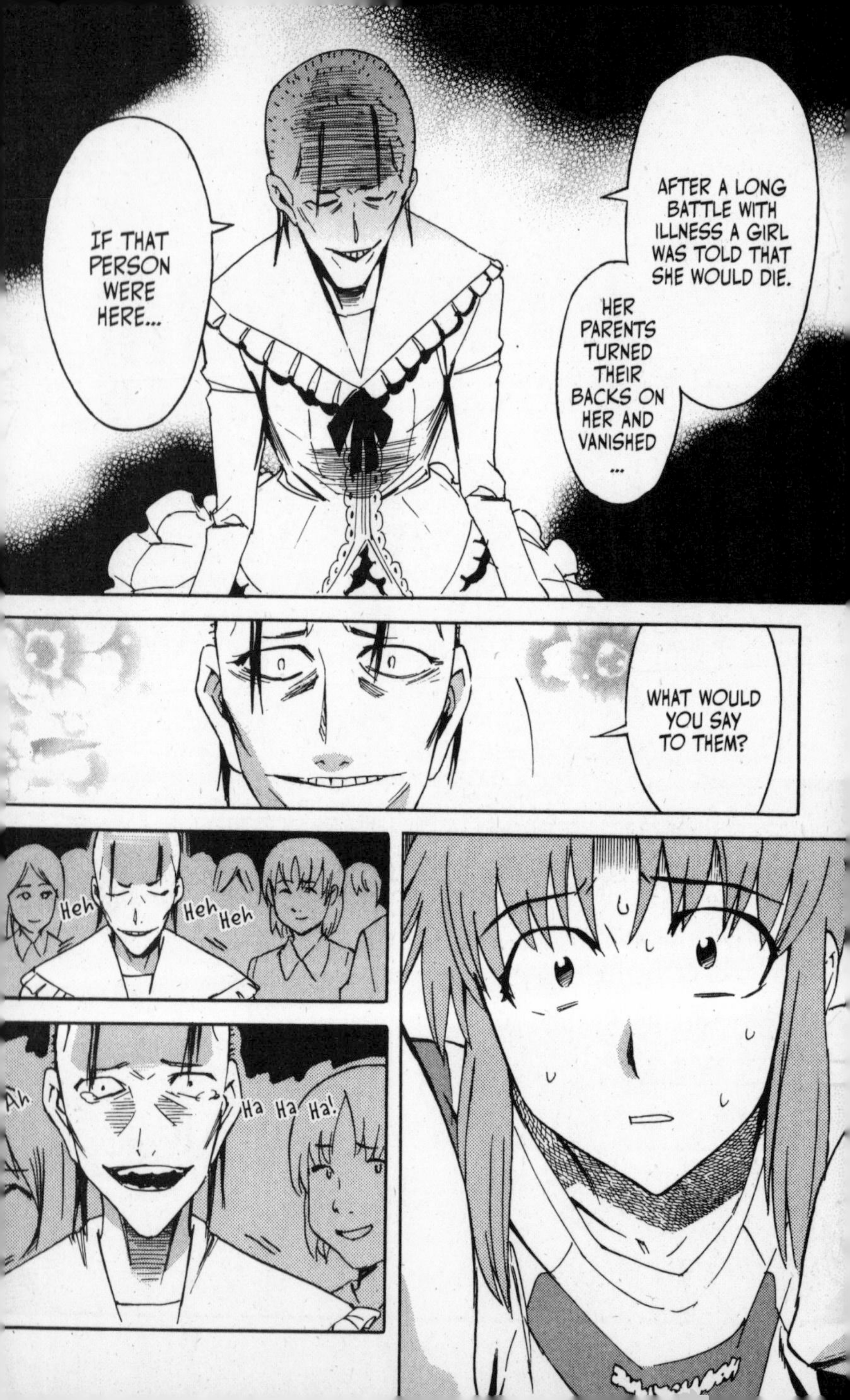
AFTER A LONG BATTLE WITH ILLNESS A GIRL WAS TOLD THAT SHE WOULD DIE.
HER PARENTS TURNED THEIR BACKS ON HER AND VANISHED ...
IF THAT PERSON WERE HERE...
WHAT WOULD YOU SAY TO THEM?
Heh Heh Heh
Ah Ha Ha Ha!

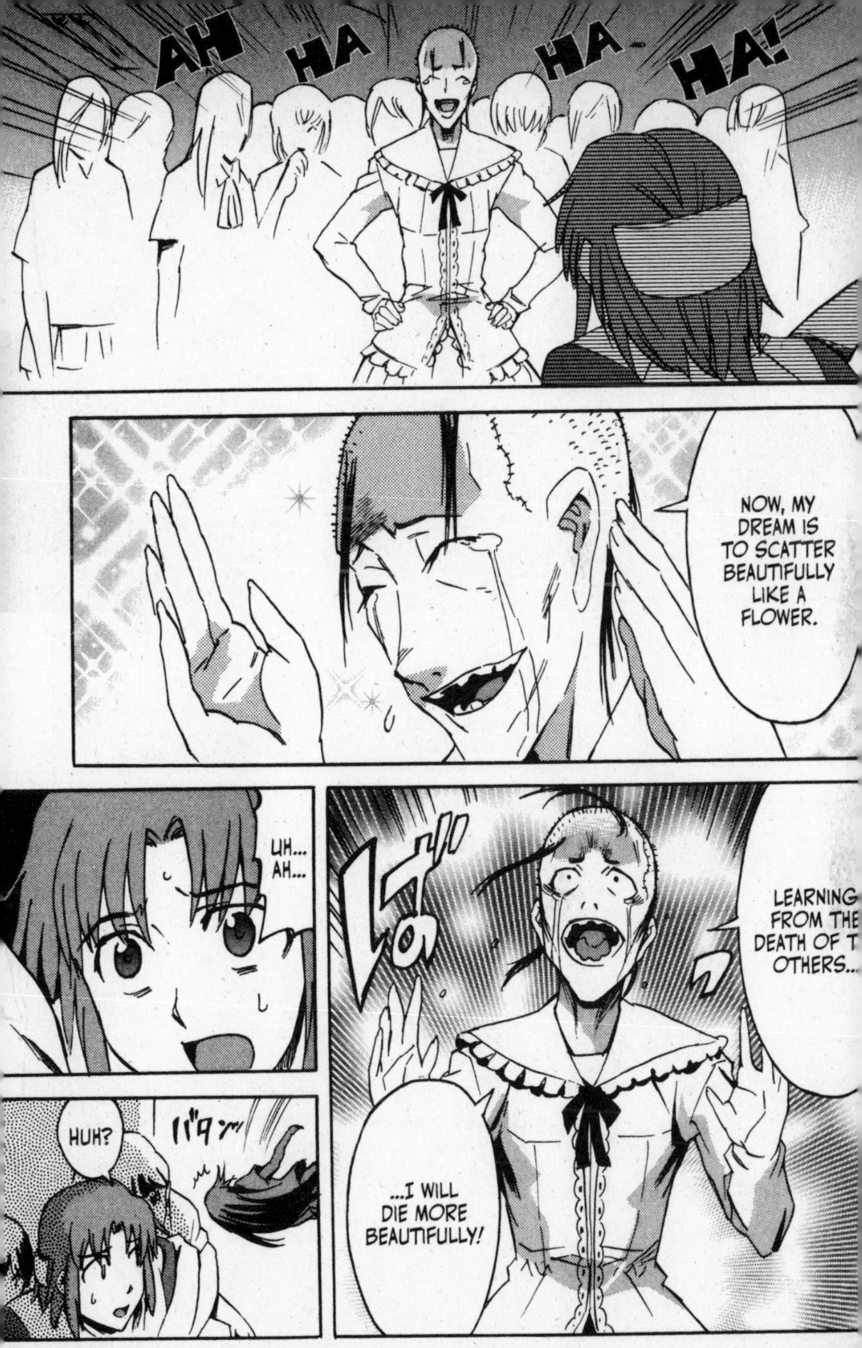
AH HA HA HA!
NOW, MY DREAM IS TO SCATTER BEAUTIFULLY LIKE A FLOWER.
LEARNING FROM THE DEATH OF T
OTHERS...
...I WILL DIE MORE BEAUTIFULLY!
UH... AH...
HUH?

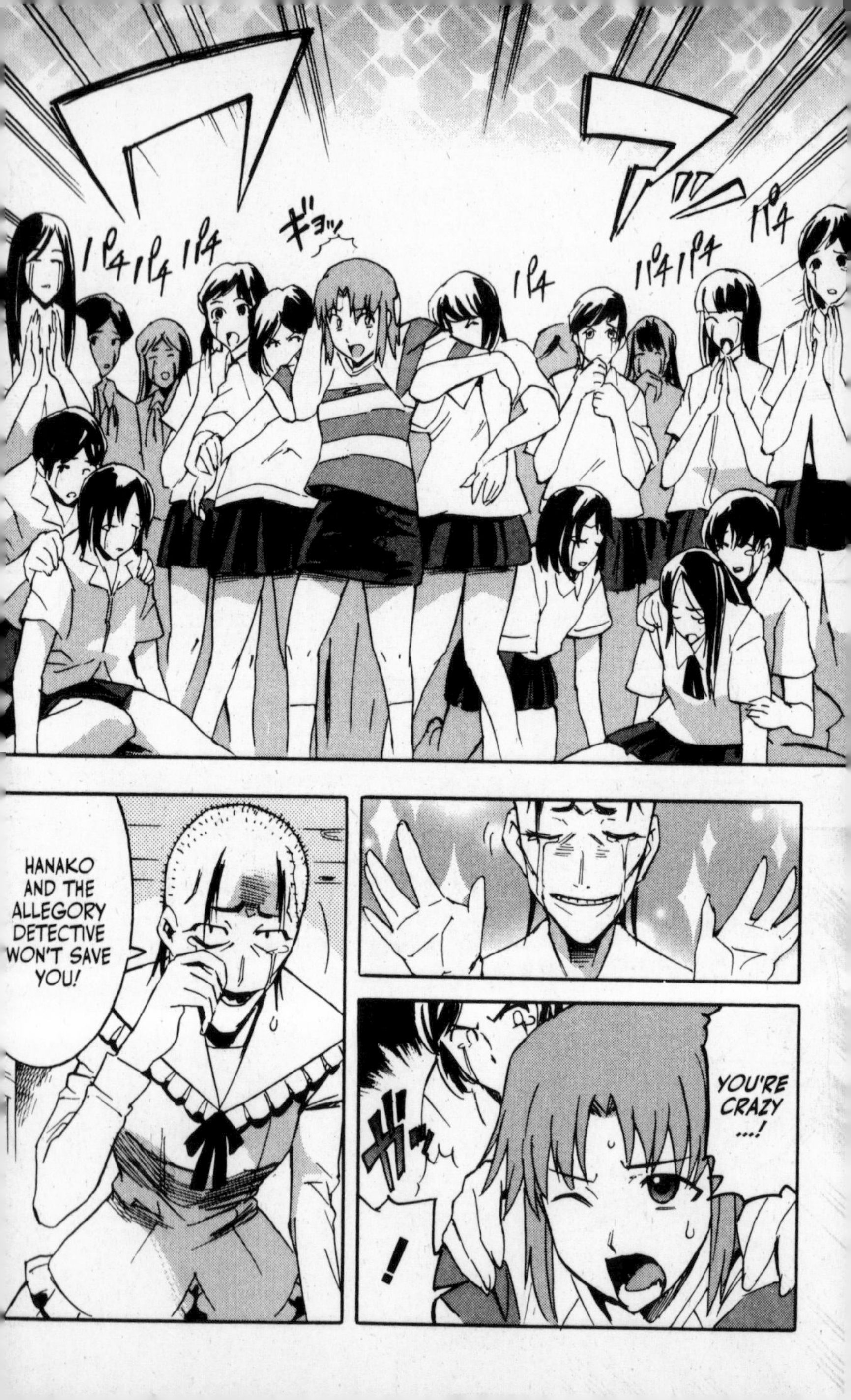
ギョッ!
YOU'RE CRAZY ...!
HANAKO AND THE ALLEGORY DETECTIVE WON'T SAVE YOU!

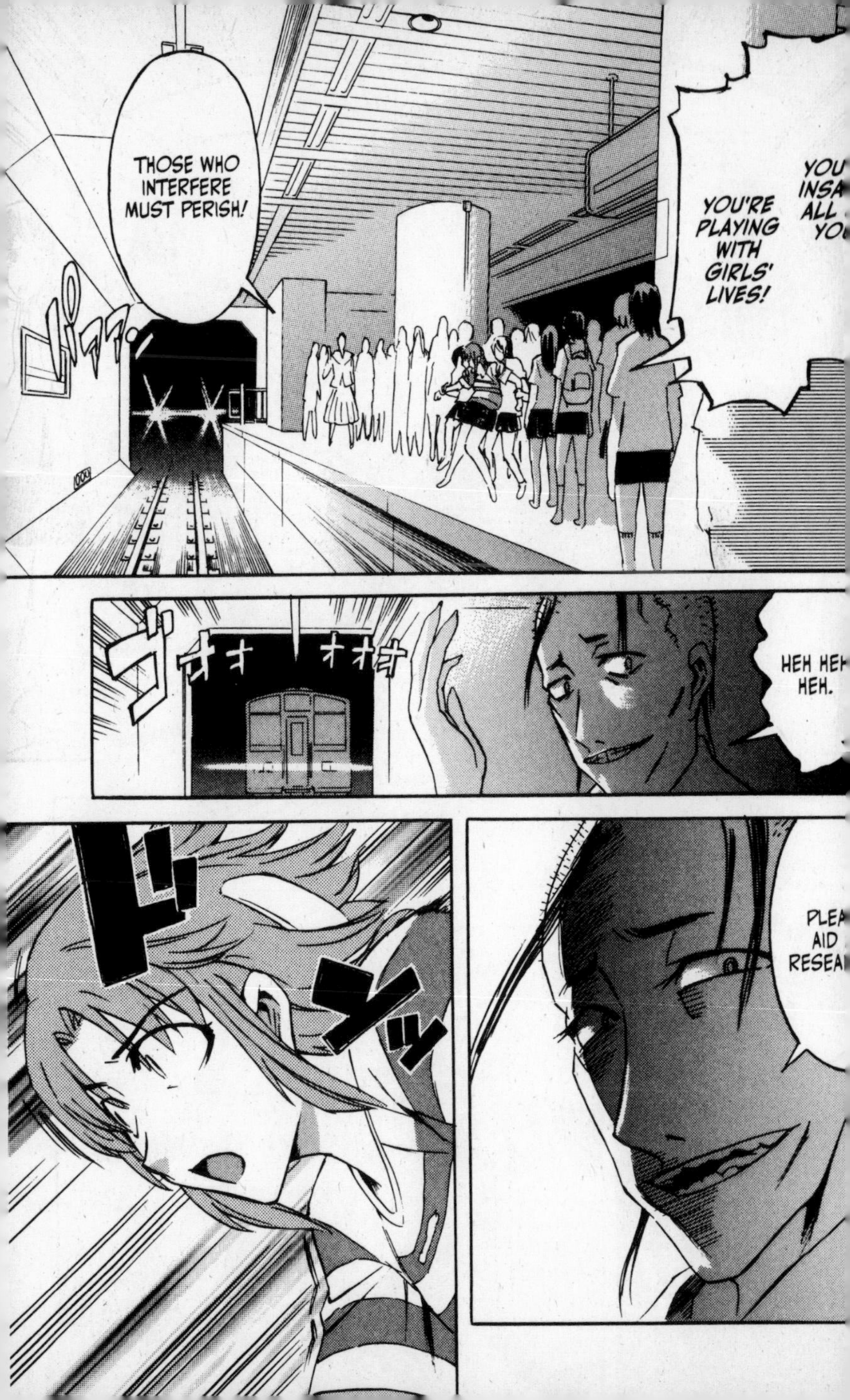
YOU INSA ALL YO
YOU'RE PLAYING WITH GIRLS' LIVES!
THOSE WHO INTERFERE MUST PERISH!
HEH HEH HEH.
ゴォォ オォォ
PLEA AID RESEA

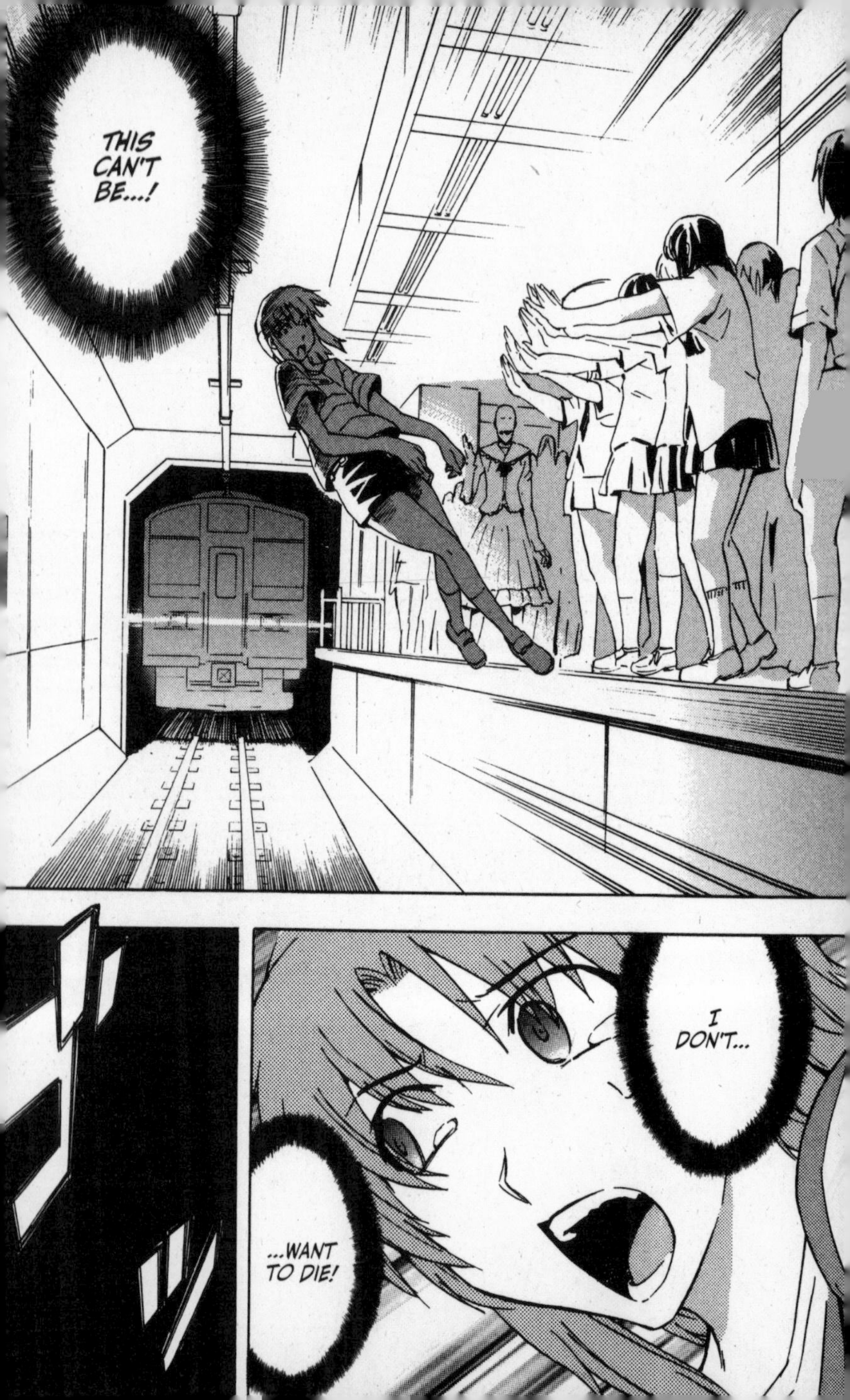
THIS CAN'T BE...!
I DON'T...
...WANT TO DIE!

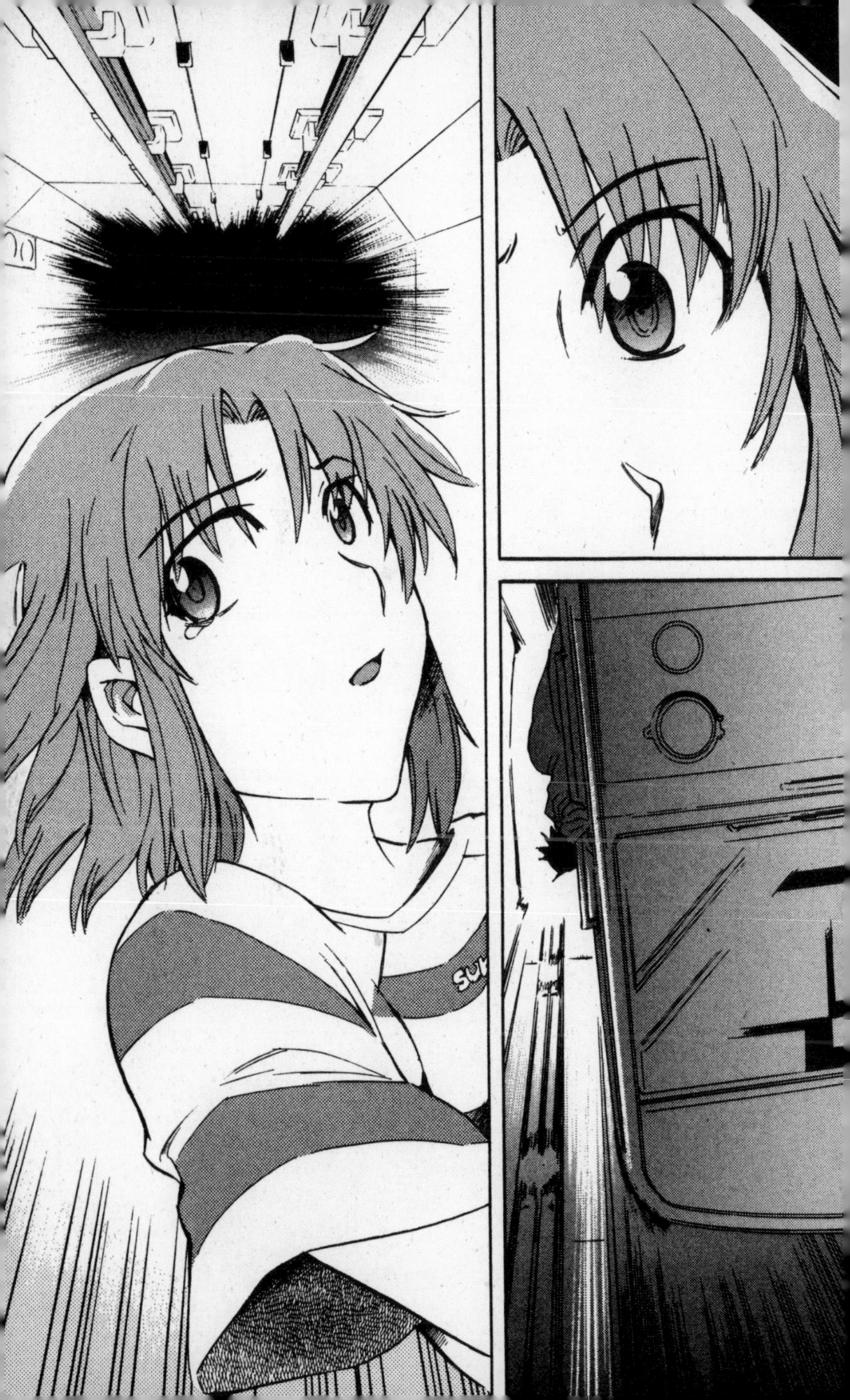

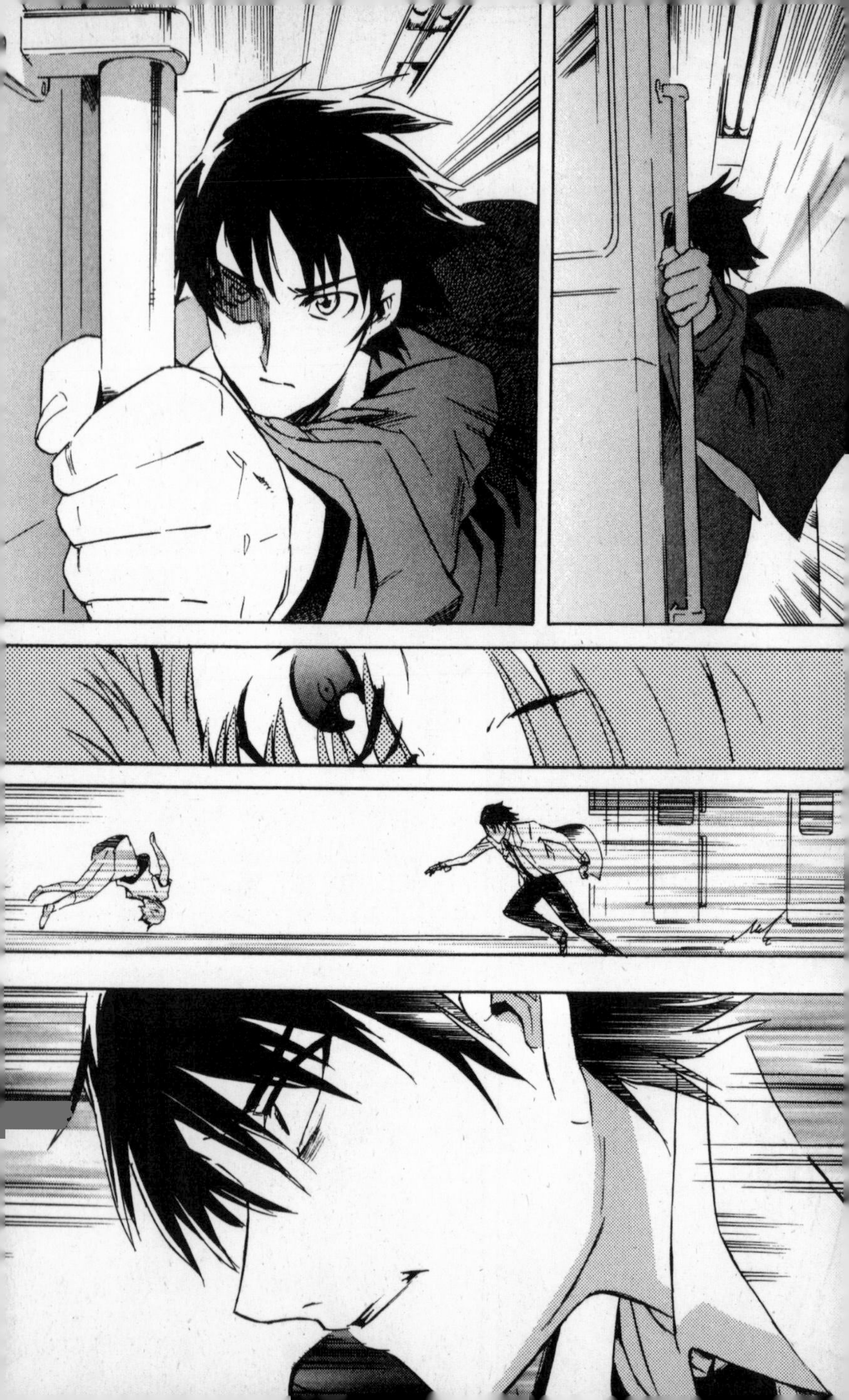

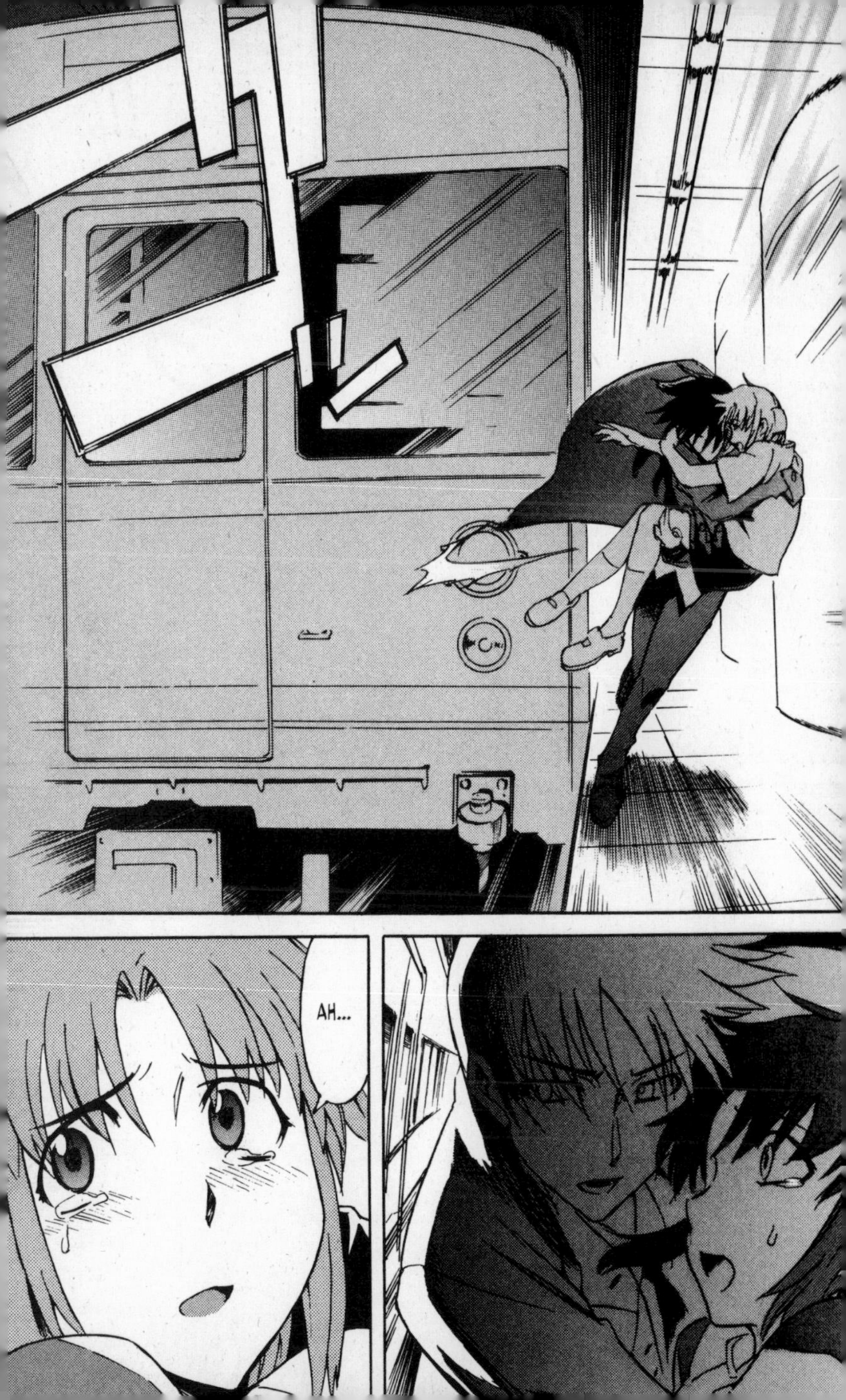
AH...

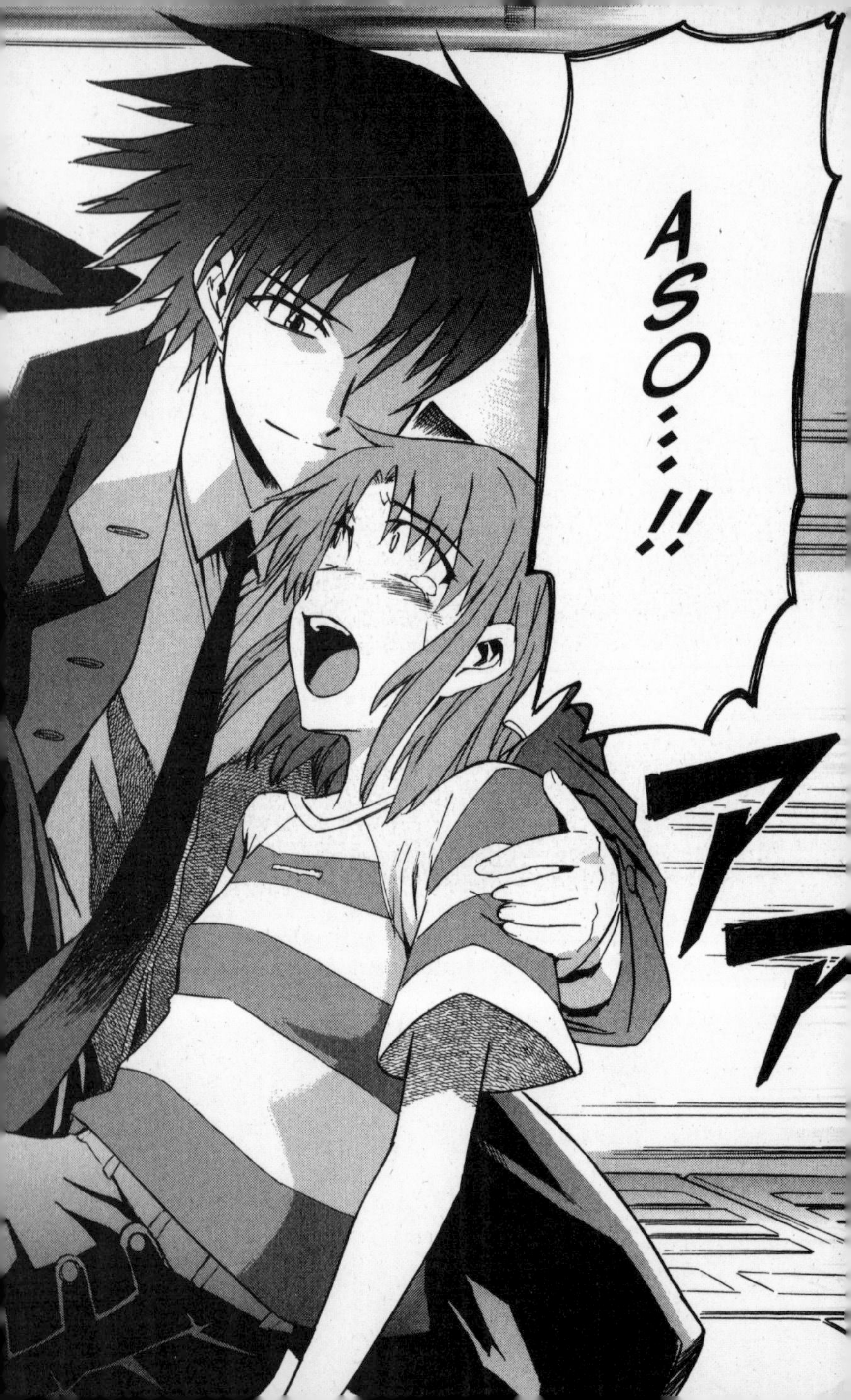
ASO...!!
ア

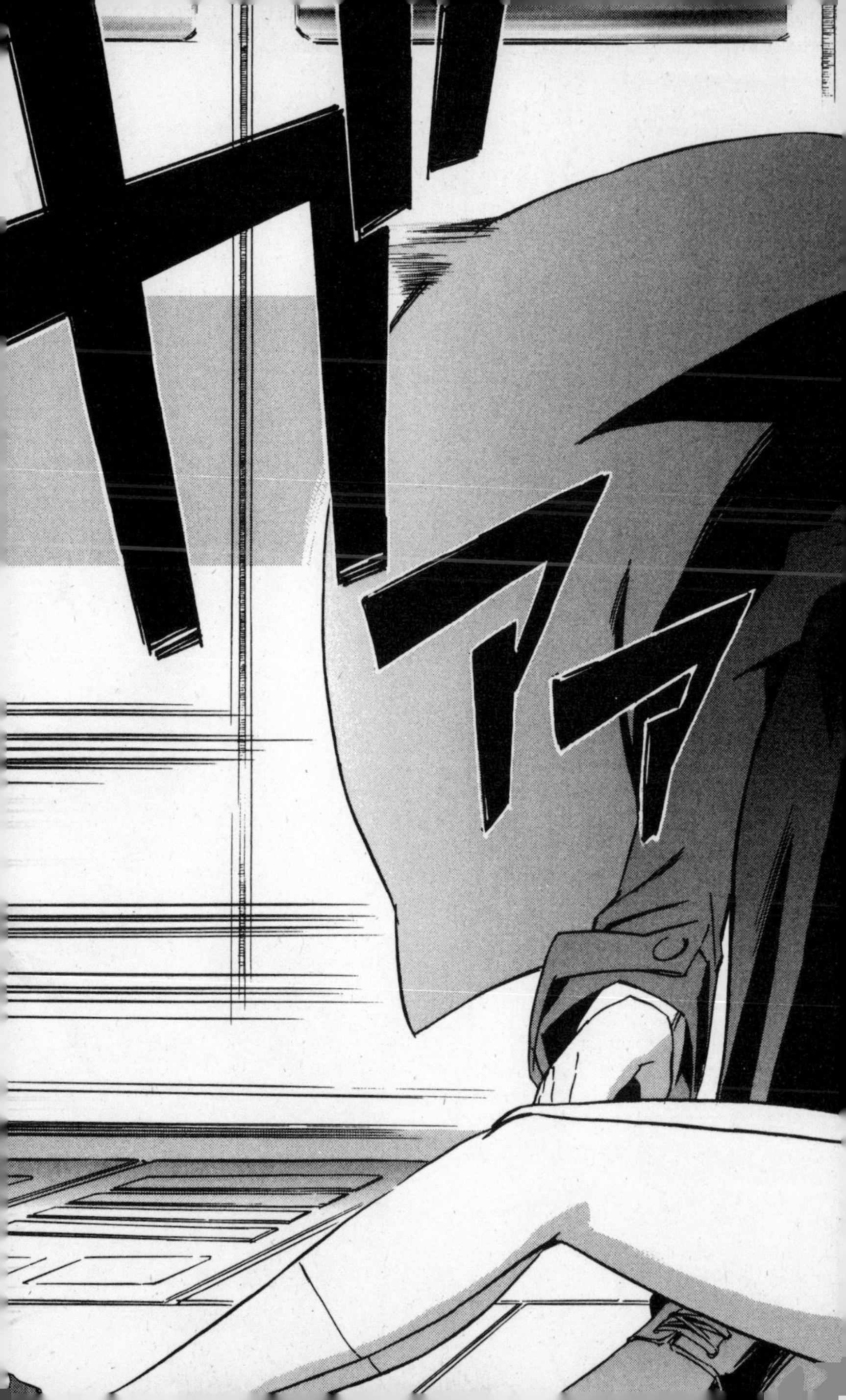
ガアア

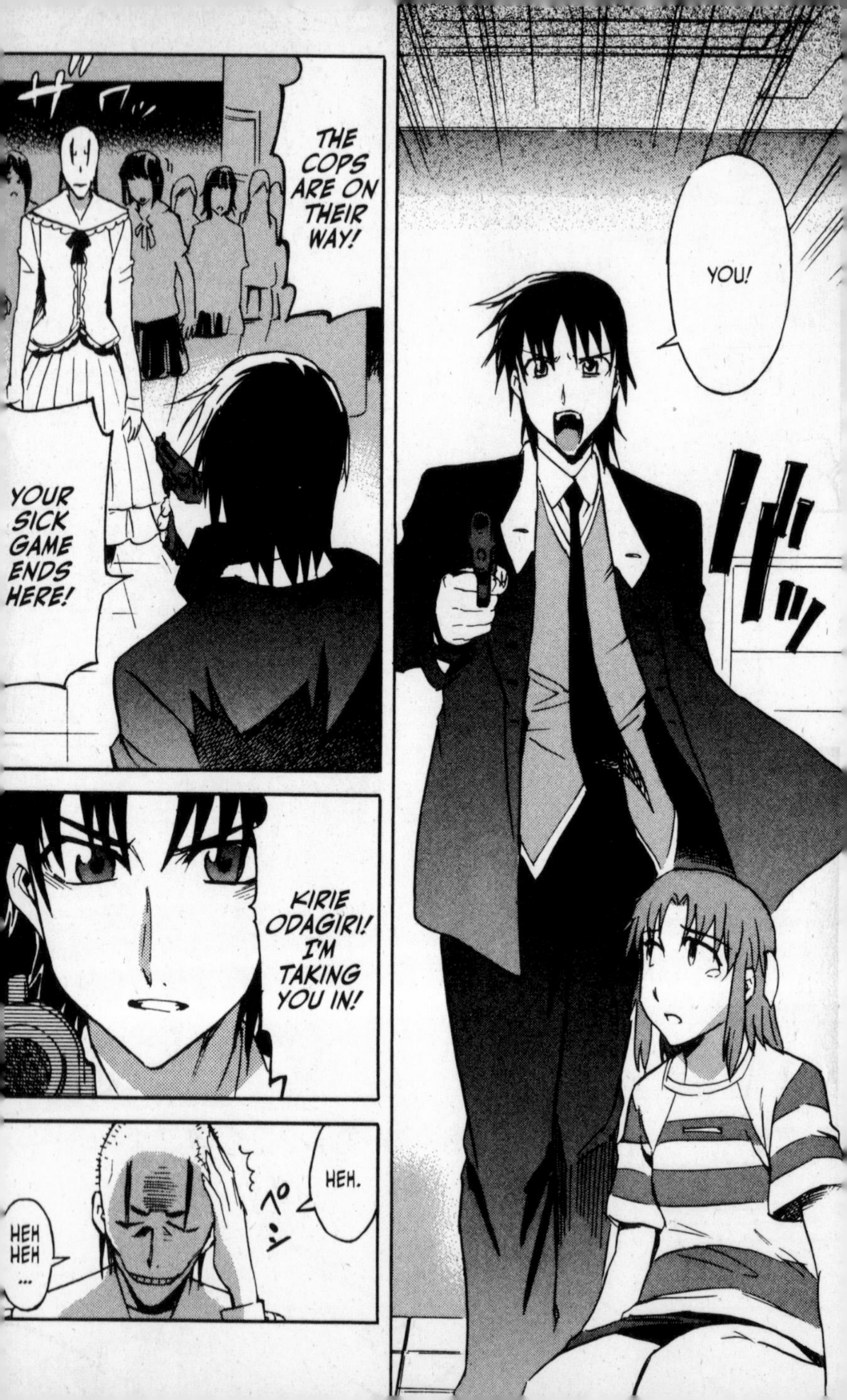
YOU!
THE COPS ARE ON THEIR WAY!
YOUR SICK GAME ENDS HERE!
KIRIE ODAGIRI! I'M TAKING YOU IN!
HEH.
HEH HEH ...

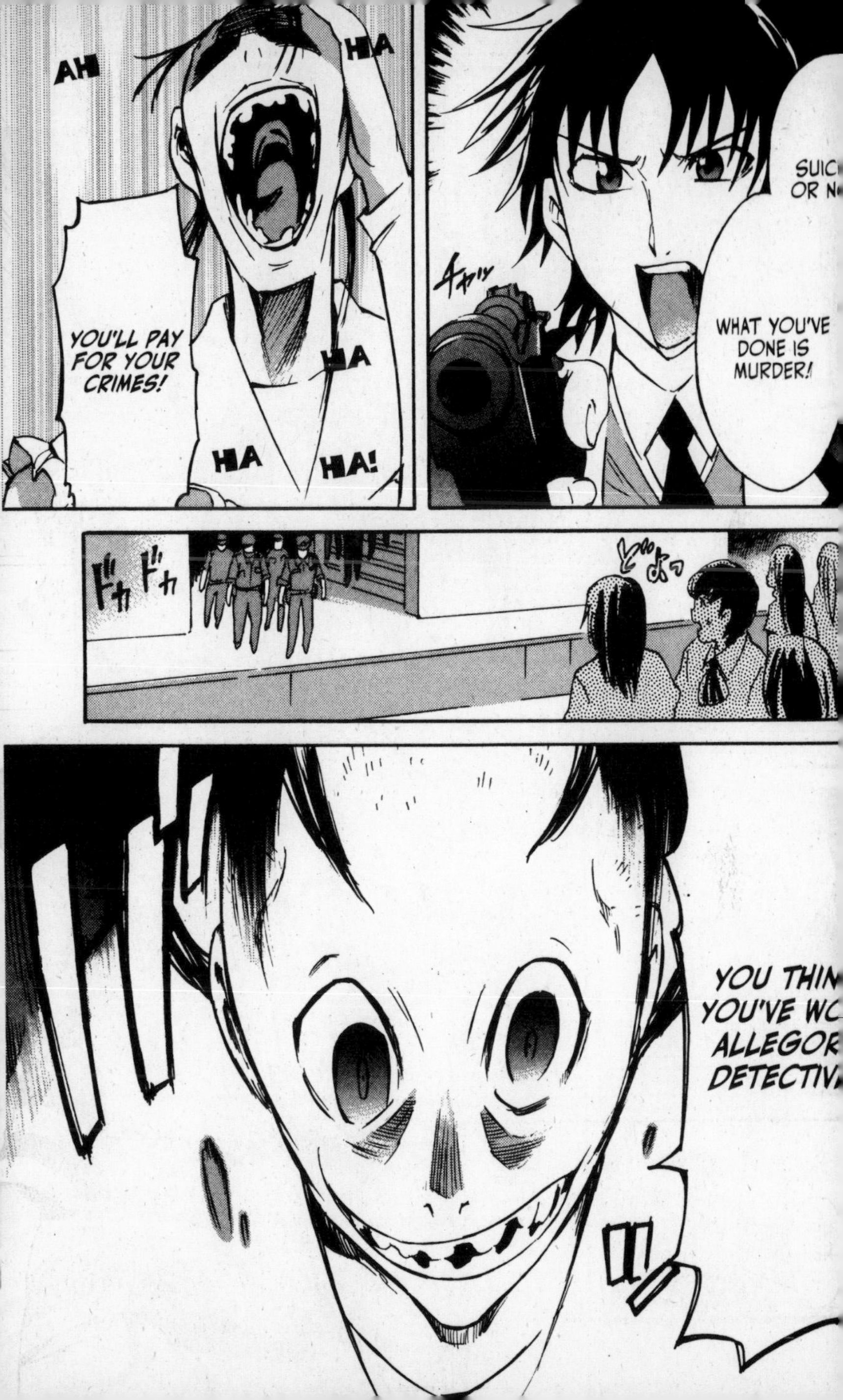

SUIC
OR N
WHAT YOU'VE DONE IS MURDER!
HA
AH
HA
HA
HA!
YOU'LL PAY FOR YOUR CRIMES!
ドカ ドカ
YOU THIN
YOU'VE WO
ALLEGOR
DETECTIV

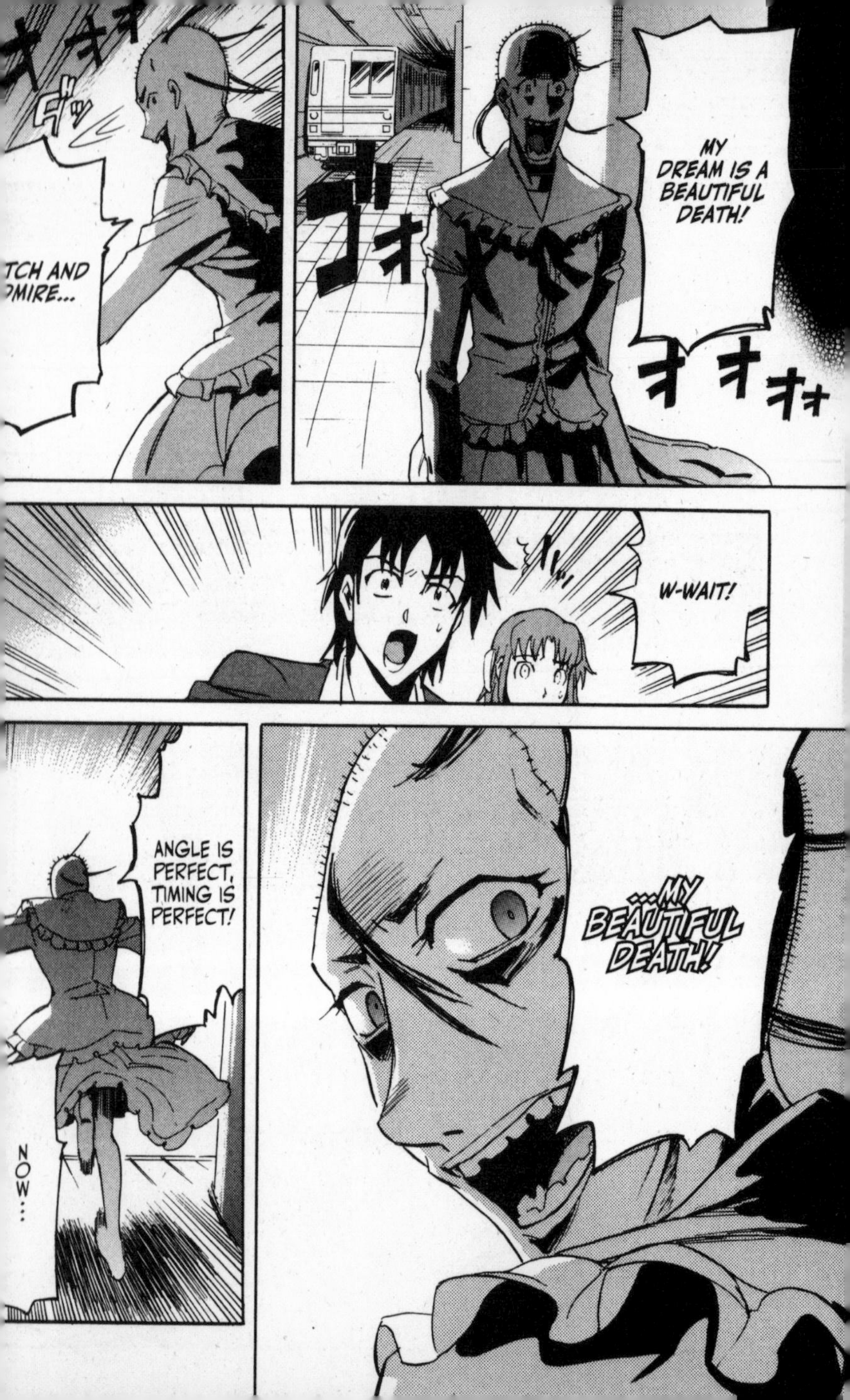
MY DREAM IS A BEAUTIFUL DEATH!
TCH AND
MIRE...
W-WAIT!
...MY BEAUTIFUL DEATH!
ANGLE IS PERFECT, TIMING IS PERFECT!
NOW...

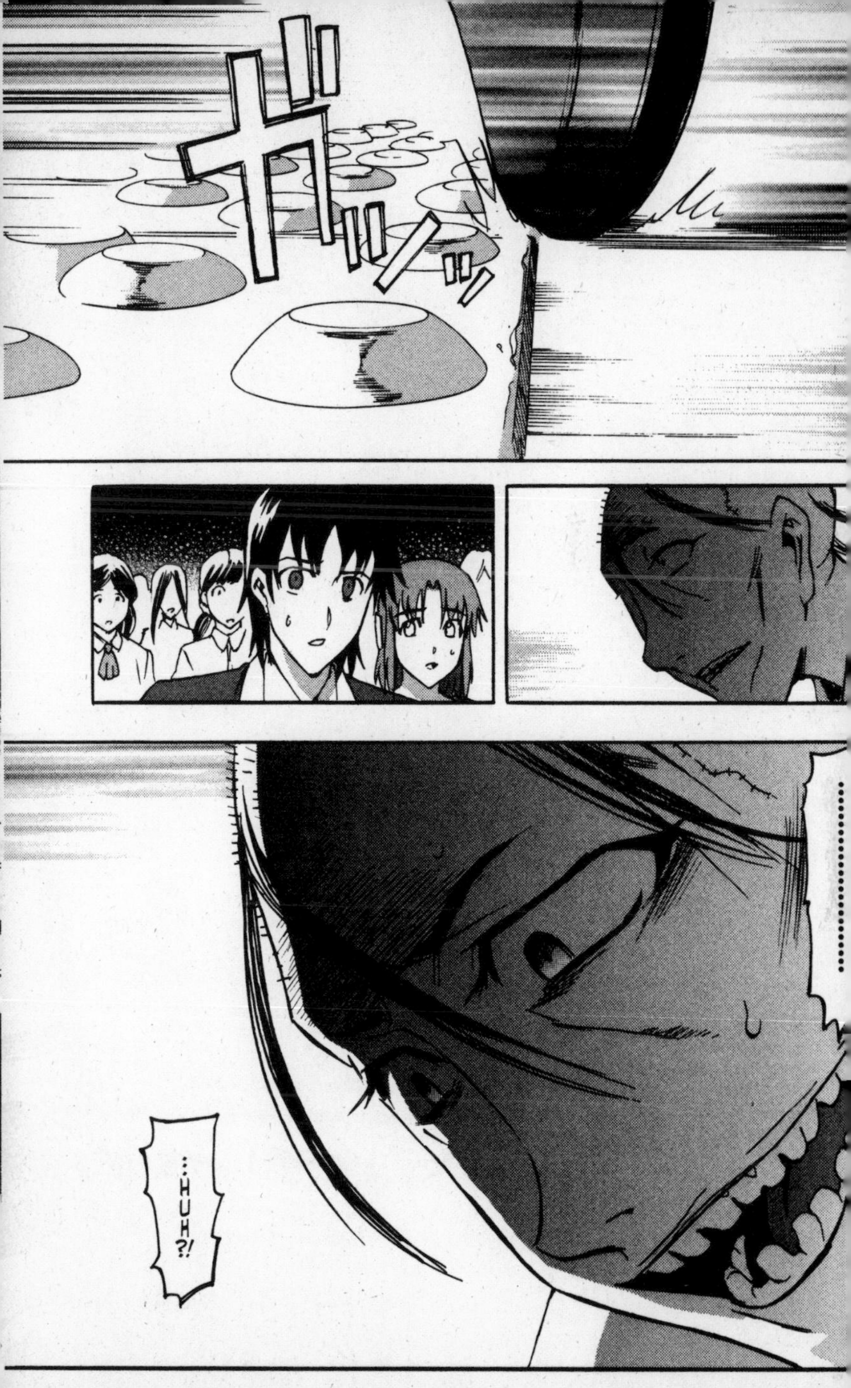
...HUH?!

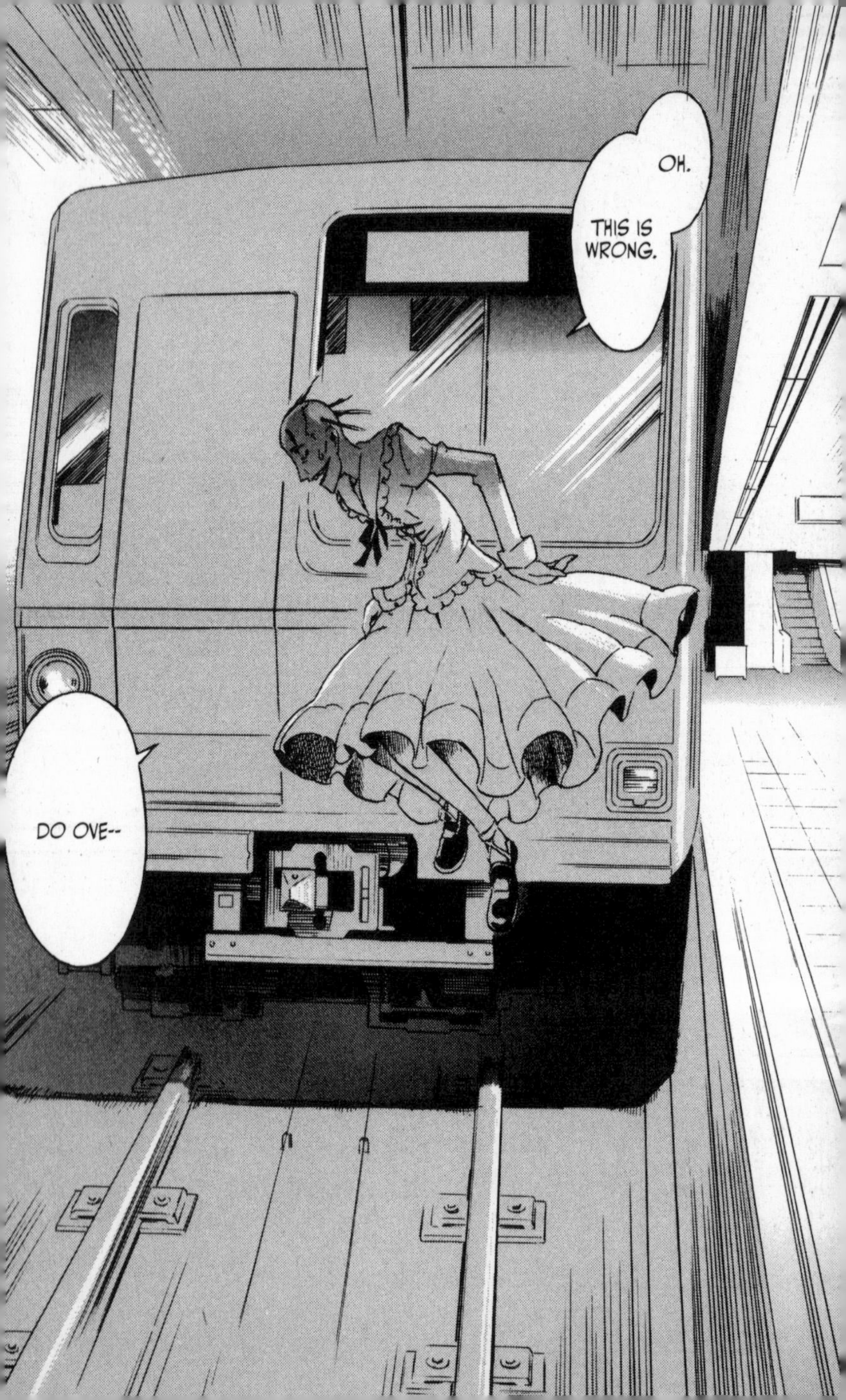
OH.
THIS IS WRONG.
DO OVE--

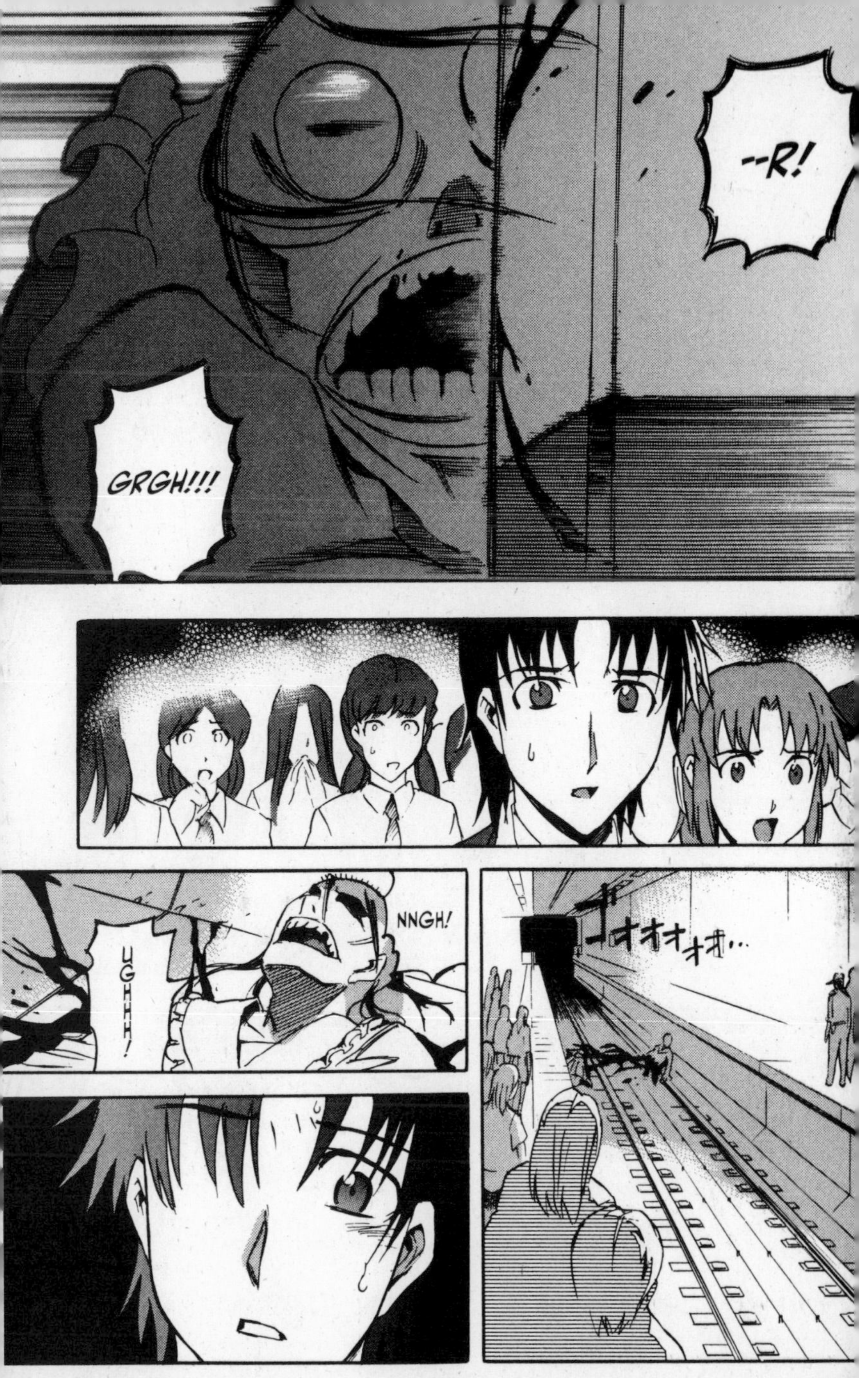
--R!
GRGH!!!
ゴオオオオオ…
NNGH!
UGHHH!

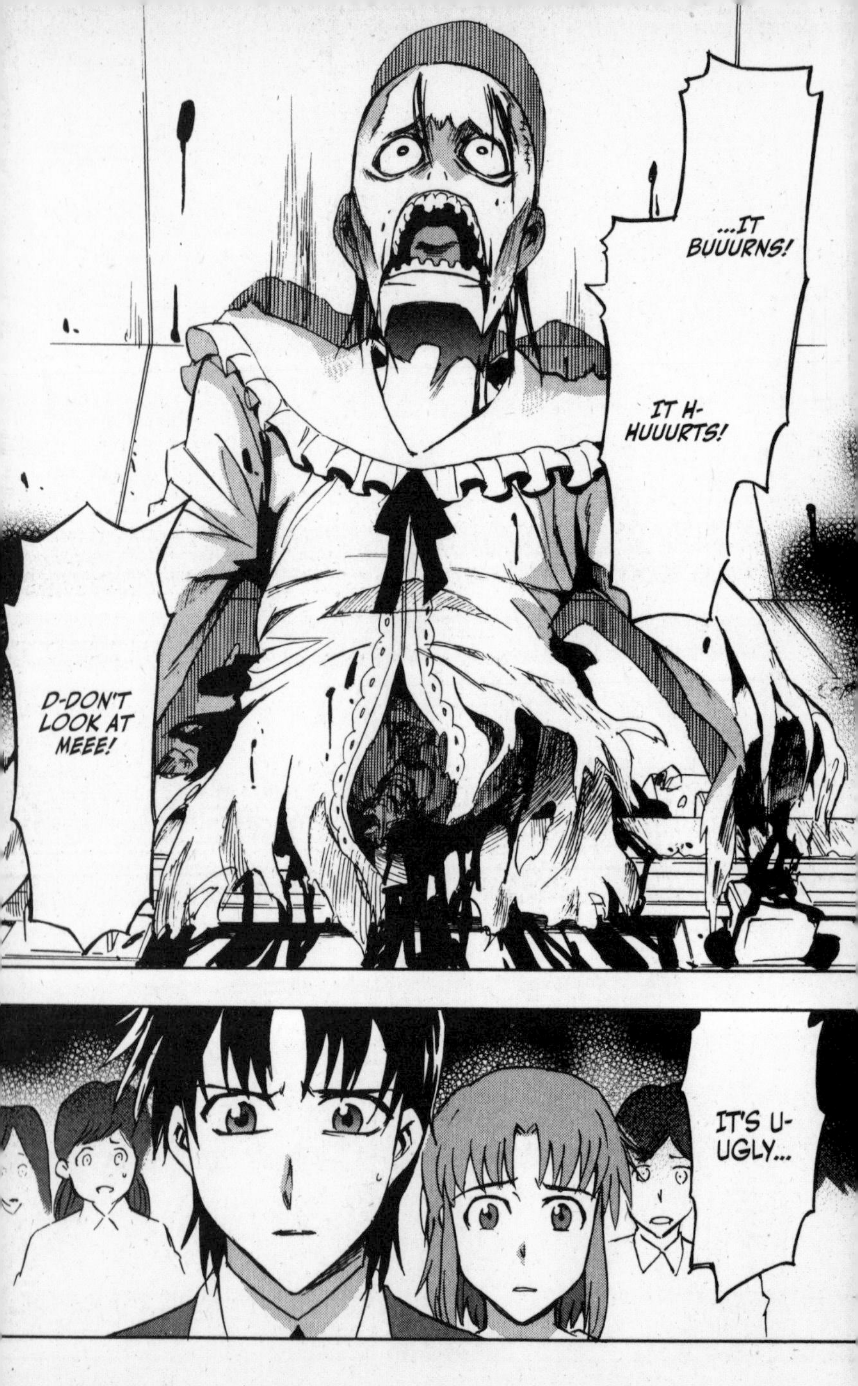
...IT BUUURNS!
IT H-HUUURTS!
D-DON'T LOOK AT MEEE!
IT'S U-UGLY...

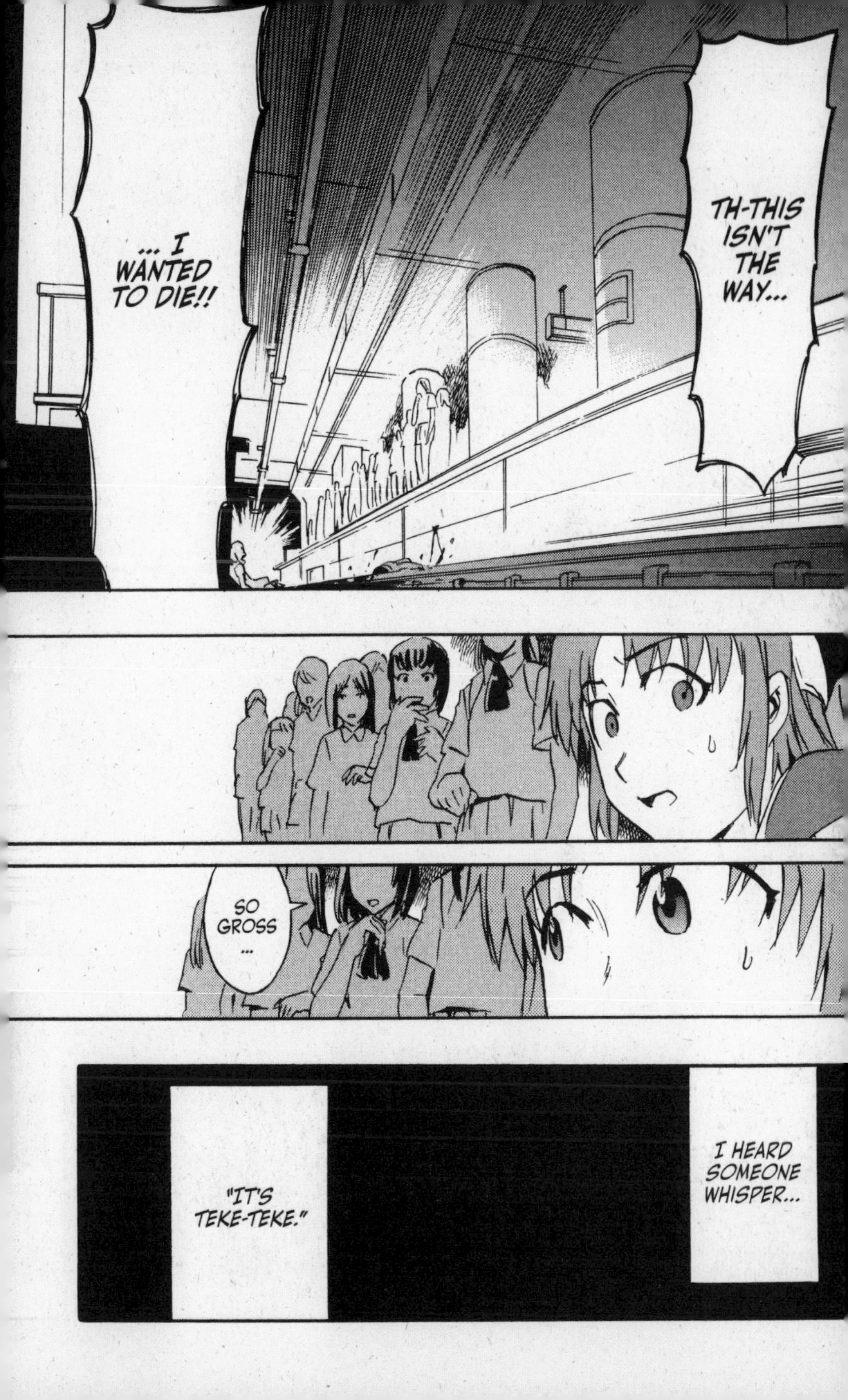
TH-THIS ISN'T THE WAY...
... I WANTED TO DIE!!
SO GROSS ...
I HEARD SOMEONE WHISPER...
"IT'S TEKE-TEKE."

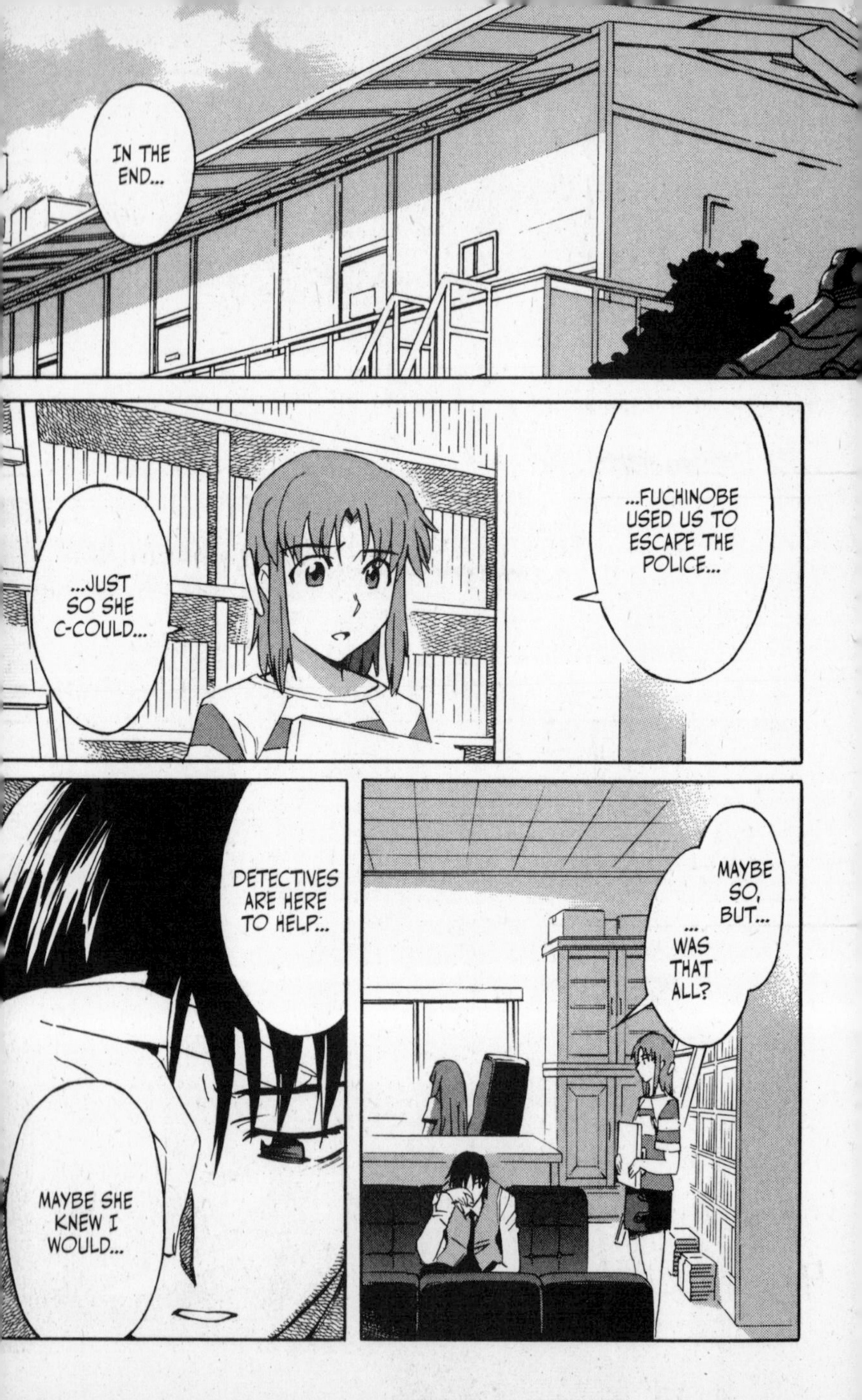
IN THE END...
...FUCHINOBE USED US TO ESCAPE THE POLICE...
...JUST SO SHE C-COULD...
MAYBE SO, BUT...
...WAS THAT ALL?
DETECTIVES ARE HERE TO HELP...
MAYBE SHE KNEW I WOULD...

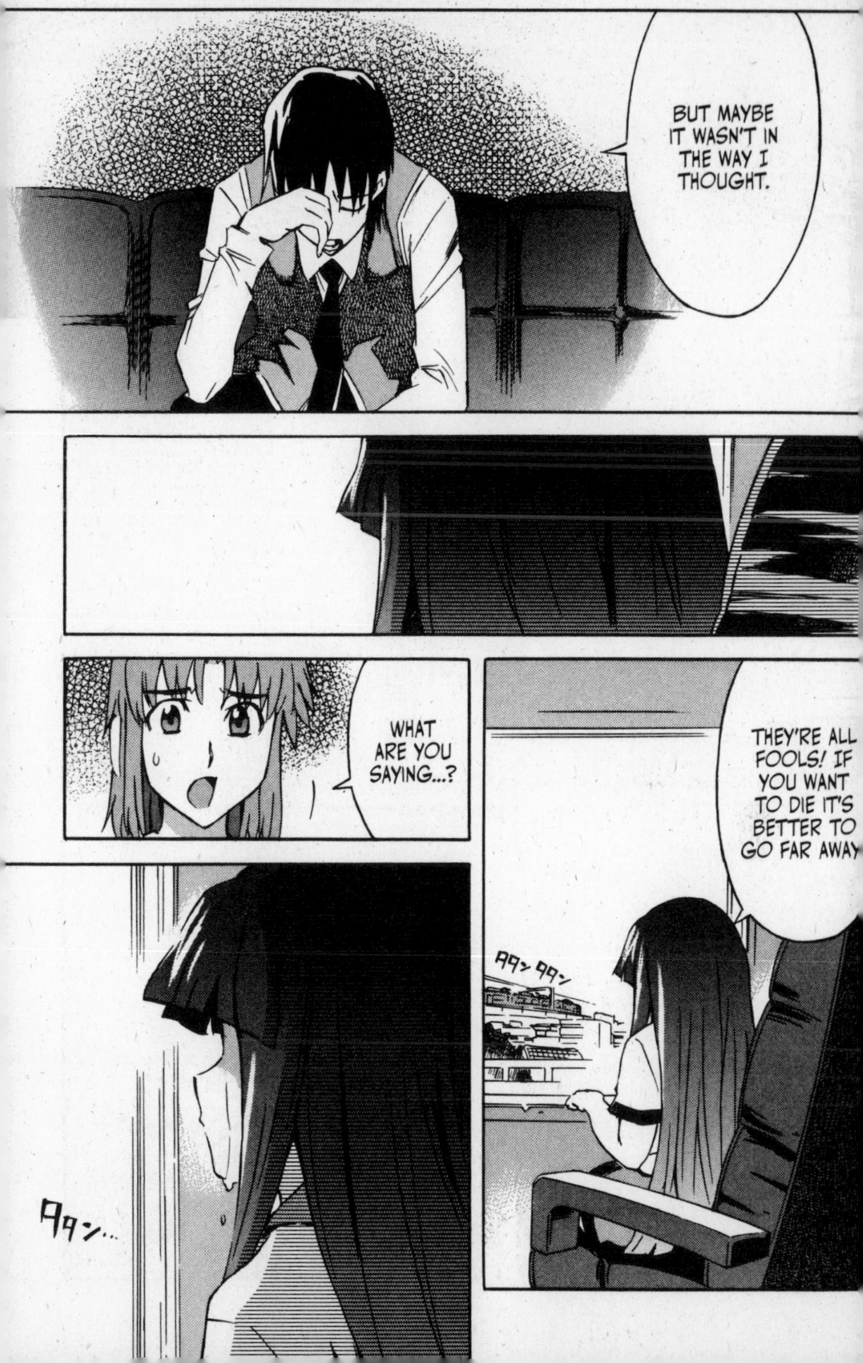
BUT MAYBE IT WASN'T IN THE WAY I THOUGHT.
THEY'RE ALL FOOLS! IF YOU WANT TO DIE IT'S BETTER TO GO FAR AWAY
タタン タタン
WHAT ARE YOU SAYING...?
タタン…

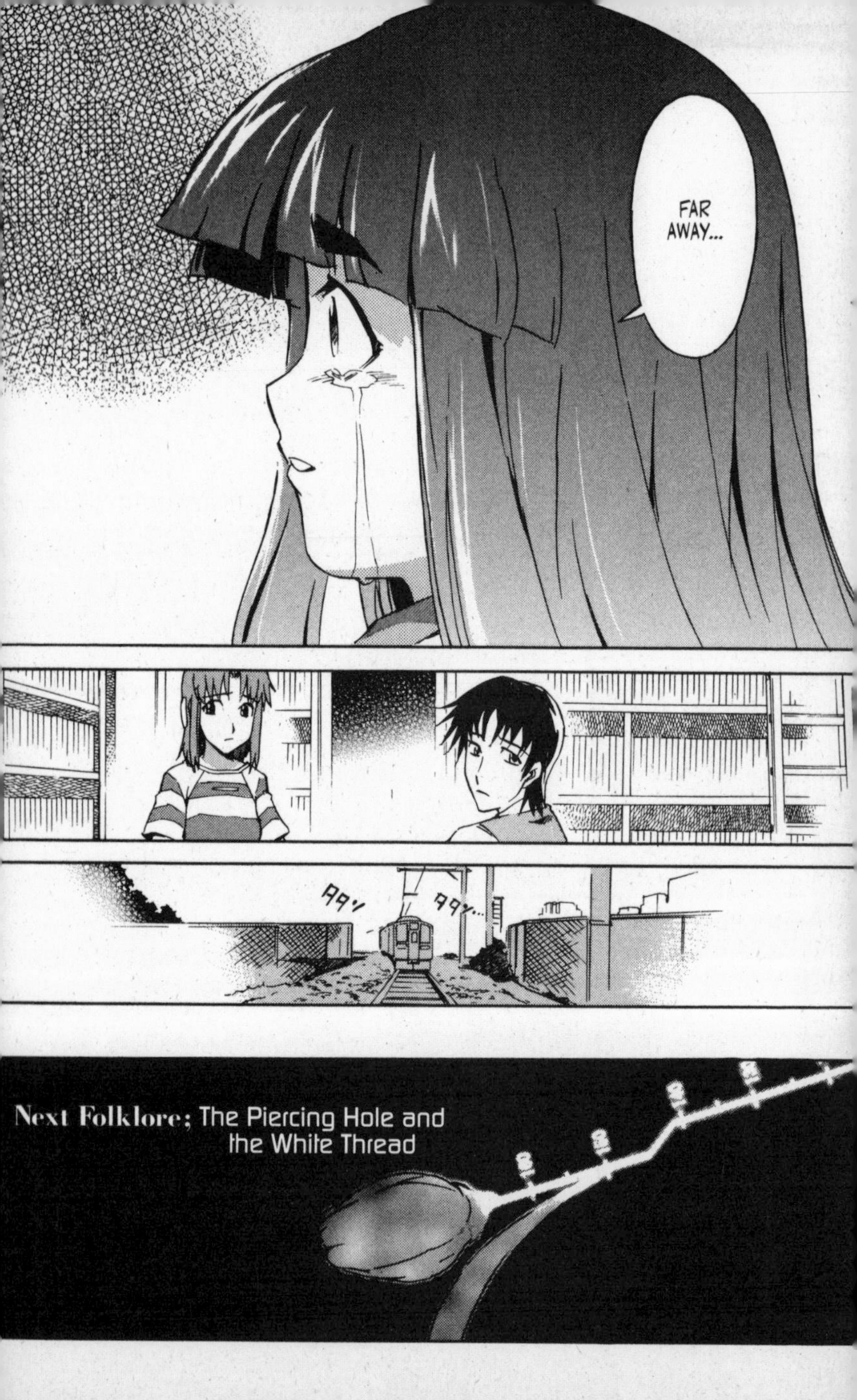
FAR AWAY...
Next Folklore; The Piercing Hole and the White Thread

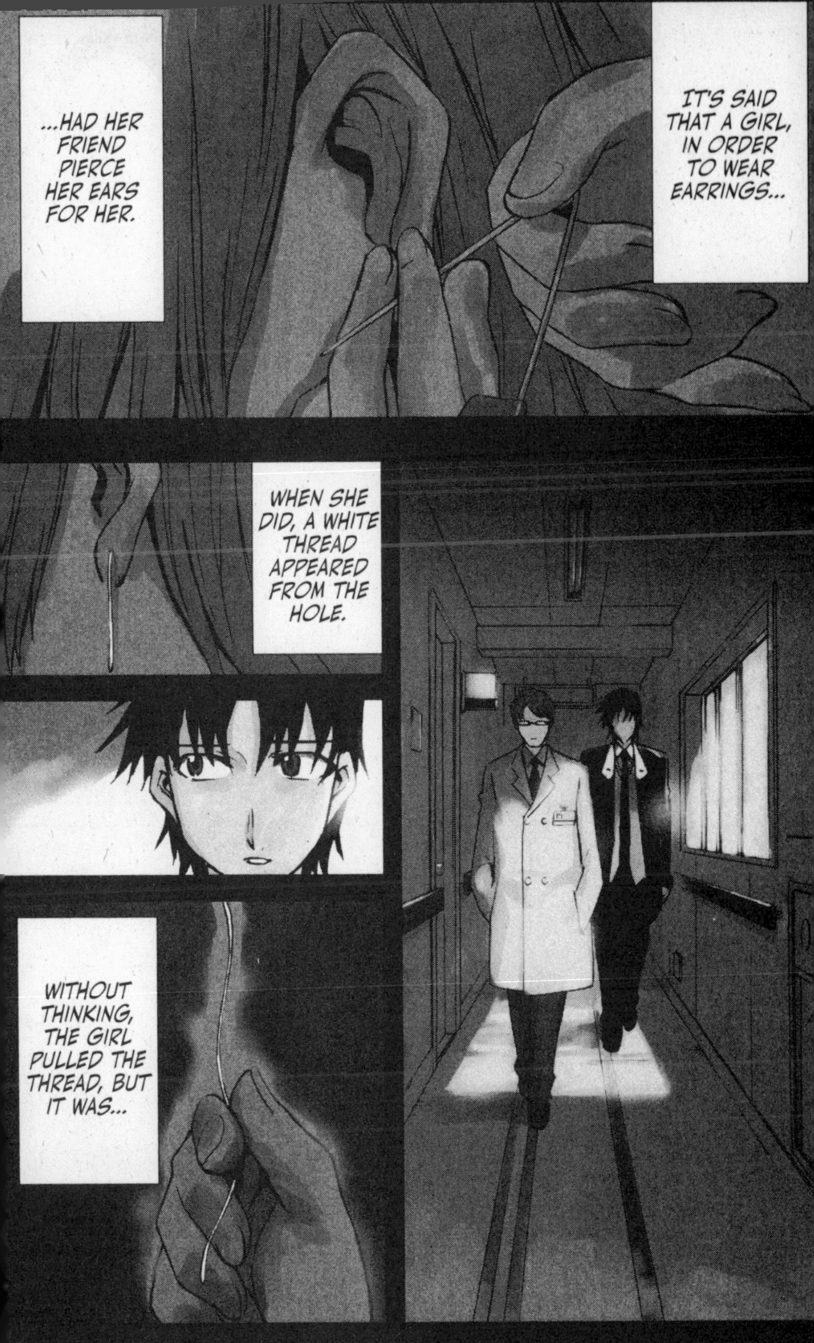
IT'S SAID THAT A GIRL, IN ORDER TO WEAR EARRINGS...
...HAD HER FRIEND PIERCE HER EARS FOR HER.
WHEN SHE DID, A WHITE THREAD APPEARED FROM THE HOLE.
WITHOUT THINKING, THE GIRL PULLED THE THREAD, BUT IT WAS...

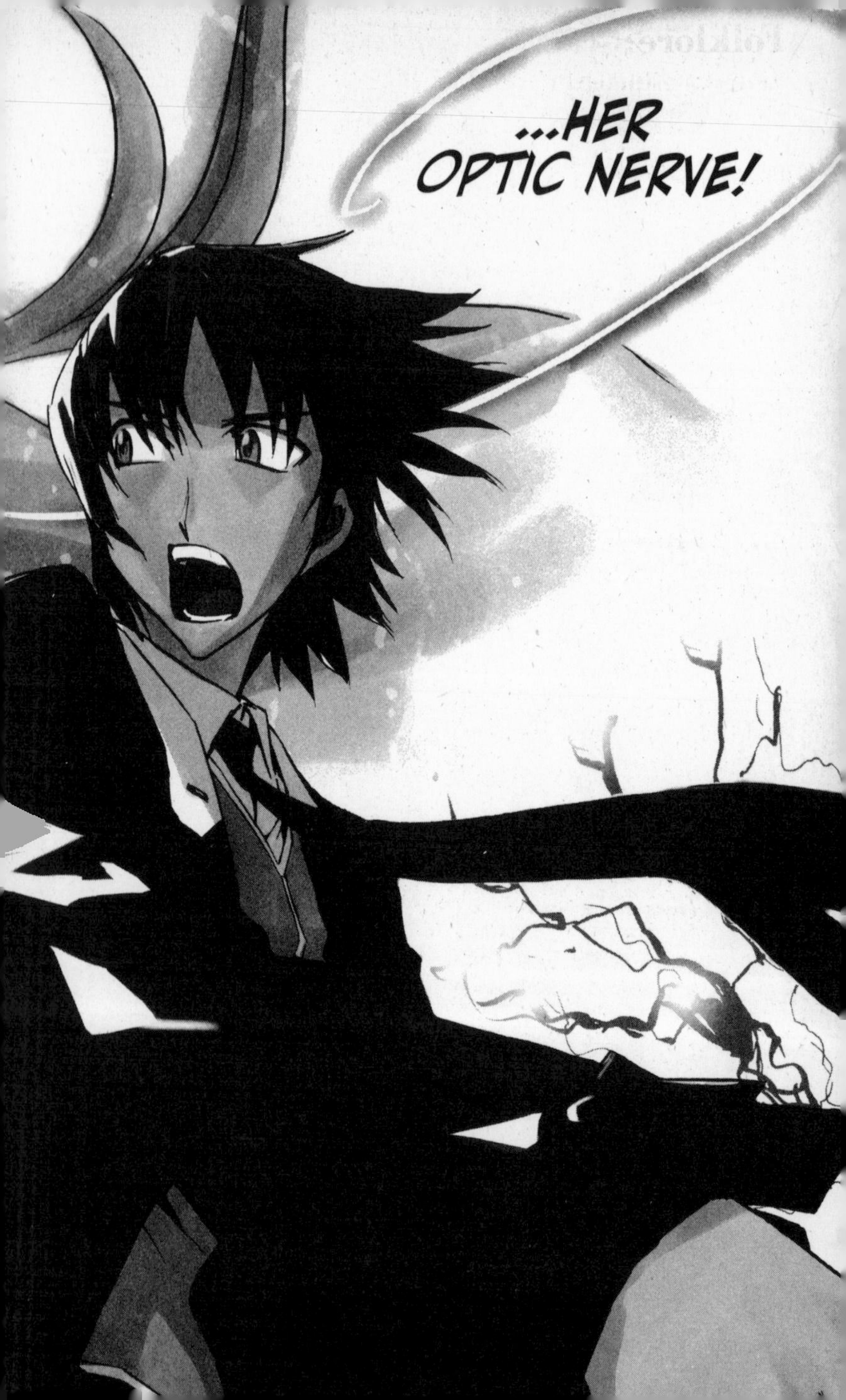
...HER
OPTIC NERVE!

Folklore;
The Piercing Hole and the White Thread

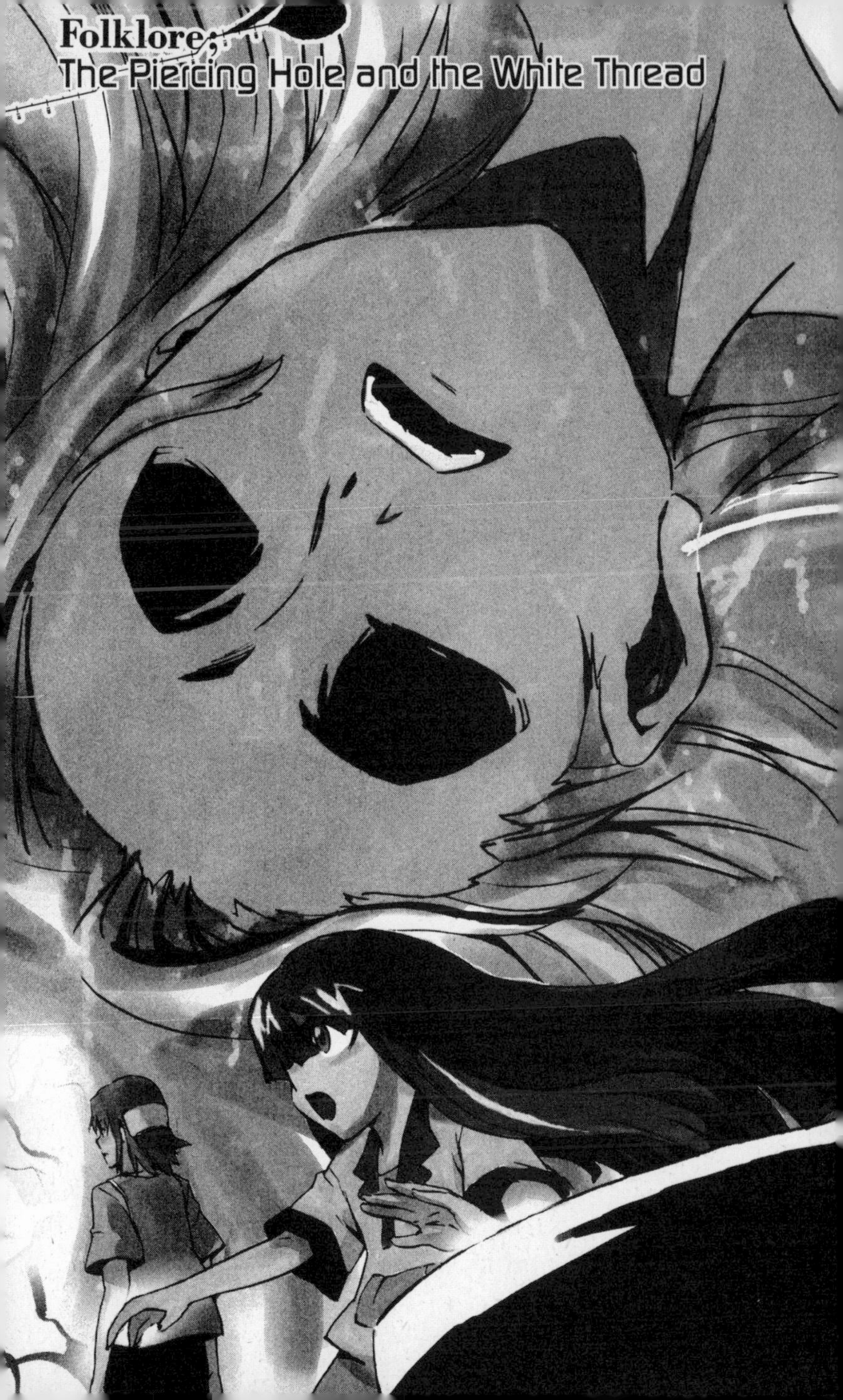

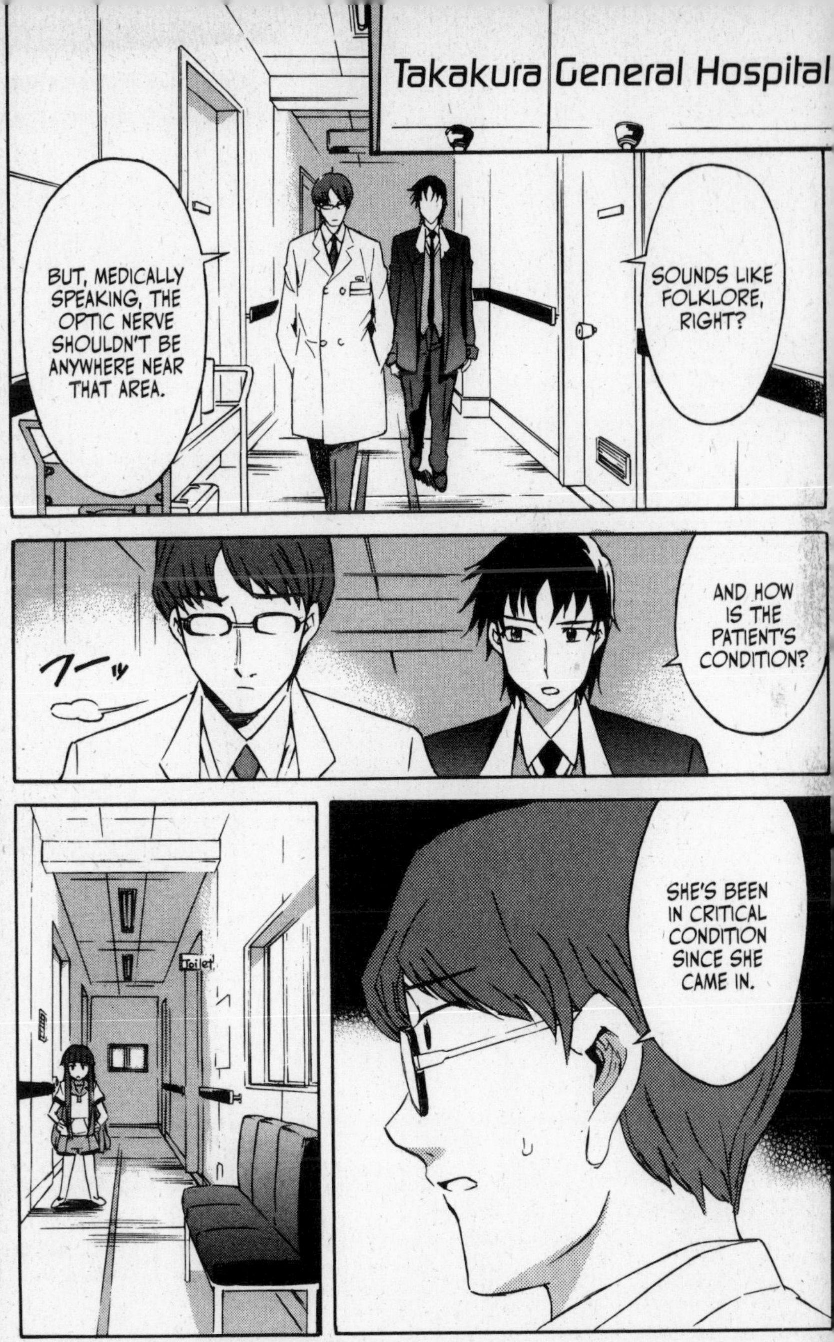
Takakura General Hospital
SOUNDS LIKE FOLKLORE, RIGHT?
BUT, MEDICALLY SPEAKING, THE OPTIC NERVE SHOULDN'T BE ANYWHERE NEAR THAT AREA.
AND HOW IS THE PATIENT'S CONDITION?
フーッ
SHE'S BEEN IN CRITICAL CONDITION SINCE SHE CAME IN.
Toilet

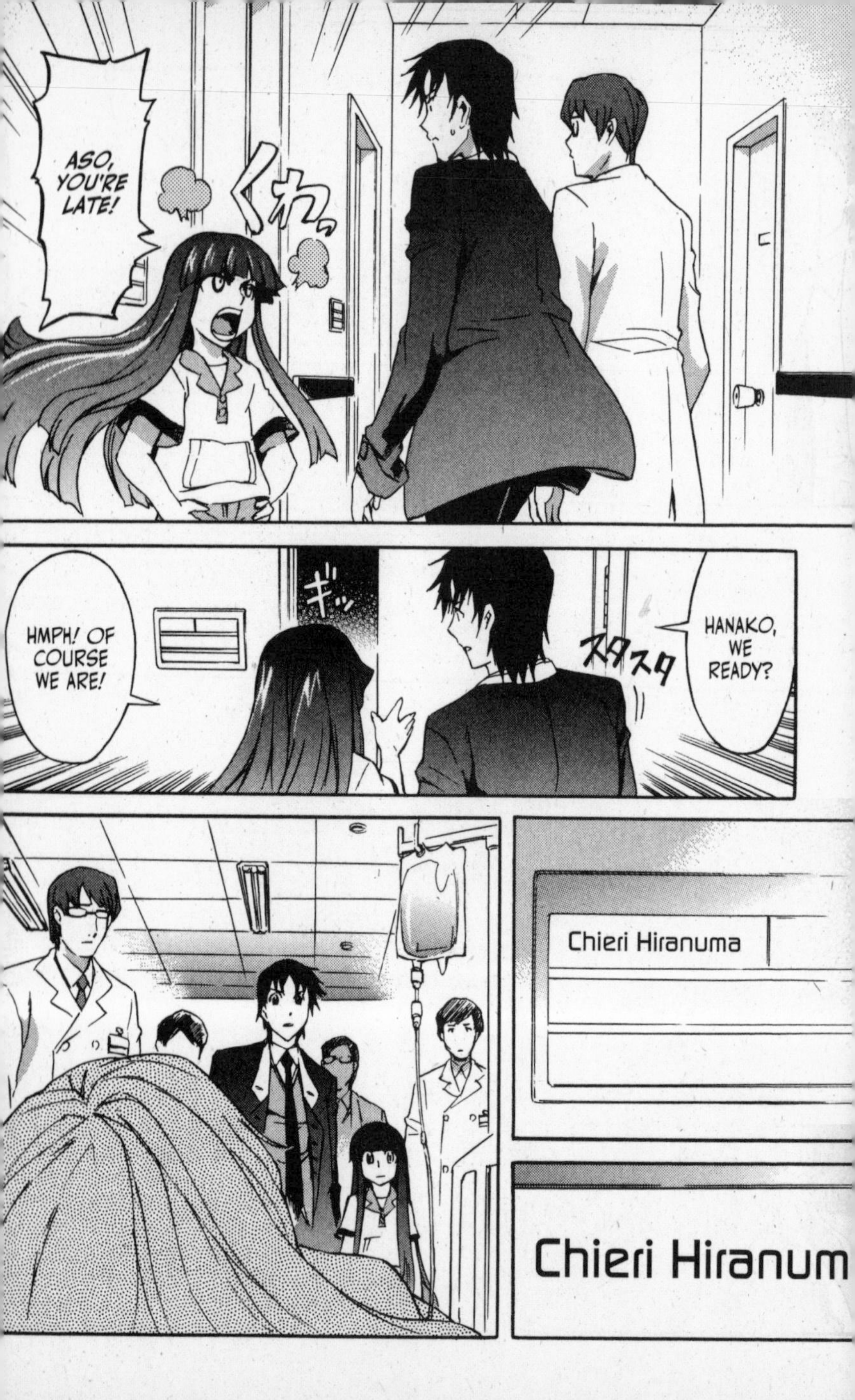
ASO, YOU'RE LATE!
くわっ
HANAKO, WE READY?
スタスタ
ギッ
HMPH! OF COURSE WE ARE!
Chieri Hiranuma
Chieri Hiranum

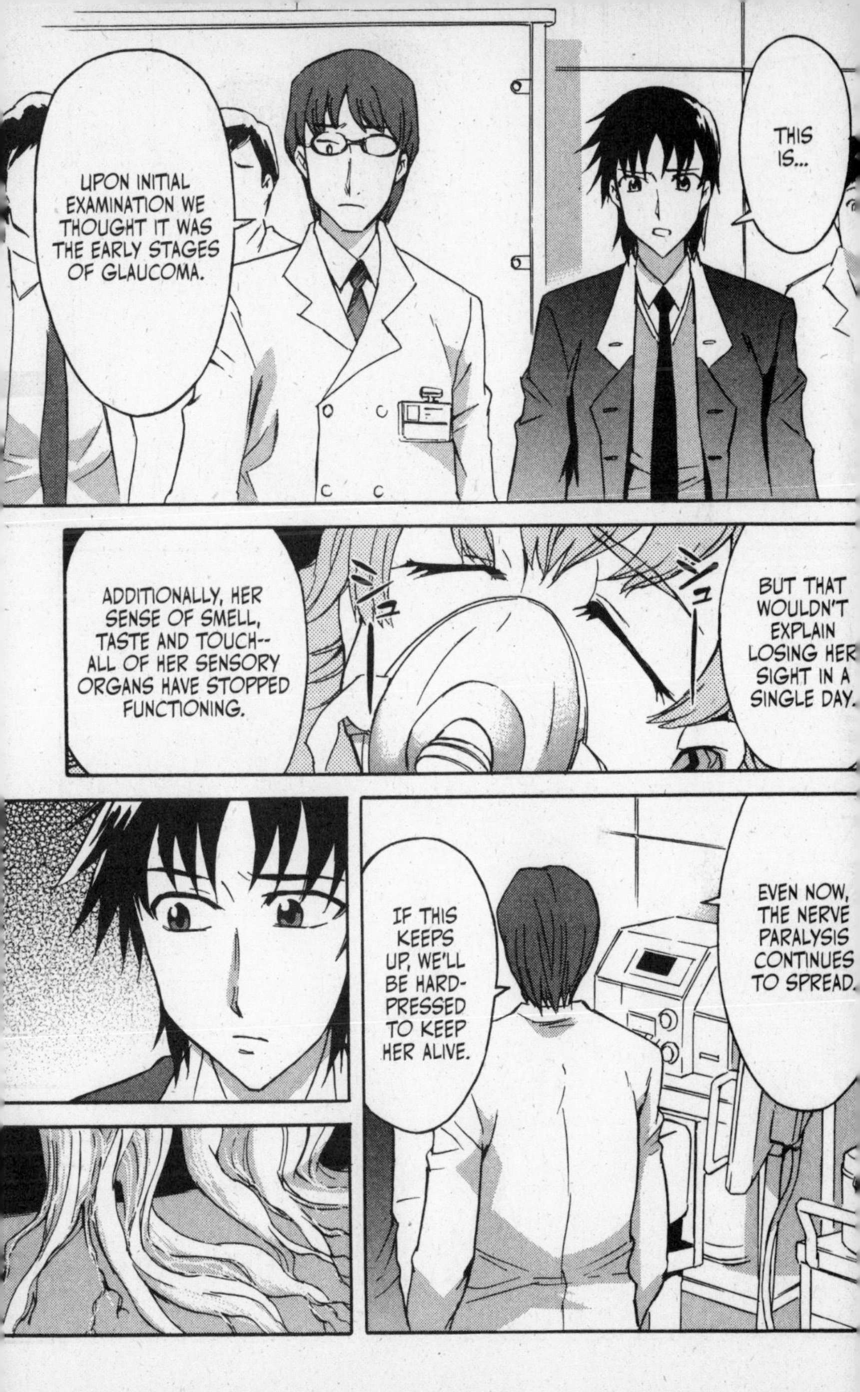
THIS IS...
UPON INITIAL EXAMINATION WE THOUGHT IT WAS THE EARLY STAGES OF GLAUCOMA.
BUT THAT WOULDN'T EXPLAIN LOSING HER SIGHT IN A SINGLE DAY.
ADDITIONALLY, HER SENSE OF SMELL, TASTE AND TOUCH-- ALL OF HER SENSORY ORGANS HAVE STOPPED FUNCTIONING.
EVEN NOW, THE NERVE PARALYSIS CONTINUES TO SPREAD.
IF THIS KEEPS UP, WE'LL BE HARD-PRESSED TO KEEP HER ALIVE.

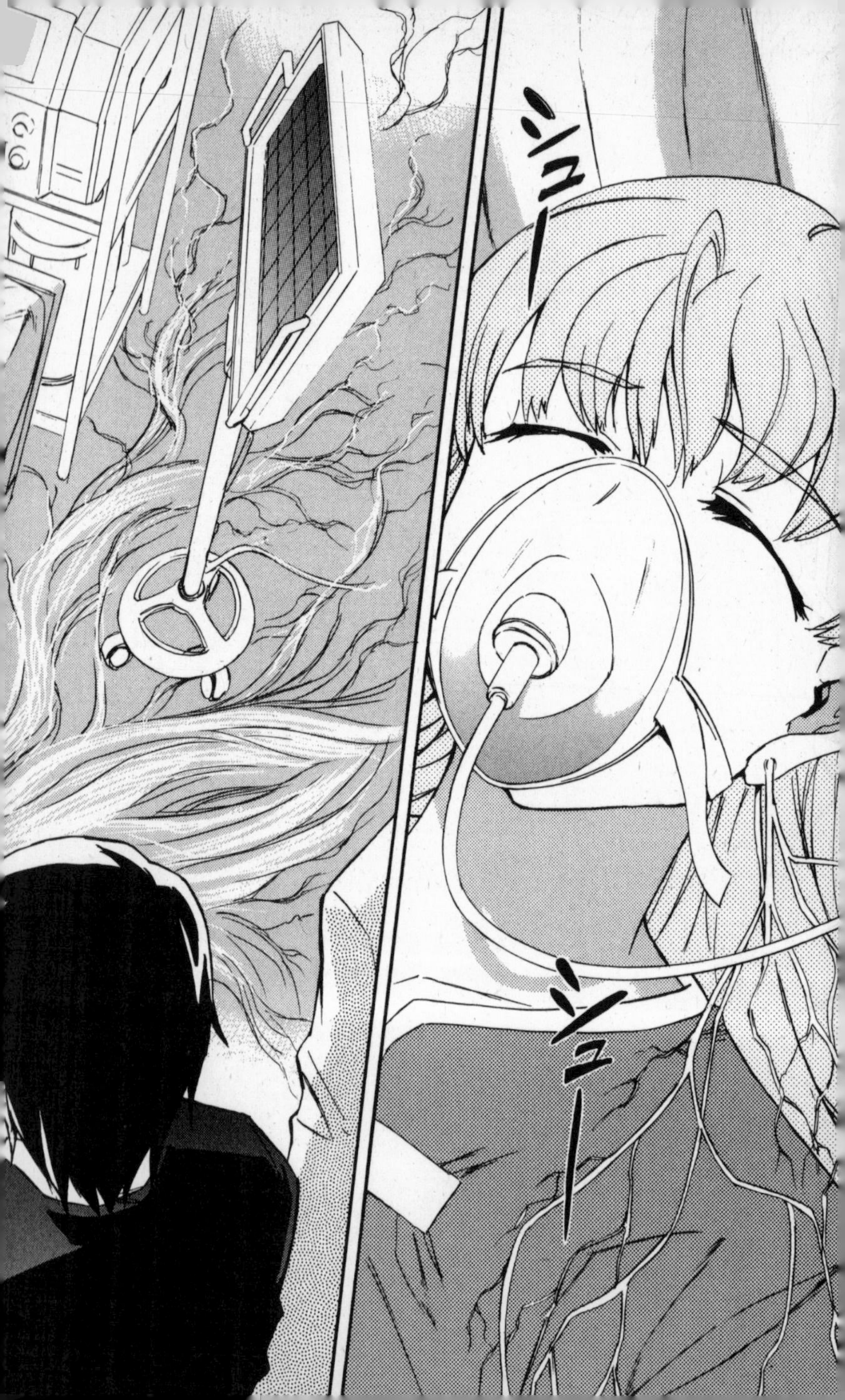
シュー
シュー

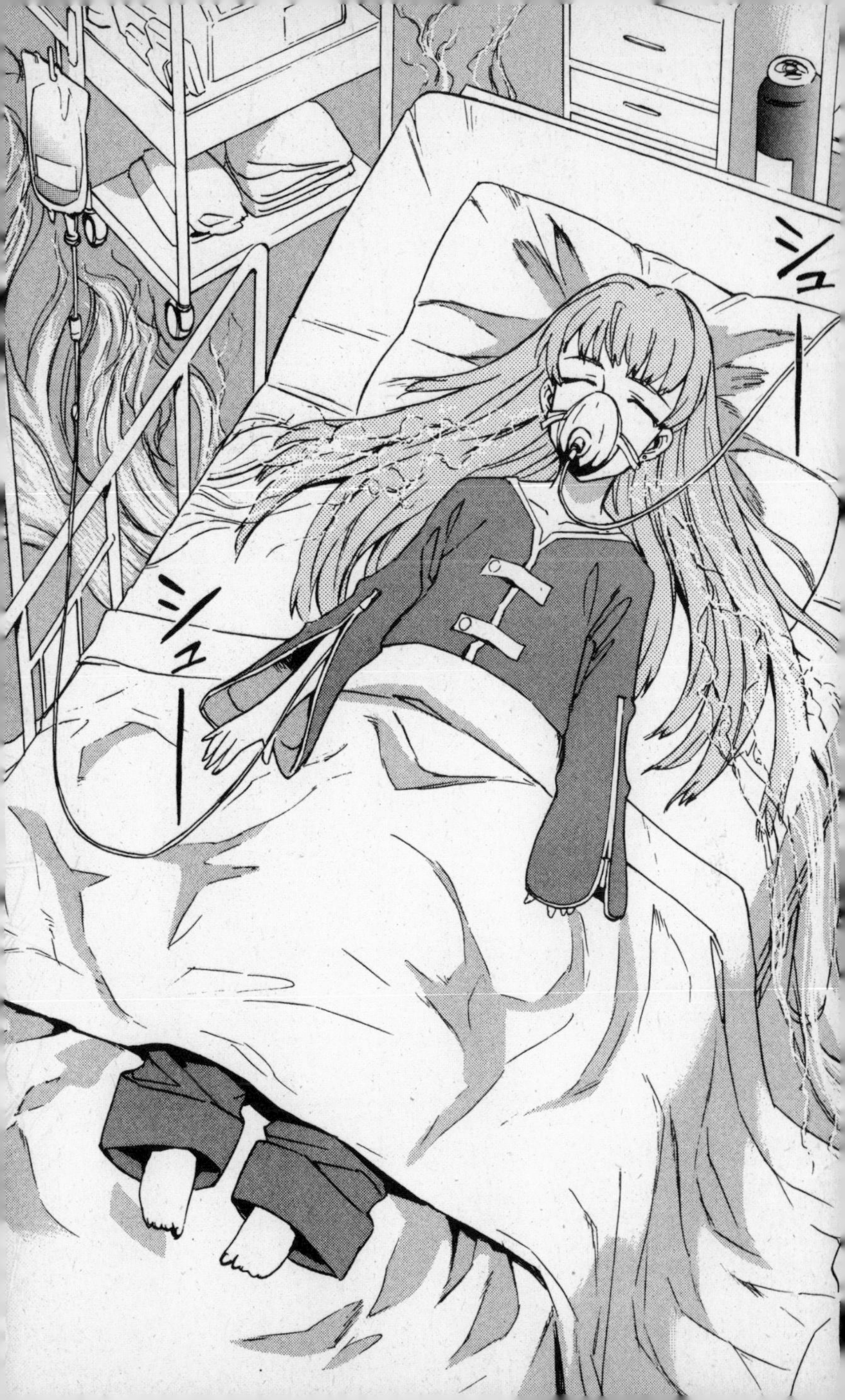
シュー
シュー

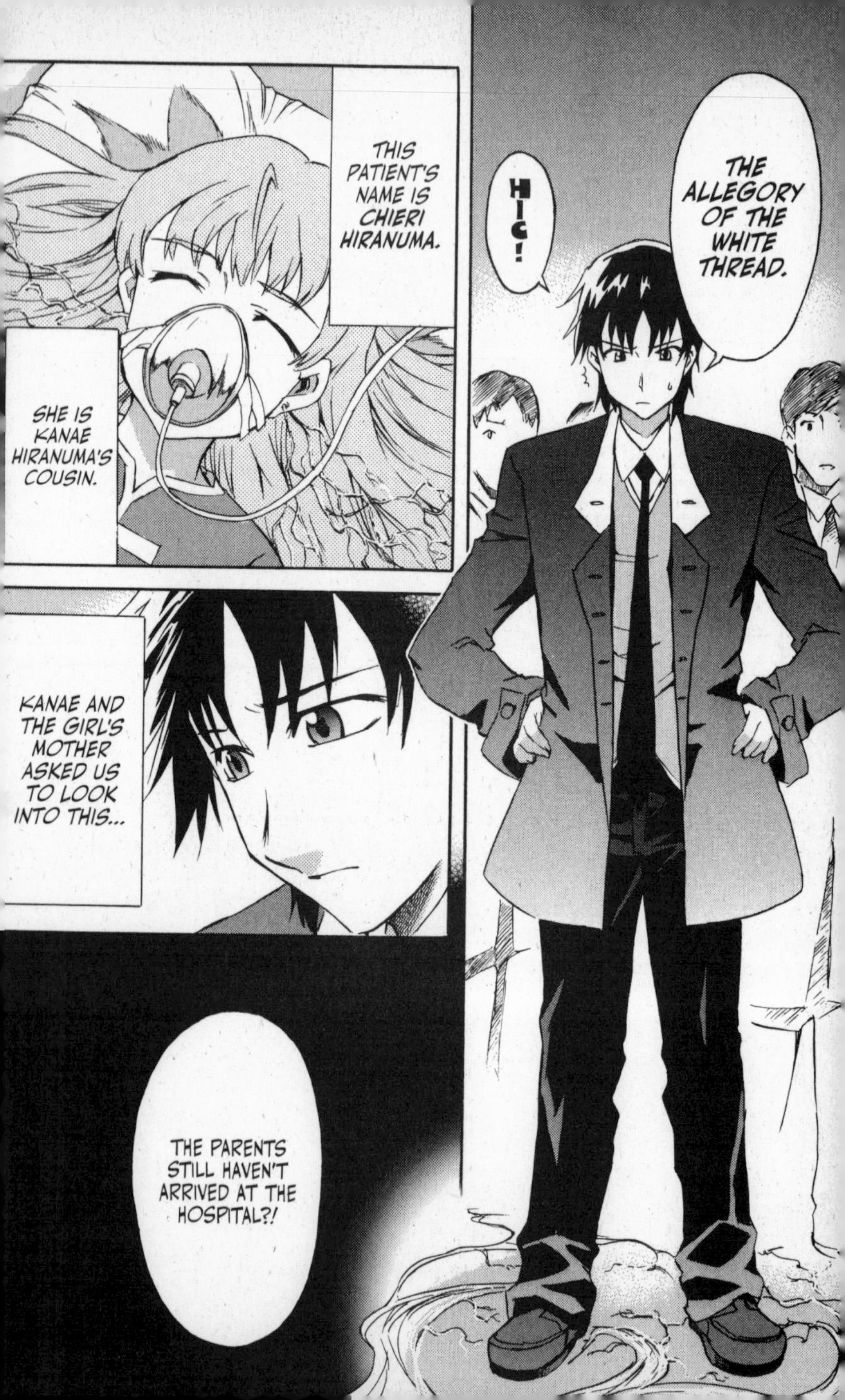
THE ALLEGORY OF THE WHITE THREAD.
HIC!
THIS PATIENT'S NAME IS CHIERI HIRANUMA.
SHE IS KANAE HIRANUMA'S COUSIN.
KANAE AND THE GIRL'S MOTHER ASKED US TO LOOK INTO THIS...
THE PARENTS STILL HAVEN'T ARRIVED AT THE HOSPITAL?!

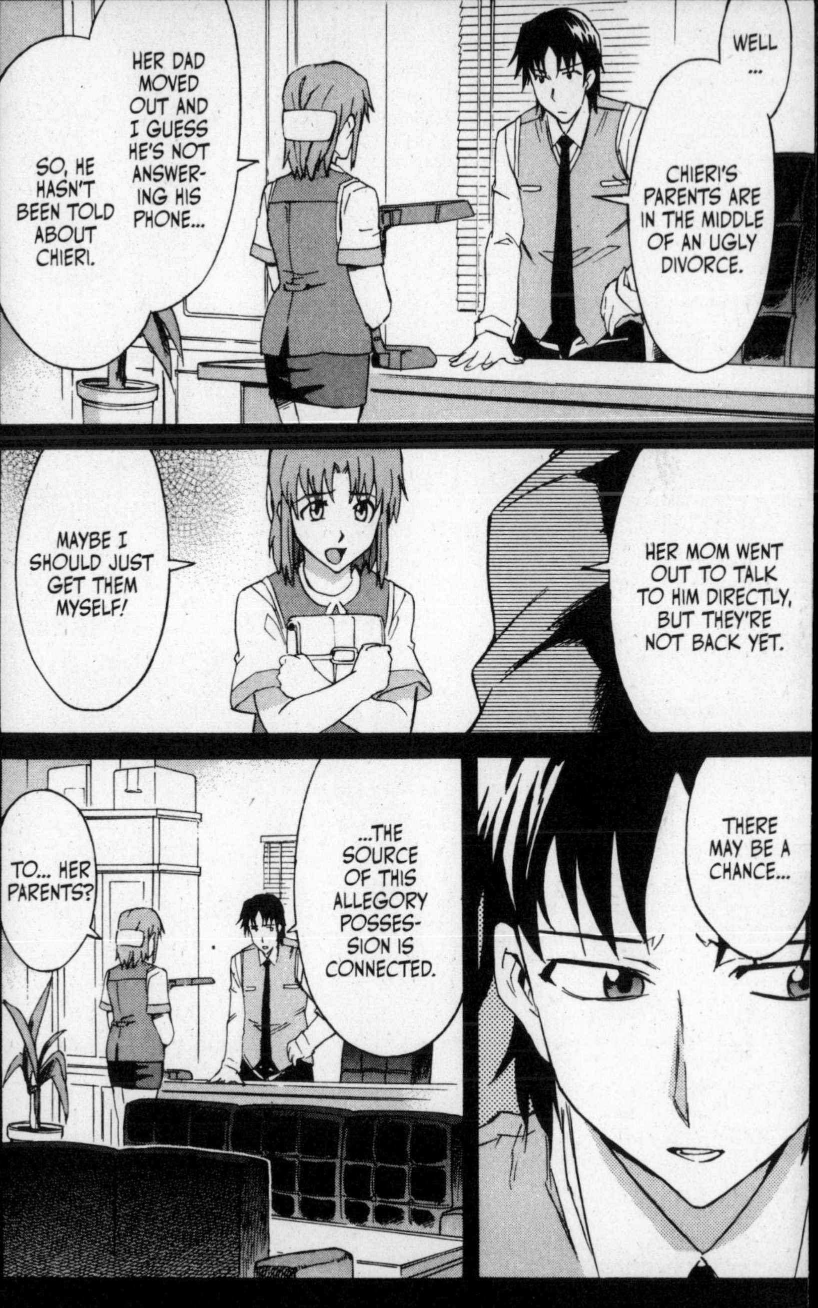
WELL ...
CHIERI'S PARENTS ARE IN THE MIDDLE OF AN UGLY DIVORCE.
HER DAD MOVED OUT AND I GUESS HE'S NOT ANSWERING HIS PHONE...
SO, HE HASN'T BEEN TOLD ABOUT CHIERI.
HER MOM WENT OUT TO TALK TO HIM DIRECTLY, BUT THEY'RE NOT BACK YET.
MAYBE I SHOULD JUST GET THEM MYSELF!
THERE MAY BE A CHANCE...
...THE SOURCE OF THIS ALLEGORY POSSESSION IS CONNECTED.
TO... HER PARENTS?

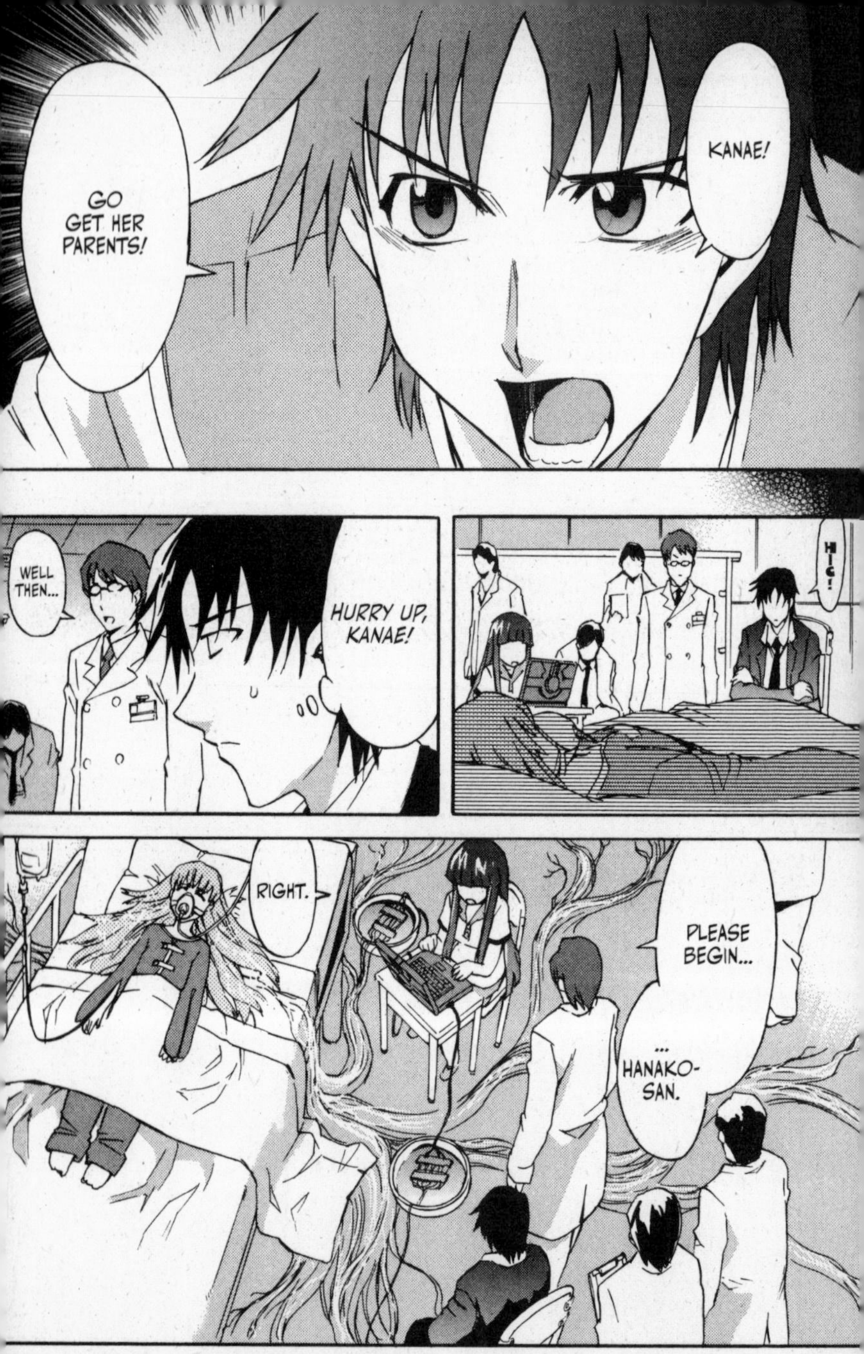
KANAE!
GO GET HER PARENTS!
HIC!
HURRY UP, KANAE!
WELL THEN...
PLEASE BEGIN...
...HANAKO-SAN.
RIGHT.

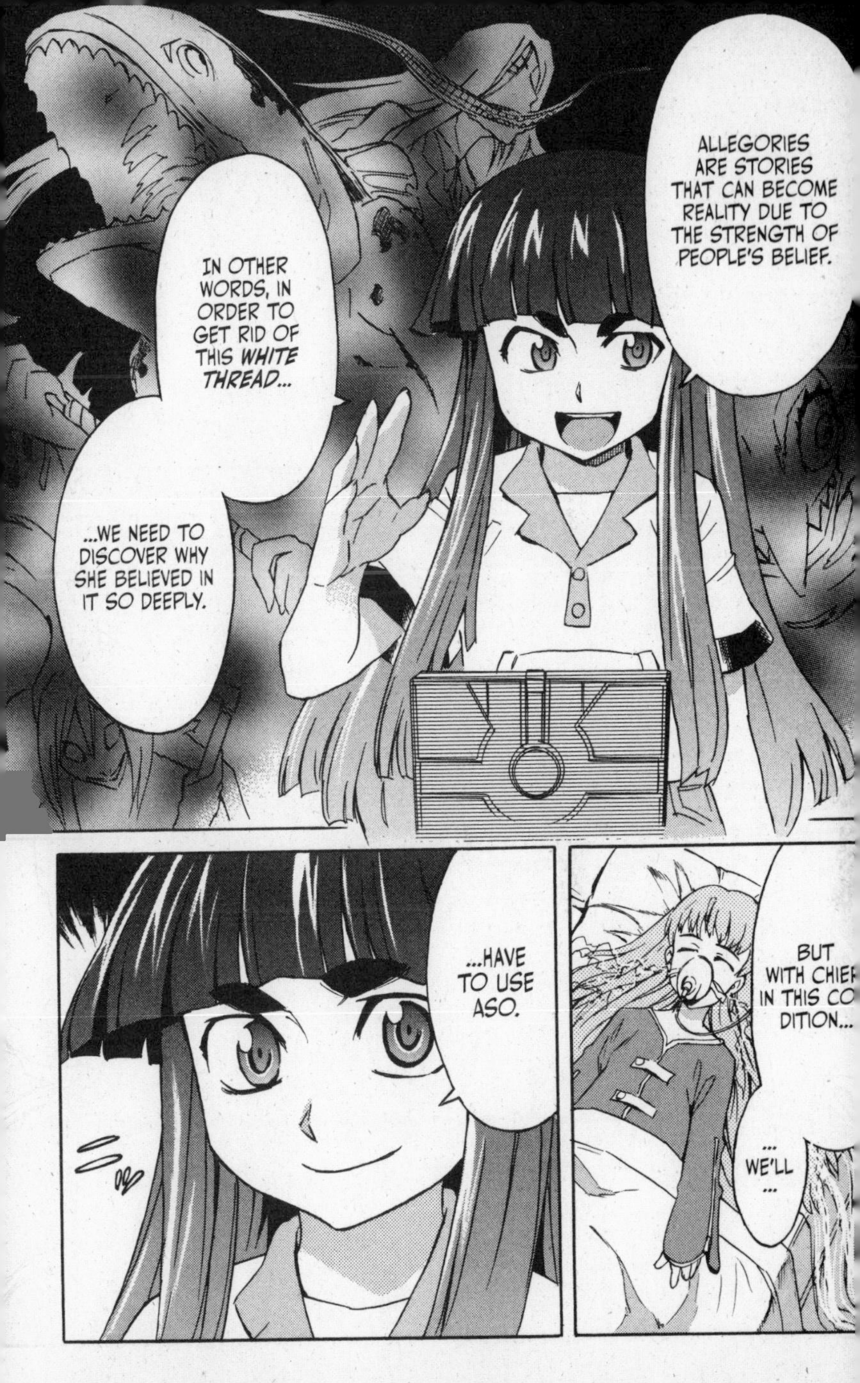
ALLEGORIES ARE STORIES THAT CAN BECOME REALITY DUE TO THE STRENGTH OF PEOPLE'S BELIEF.
IN OTHER WORDS, IN ORDER TO GET RID OF THIS *WHITE THREAD*...
...WE NEED TO DISCOVER WHY SHE BELIEVED IN IT SO DEEPLY.
BUT WITH CHIEF IN THIS CO DITION...
... WE'LL ...
...HAVE TO USE ASO.

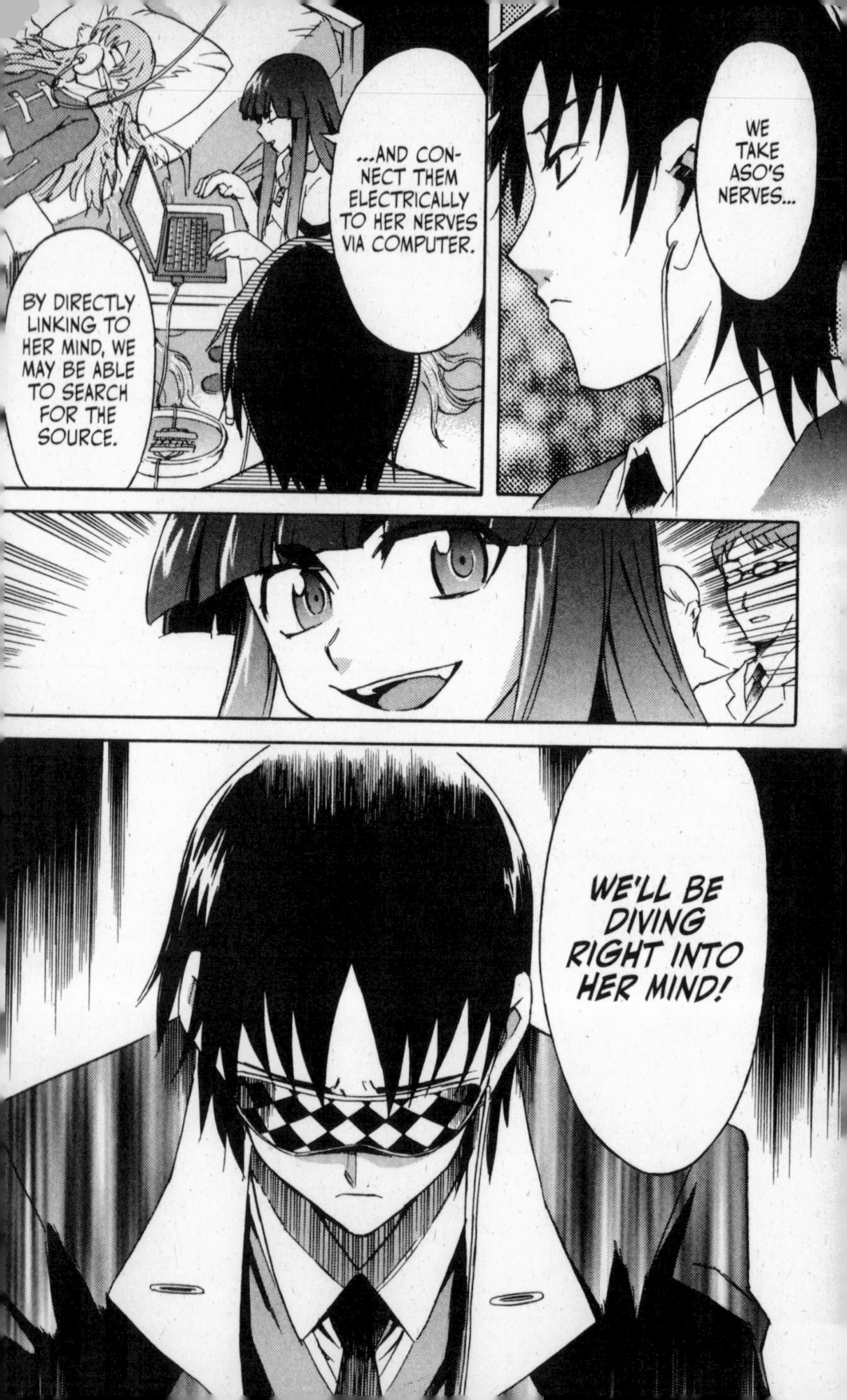
WE TAKE ASO'S NERVES...
...AND CON-NECT THEM ELECTRICALLY TO HER NERVES VIA COMPUTER.
BY DIRECTLY LINKING TO HER MIND, WE MAY BE ABLE TO SEARCH FOR THE SOURCE.
WE'LL BE DIVING RIGHT INTO HER MIND!

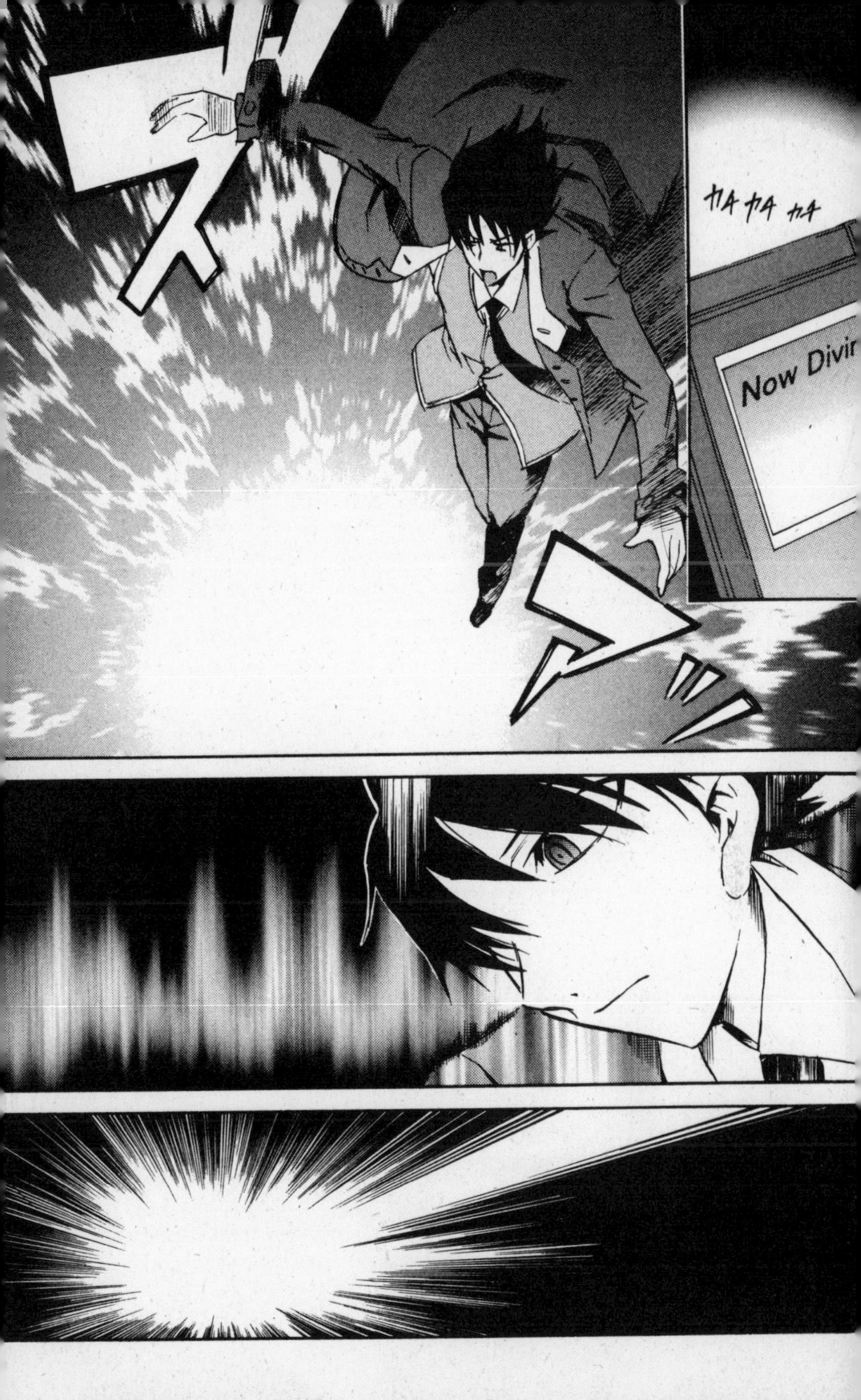
カチ カチ カチ
Now Divi

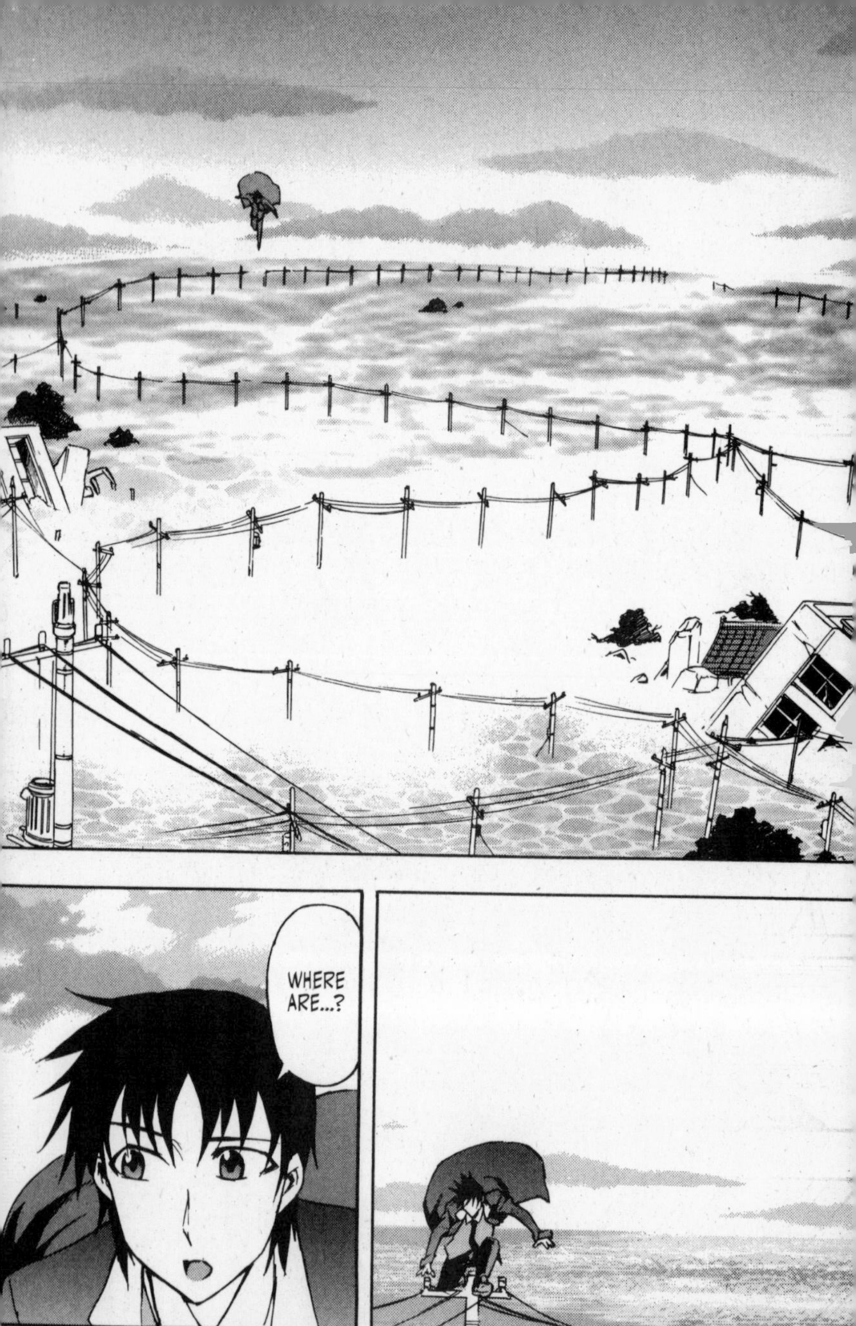
WHERE ARE...?

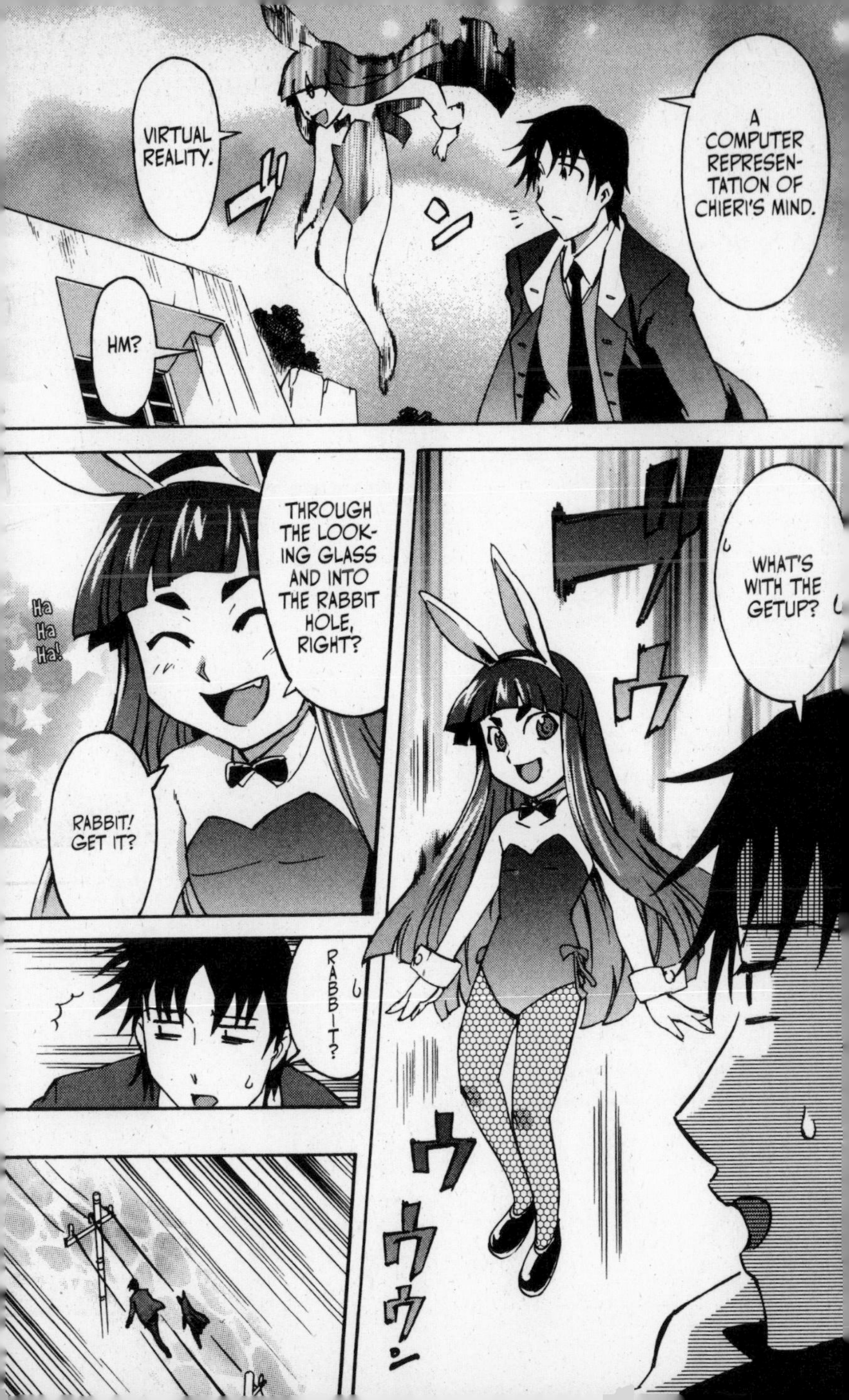
A COMPUTER REPRESENTATION OF CHIERI'S MIND.
VIRTUAL REALITY.
HM?
WHAT'S WITH THE GETUP?
THROUGH THE LOOKING GLASS AND INTO THE RABBIT HOLE, RIGHT?
Ha Ha Ha!
RABBIT! GET IT?
RABBIT?

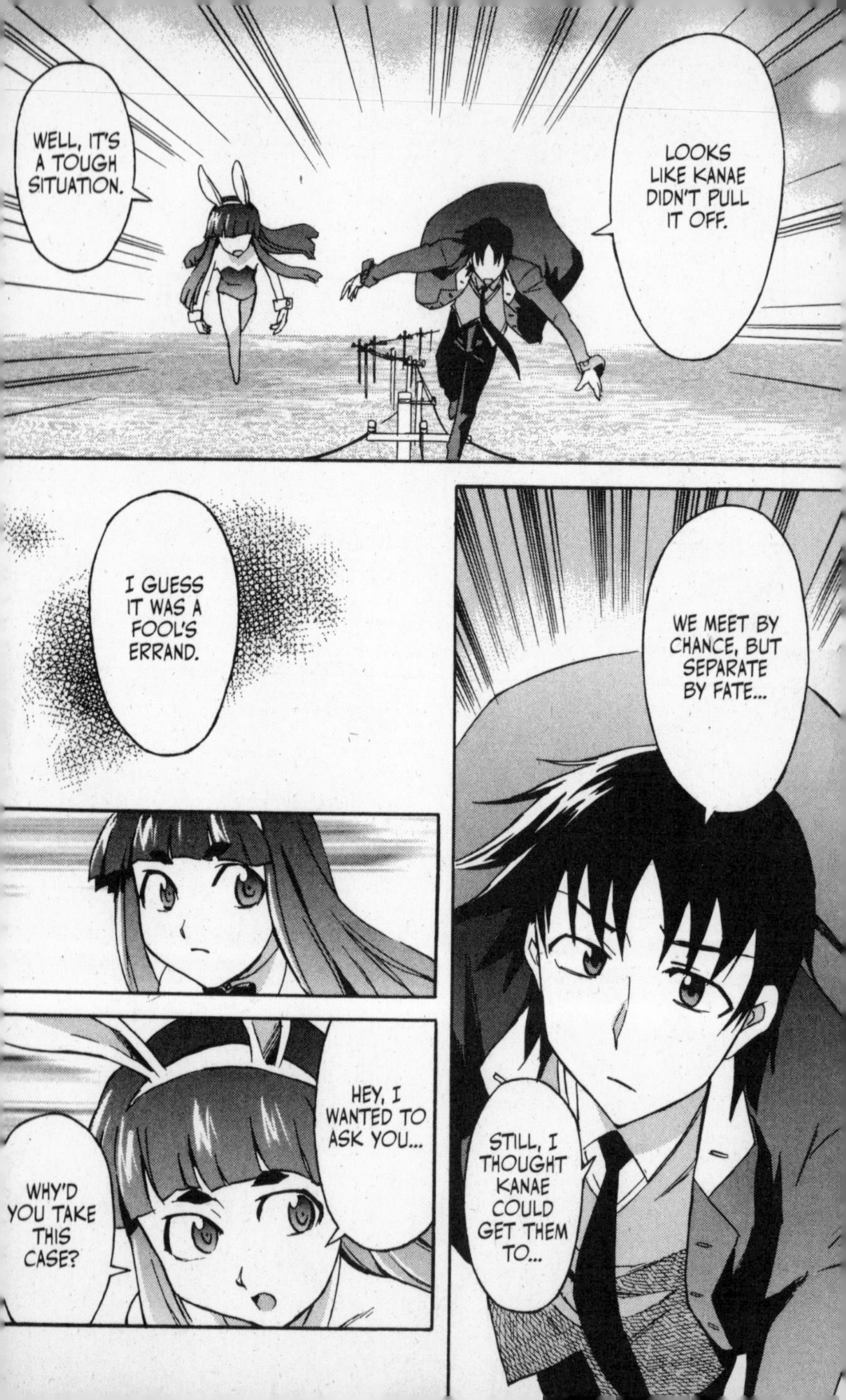
LOOKS LIKE KANAE DIDN'T PULL IT OFF.
WELL, IT'S A TOUGH SITUATION.
WE MEET BY CHANCE, BUT SEPARATE BY FATE...
STILL, I THOUGHT KANAE COULD GET THEM TO...
I GUESS IT WAS A FOOL'S ERRAND.
HEY, I WANTED TO ASK YOU...
WHY'D YOU TAKE THIS CASE?

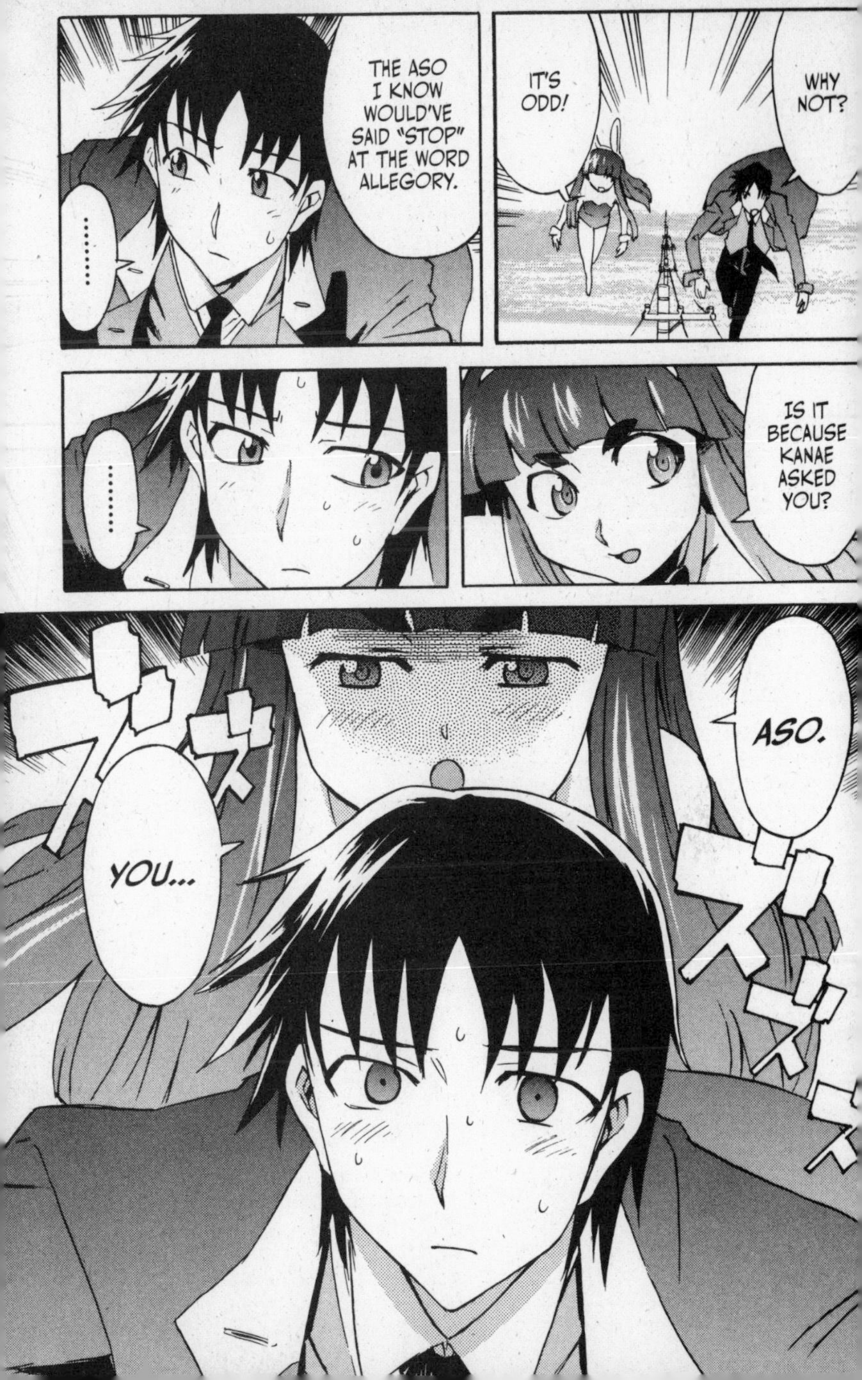
WHY NOT?
IT'S ODD!
THE ASO I KNOW WOULD'VE SAID "STOP" AT THE WORD ALLEGORY.
......
IS IT BECAUSE KANAE ASKED YOU?
......
ASO.
YOU...

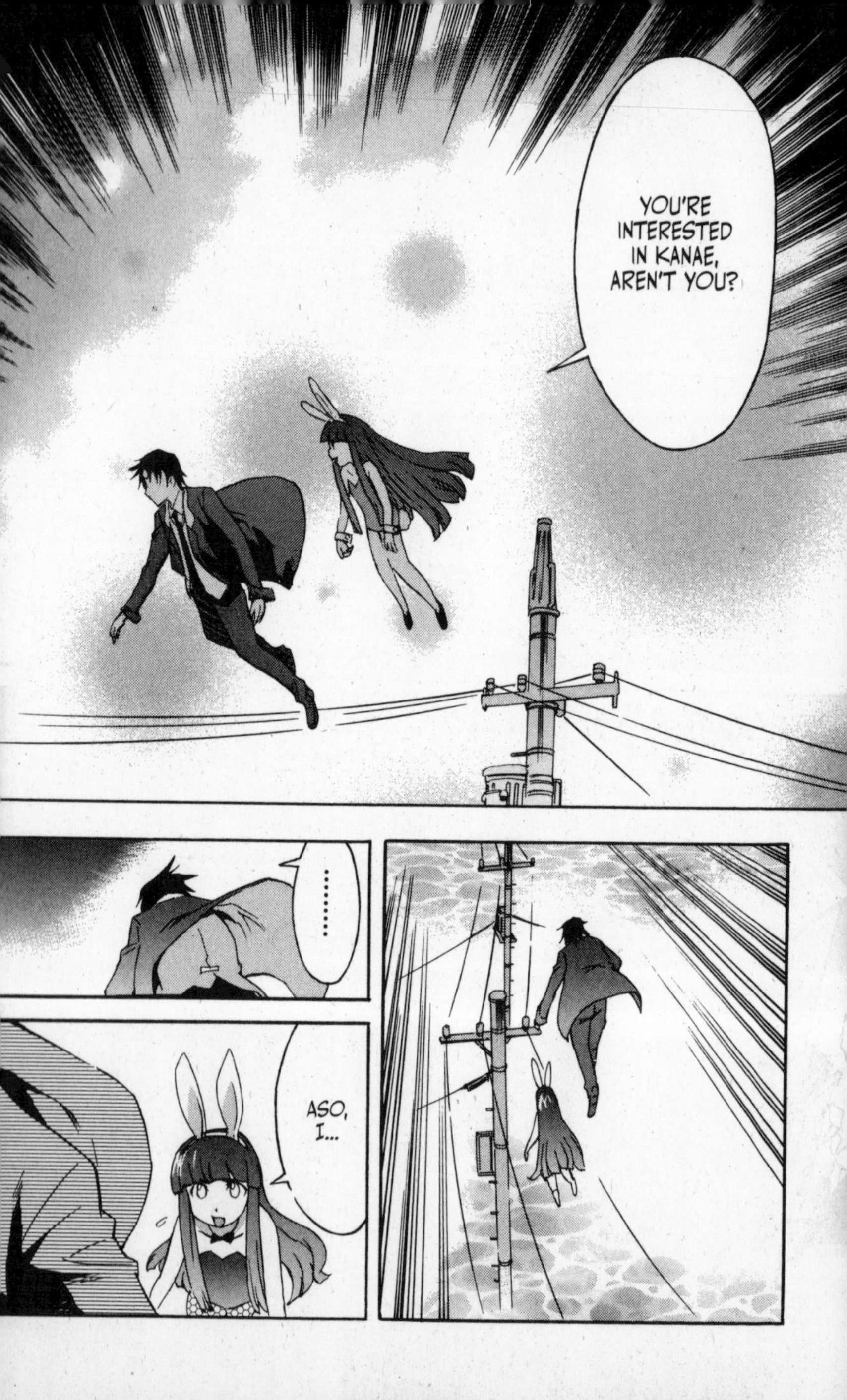
YOU'RE INTERESTED IN KANAE, AREN'T YOU?
......
ASO, I...

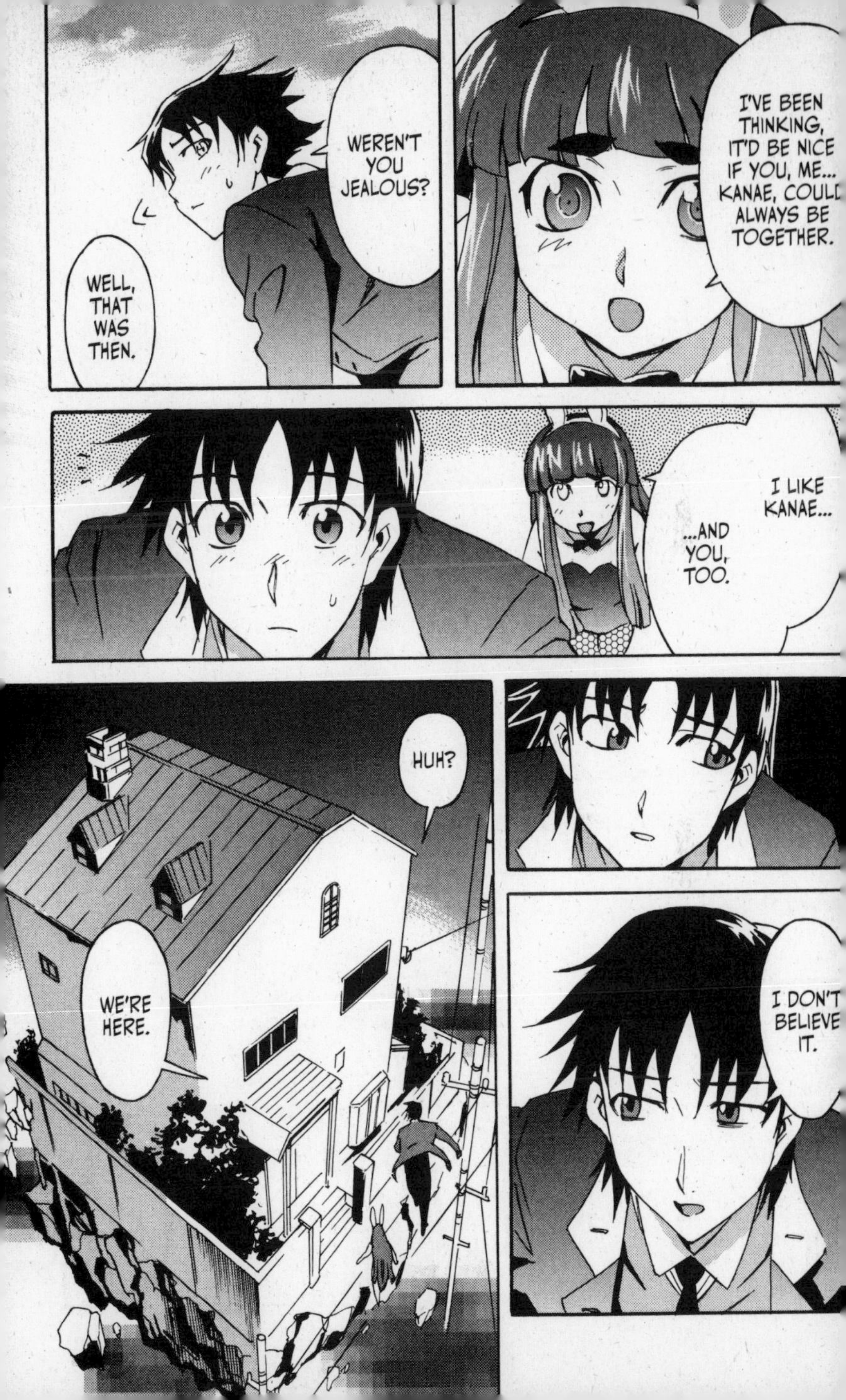
I'VE BEEN THINKING, IT'D BE NICE IF YOU, ME... KANAE, COULD ALWAYS BE TOGETHER.
WEREN'T YOU JEALOUS?
WELL, THAT WAS THEN.
I LIKE KANAE...
...AND YOU, TOO.
I DON'T BELIEVE IT.
HUH?
WE'RE HERE.

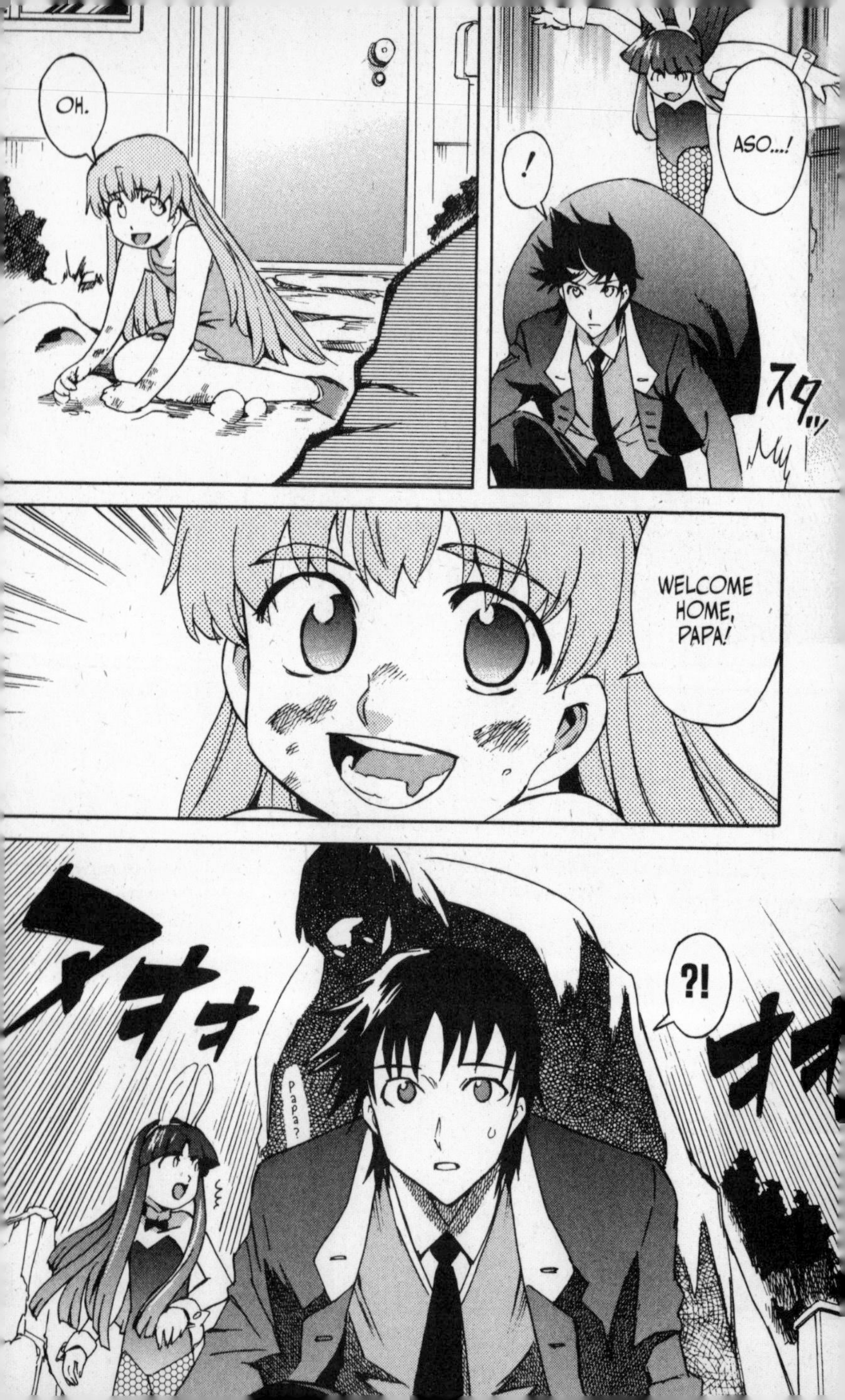
ASO...!
!
スタッ
OH.
WELCOME HOME, PAPA!
?!
Papa?

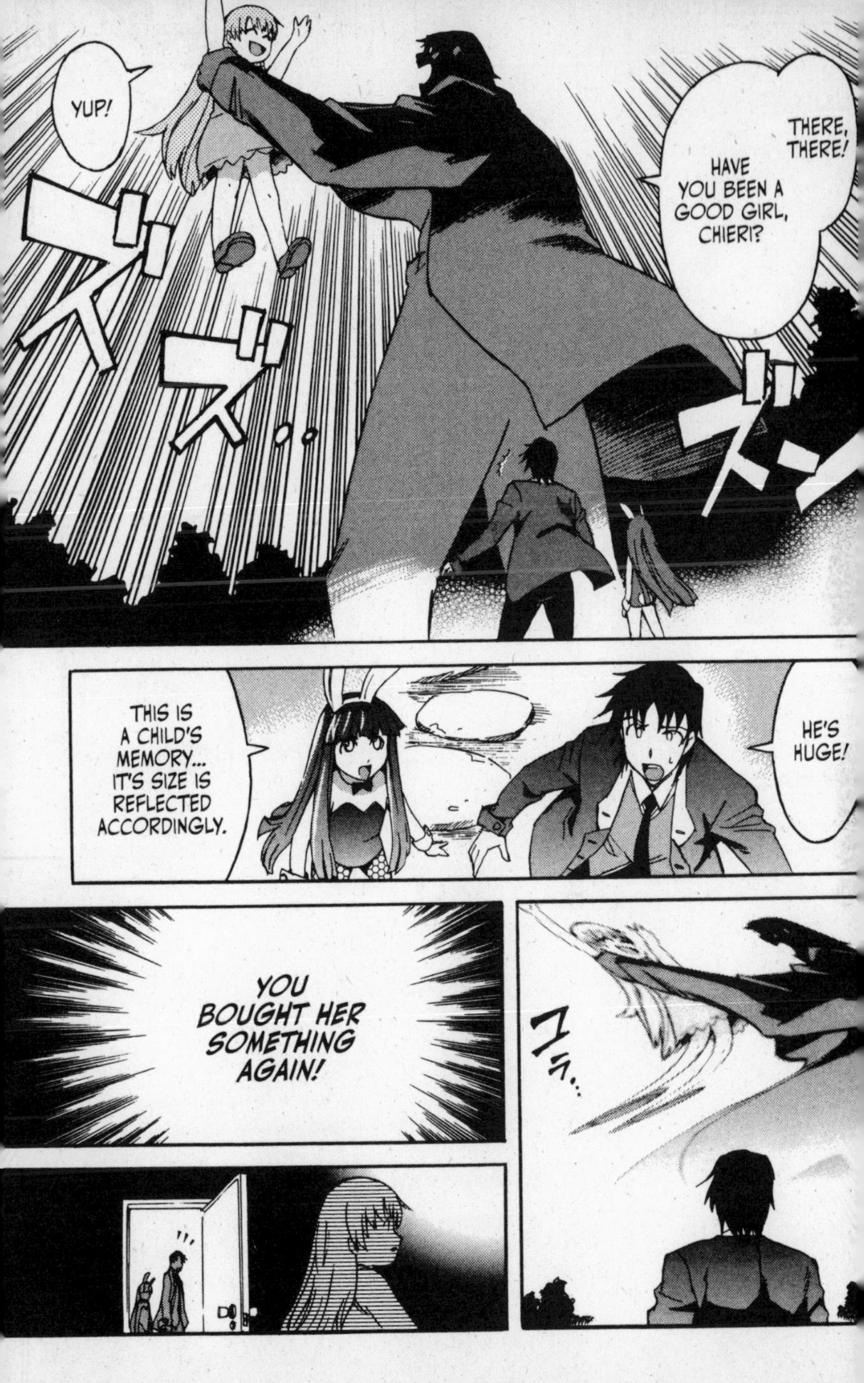
THERE, THERE! HAVE YOU BEEN A GOOD GIRL, CHIERI?
YUP!
HE'S HUGE!
THIS IS A CHILD'S MEMORY... IT'S SIZE IS REFLECTED ACCORDINGLY.
YOU BOUGHT HER SOMETHING AGAIN!

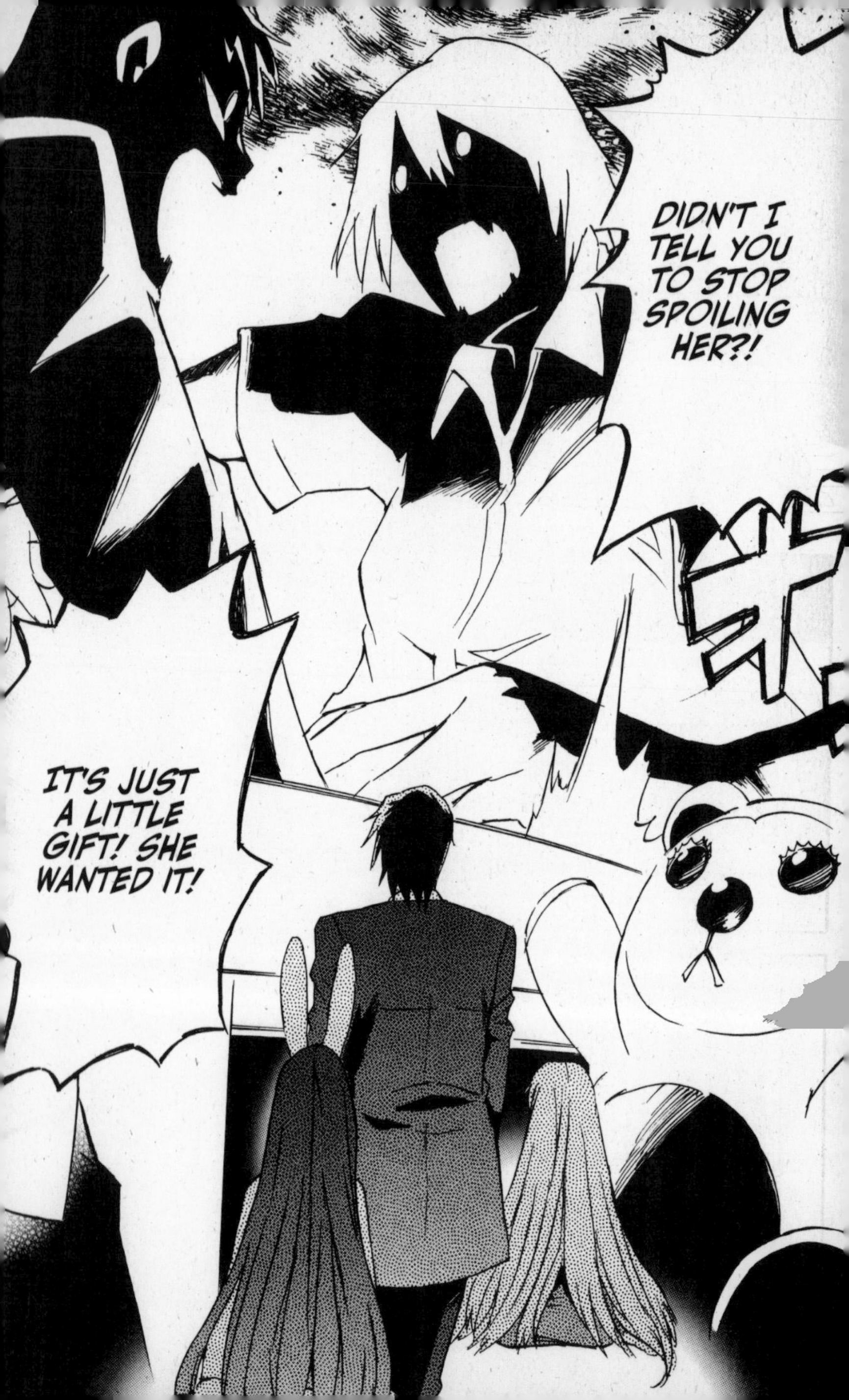
DIDN'T I TELL YOU TO STOP SPOILING HER?!
IT'S JUST A LITTLE GIFT! SHE WANTED IT!

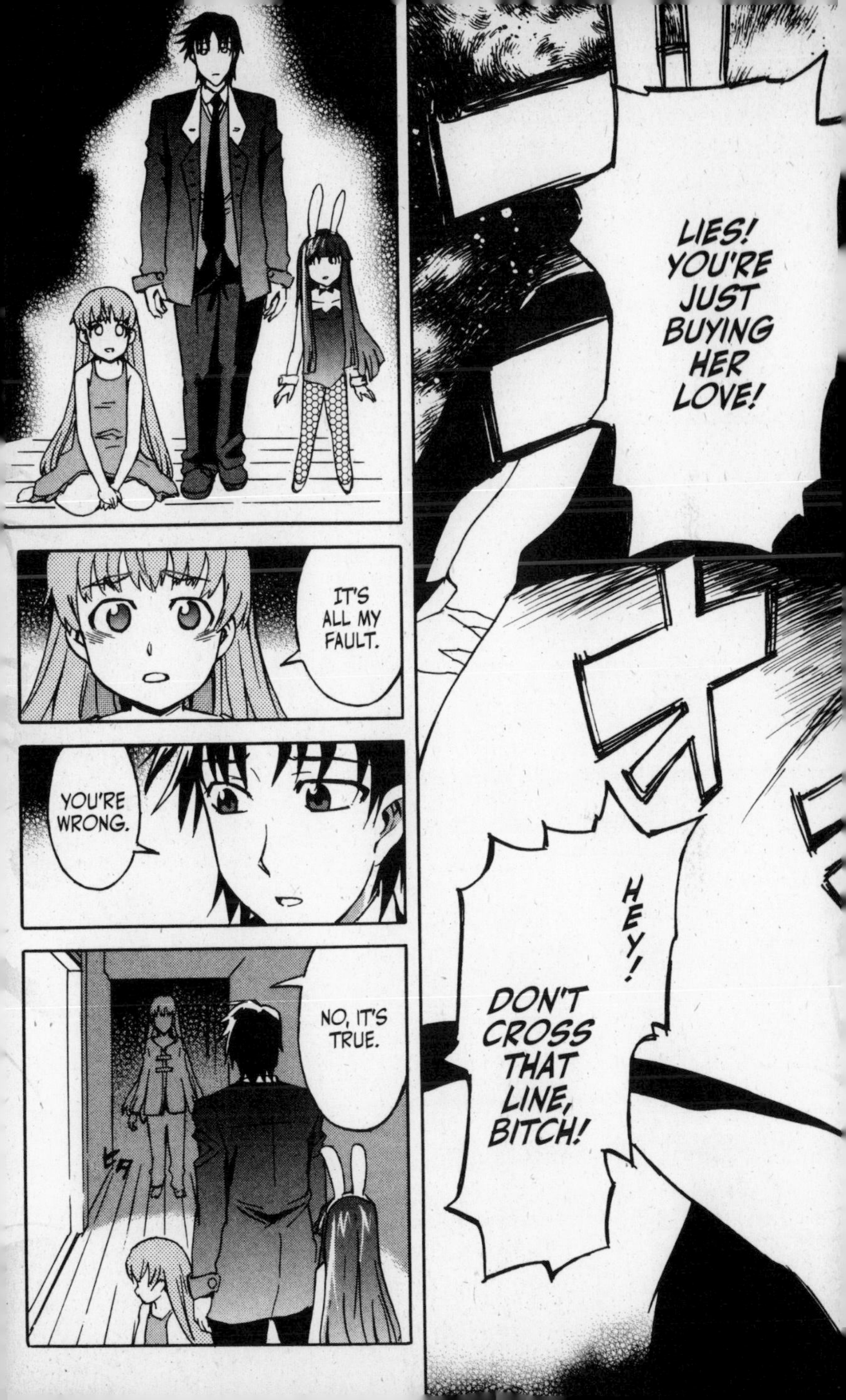
LIES! YOU'RE JUST BUYING HER LOVE!
HEY!
DON'T CROSS THAT LINE, BITCH!
IT'S ALL MY FAULT.
YOU'RE WRONG.
NO, IT'S TRUE.

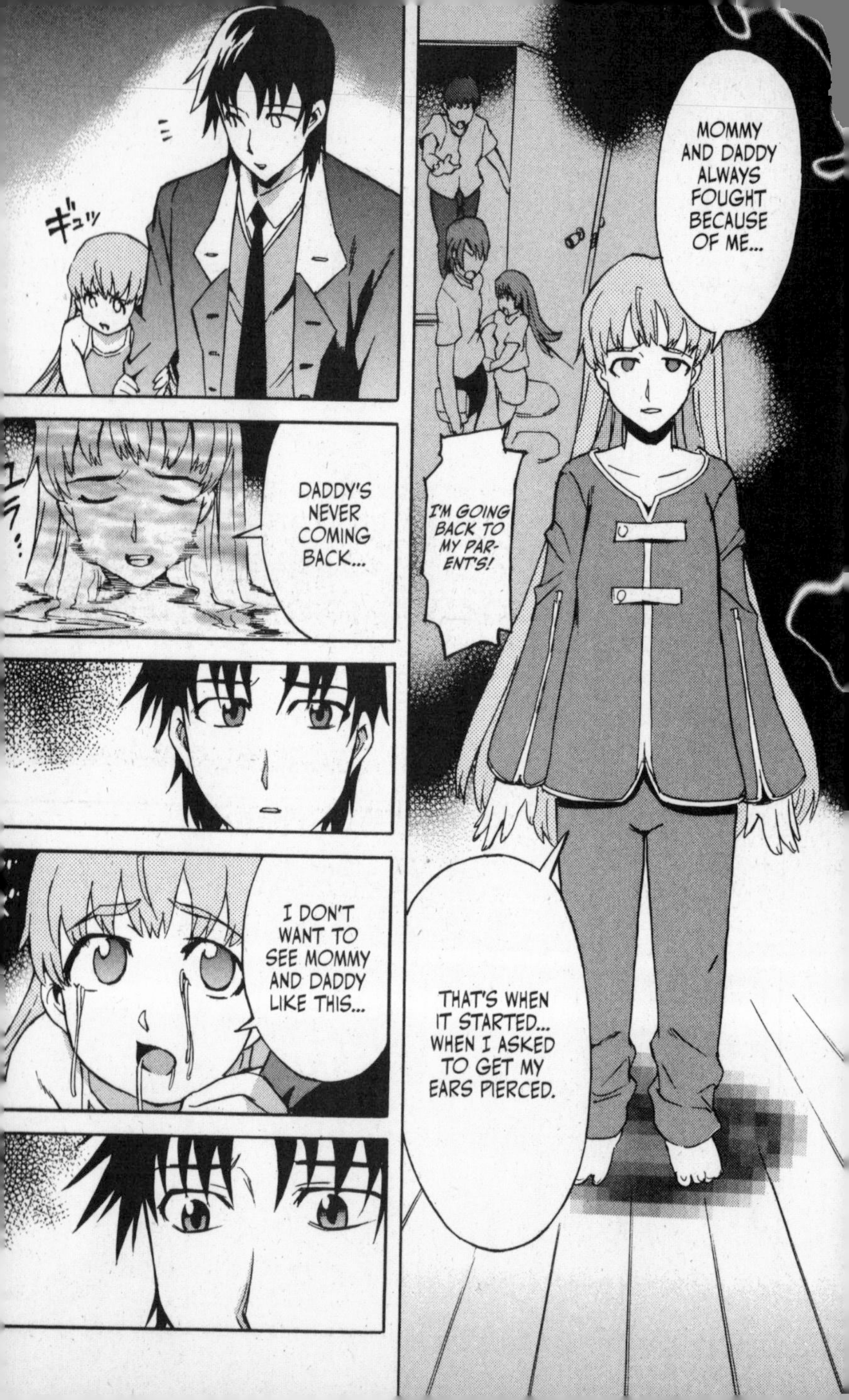
MOMMY AND DADDY ALWAYS FOUGHT BECAUSE OF ME...
I'M GOING BACK TO MY PAR- ENT'S!
THAT'S WHEN IT STARTED... WHEN I ASKED TO GET MY EARS PIERCED.
ギュッ
DADDY'S NEVER COMING BACK...
I DON'T WANT TO SEE MOMMY AND DADDY LIKE THIS...

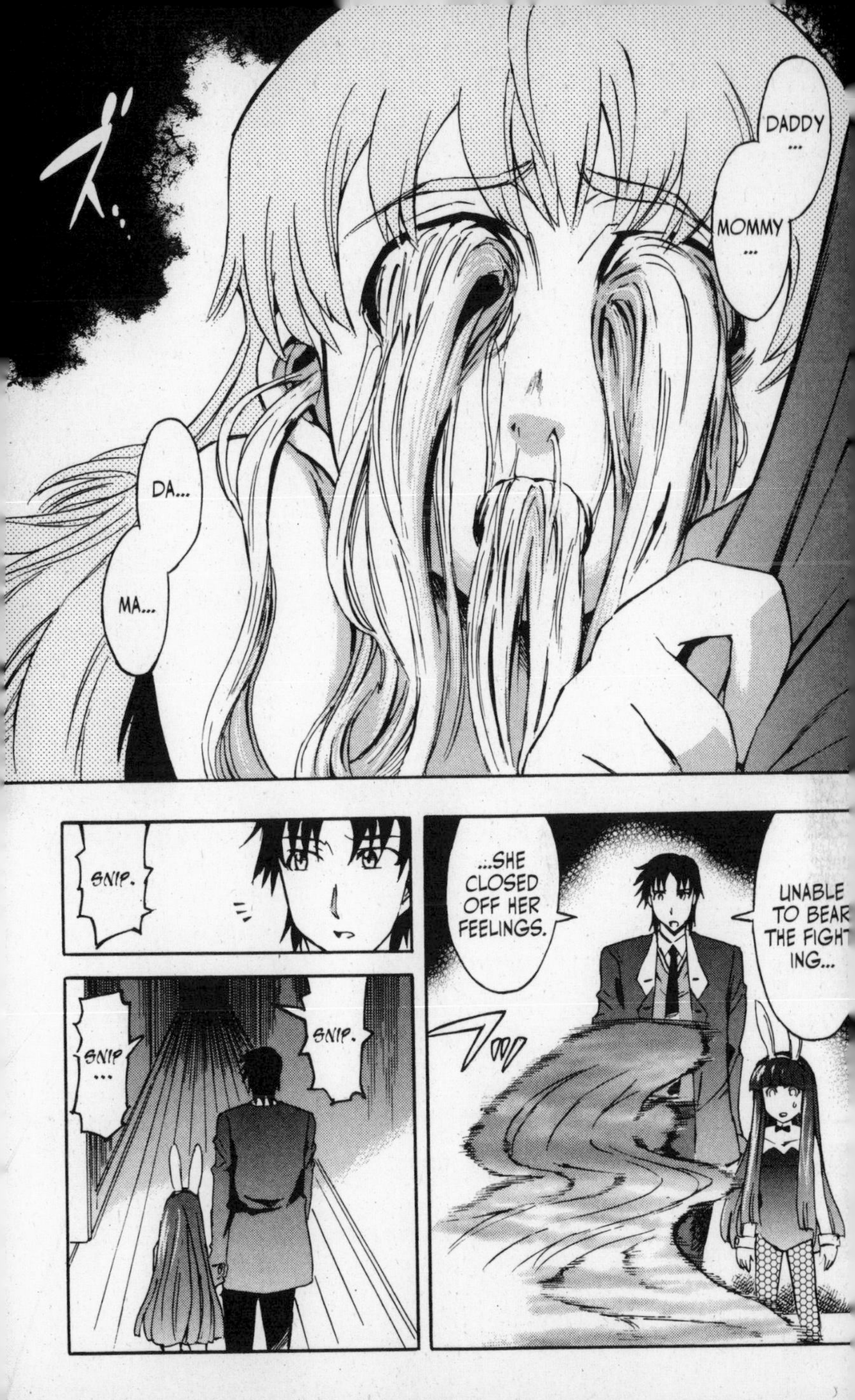
DADDY ...
MOMMY ...
ズ...
DA...
MA...
UNABLE TO BEAR THE FIGHT ING...
...SHE CLOSED OFF HER FEELINGS.
SNIP.
SNIP.
SNIP ...

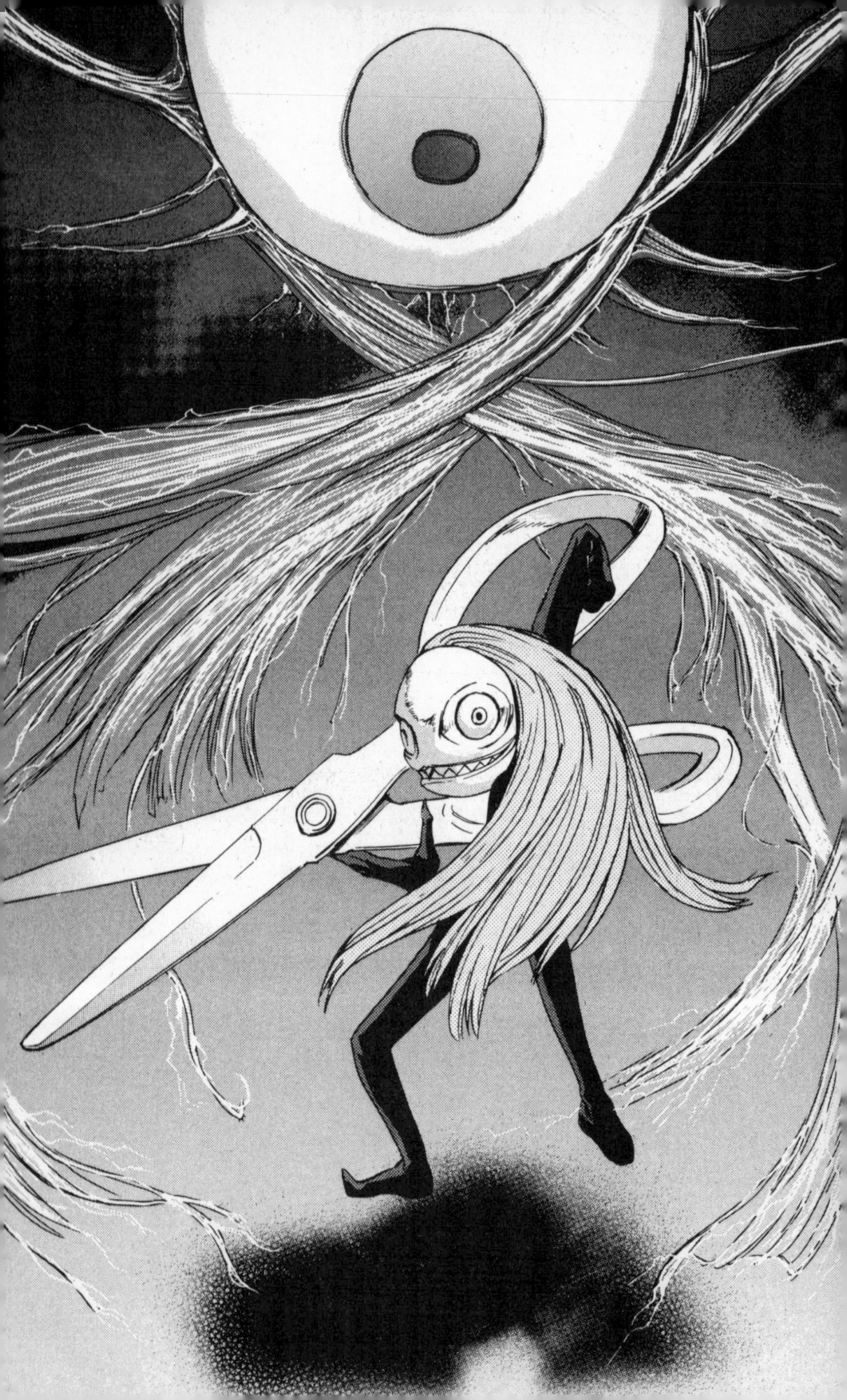

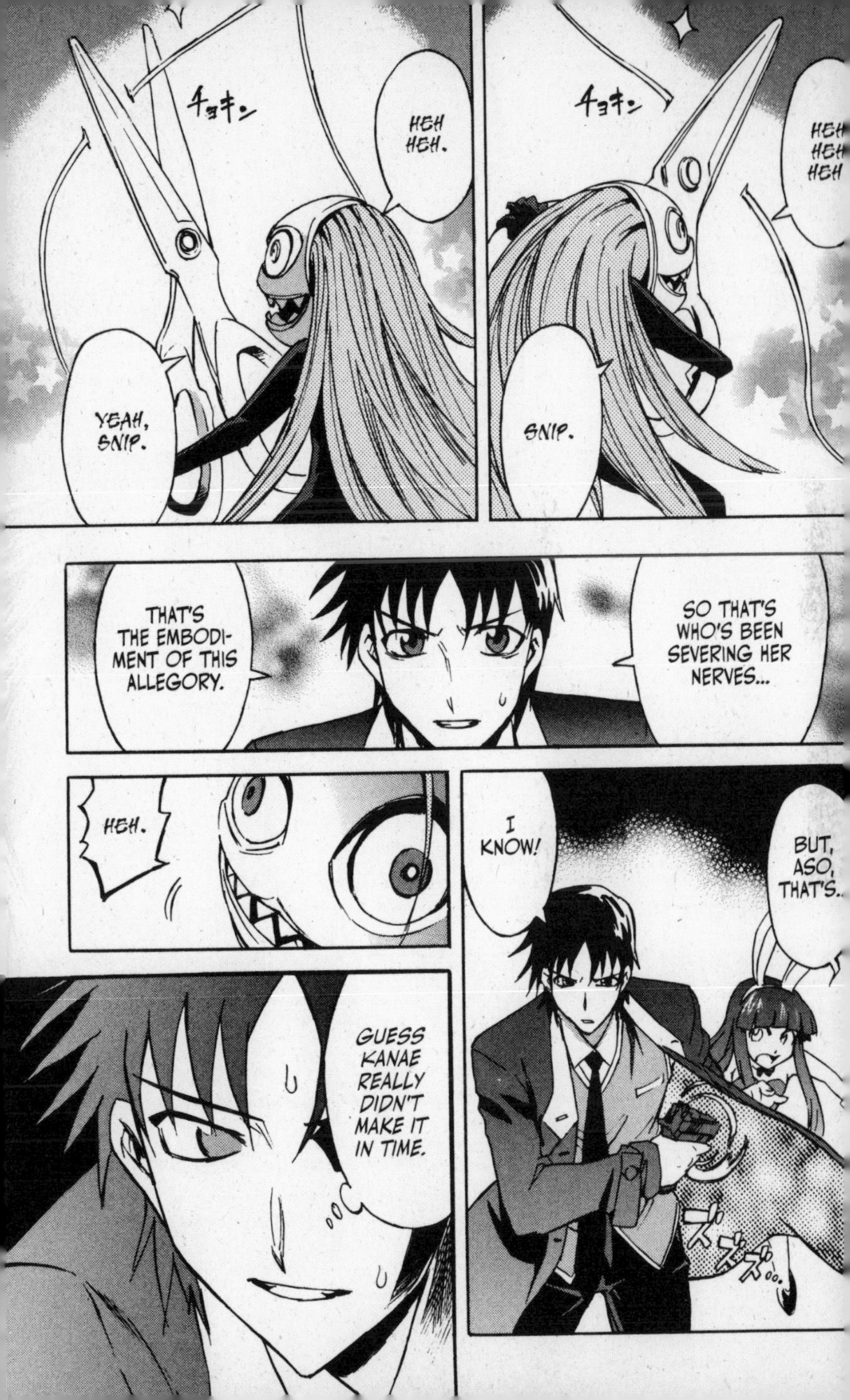
HEH HEH HEH
チョキン
SNIP.
チョキン
HEH HEH.
YEAH, SNIP.
SO THAT'S WHO'S BEEN SEVERING HER NERVES...
THAT'S THE EMBODIMENT OF THIS ALLEGORY.
BUT, ASO, THAT'S...
I KNOW!
ズズズ
HEH.
GUESS KANAE REALLY DIDN'T MAKE IT IN TIME.

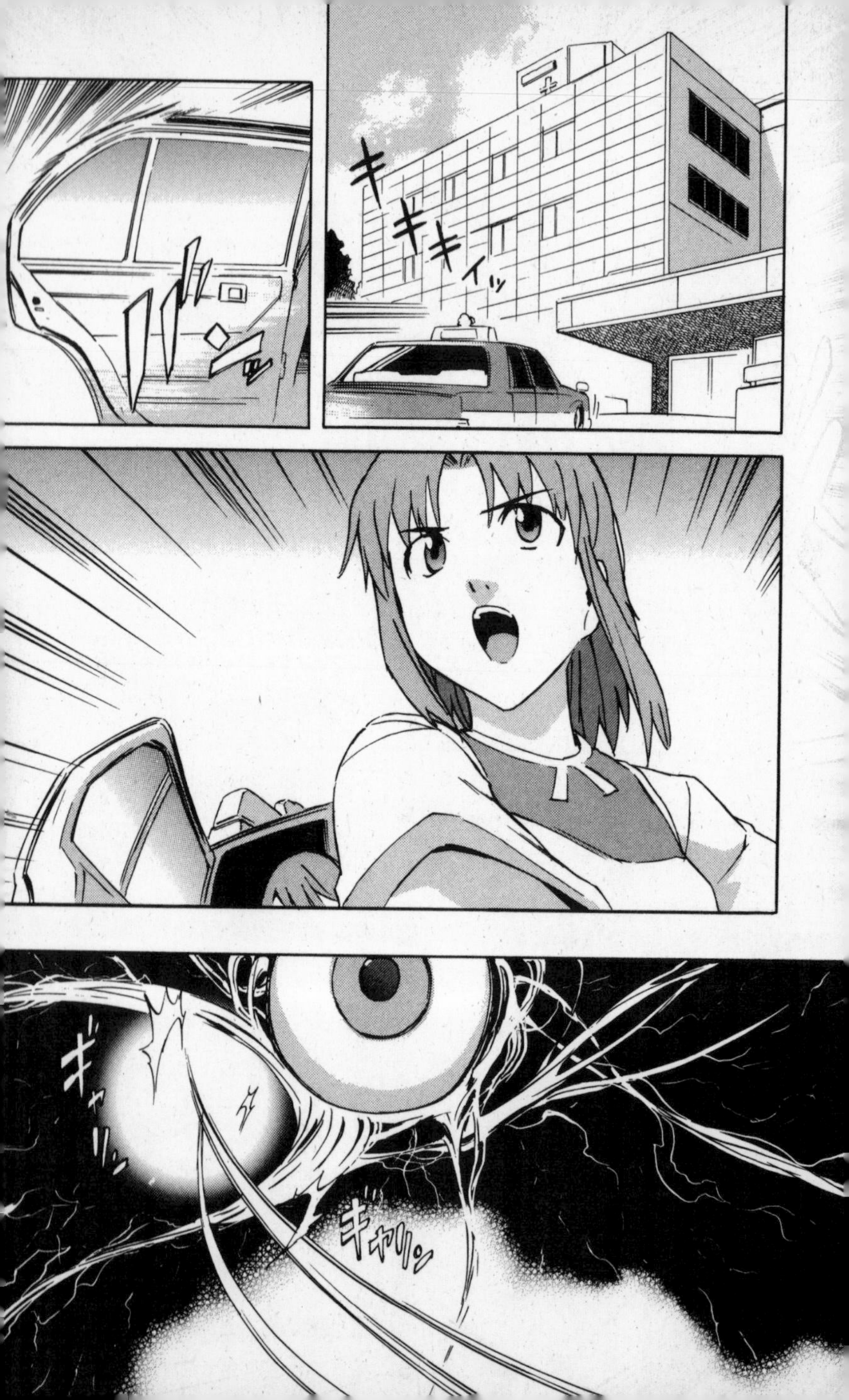
ギギギイッ
バンッ
ギャルン
ギャルン

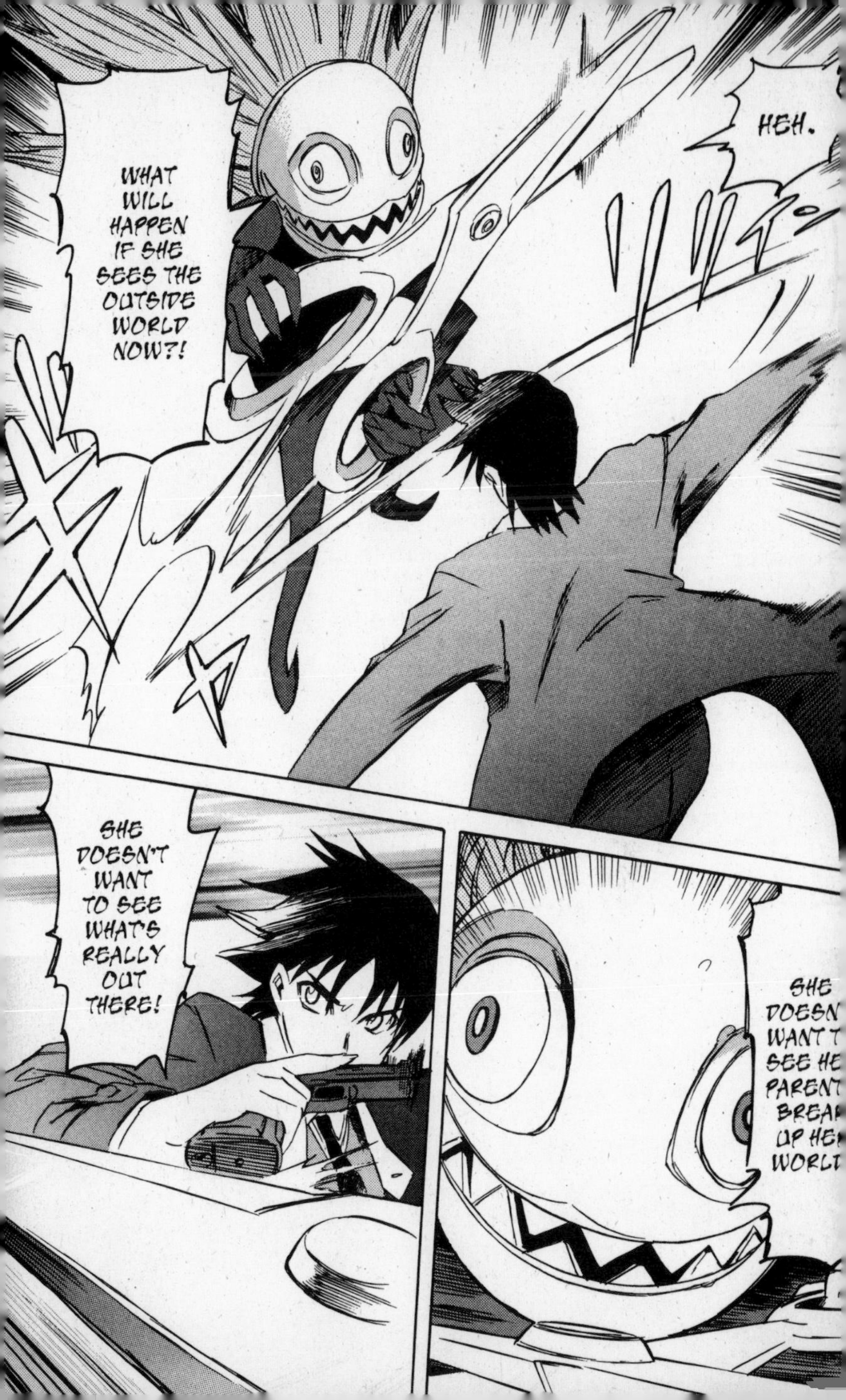
HEH.
WHAT WILL HAPPEN IF SHE SEES THE OUTSIDE WORLD NOW?!
SHE DOESN WANT T SEE HE PARENT BREA UP HE WORLD
SHE DOESN'T WANT TO SEE WHAT'S REALLY OUT THERE!

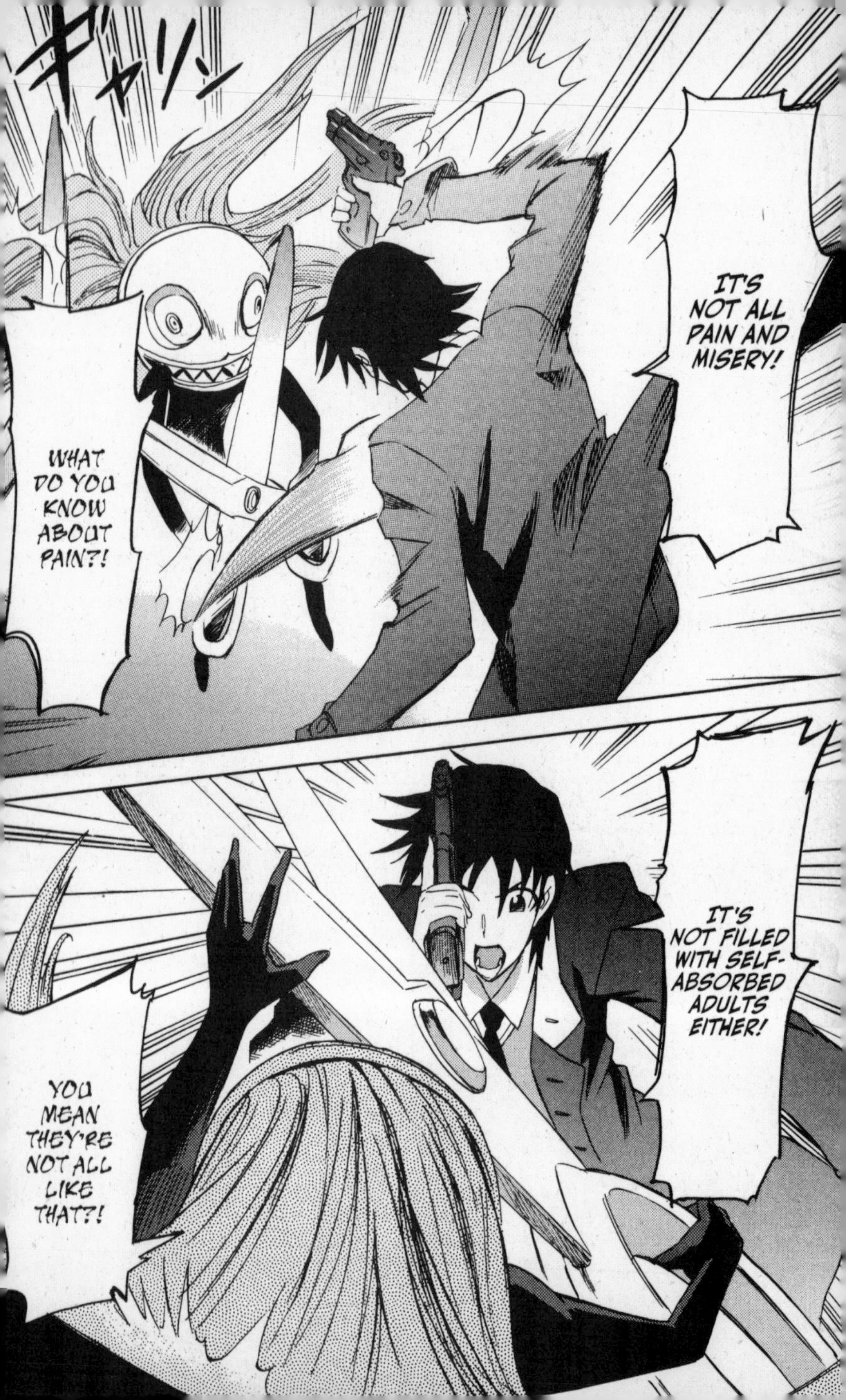
IT'S NOT ALL PAIN AND MISERY!
ギャリン
WHAT DO YOU KNOW ABOUT PAIN?!
IT'S NOT FILLED WITH SELF-ABSORBED ADULTS EITHER!
YOU MEAN THEY'RE NOT ALL LIKE THAT?!

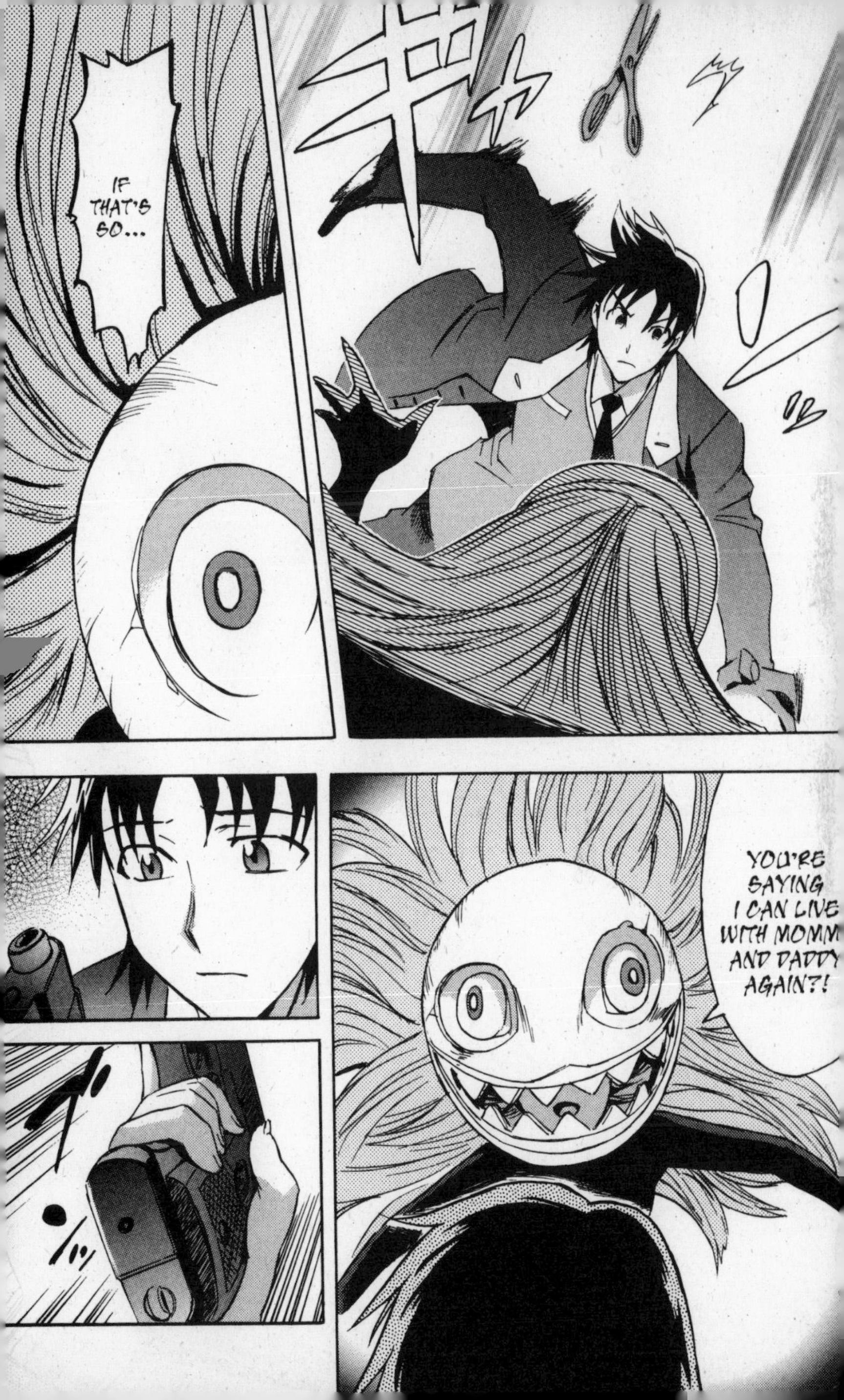
IF THAT'S SO...
YOU'RE SAYING I CAN LIVE WITH MOMM AND DADDY AGAIN?!

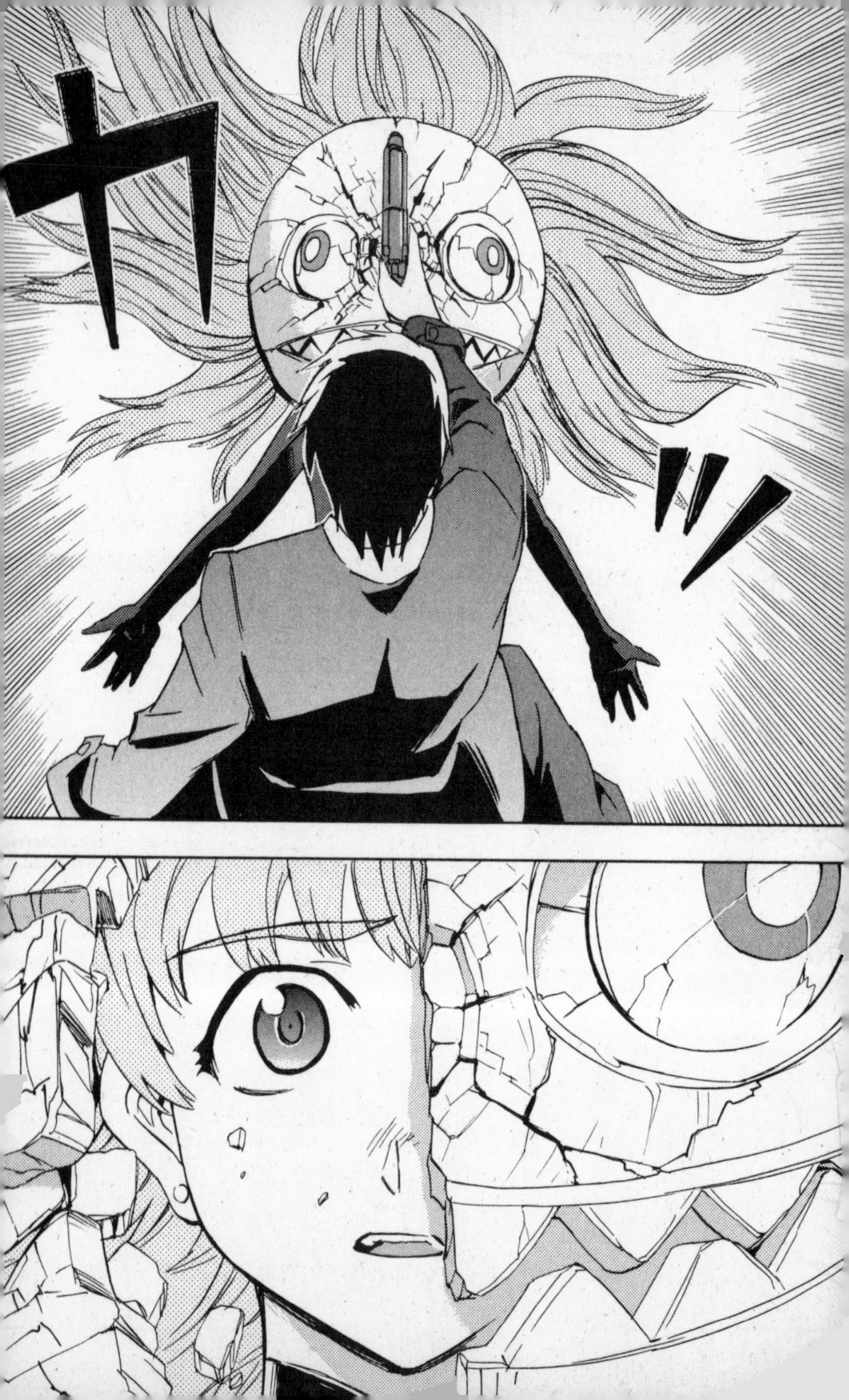

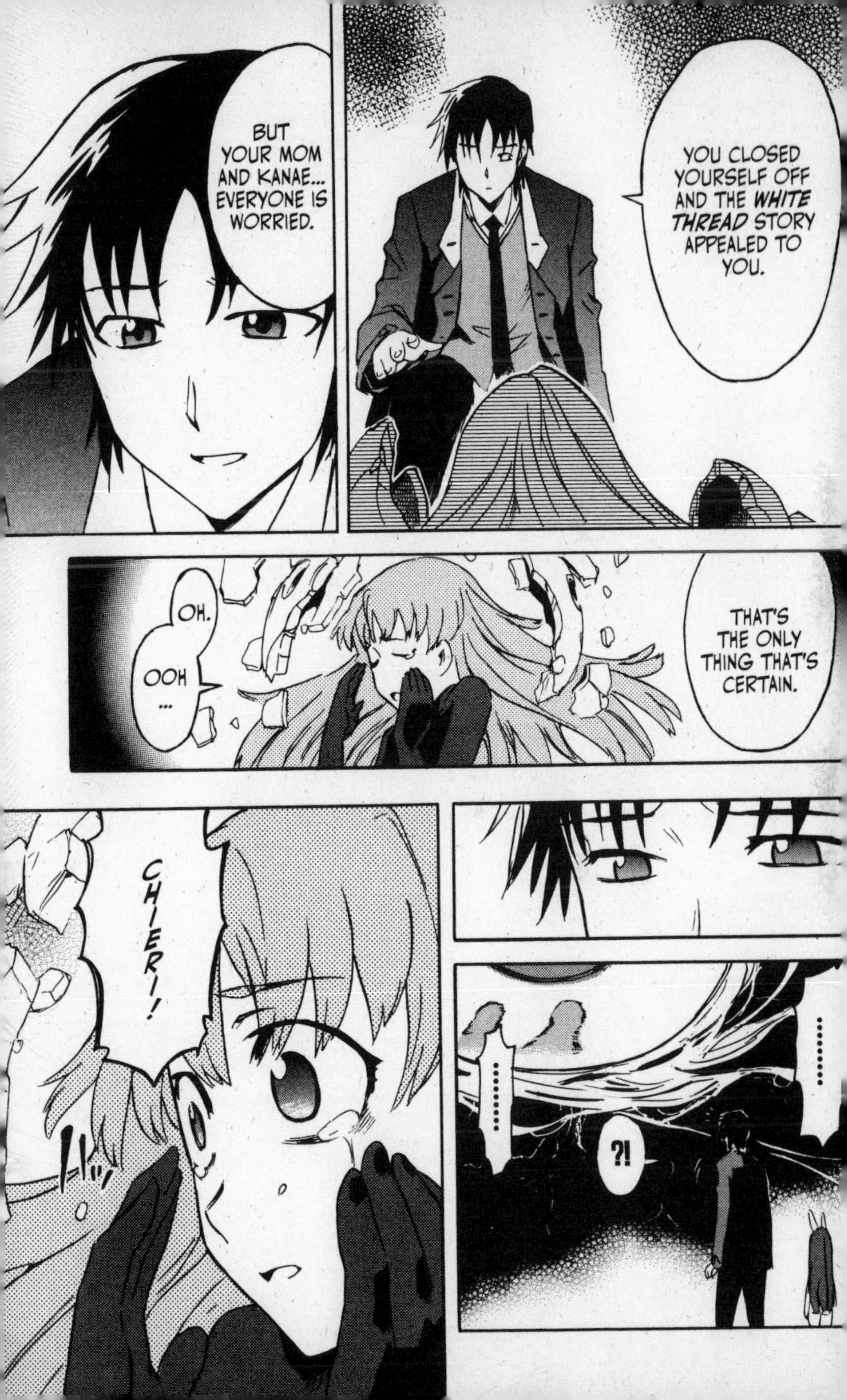

YOU CLOSED YOURSELF OFF AND THE *WHITE THREAD* STORY APPEALED TO YOU.
BUT YOUR MOM AND KANAE... EVERYONE IS WORRIED.
THAT'S THE ONLY THING THAT'S CERTAIN.
OH.
OOH ...
....
....
?!
CHIERI!

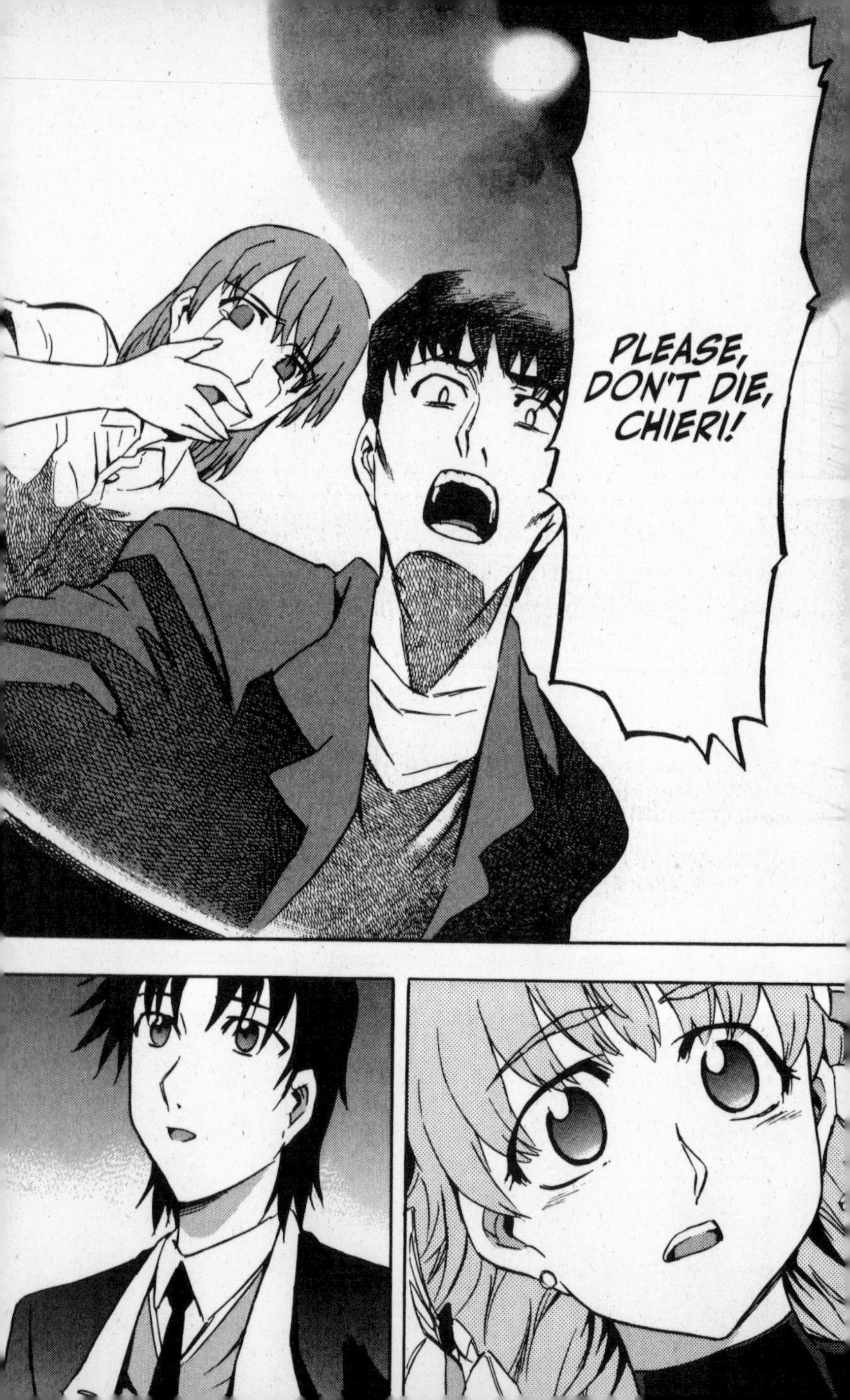
PLEASE, DON'T DIE, CHIERI!

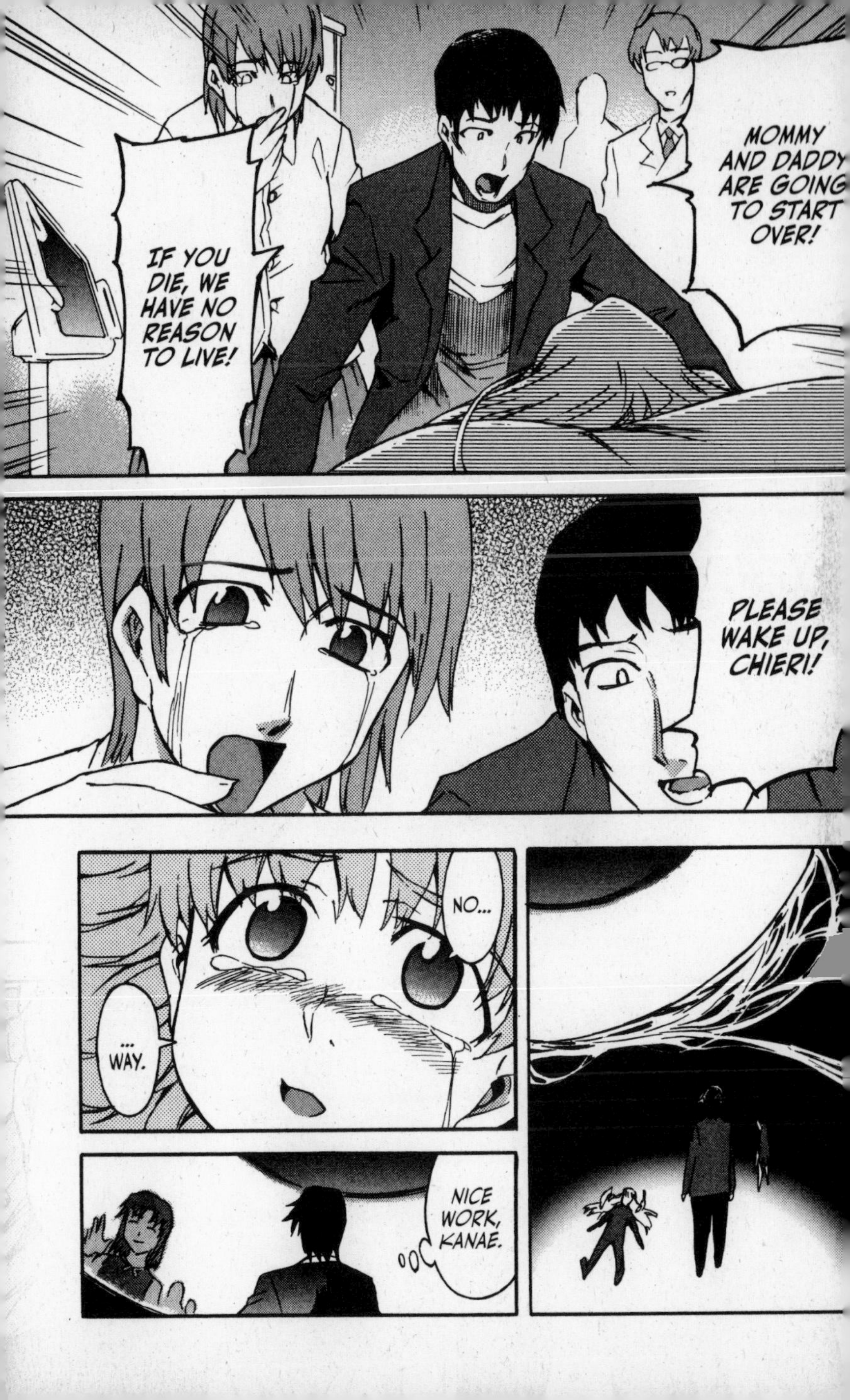
MOMMY AND DADDY ARE GOING TO START OVER!
IF YOU DIE, WE HAVE NO REASON TO LIVE!
PLEASE WAKE UP, CHIERI!
NO...
...WAY.
NICE WORK, KANAE.

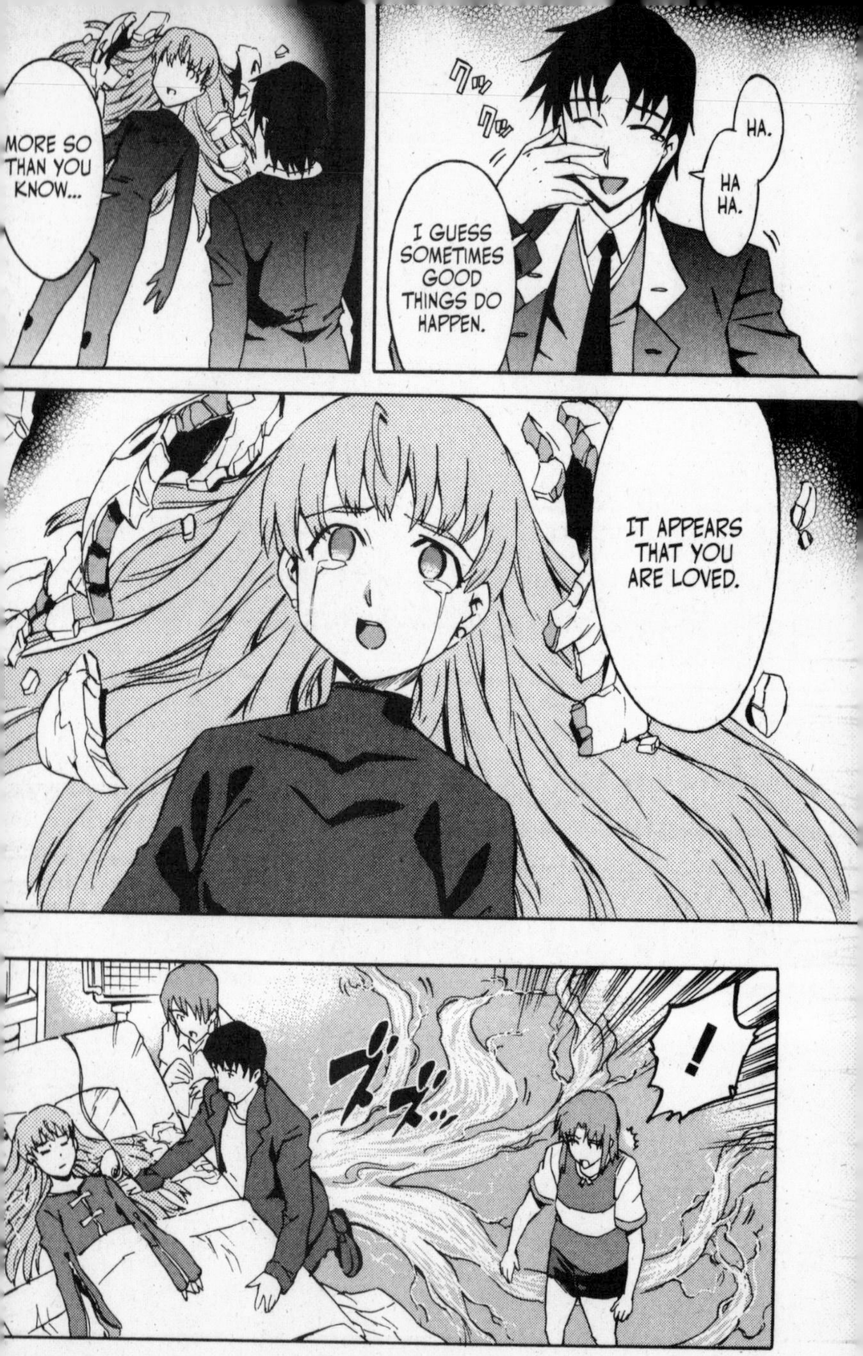
HA.
HA HA.
クッ
クッ
I GUESS SOMETIMES GOOD THINGS DO HAPPEN.
MORE SO THAN YOU KNOW...
IT APPEARS THAT YOU ARE LOVED.
!

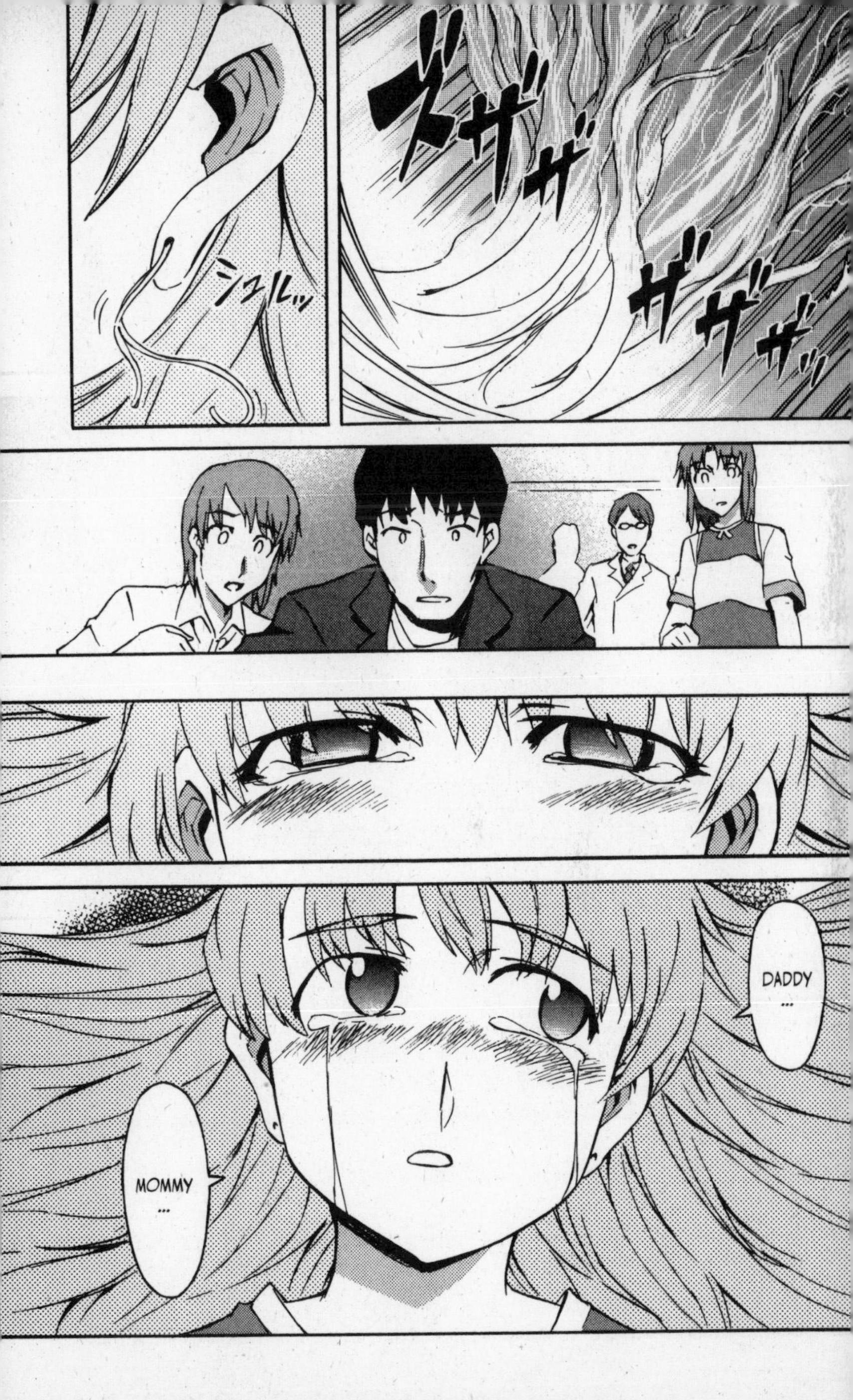
ズザザ
ザザザッ
シュルッ
DADDY ...
MOMMY ...

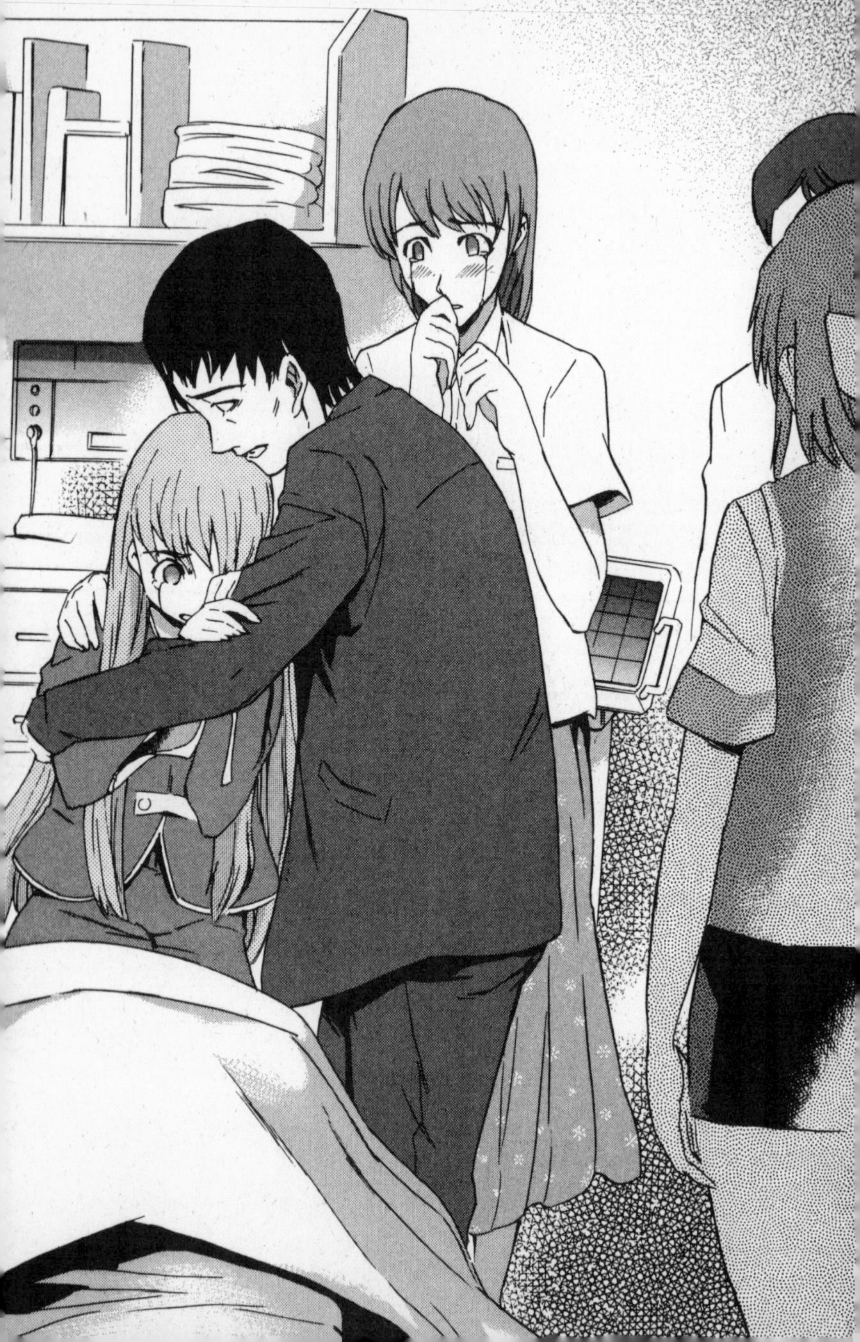

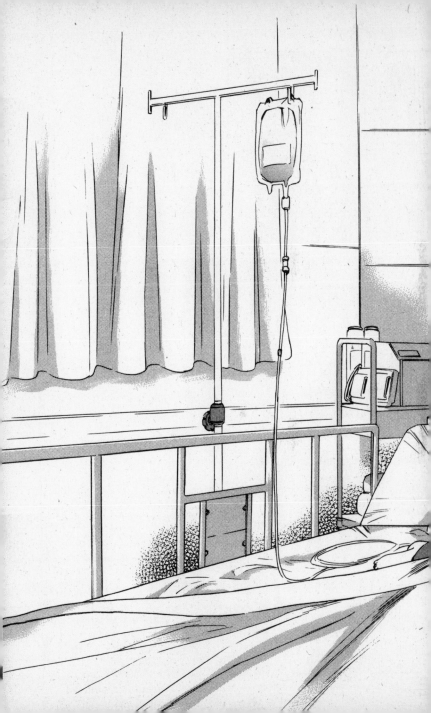

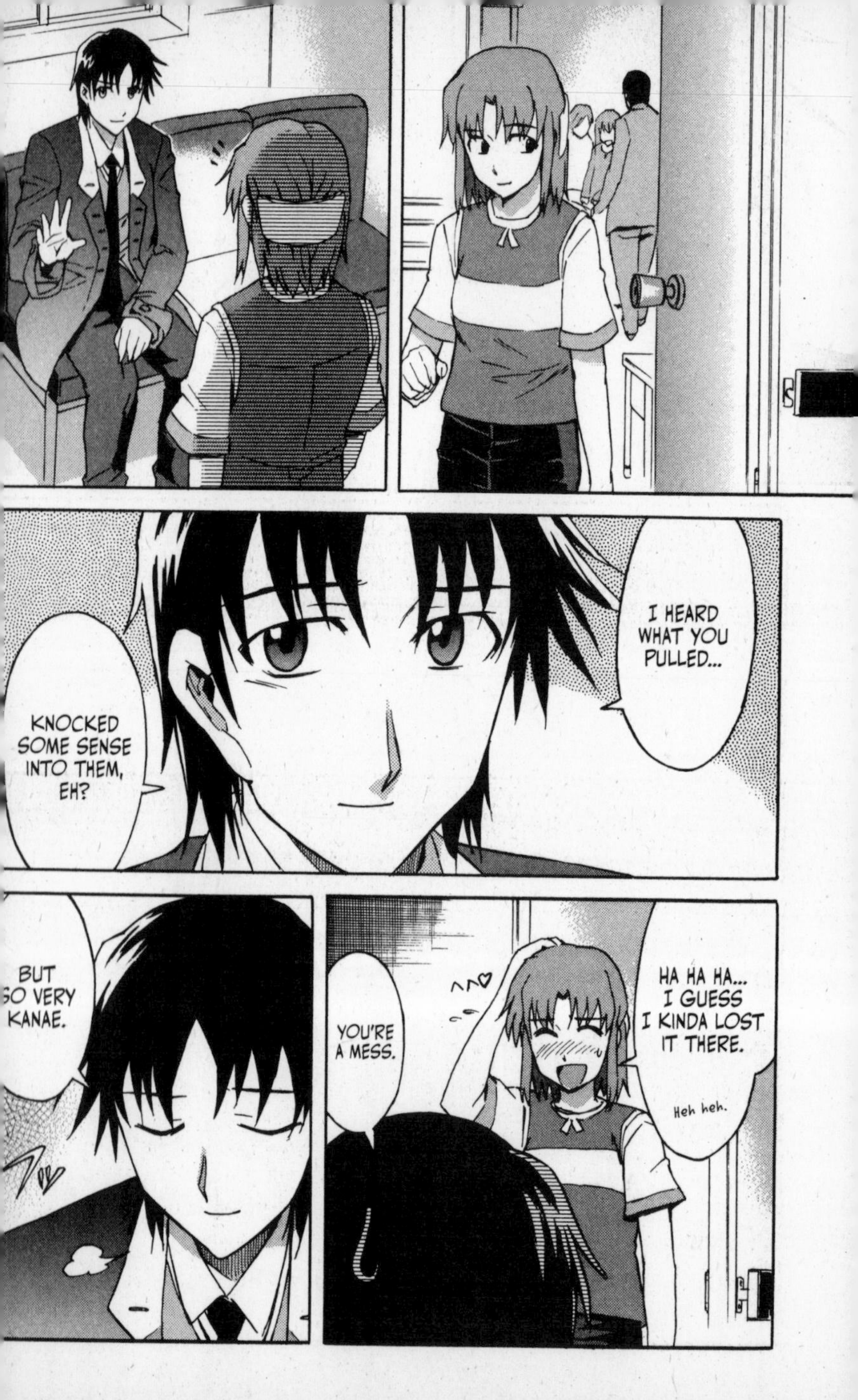
I HEARD WHAT YOU PULLED...
KNOCKED SOME SENSE INTO THEM, EH?
HA HA HA... I GUESS I KINDA LOST IT THERE.
Heh heh.
YOU'RE A MESS.
BUT SO VERY KANAE.

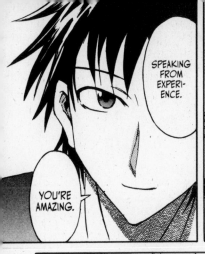

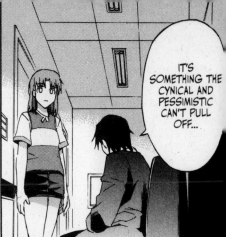

IT'S SOMETHING THE CYNICAL AND PESSIMISTIC CAN'T PULL OFF...
SPEAKING FROM EXPERI-ENCE.
YOU'RE AMAZING.
OH? I, UH...
WAS THAT A COMPLI-MENT?
EVEN SO...

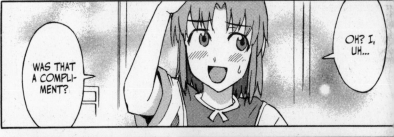

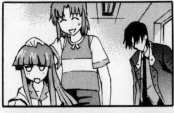

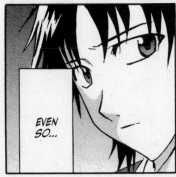

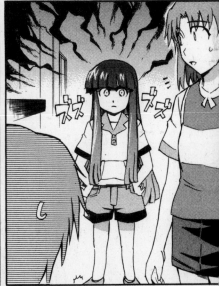

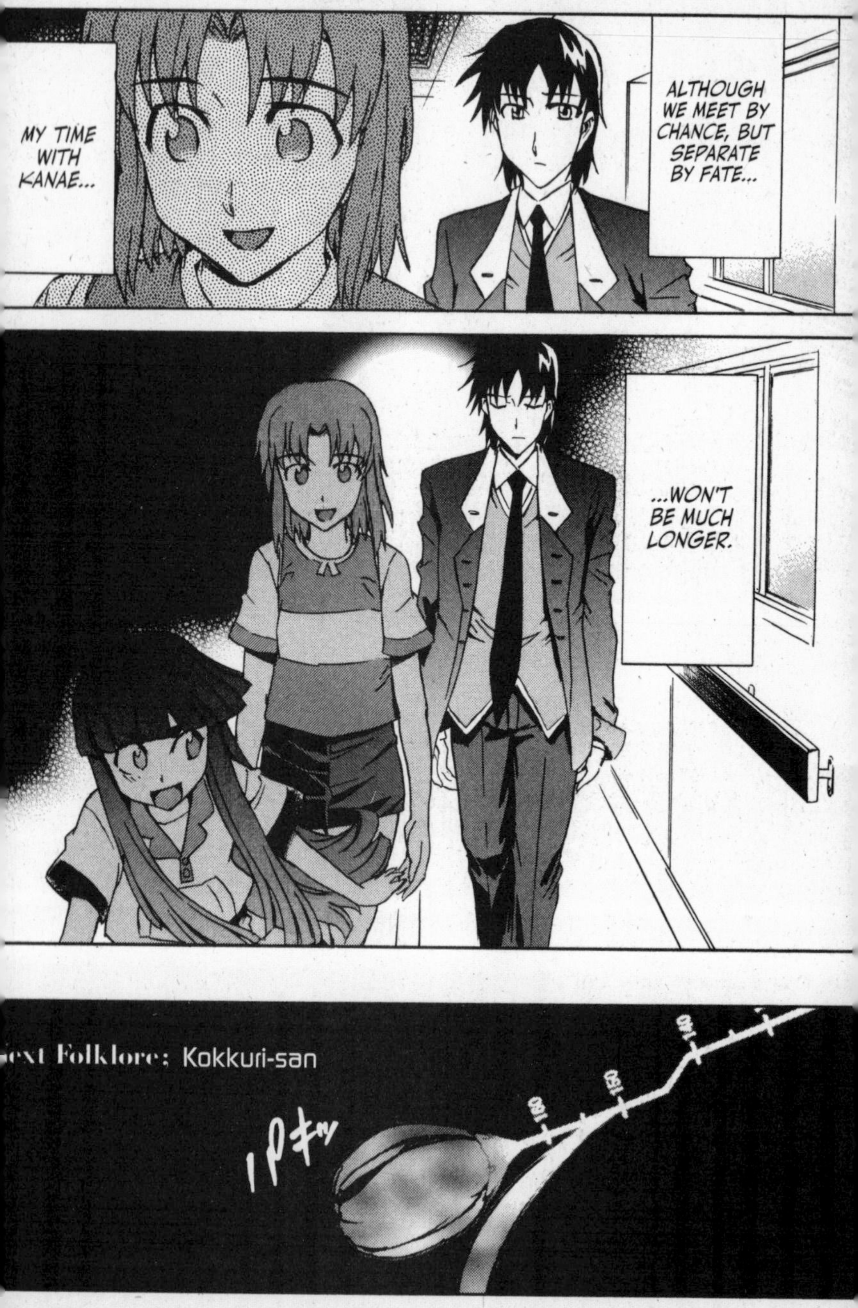
ALTHOUGH WE MEET BY CHANCE, BUT SEPARATE BY FATE...
MY TIME WITH KANAE...
...WON'T BE MUCH LONGER.
ext Folklore: Kokkuri-san
パキッ

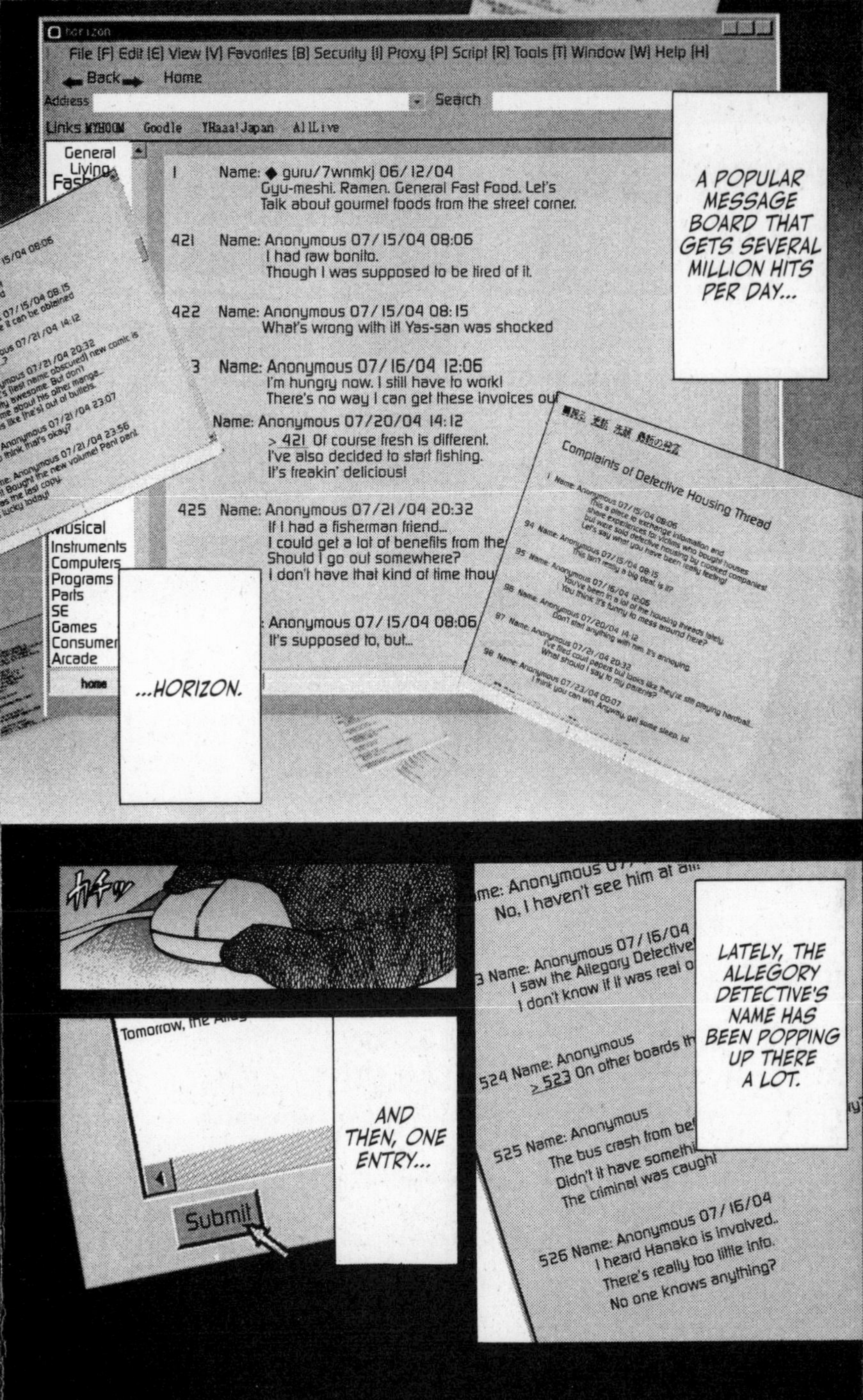
A POPULAR MESSAGE BOARD THAT GETS SEVERAL MILLION HITS PER DAY...
File [F] Edit [E] View [V] Favorites [B] Security [I] Proxy [P] Script [R] Tools [T] Window [W] Help [H]
Back Home
Address Search
Links Goodle YHaaa!Japan AllLive
1 Name: ◆ guru/7wnmkj 06/12/04
Gyu-meshi. Ramen. General Fast Food. Let's Talk about gourmet foods from the street corner.
421 Name: Anonymous 07/15/04 08:06
I had raw bonito.
Though I was supposed to be tired of it.
422 Name: Anonymous 07/15/04 08:15
What's wrong with it! Yas-san was shocked
Name: Anonymous 07/16/04 12:06
I'm hungry now. I still have to work!
There's no way I can get these invoices ou
Name: Anonymous 07/20/04 14:12
> 421 Of course fresh is different.
I've also decided to start fishing.
It's freakin' delicious!
425 Name: Anonymous 07/21/04 20:32
If I had a fisherman friend...
I could get a lot of benefits from the
Should I go out somewhere?
I don't have that kind of time thou
Anonymous 07/15/04 08:06
It's supposed to, but...
General
Living
Musical Instruments
Computers
Programs
Parts
SE
Games
Consumer
Arcade
home
Complaints of Defective Housing Thread
...HORIZON.
LATELY, THE ALLEGORY DETECTIVE'S NAME HAS BEEN POPPING UP THERE A LOT.
me: Anonymous
No, I haven't see him at all!
3 Name: Anonymous 07/16/04
I saw the Allegory Detective
I don't know if it was real o
524 Name: Anonymous
> 523 On other boards th
525 Name: Anonymous
The bus crash from be
Didn't it have somethi
The criminal was caught
526 Name: Anonymous 07/16/04
I heard Hanako is involved.
There's really too little info.
No one knows anything?
カチッ
Tomorrow, the
Submit
AND THEN, ONE ENTRY...

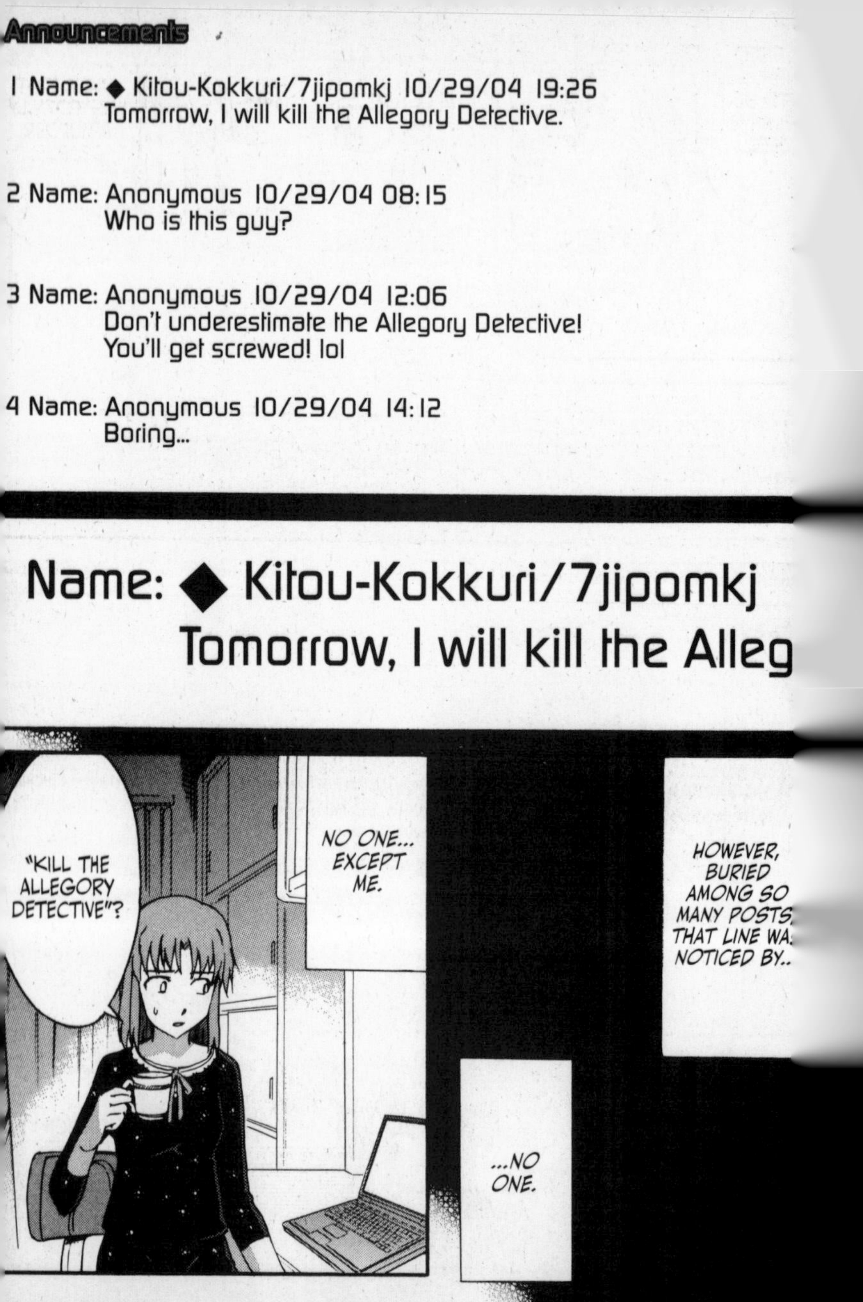
Announcements
1 Name: ◆ Kitou-Kokkuri/7jipomkj 10/29/04 19:26
Tomorrow, I will kill the Allegory Detective.
2 Name: Anonymous 10/29/04 08:15
Who is this guy?
3 Name: Anonymous 10/29/04 12:06
Don't underestimate the Allegory Detective!
You'll get screwed! lol
4 Name: Anonymous 10/29/04 14:12
Boring...
Name: ◆ Kitou-Kokkuri/7jipomkj
Tomorrow, I will kill the Alleg
HOWEVER, BURIED AMONG SO MANY POSTS THAT LINE WA NOTICED BY..
...NO ONE.
NO ONE... EXCEPT ME.
"KILL THE ALLEGORY DETECTIVE"?

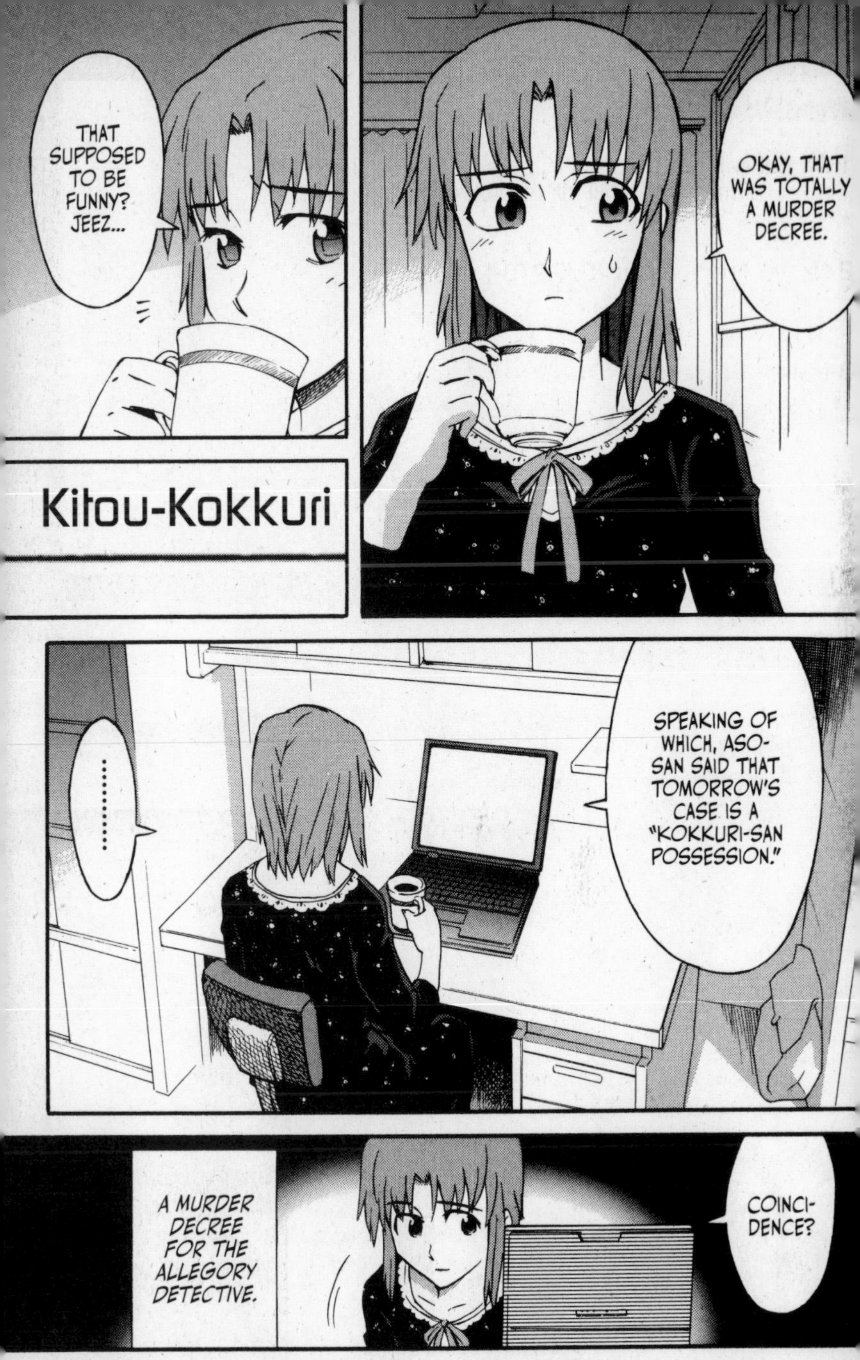

OKAY, THAT WAS TOTALLY A MURDER DECREE.
THAT SUPPOSED TO BE FUNNY? JEEZ...
Kitou-Kokkuri
SPEAKING OF WHICH, ASO-SAN SAID THAT TOMORROW'S CASE IS A "KOKKURI-SAN POSSESSION."
....
COINCI-DENCE?
A MURDER DECREE FOR THE ALLEGORY DETECTIVE.

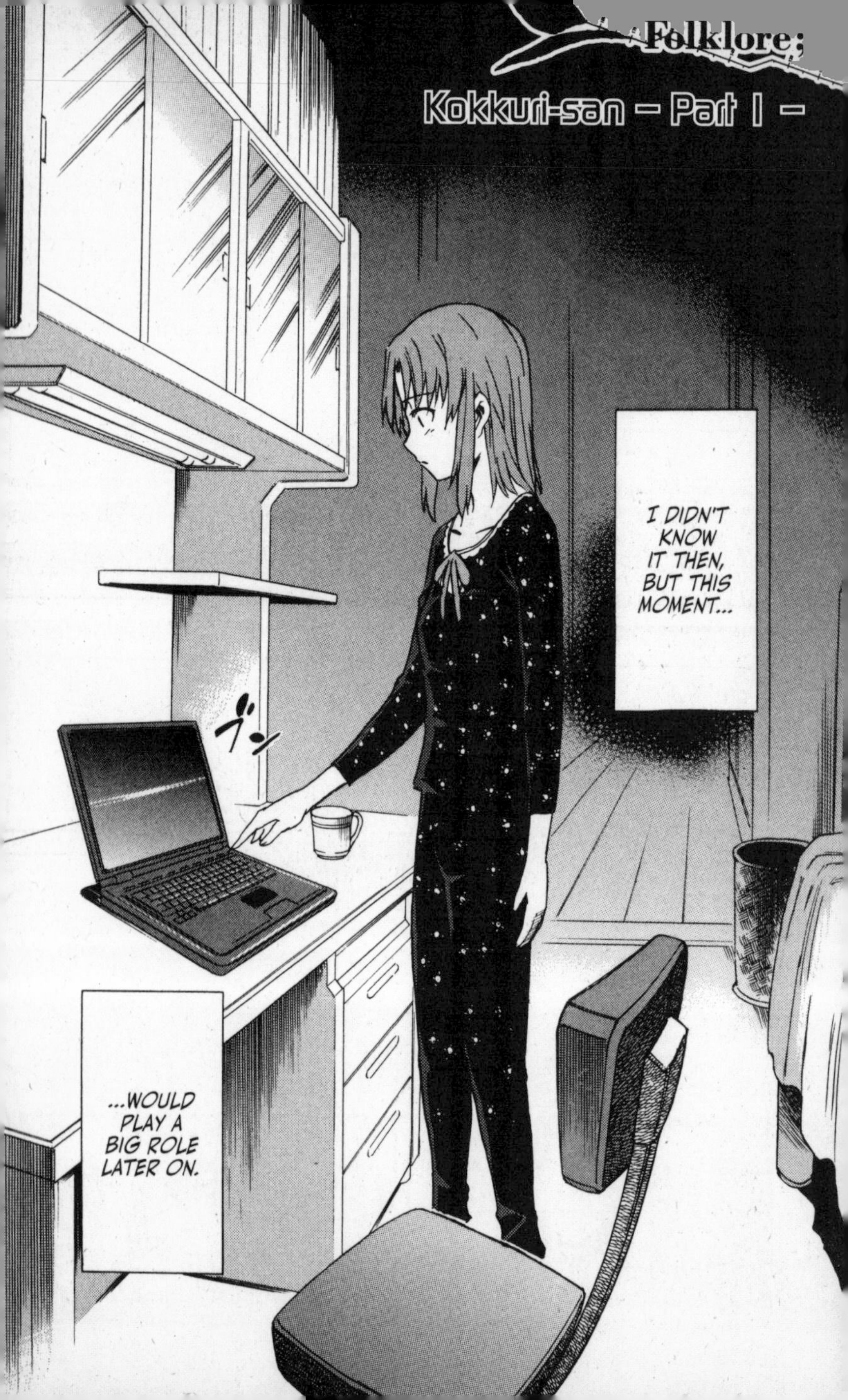
Folklore;
Kokkuri-san – Part 1 –
I DIDN'T KNOW IT THEN, BUT THIS MOMENT...
ブン
...WOULD PLAY A BIG ROLE LATER ON.

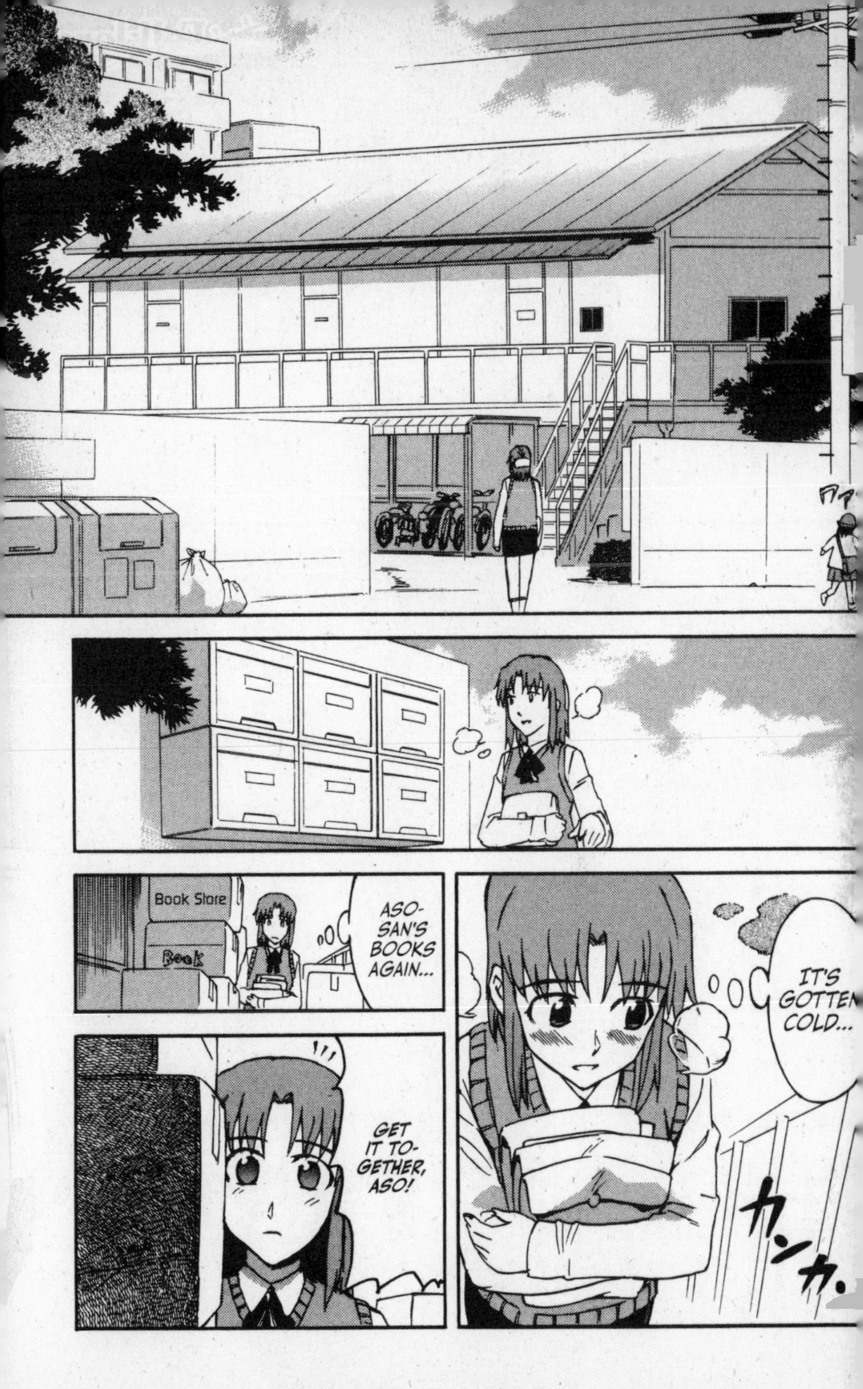
ワァ
IT'S GOTTEN COLD...
カンカ
Book Store
Book
ASO-SAN'S BOOKS AGAIN...
GET IT TO-GETHER, ASO!

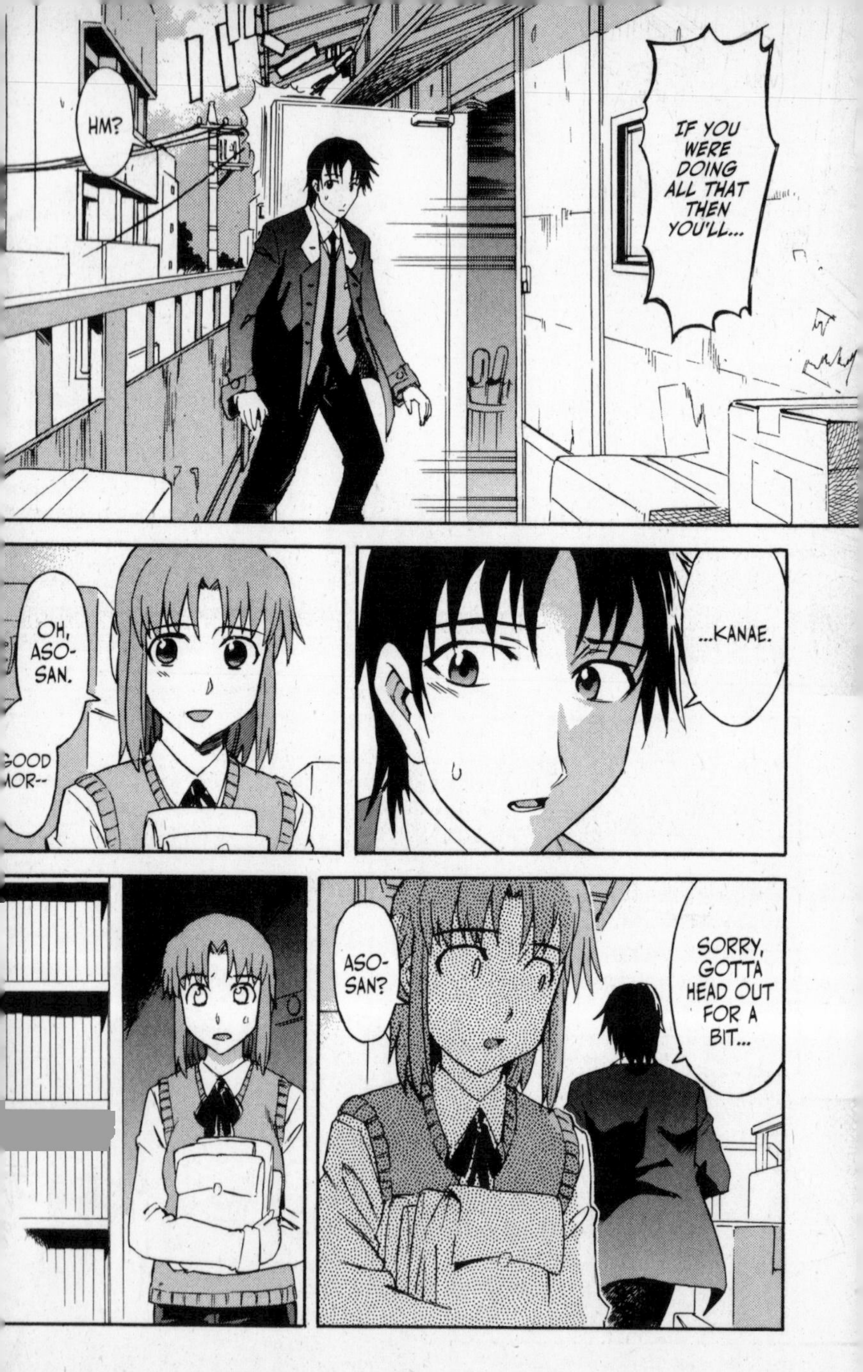
IF YOU WERE DOING ALL THAT THEN YOU'LL...
HM?
...KANAE.
OH, ASO-SAN.
GOOD MOR--
SORRY, GOTTA HEAD OUT FOR A BIT...
ASO-SAN?

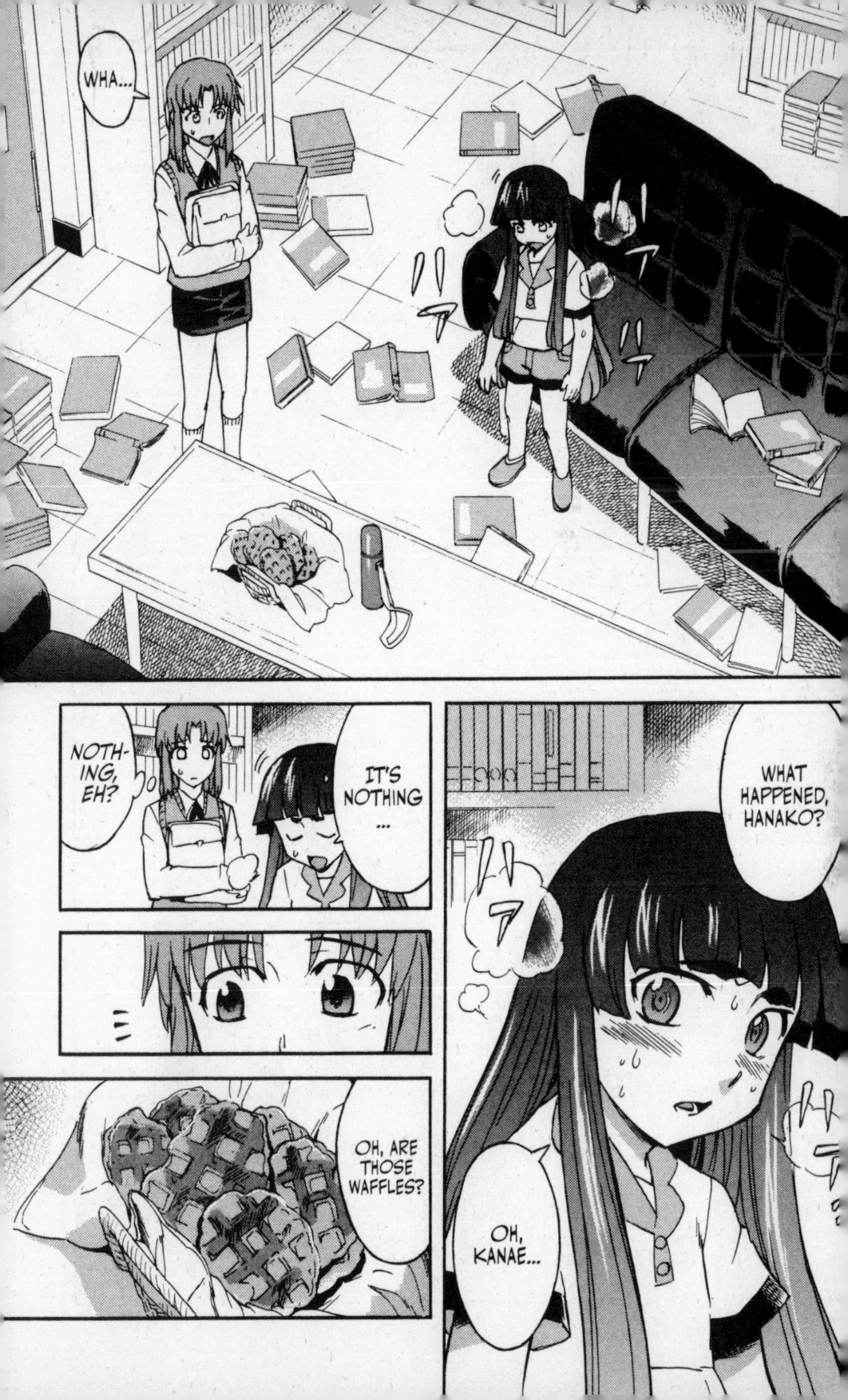
WHA...
WHAT HAPPENED, HANAKO?
OH, KANAE...
IT'S NOTHING ...
NOTHING, EH?
OH, ARE THOSE WAFFLES?

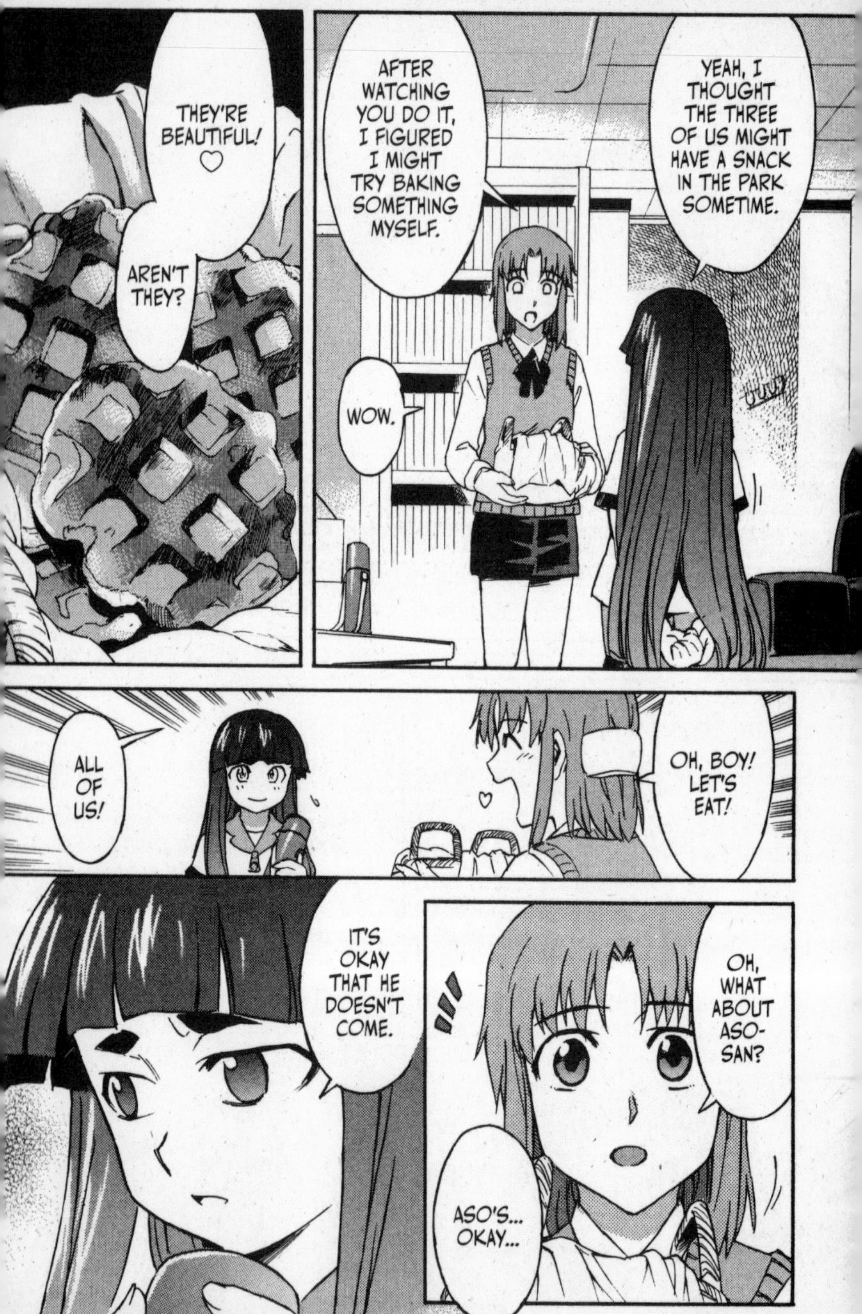

YEAH, I THOUGHT THE THREE OF US MIGHT HAVE A SNACK IN THE PARK SOMETIME.
AFTER WATCHING YOU DO IT, I FIGURED I MIGHT TRY BAKING SOMETHING MYSELF.
WOW.
THEY'RE BEAUTIFUL! ♡
AREN'T THEY?
OH, BOY! LET'S EAT!
ALL OF US!
OH, WHAT ABOUT ASO-SAN?
ASO'S... OKAY...
IT'S OKAY THAT HE DOESN'T COME.

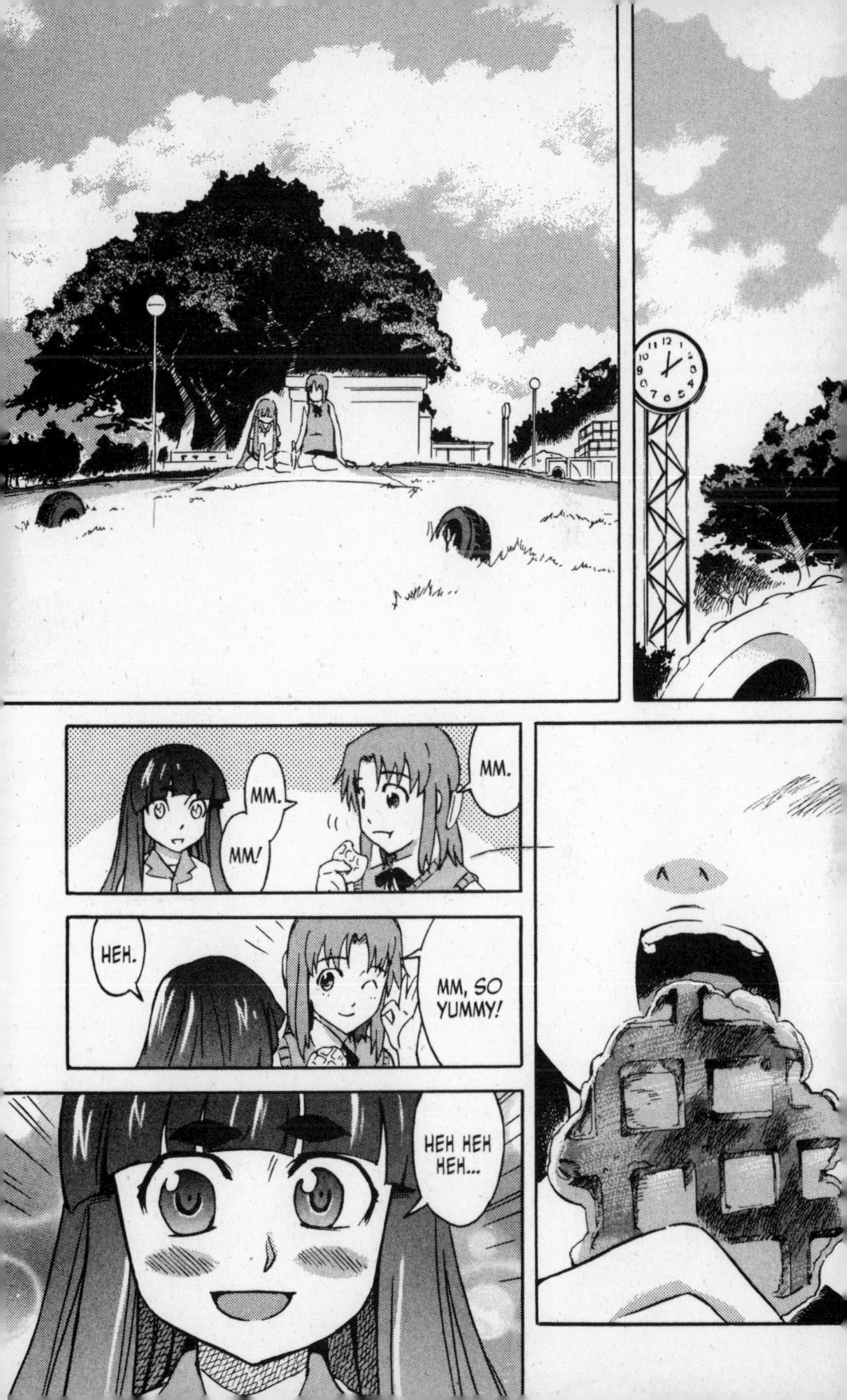
MM.
MM.
MM!
MM, SO YUMMY!
HEH.
HEH HEH HEH...

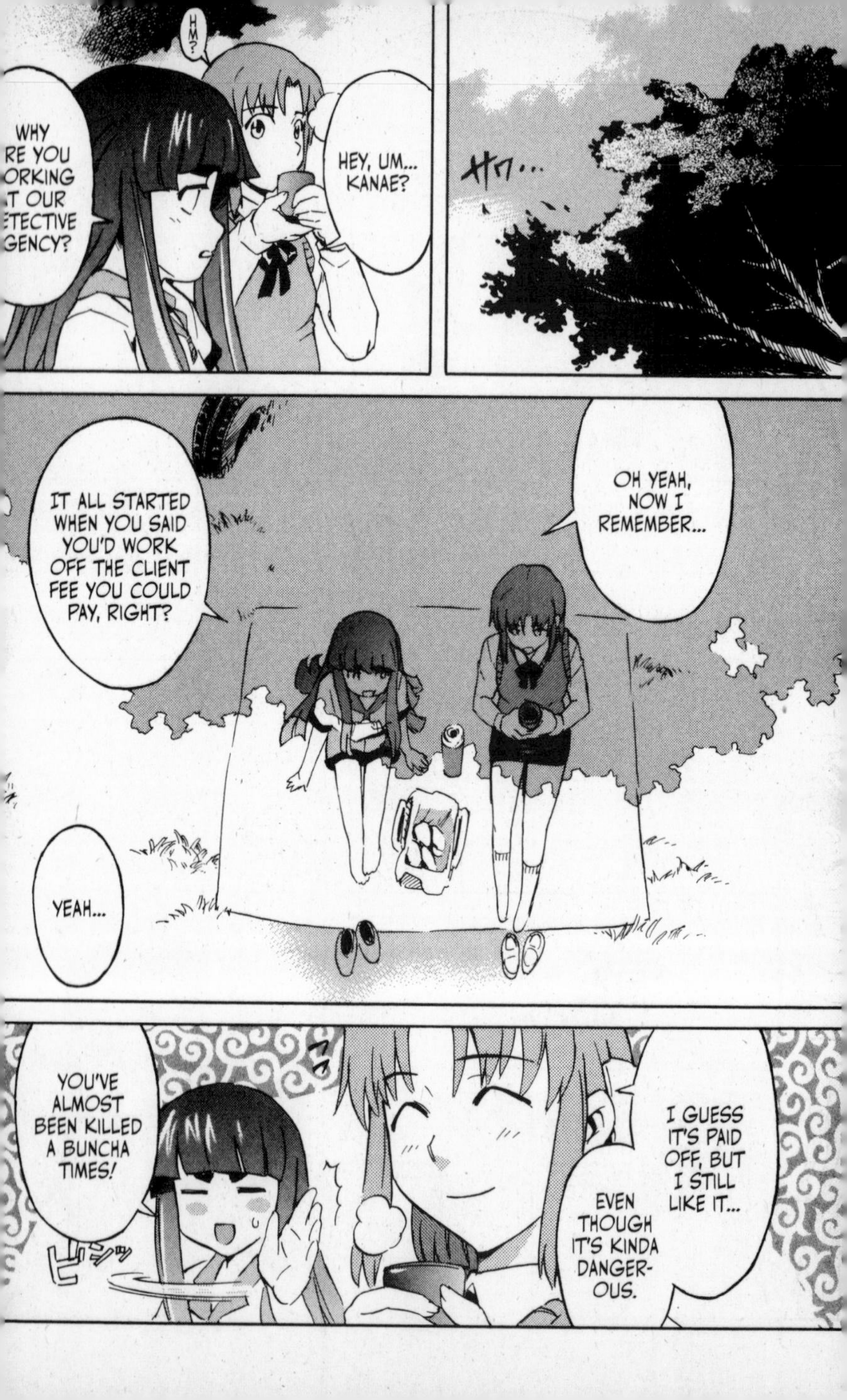
サワ…
HEY, UM... KANAE?
HM?
WHY RE YOU ORKING T OUR ETECTIVE GENCY?
OH YEAH, NOW I REMEMBER...
IT ALL STARTED WHEN YOU SAID YOU'D WORK OFF THE CLIENT FEE YOU COULD PAY, RIGHT?
YEAH...
I GUESS IT'S PAID OFF, BUT I STILL LIKE IT...
EVEN THOUGH IT'S KINDA DANGER-OUS.
YOU'VE ALMOST BEEN KILLED A BUNCHA TIMES!
ビシッ

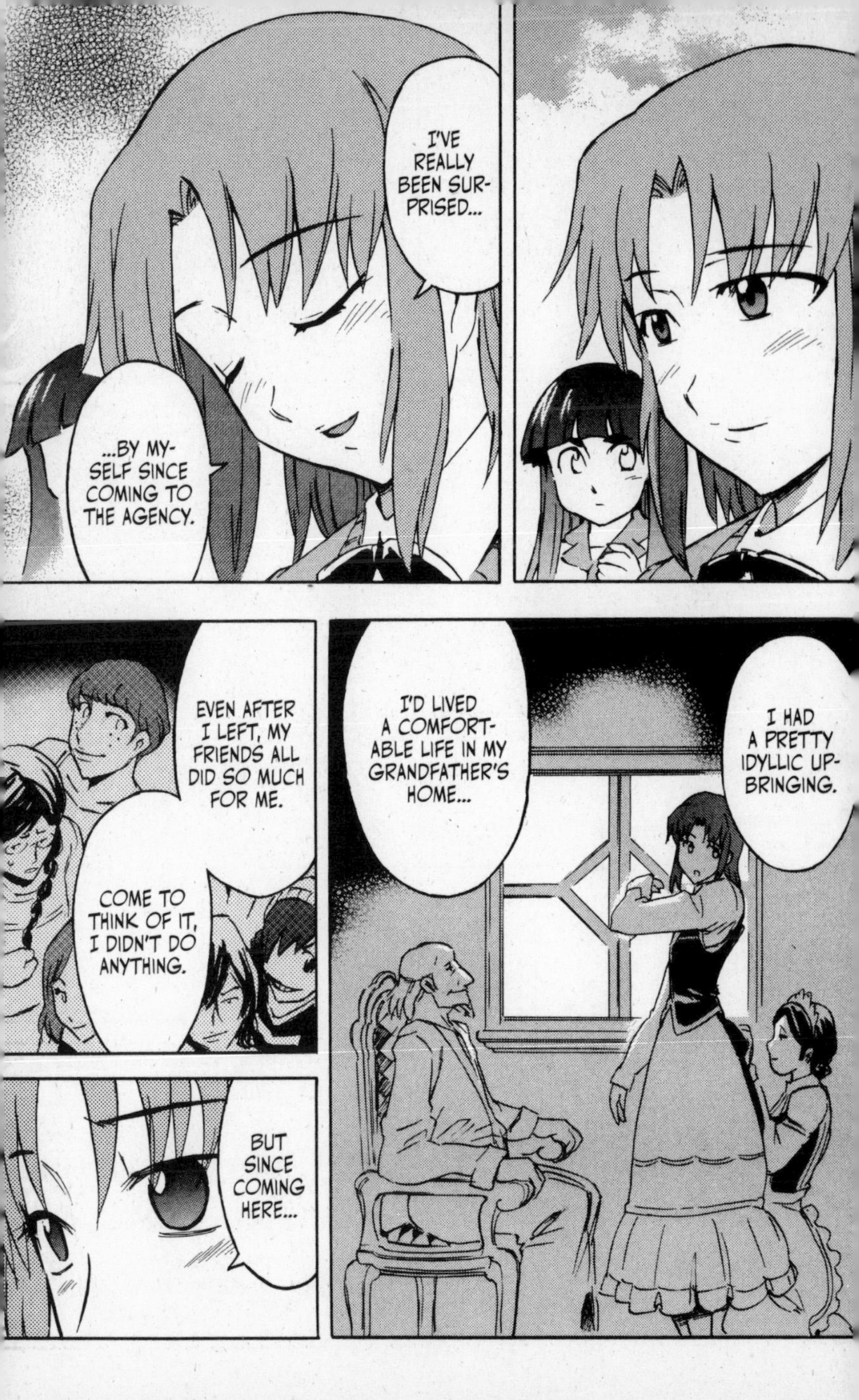
I'VE REALLY BEEN SUR-PRISED...
...BY MY-SELF SINCE COMING TO THE AGENCY.
I HAD A PRETTY IDYLLIC UP-BRINGING.
I'D LIVED A COMFORT-ABLE LIFE IN MY GRANDFATHER'S HOME...
EVEN AFTER I LEFT, MY FRIENDS ALL DID SO MUCH FOR ME.
COME TO THINK OF IT, I DIDN'T DO ANYTHING.
BUT SINCE COMING HERE...

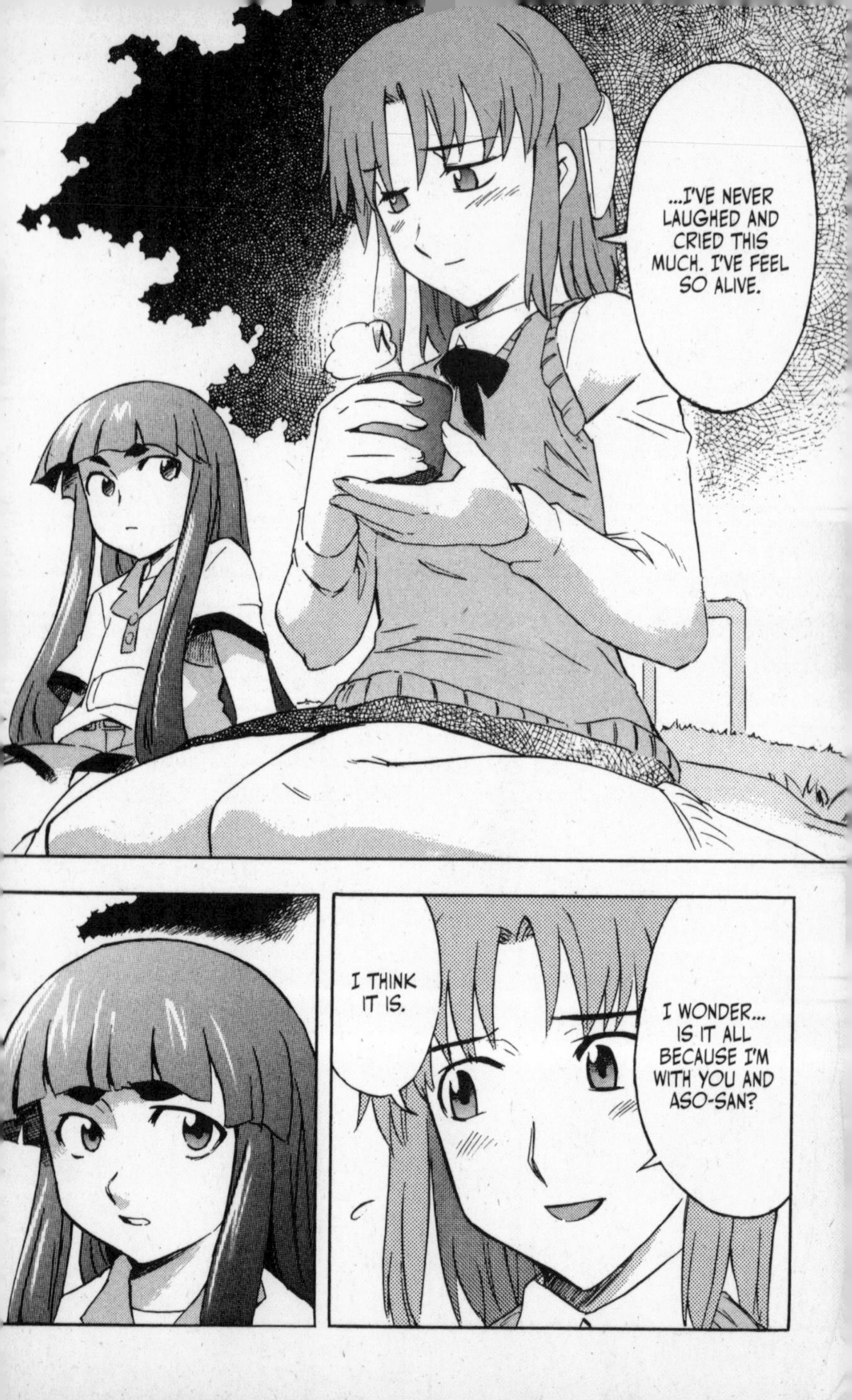
...I'VE NEVER LAUGHED AND CRIED THIS MUCH. I'VE FEEL SO ALIVE.
I WONDER... IS IT ALL BECAUSE I'M WITH YOU AND ASO-SAN?
I THINK IT IS.

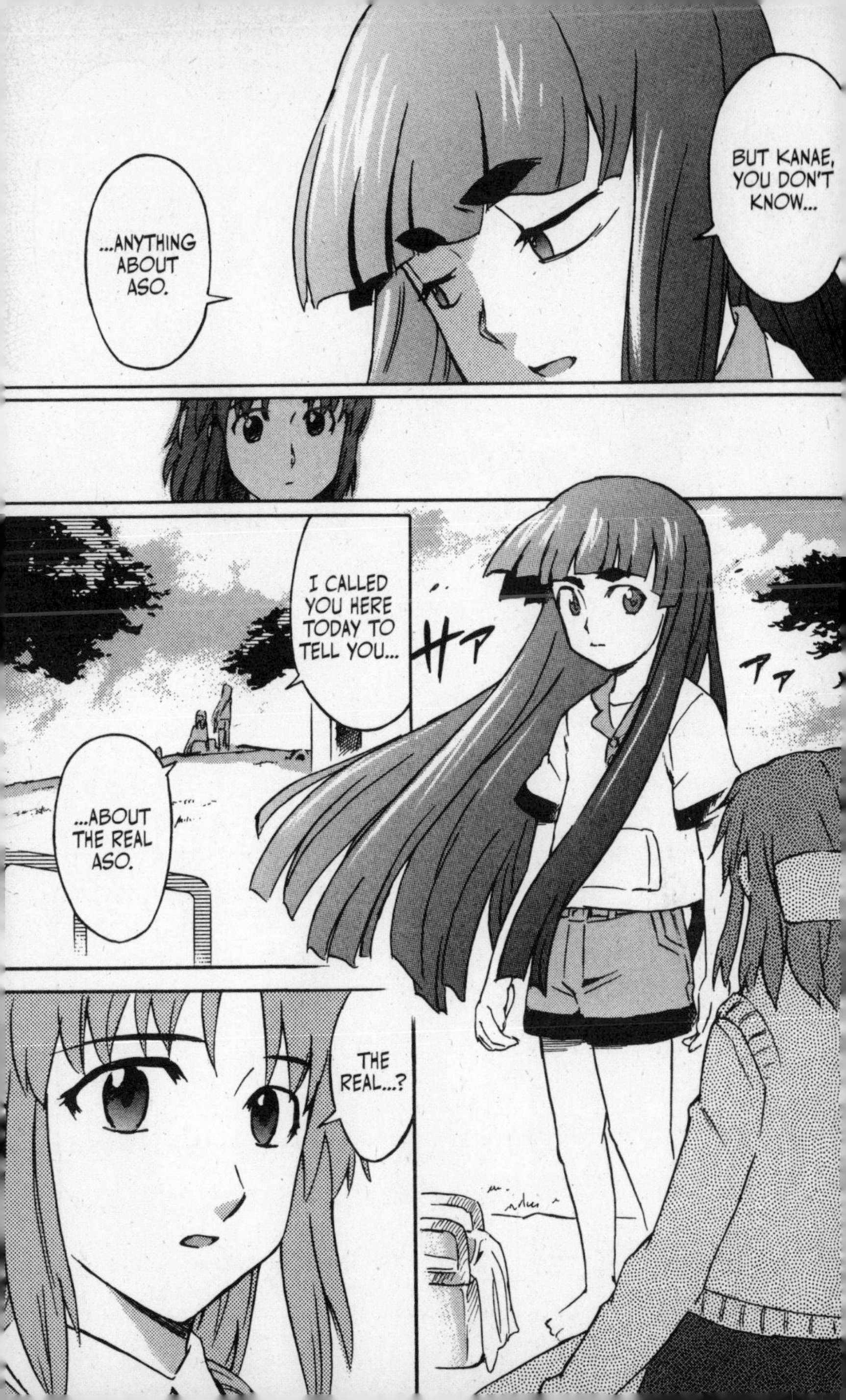
BUT KANAE, YOU DON'T KNOW...
...ANYTHING ABOUT ASO.
ァァ
サァ
I CALLED YOU HERE TODAY TO TELL YOU...
...ABOUT THE REAL ASO.
THE REAL...?

KOKKURI-SAN...?

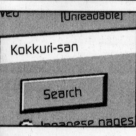

[Unreadable]

Kokkuri-san

Search

Japanese pages

MY CLIENT IS THE MOTHER OF A YOUNG GIRL WHO'S BEEN POSSESSED BY KOKKURI-SAN.

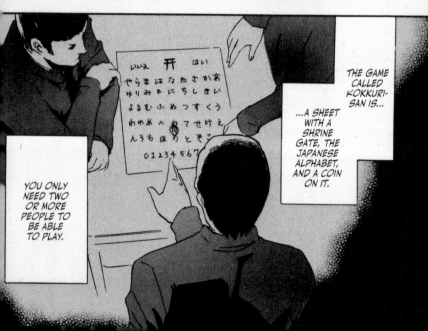

THE GAME CALLED KOKKURI-SAN IS...

...A SHEET WITH A SHRINE GATE, THE JAPANESE ALPHABET, AND A COIN ON IT.

YOU ONLY NEED TWO OR MORE PEOPLE TO BE ABLE TO PLAY.

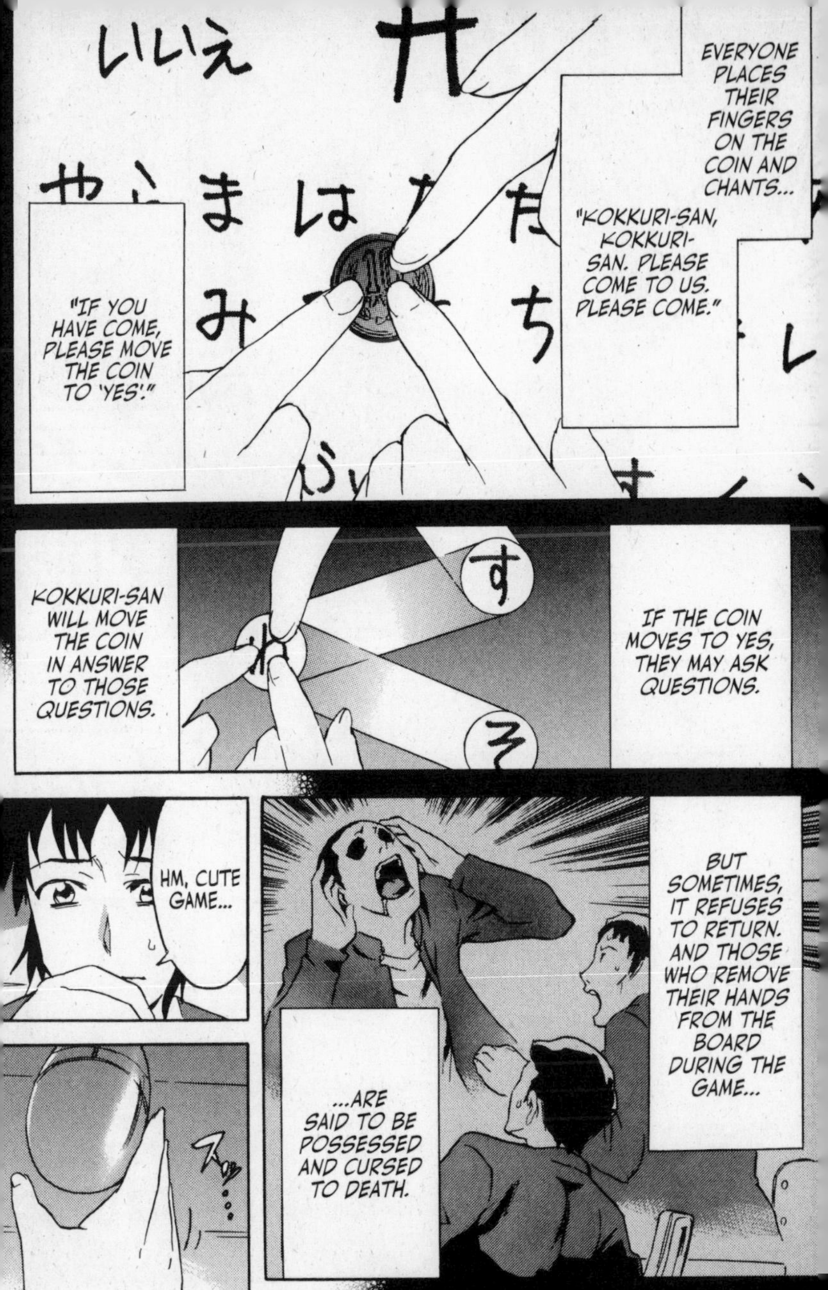
EVERYONE PLACES THEIR FINGERS ON THE COIN AND CHANTS...
"KOKKURI-SAN, KOKKURI-SAN. PLEASE COME TO US. PLEASE COME."
"IF YOU HAVE COME, PLEASE MOVE THE COIN TO 'YES'."
IF THE COIN MOVES TO YES, THEY MAY ASK QUESTIONS.
KOKKURI-SAN WILL MOVE THE COIN IN ANSWER TO THOSE QUESTIONS.
BUT SOMETIMES, IT REFUSES TO RETURN. AND THOSE WHO REMOVE THEIR HANDS FROM THE BOARD DURING THE GAME...
...ARE SAID TO BE POSSESSED AND CURSED TO DEATH.
HM, CUTE GAME...

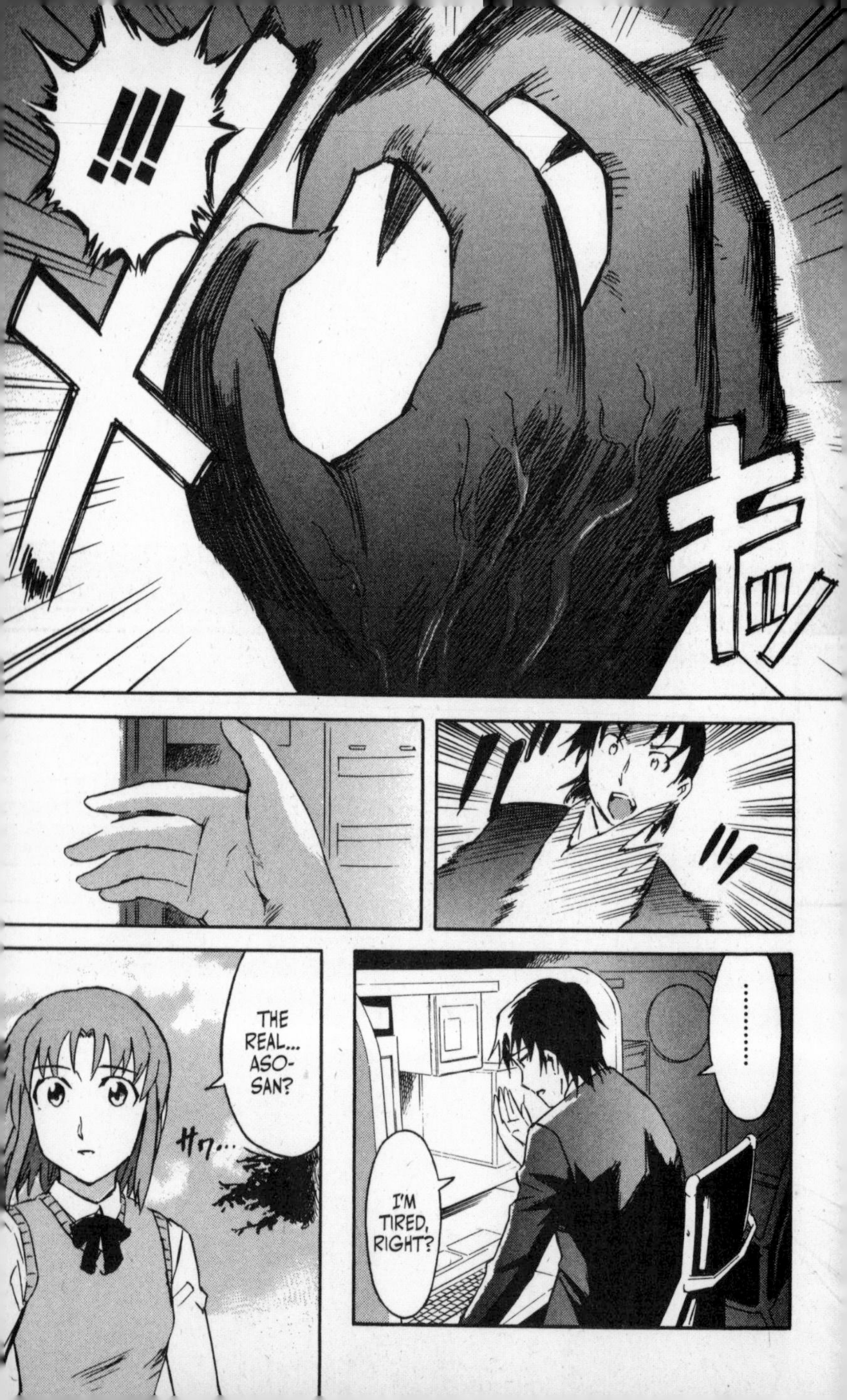
!!!
......
I'M TIRED, RIGHT?
THE REAL... ASO-SAN?

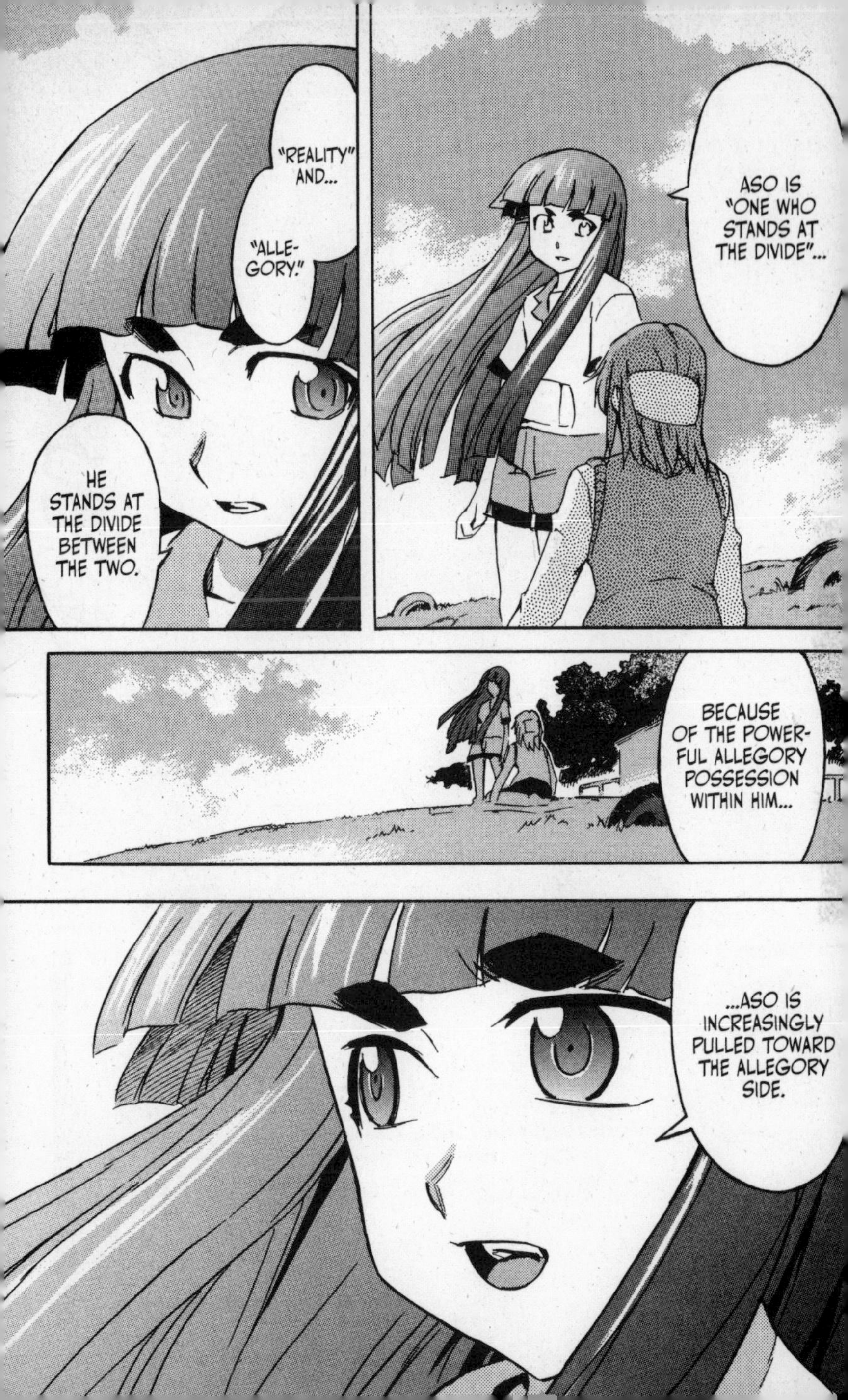
ASO IS "ONE WHO STANDS AT THE DIVIDE"...
"REALITY" AND...
"ALLE-GORY."
HE STANDS AT THE DIVIDE BETWEEN THE TWO.
BECAUSE OF THE POWER-FUL ALLEGORY POSSESSION WITHIN HIM...
...ASO IS INCREASINGLY PULLED TOWARD THE ALLEGORY SIDE.

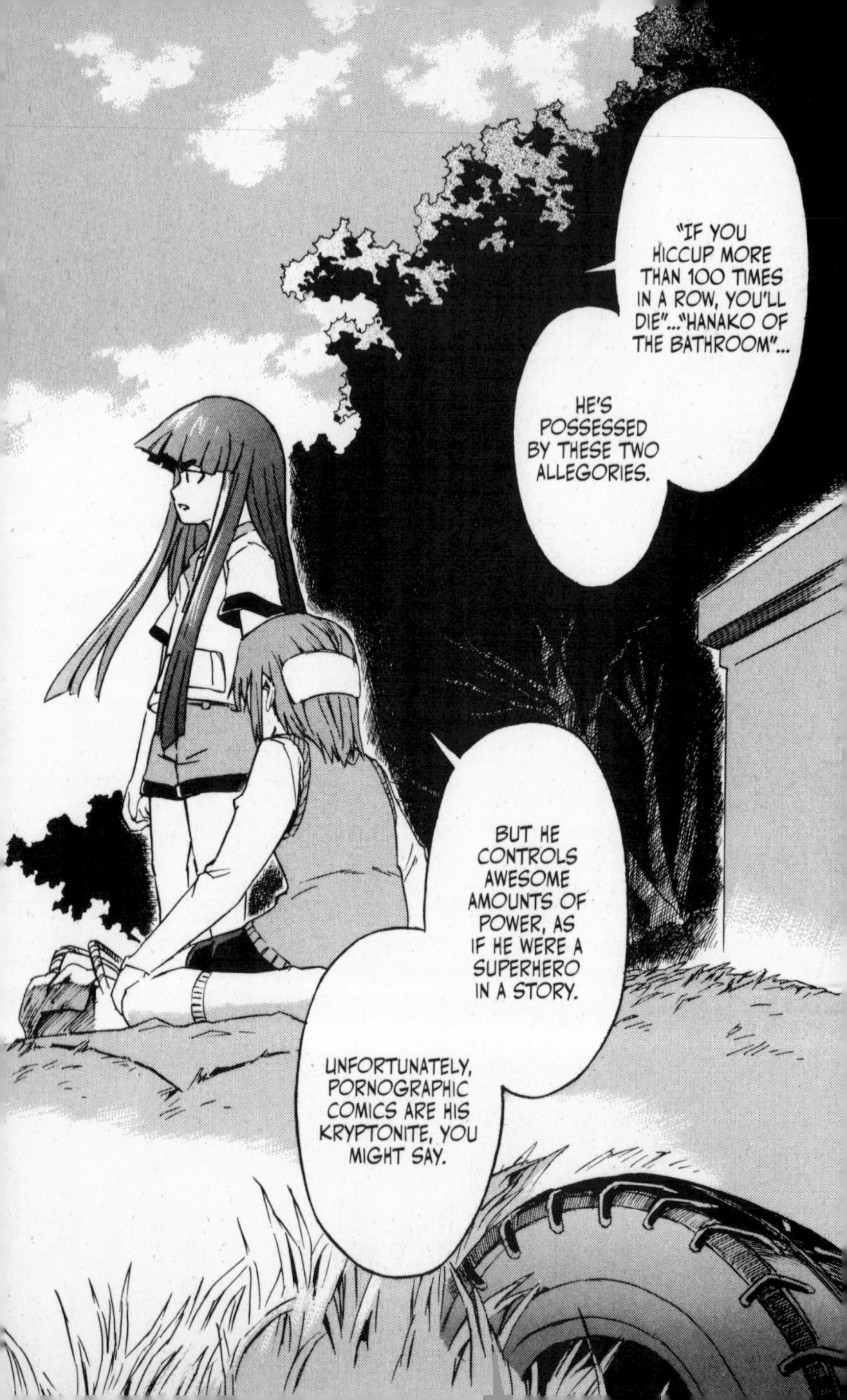
"IF YOU HICCUP MORE THAN 100 TIMES IN A ROW, YOU'LL DIE"..."HANAKO OF THE BATHROOM"...
HE'S POSSESSED BY THESE TWO ALLEGORIES.
BUT HE CONTROLS AWESOME AMOUNTS OF POWER, AS IF HE WERE A SUPERHERO IN A STORY.
UNFORTUNATELY, PORNOGRAPHIC COMICS ARE HIS KRYPTONITE, YOU MIGHT SAY.

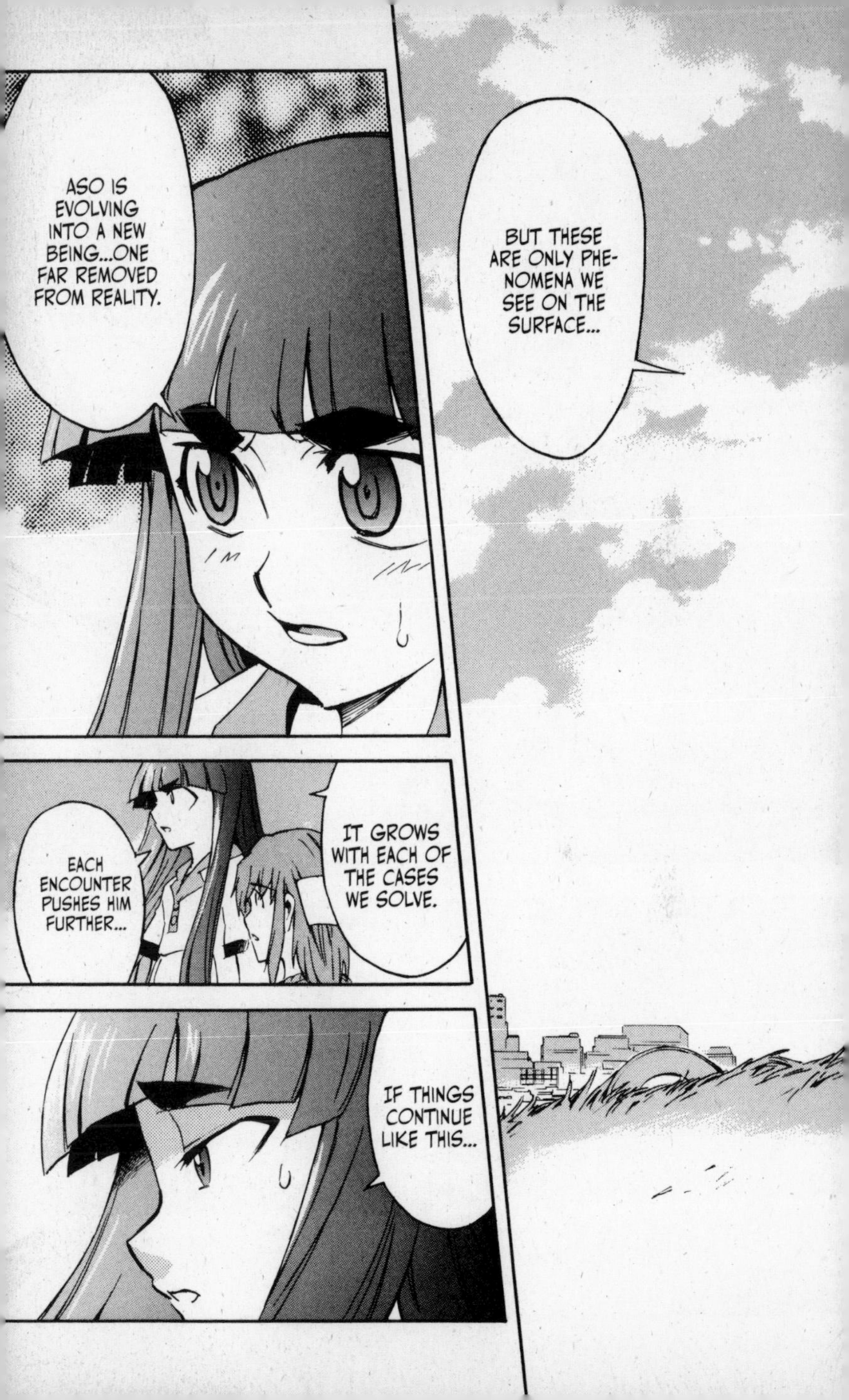
BUT THESE ARE ONLY PHE-NOMENA WE SEE ON THE SURFACE...
ASO IS EVOLVING INTO A NEW BEING...ONE FAR REMOVED FROM REALITY.
IT GROWS WITH EACH OF THE CASES WE SOLVE.
EACH ENCOUNTER PUSHES HIM FURTHER...
IF THINGS CONTINUE LIKE THIS...

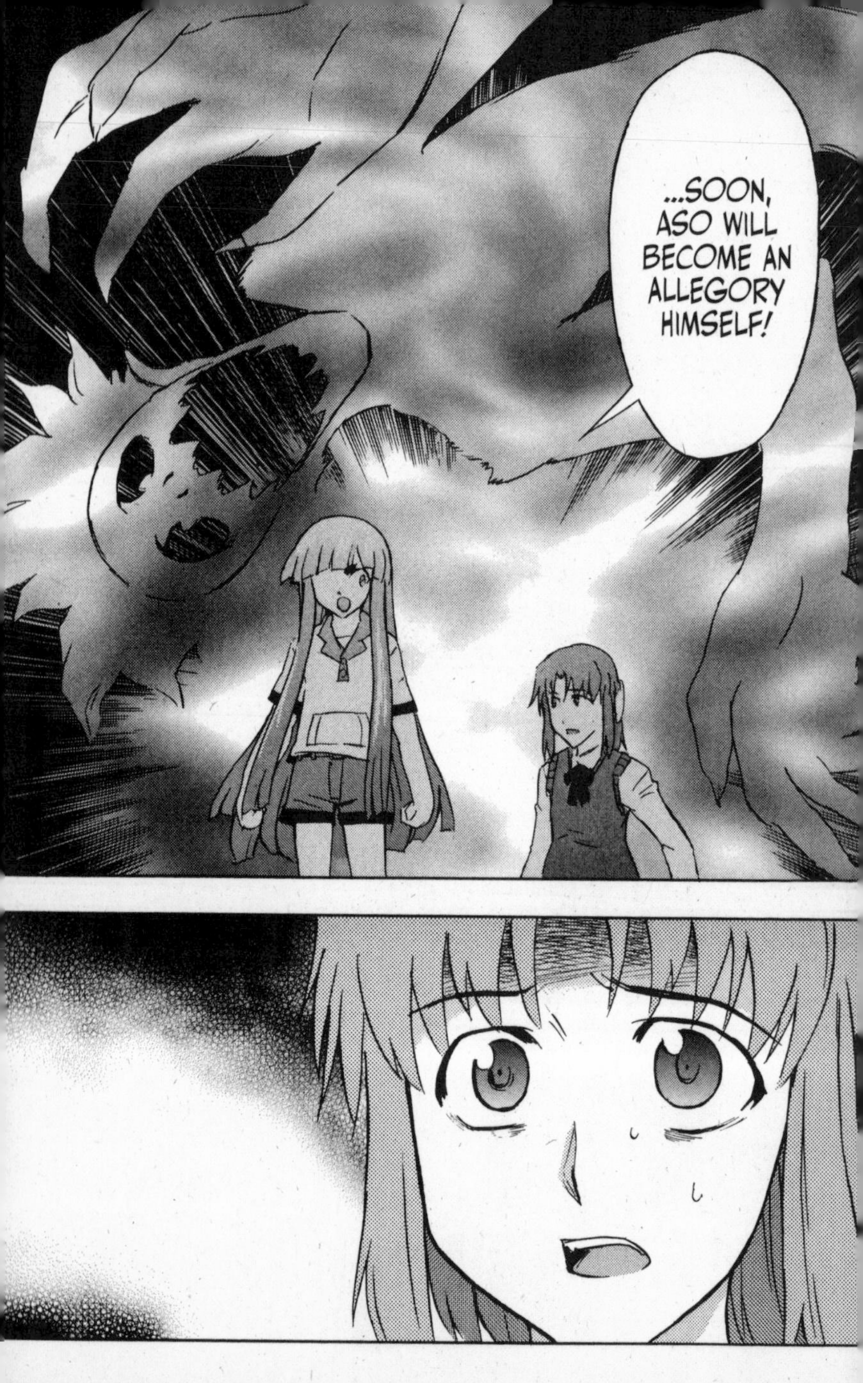
...SOON, ASO WILL BECOME AN ALLEGORY HIMSELF!

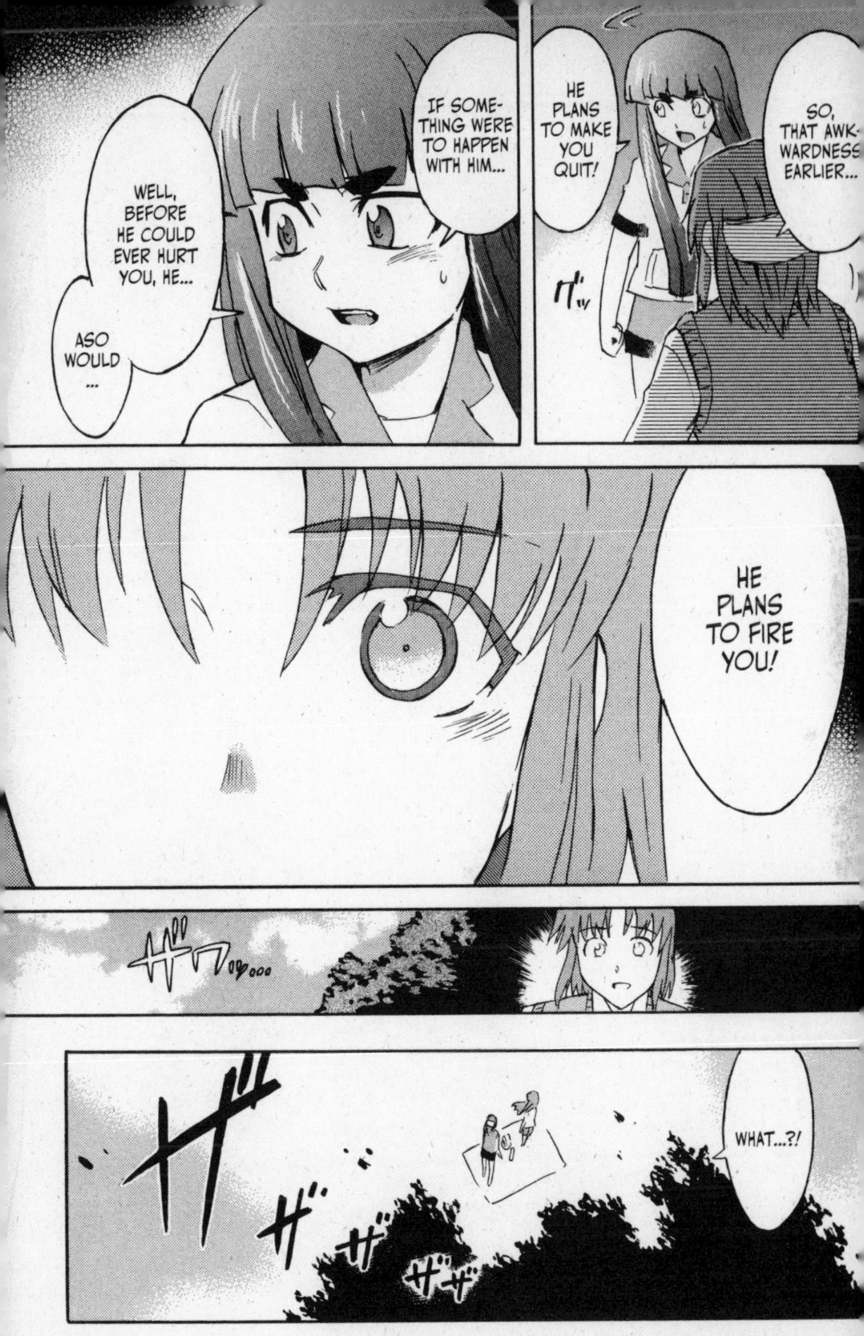
SO, THAT AWK-WARDNESS EARLIER...
HE PLANS TO MAKE YOU QUIT!
ガッ
IF SOME-THING WERE TO HAPPEN WITH HIM...
WELL, BEFORE HE COULD EVER HURT YOU, HE...
ASO WOULD ...
HE PLANS TO FIRE YOU!
ザワッ...
WHAT...?!
ザザザザ

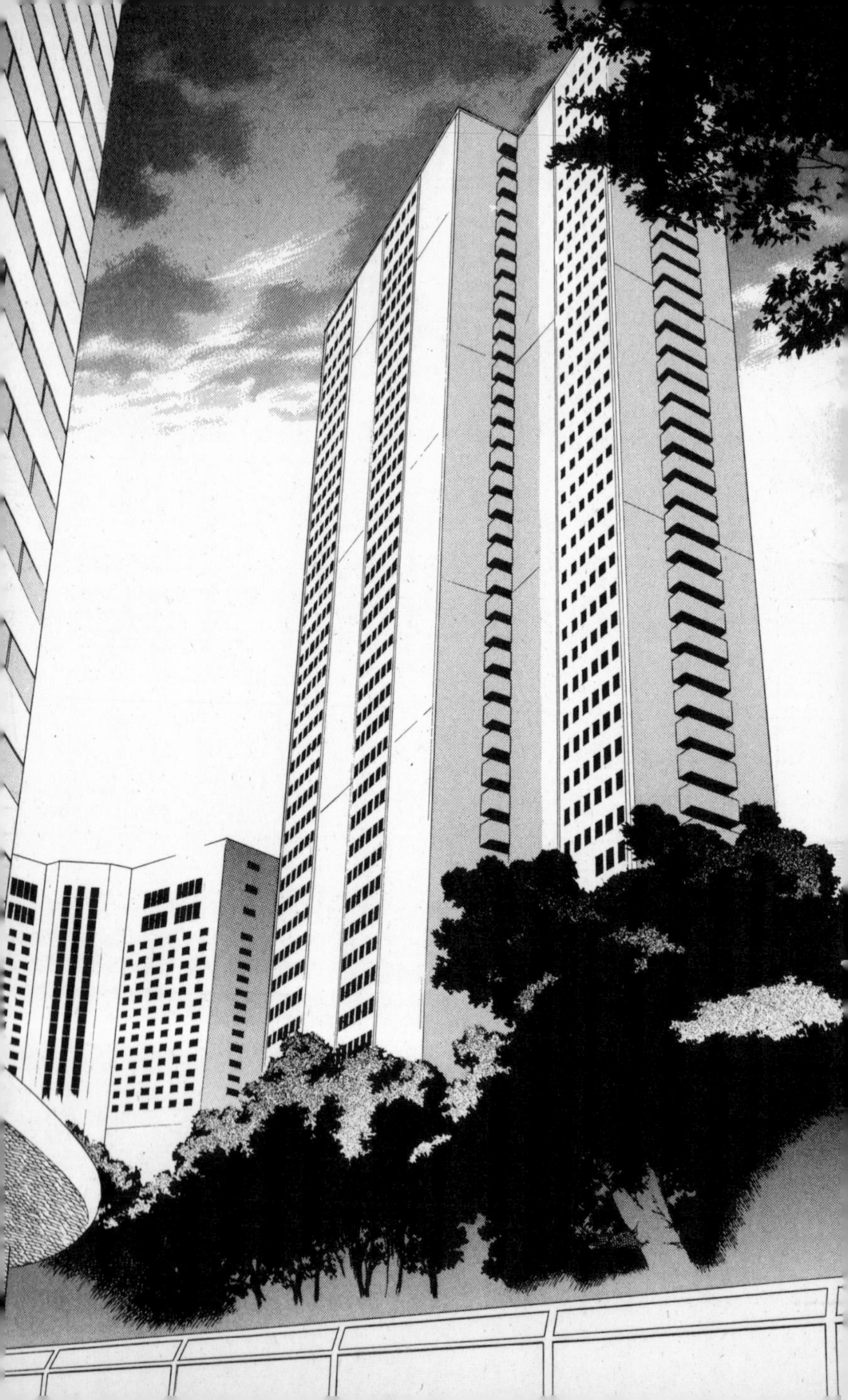

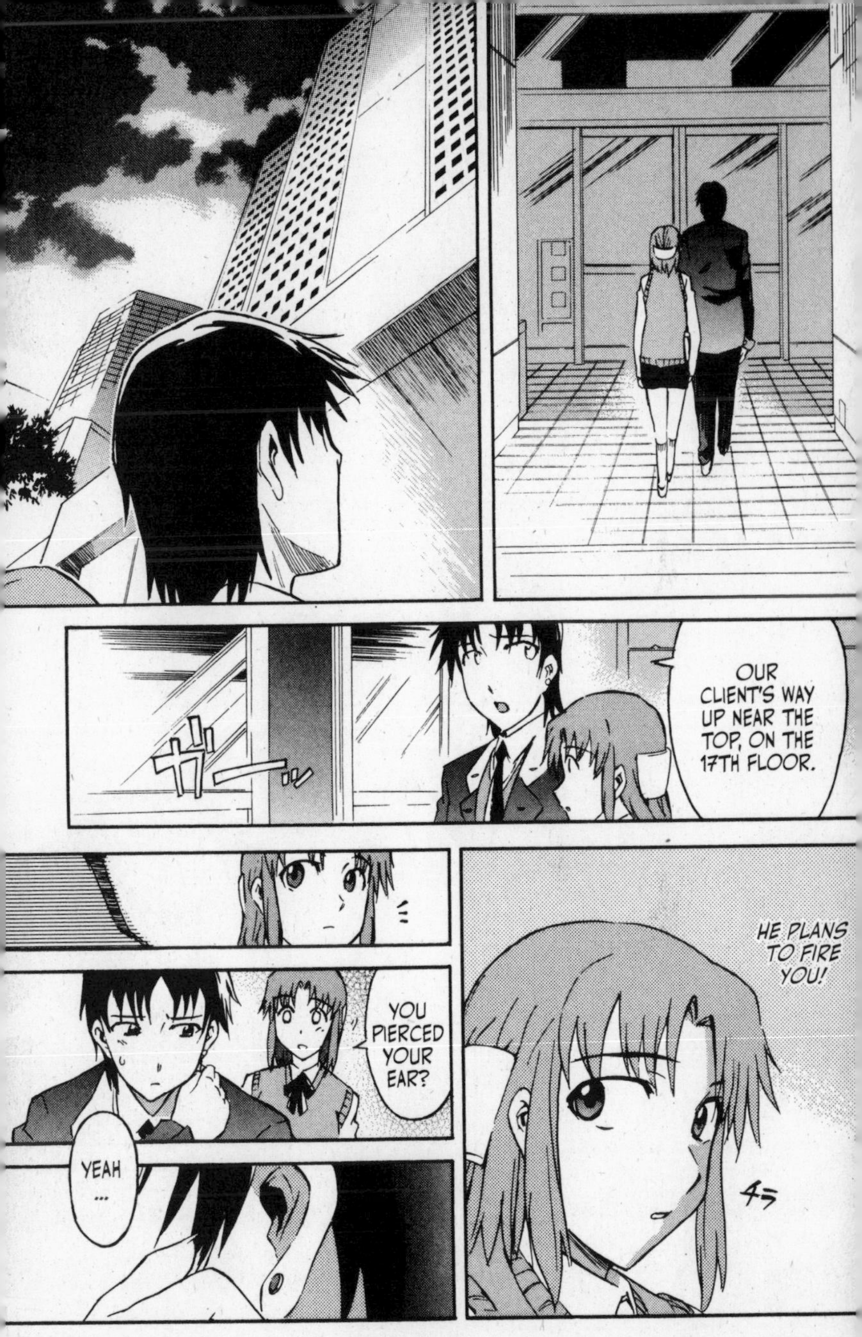
OUR CLIENT'S WAY UP NEAR THE TOP, ON THE 17TH FLOOR.
HE PLANS TO FIRE YOU!
YOU PIERCED YOUR EAR?
YEAH ...

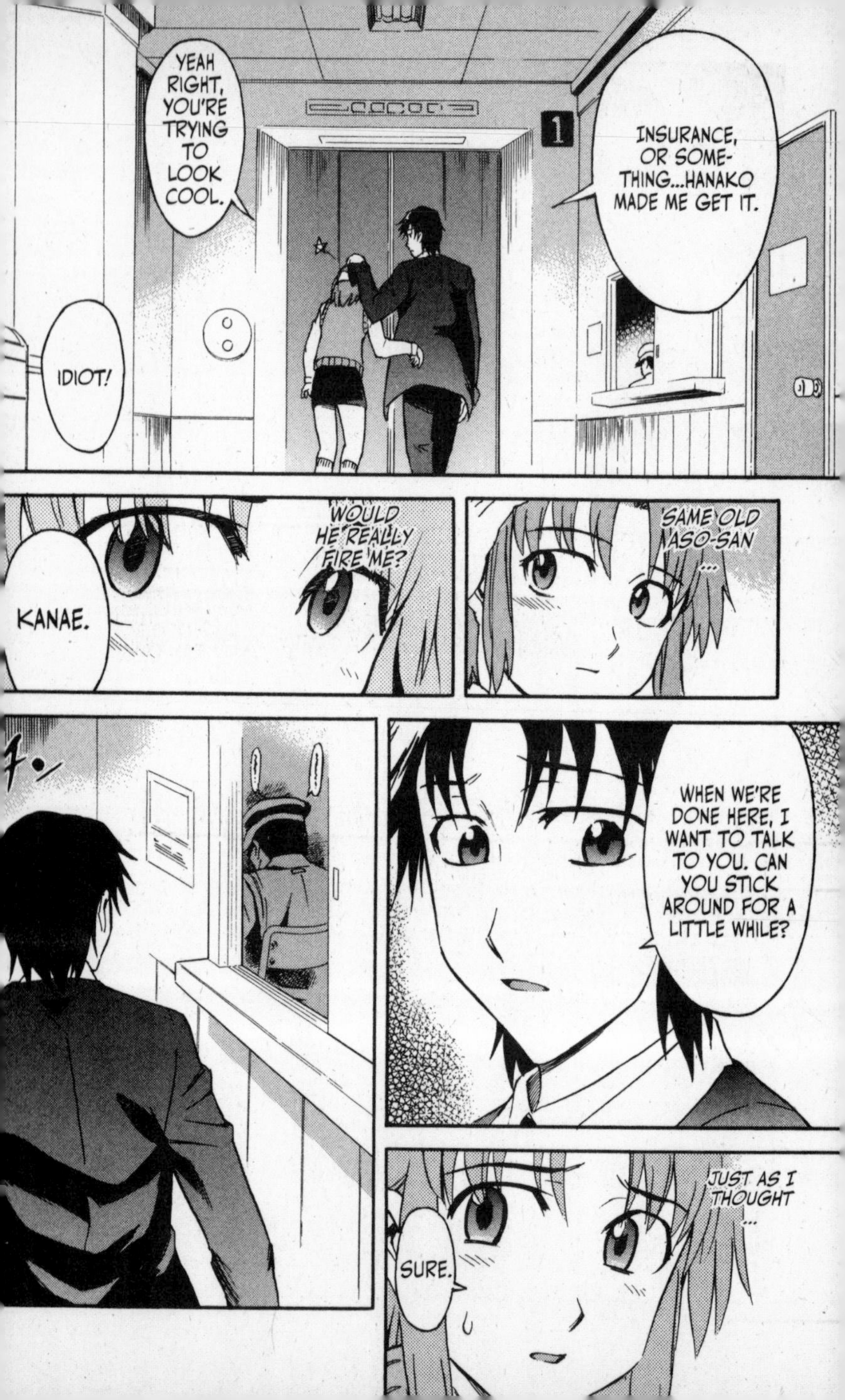
INSURANCE, OR SOME-THING...HANAKO MADE ME GET IT.
YEAH RIGHT, YOU'RE TRYING TO LOOK COOL.
IDIOT!
SAME OLD ASO-SAN ...
WOULD HE REALLY FIRE ME?
KANAE.
WHEN WE'RE DONE HERE, I WANT TO TALK TO YOU. CAN YOU STICK AROUND FOR A LITTLE WHILE?
JUST AS I THOUGHT ...
SURE.

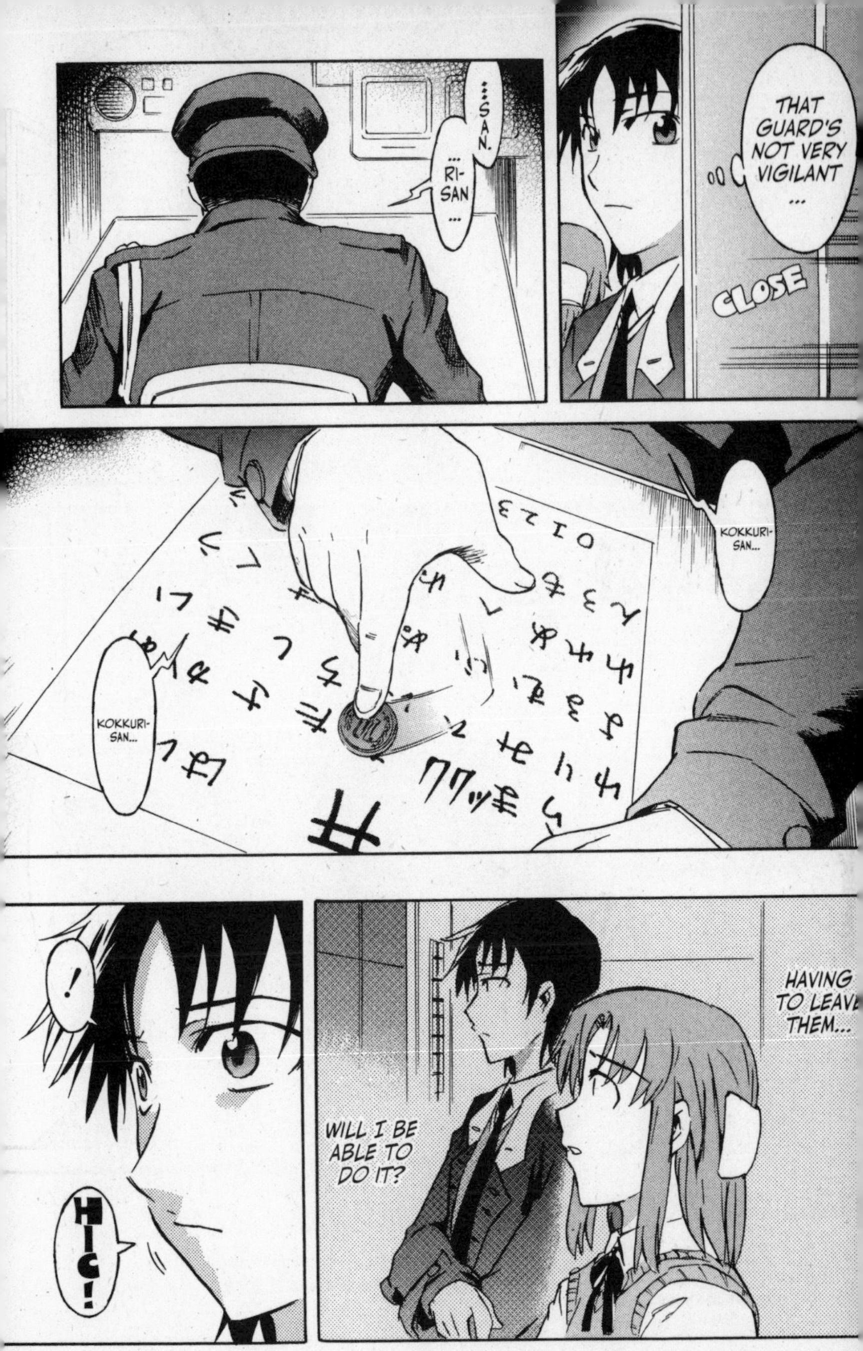

THAT GUARD'S NOT VERY VIGILANT ...
CLOSE
...SAN.
...RI-SAN...
KOKKURI-SAN...
KOKKURI-SAN...
HAVING TO LEAVE THEM...
WILL I BE ABLE TO DO IT?
!
HIC!

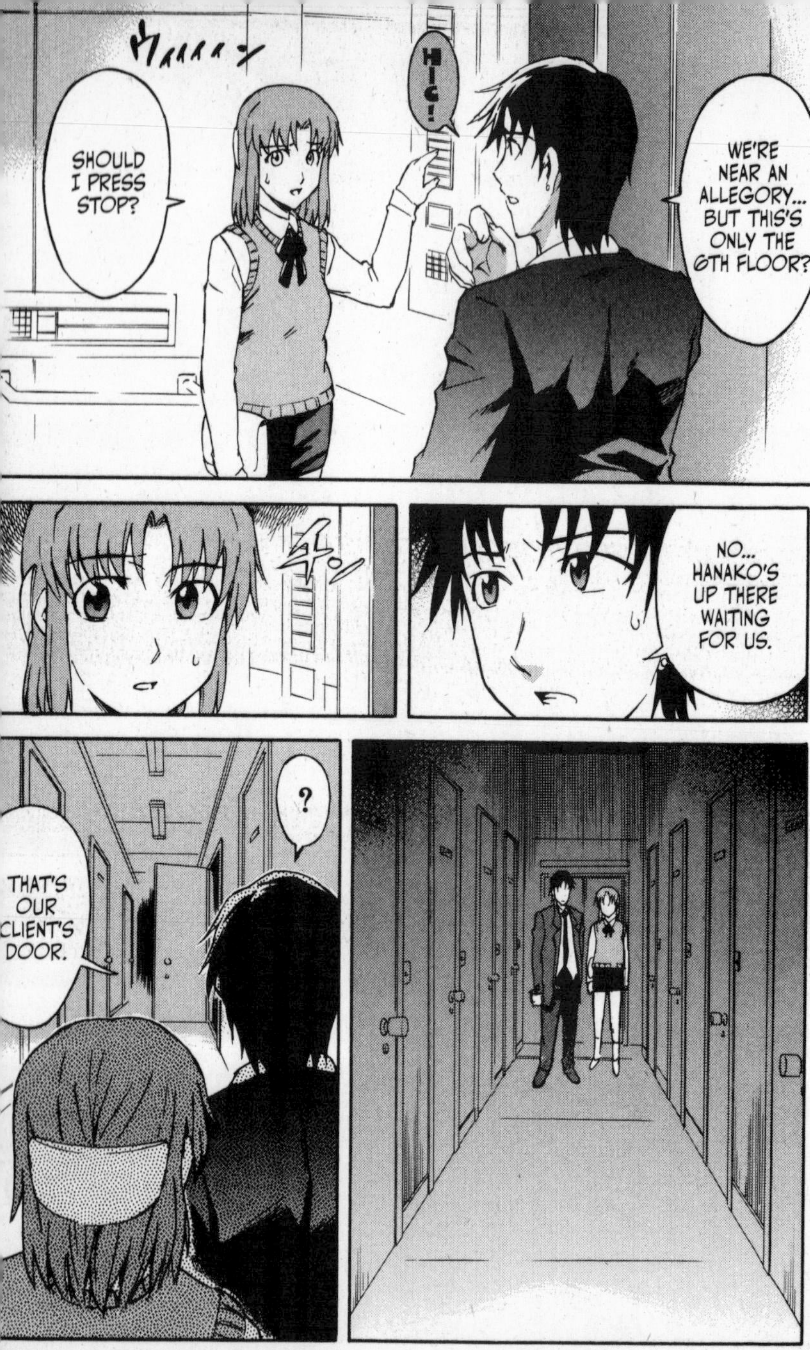
WE'RE NEAR AN ALLEGORY... BUT THIS'S ONLY THE 6TH FLOOR?
HIG!
SHOULD I PRESS STOP?
NO... HANAKO'S UP THERE WAITING FOR US.
?
THAT'S OUR CLIENT'S DOOR.

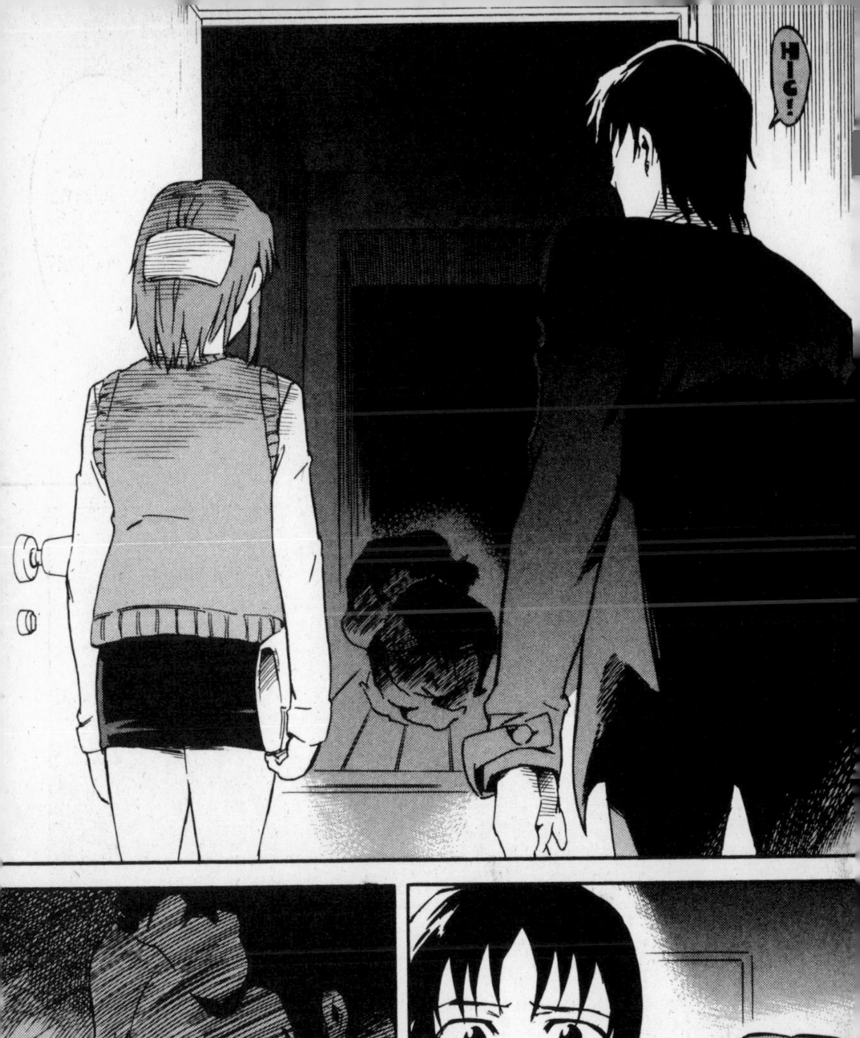
HIC!
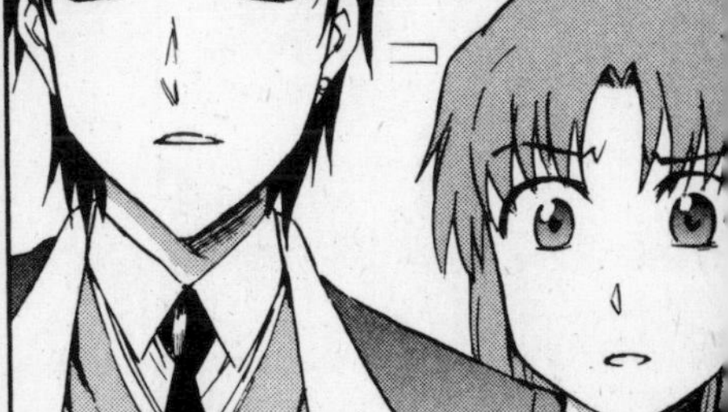
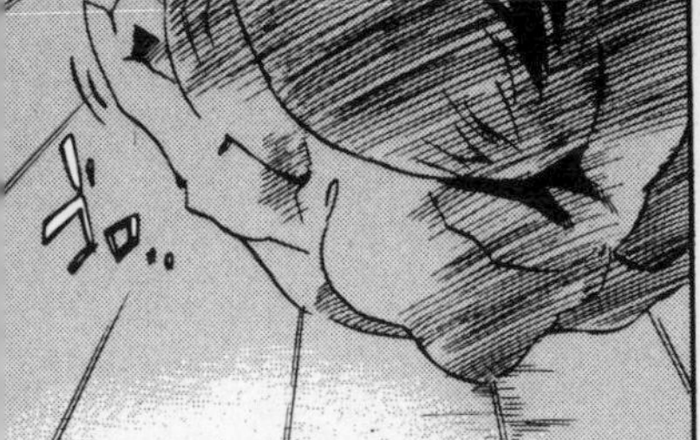
ゴロ..

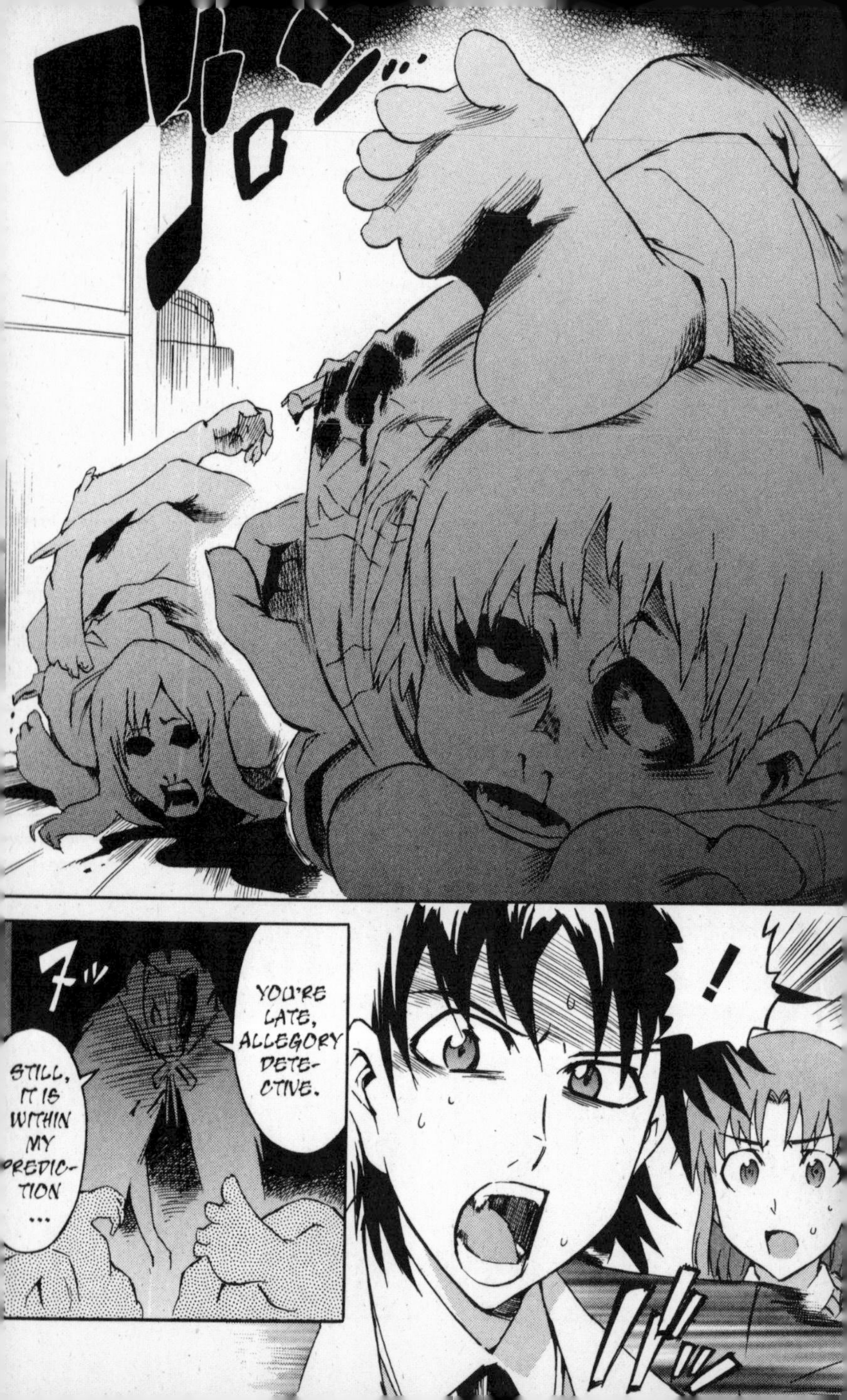
ゴロン…
!
YOU'RE LATE, ALLEGORY DETECTIVE.
フッ
STILL, IT IS WITHIN MY PREDICTION...

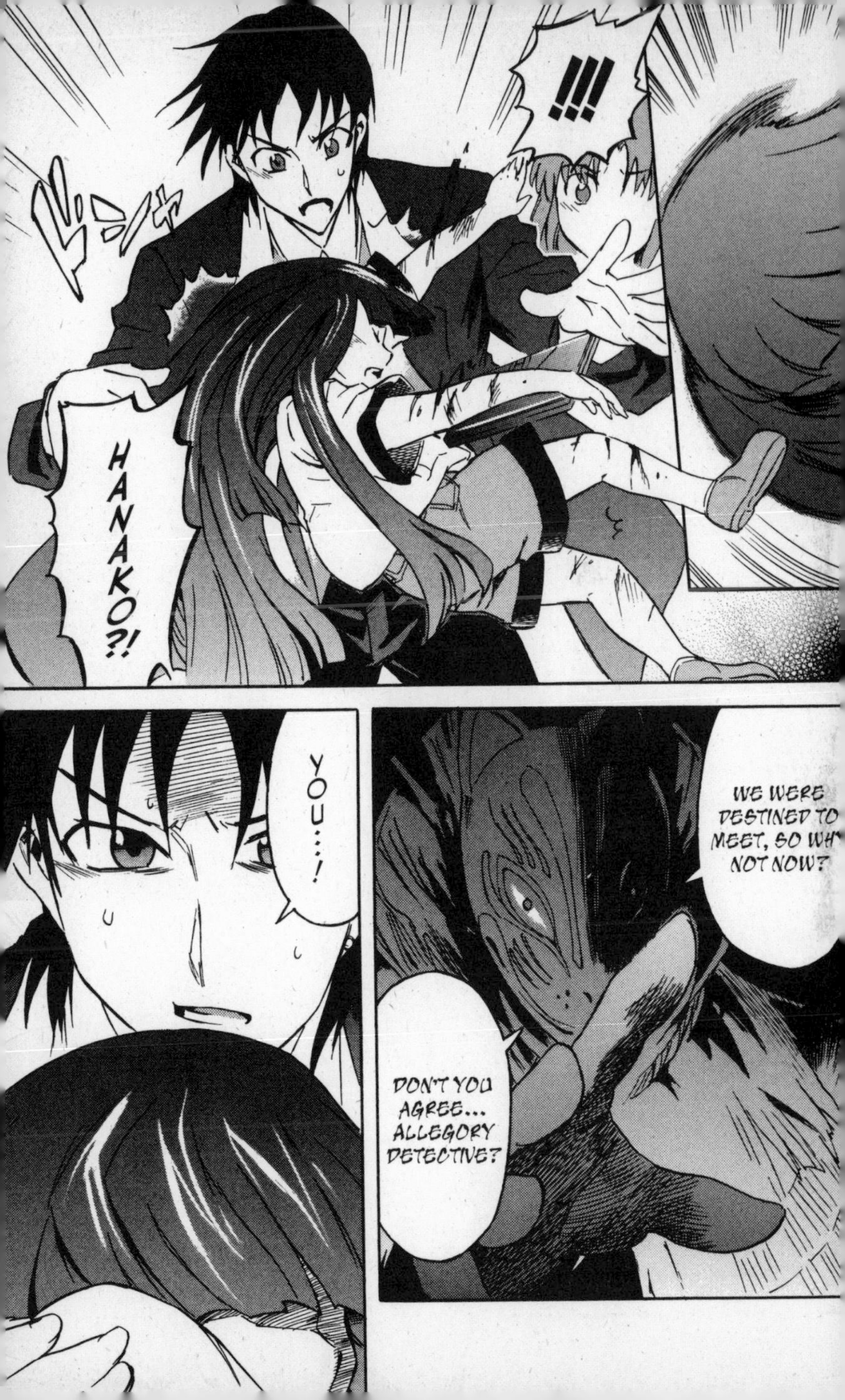
!!!
HANAKO?!
WE WERE DESTINED TO MEET, SO WHY NOT NOW?
DON'T YOU AGREE... ALLEGORY DETECTIVE?
YOU...!

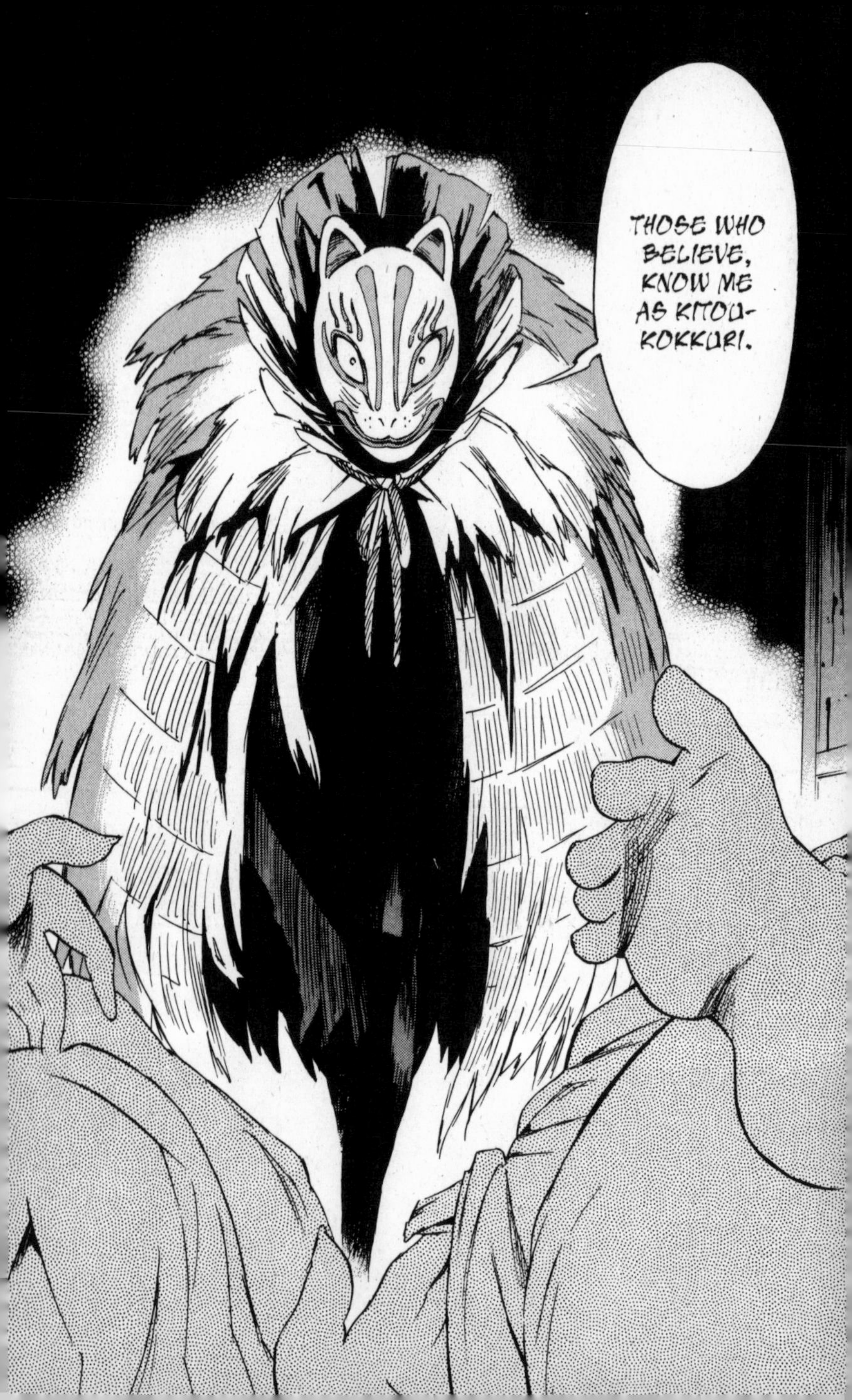
THOSE WHO BELIEVE, KNOW ME AS KITOU-KOKKURI.

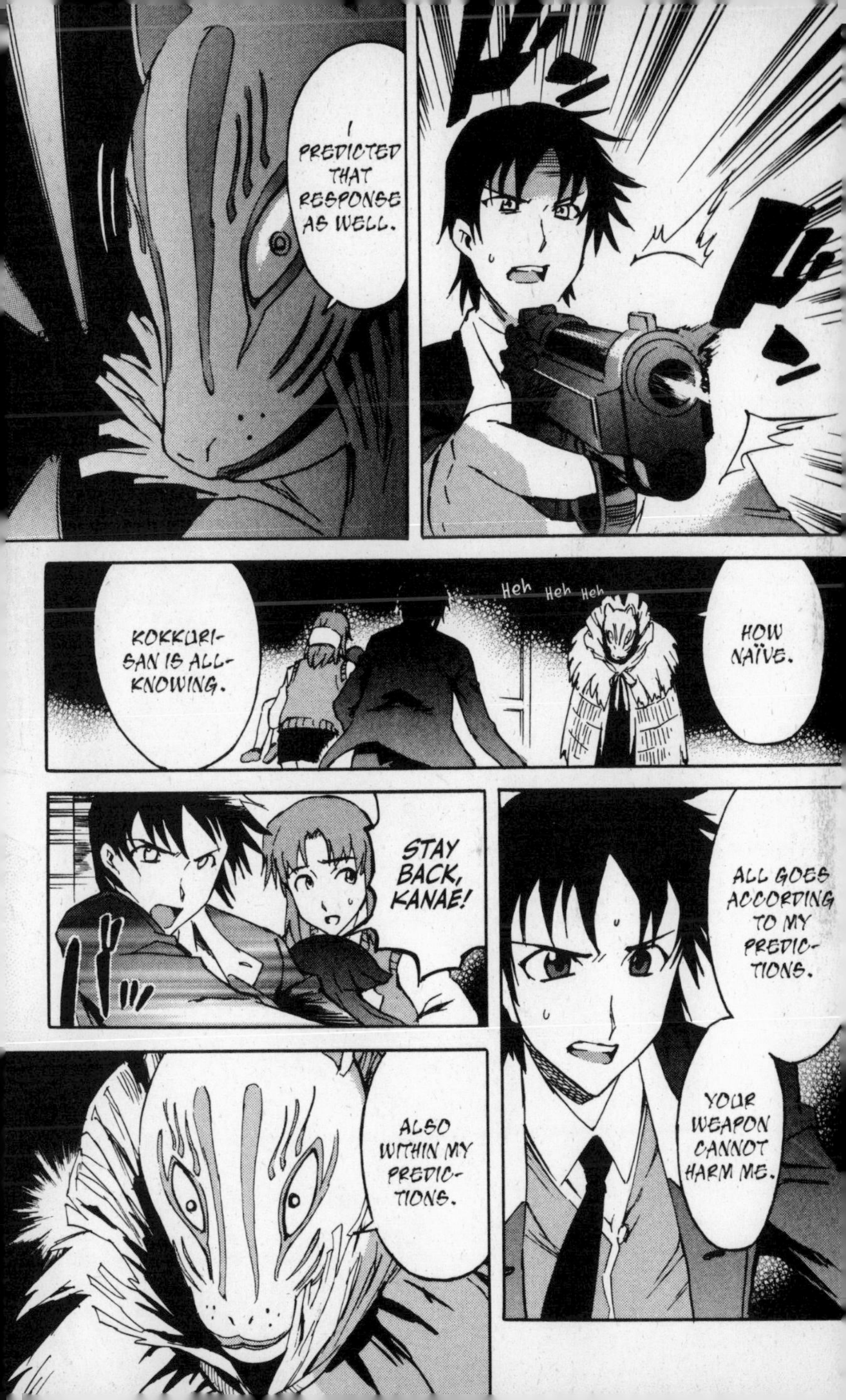
I PREDICTED THAT RESPONSE AS WELL.
HOW NAÏVE.
Heh Heh Heh
KOKKURI-SAN IS ALL-KNOWING.
ALL GOES ACCORDING TO MY PREDIC-TIONS.
YOUR WEAPON CANNOT HARM ME.
STAY BACK, KANAE!
ALSO WITHIN MY PREDIC-TIONS.

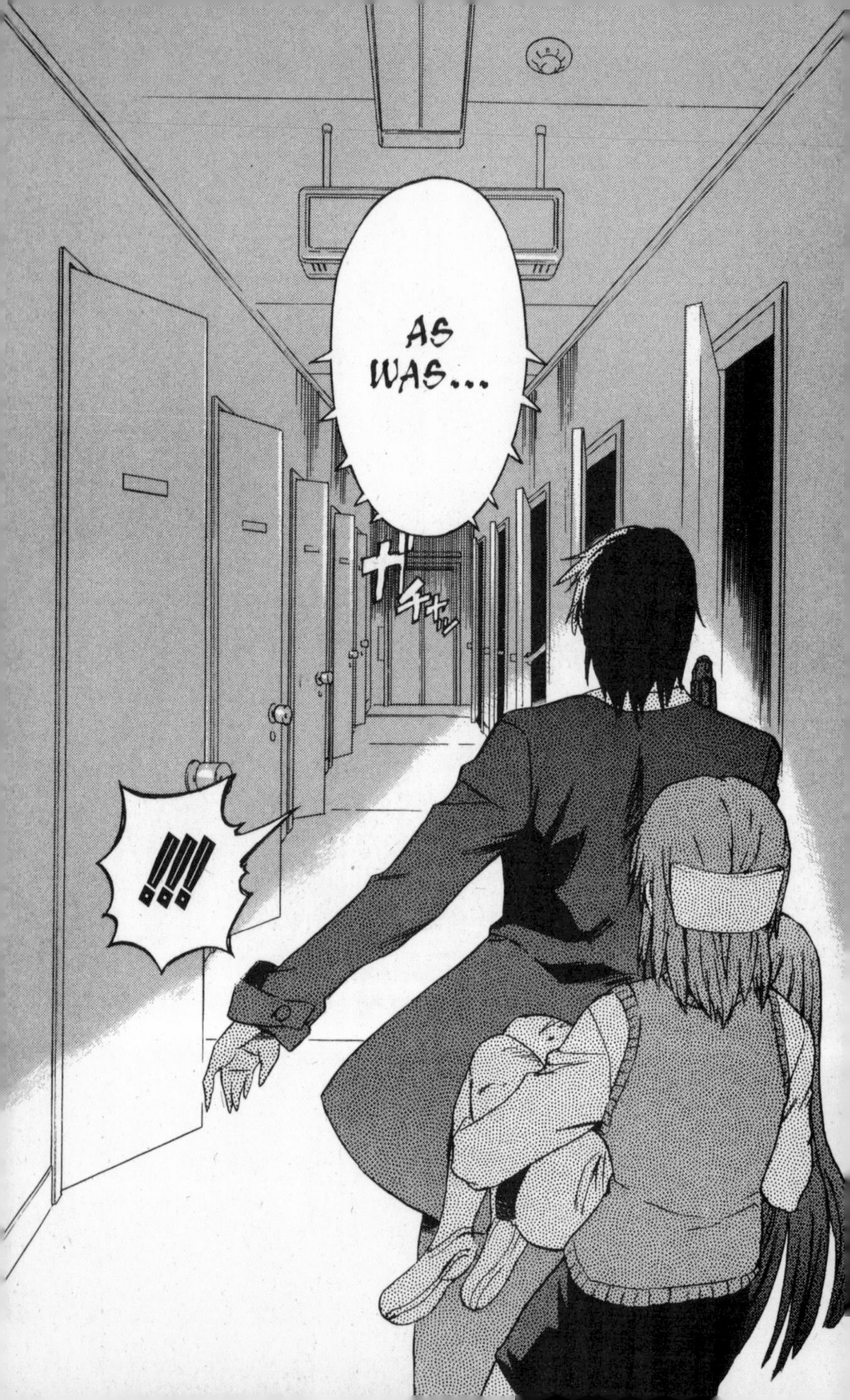
AS WAS...
ガチャン
!!!

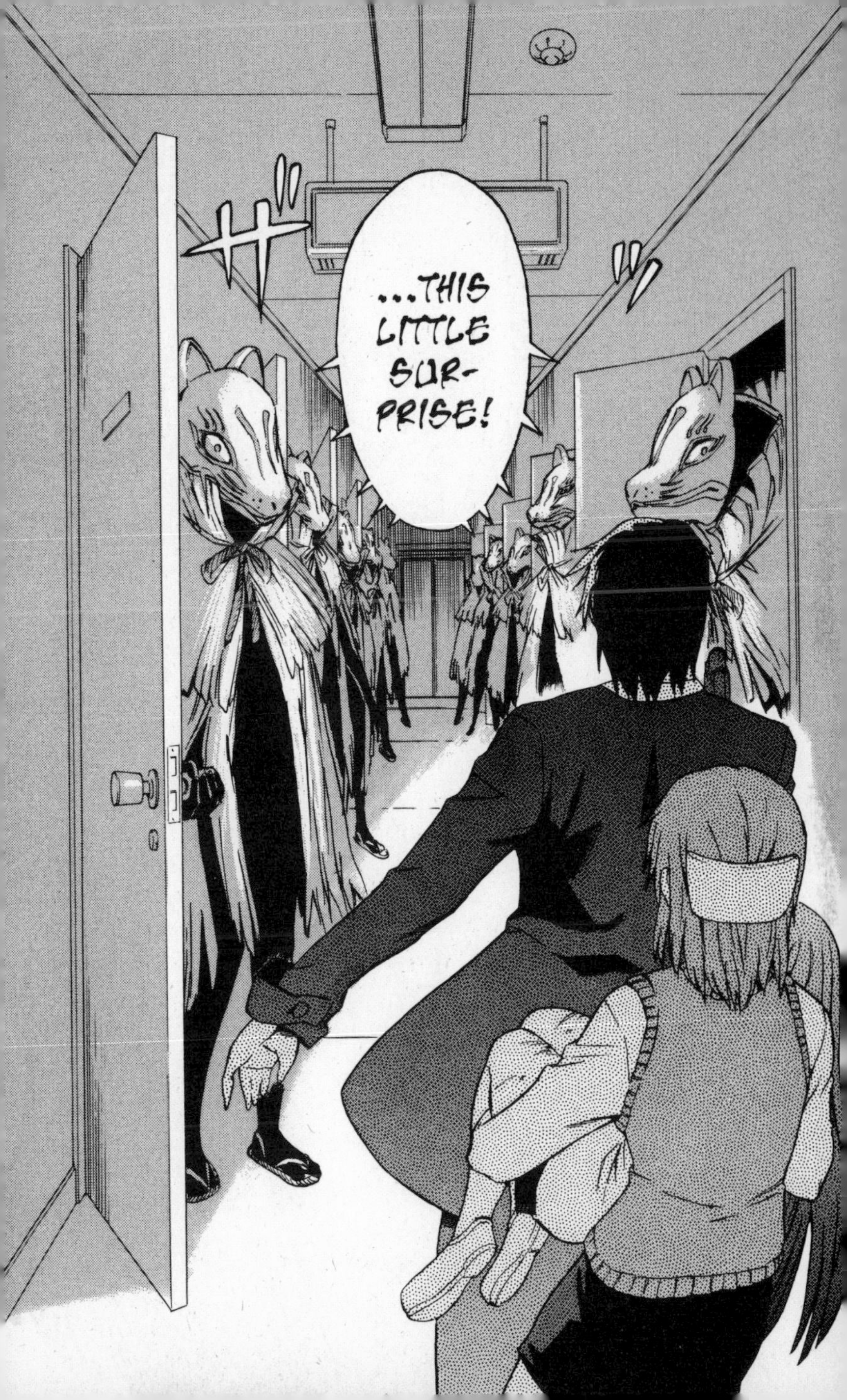
...THIS LITTLE SUR-PRISE!

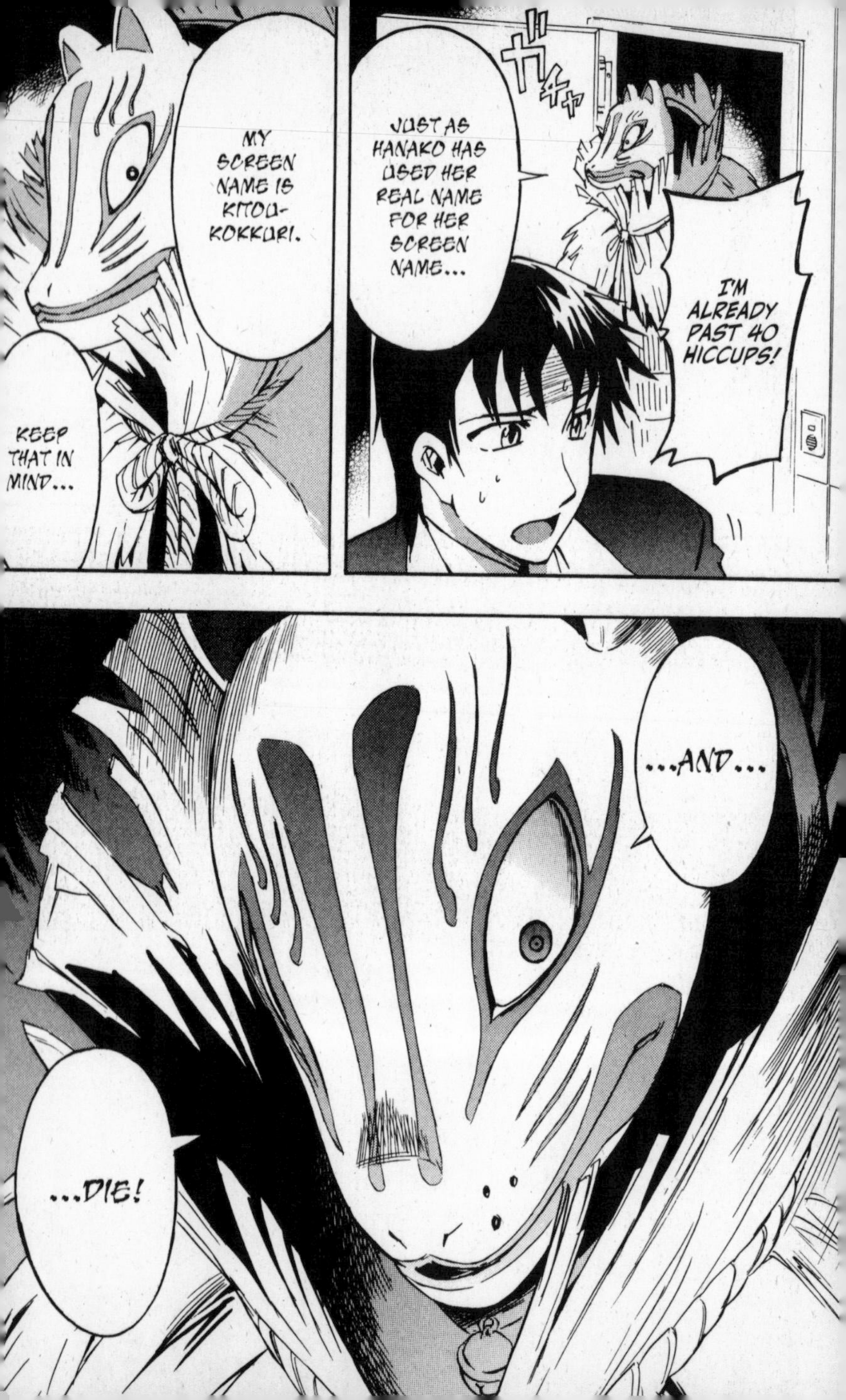

ガチャ
JUST AS HANAKO HAS USED HER REAL NAME FOR HER SCREEN NAME...
I'M ALREADY PAST 40 HICCUPS!
MY SCREEN NAME IS KITOU-KOKKURI.
KEEP THAT IN MIND...
...AND...
...DIE!

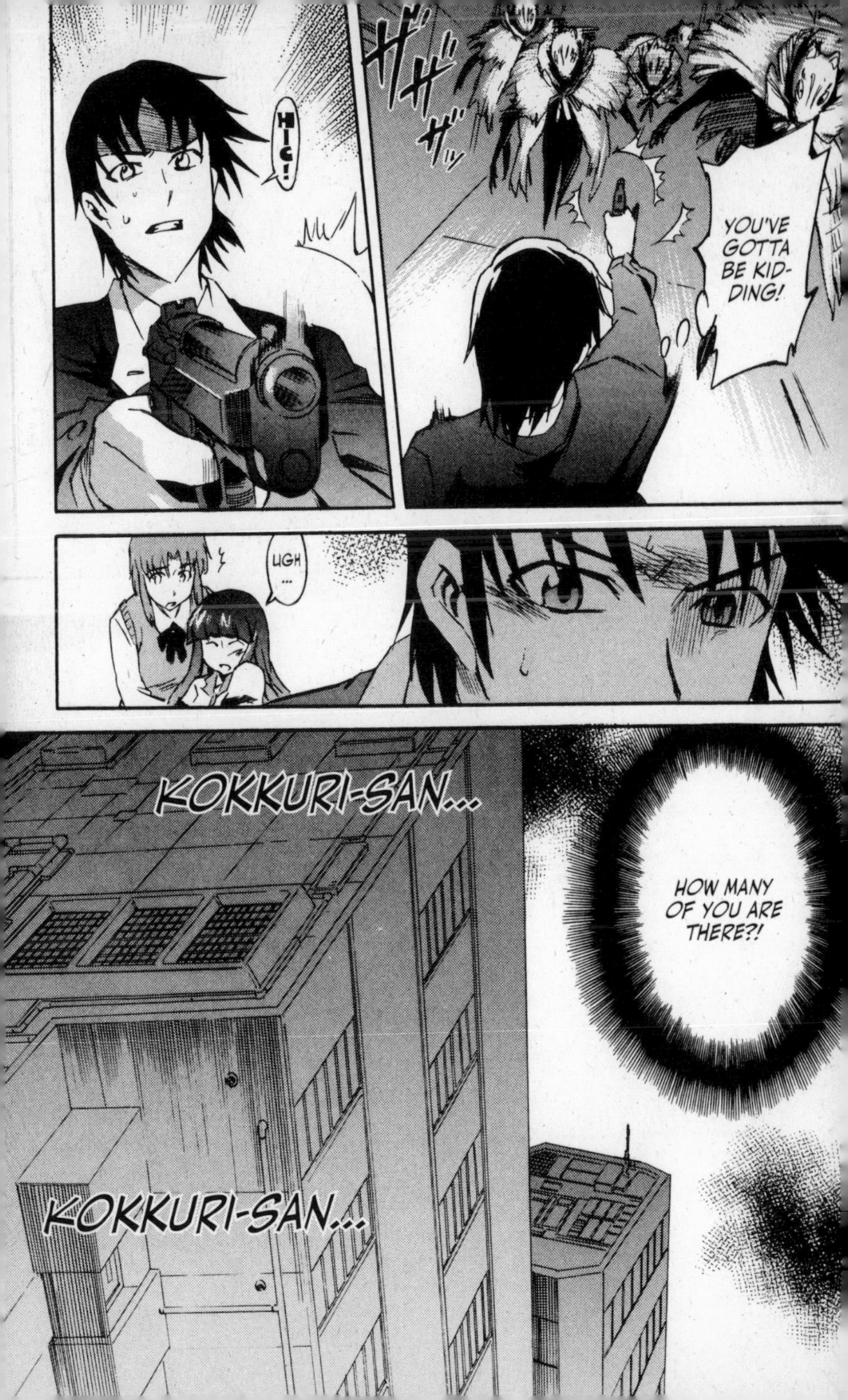
ザザザッ
YOU'VE GOTTA BE KID-DING!
HIC!
UGH ...
HOW MANY OF YOU ARE THERE?!
KOKKURI-SAN...
KOKKURI-SAN...

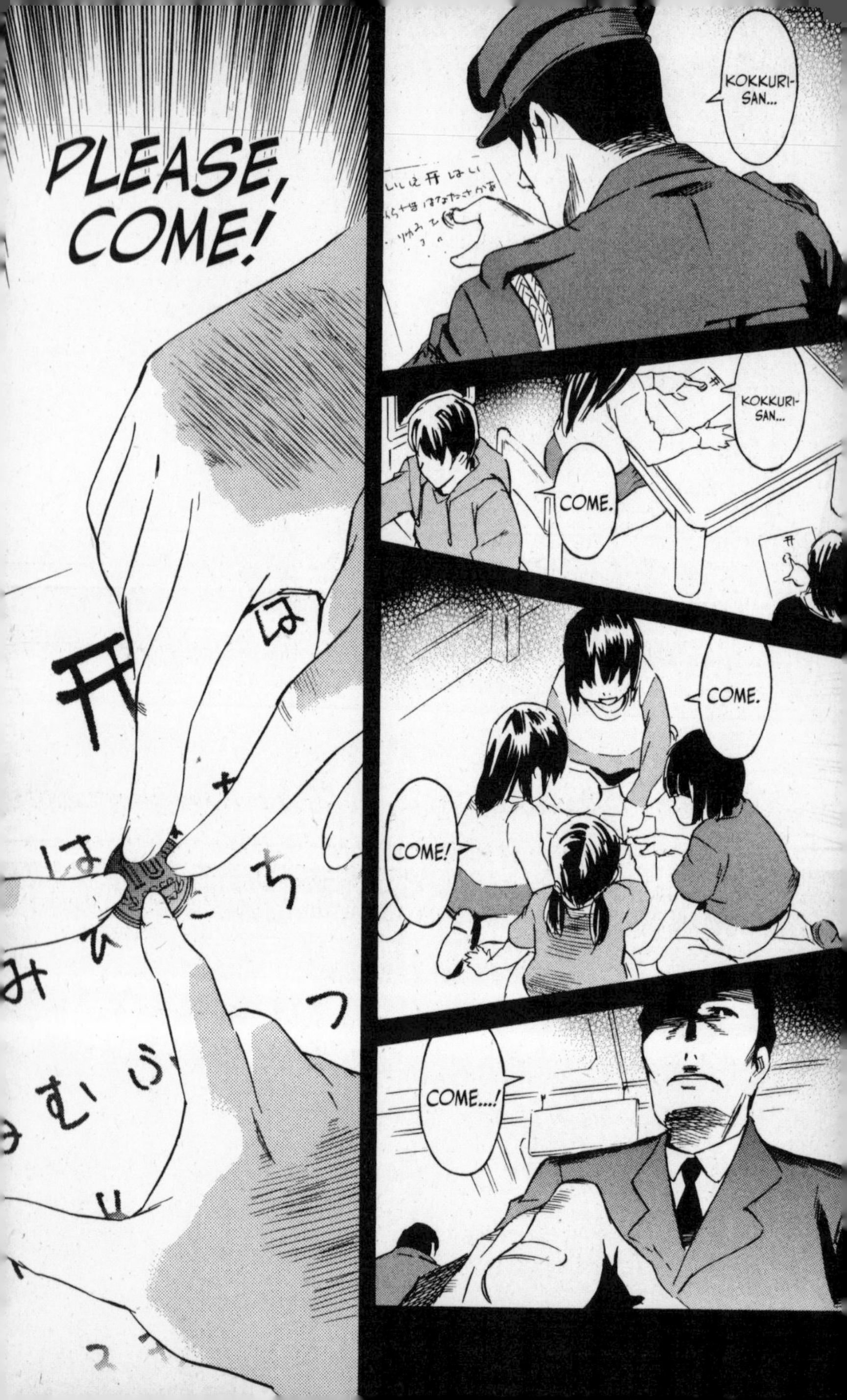
KOKKURI-SAN...
KOKKURI-SAN...
COME.
COME.
COME!
COME...!
PLEASE, COME!

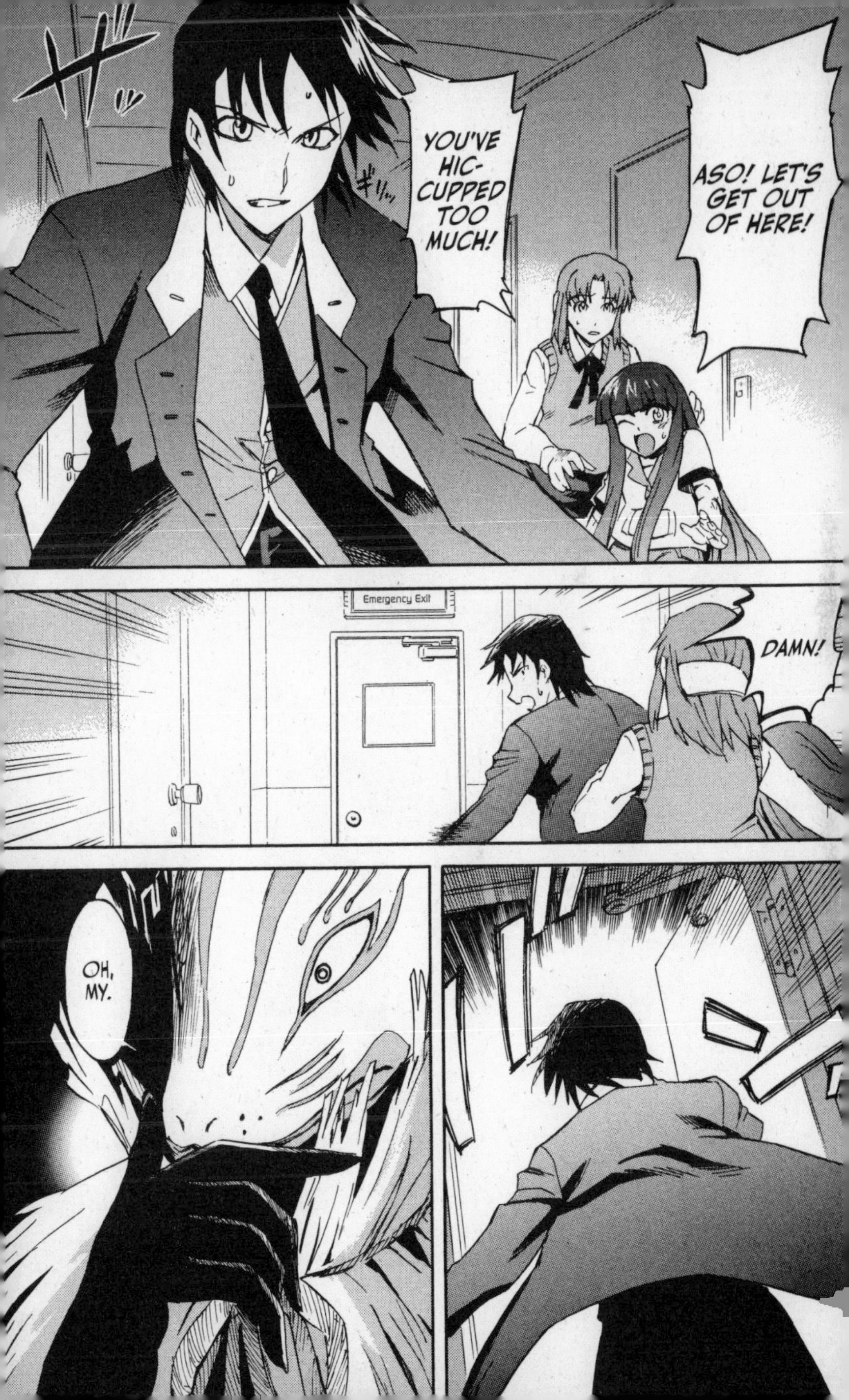

ASO! LET'S GET OUT OF HERE!
YOU'VE HIC-CUPPED TOO MUCH!
DAMN!
Emergency Exit
OH, MY.

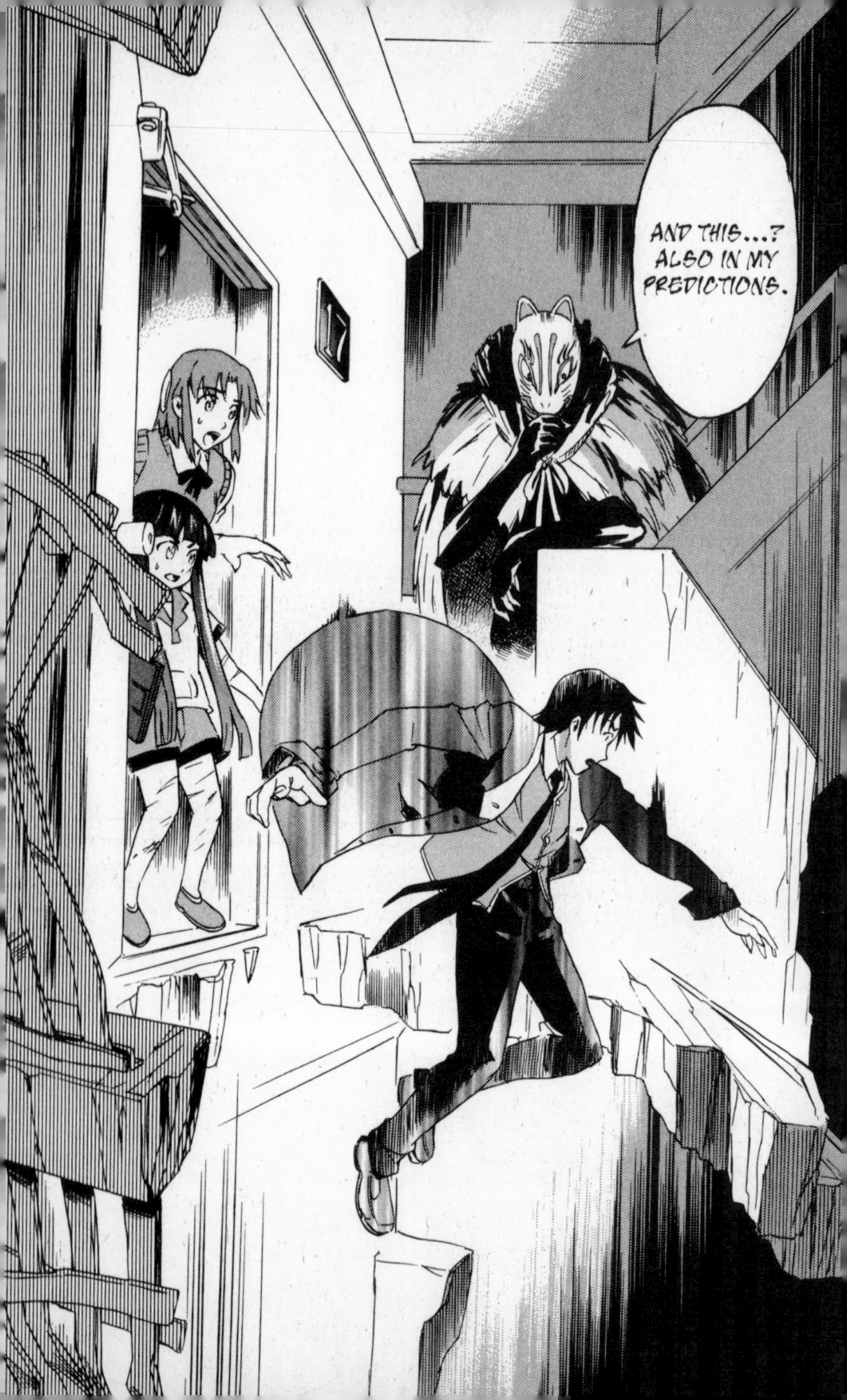
AND THIS...? ALSO IN MY PREDICTIONS.

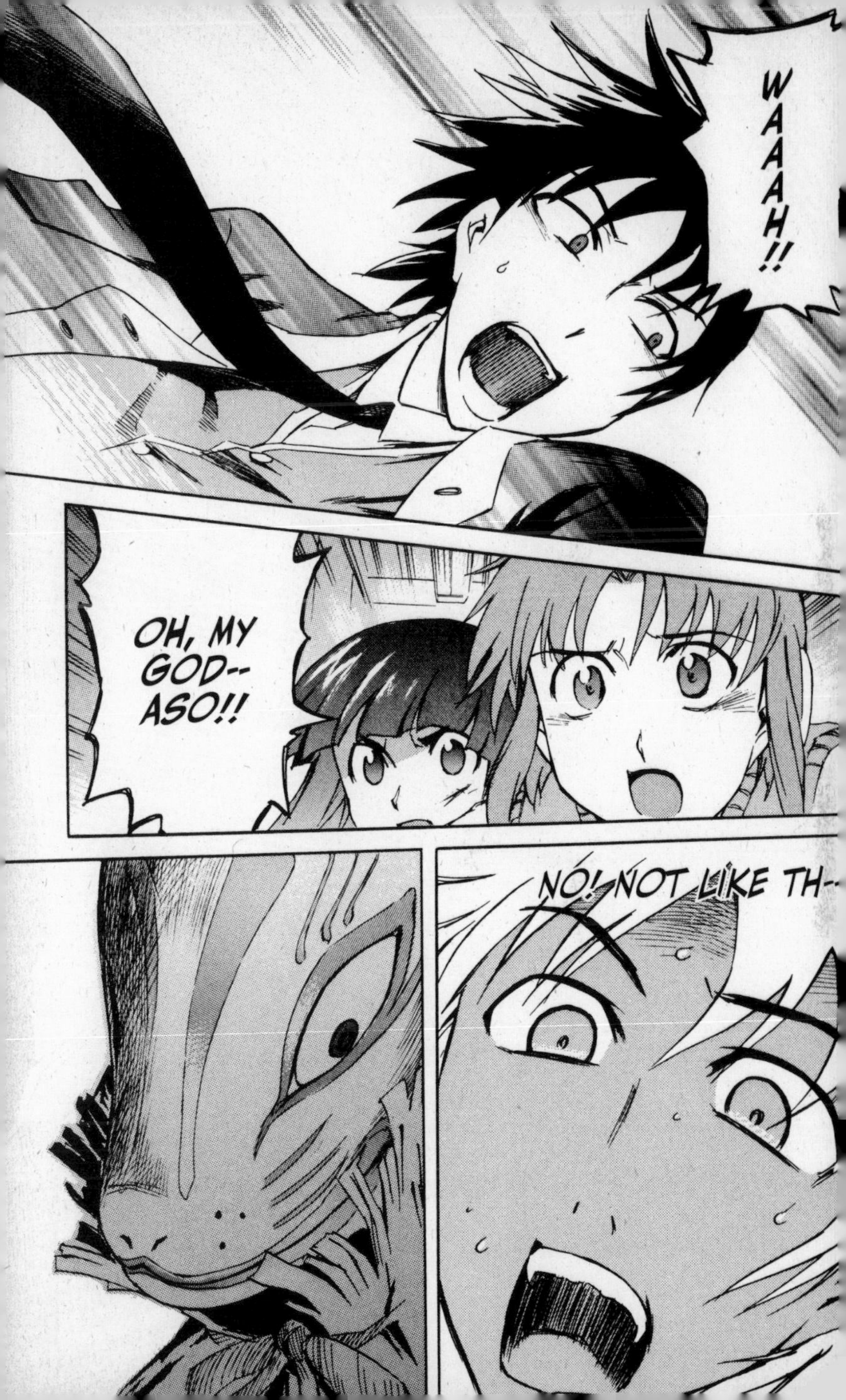
WAAAAH!!
OH, MY GOD-- ASO!!
NO! NOT LIKE TH--

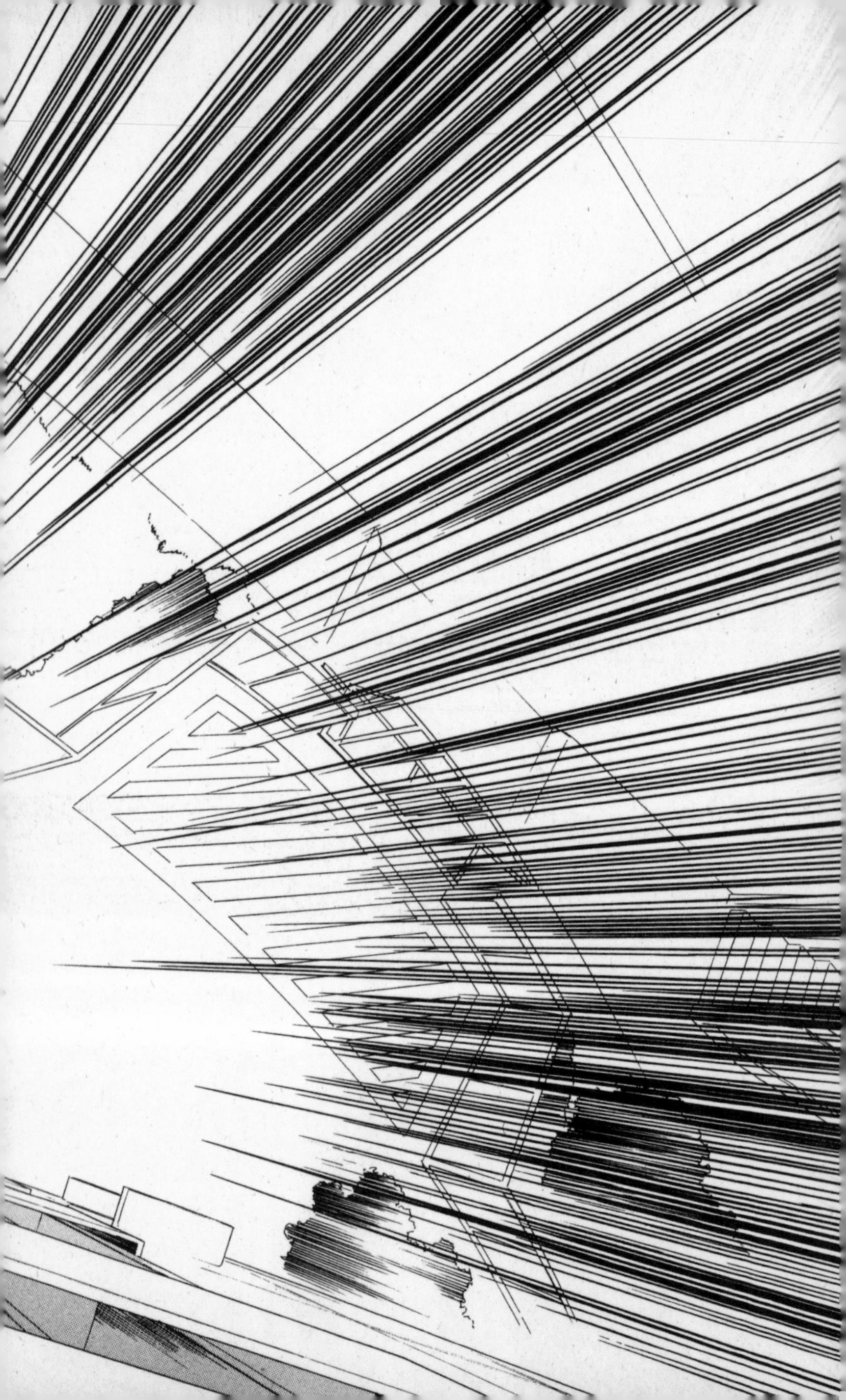

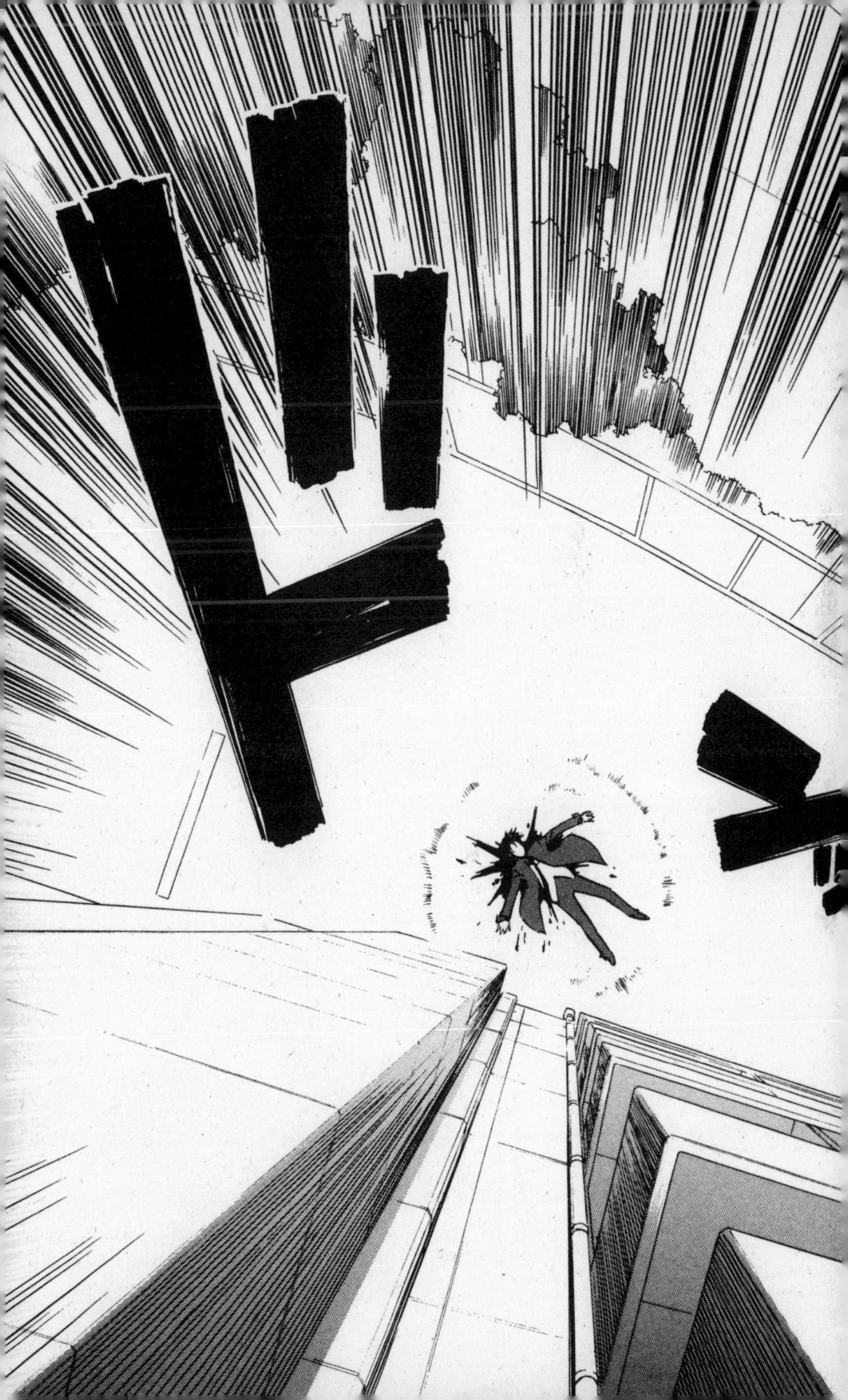
ド

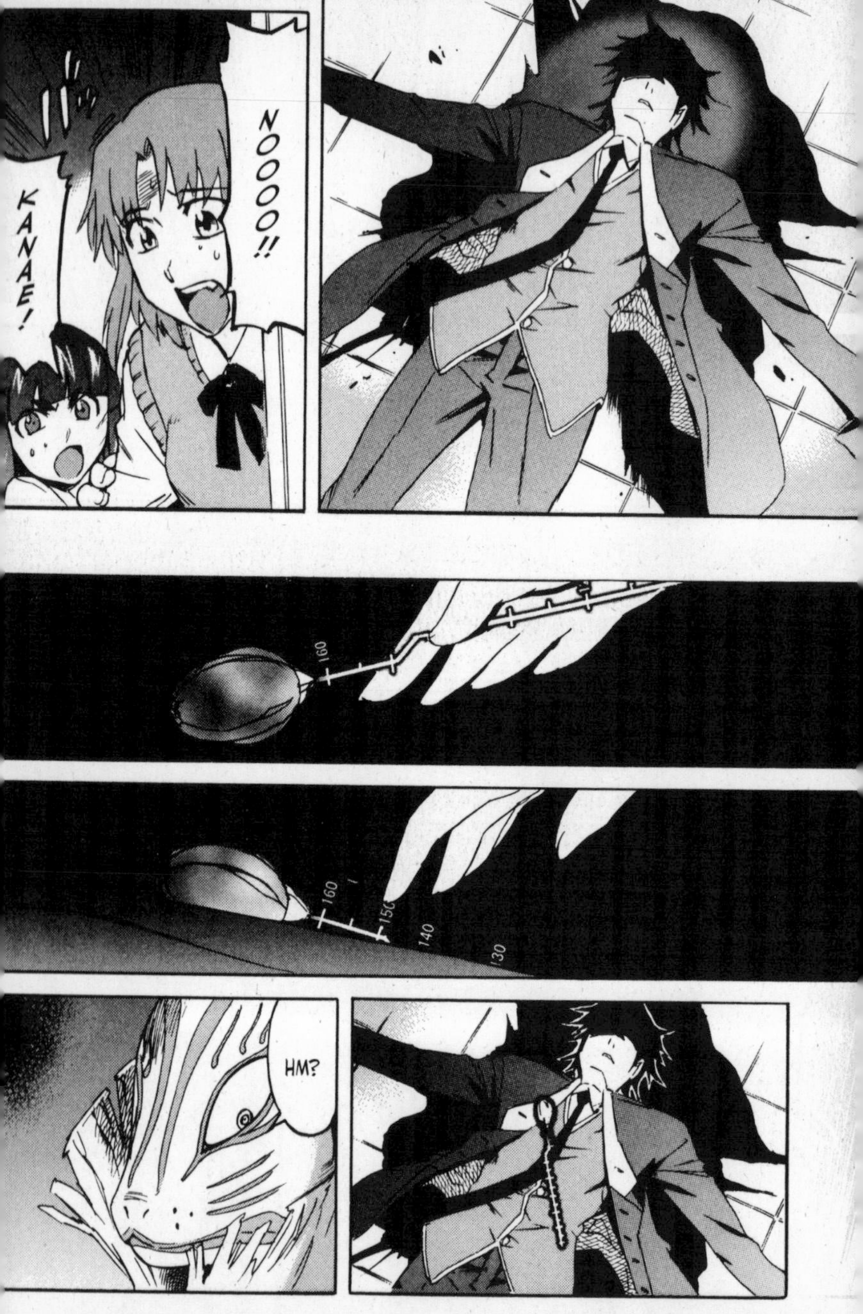
NOOOOO!!
KANAE!
160
160
150
140
130
HM?

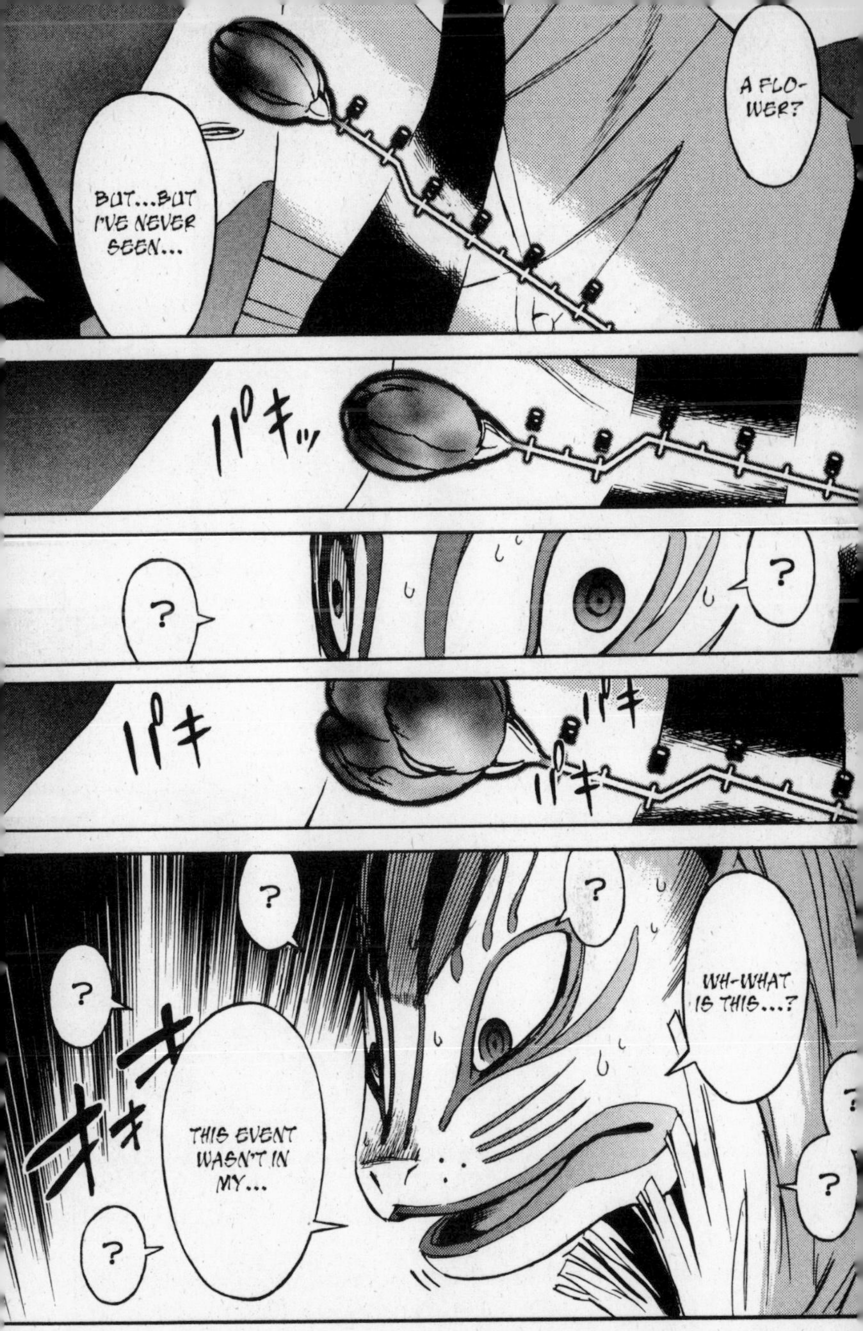
A FLO-
WER?
BUT...BUT I'VE NEVER SEEN...
パキッ
?
?
パキ
パキ
パキ
WH-WHAT IS THIS...?
?
?
?
THIS EVENT WASN'T IN MY...
?
?
オオ

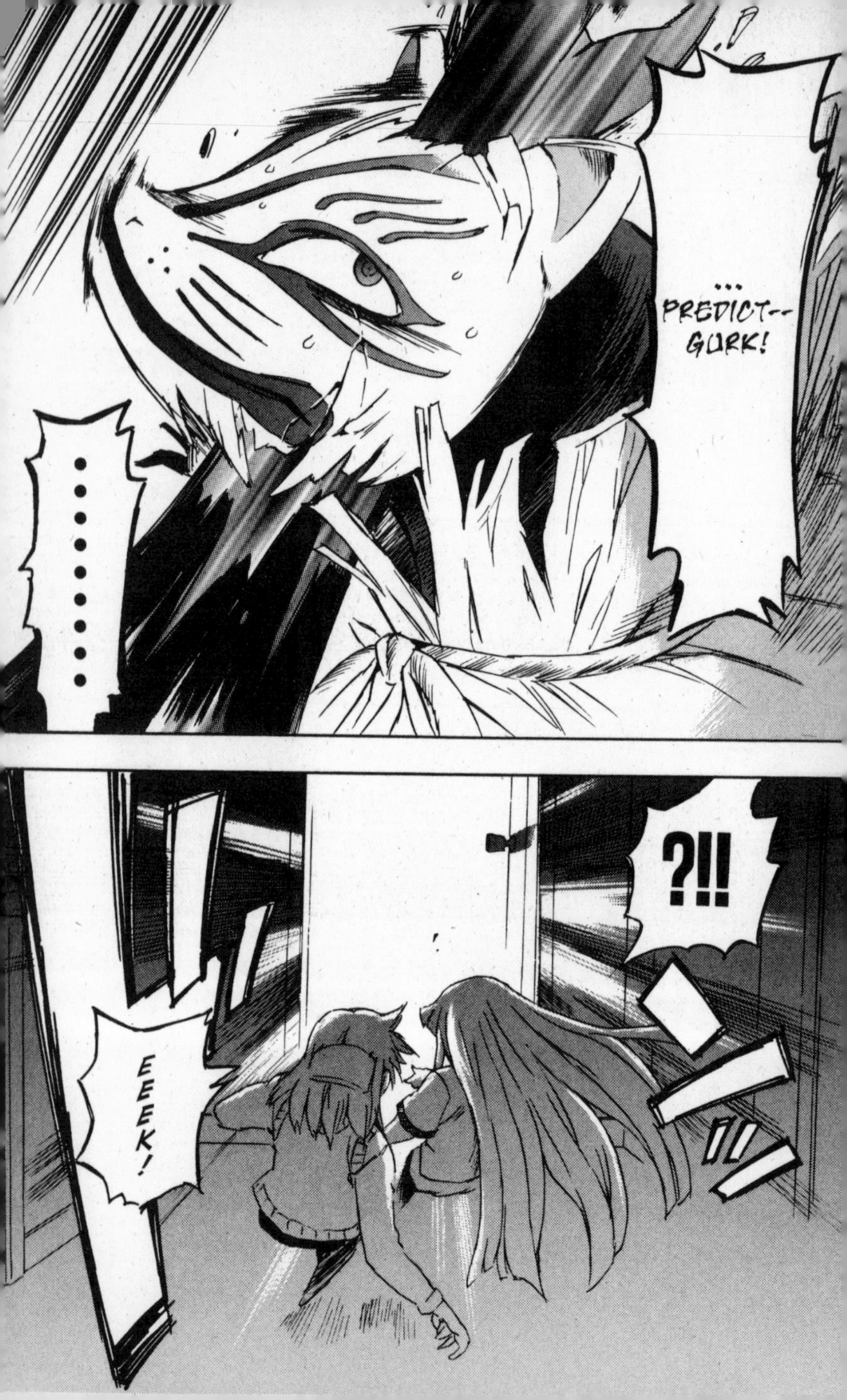
...PREDICT--GURK!
....
?!!
EEEK!

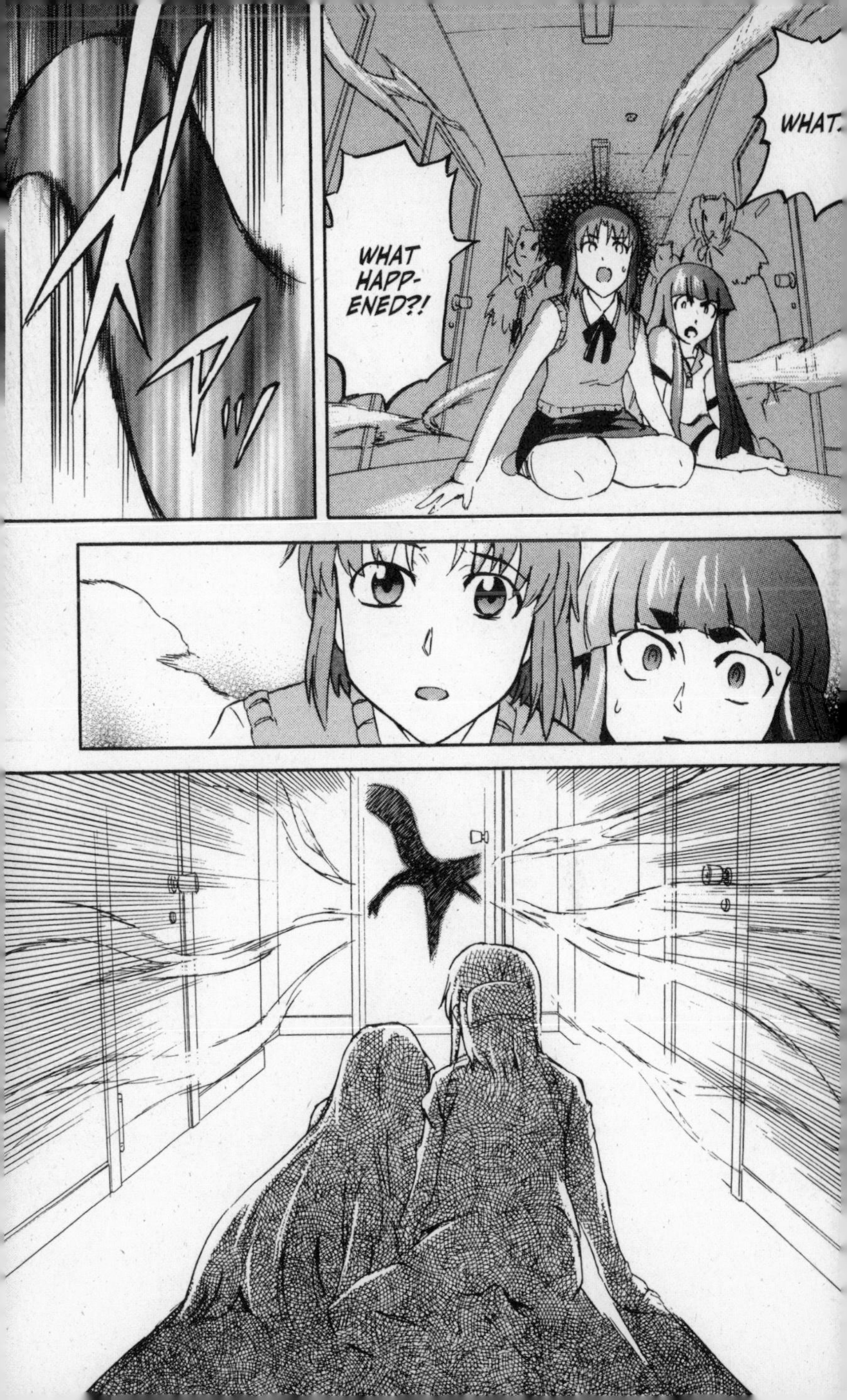
WHAT.
WHAT HAPPENED?!

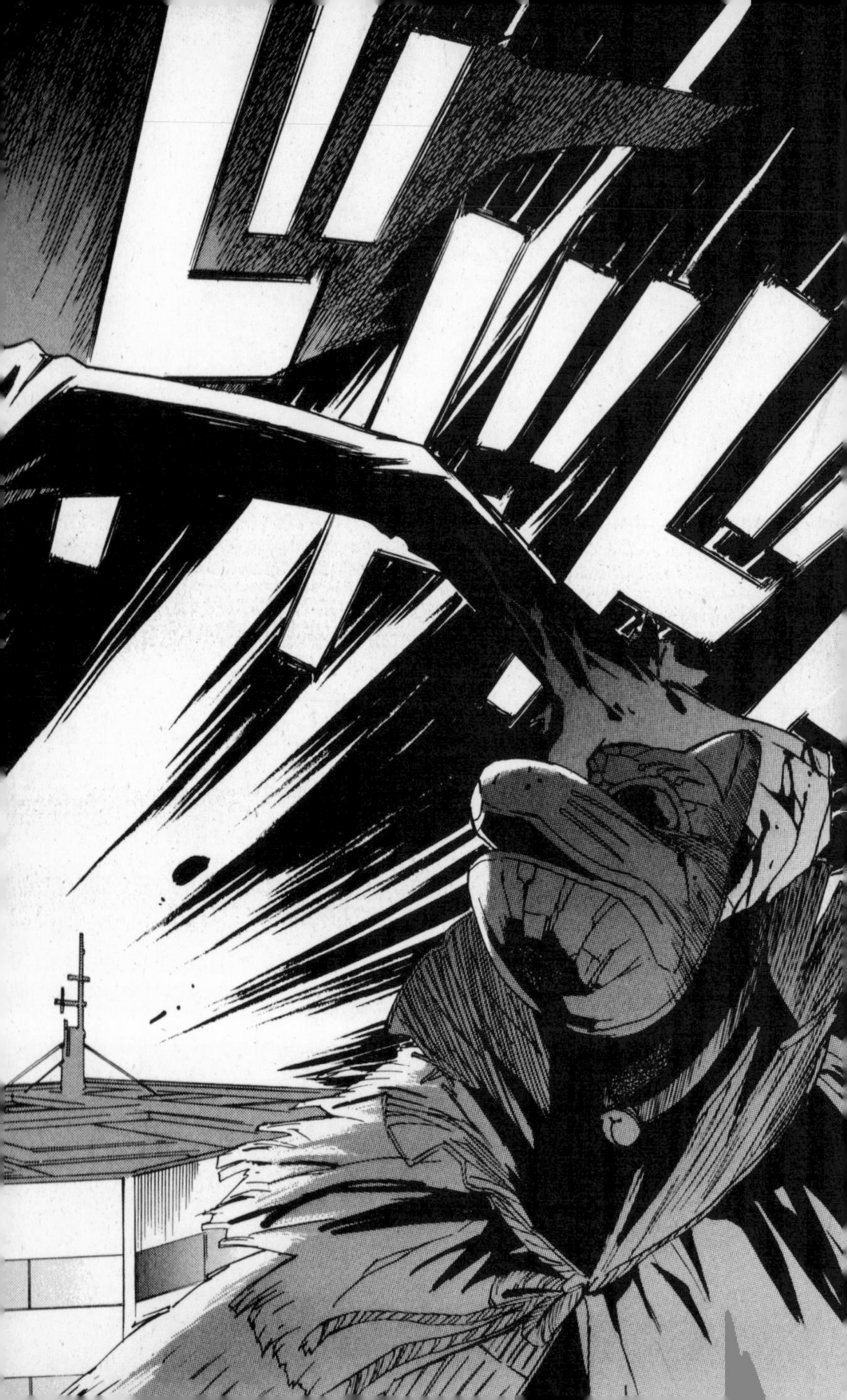

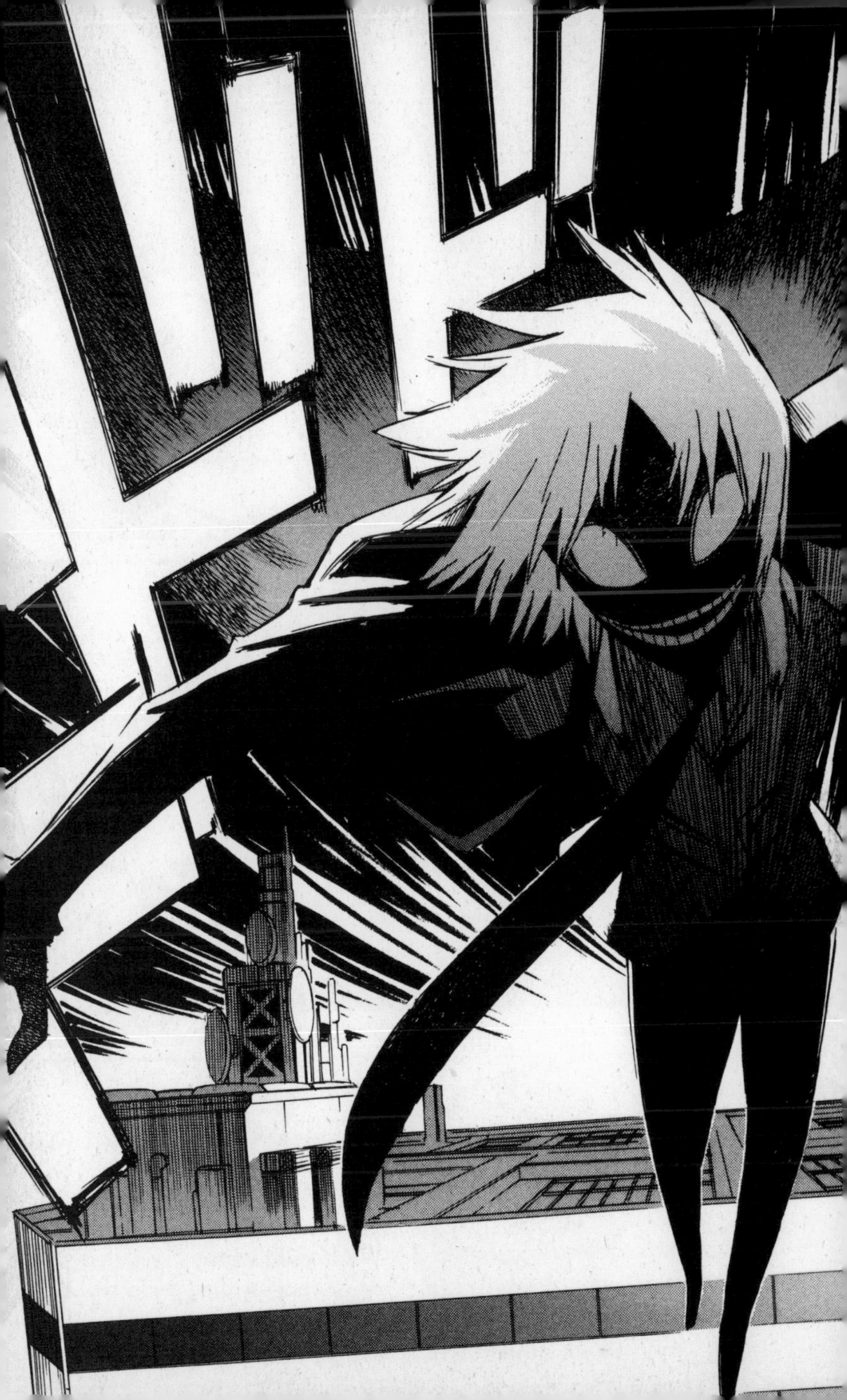

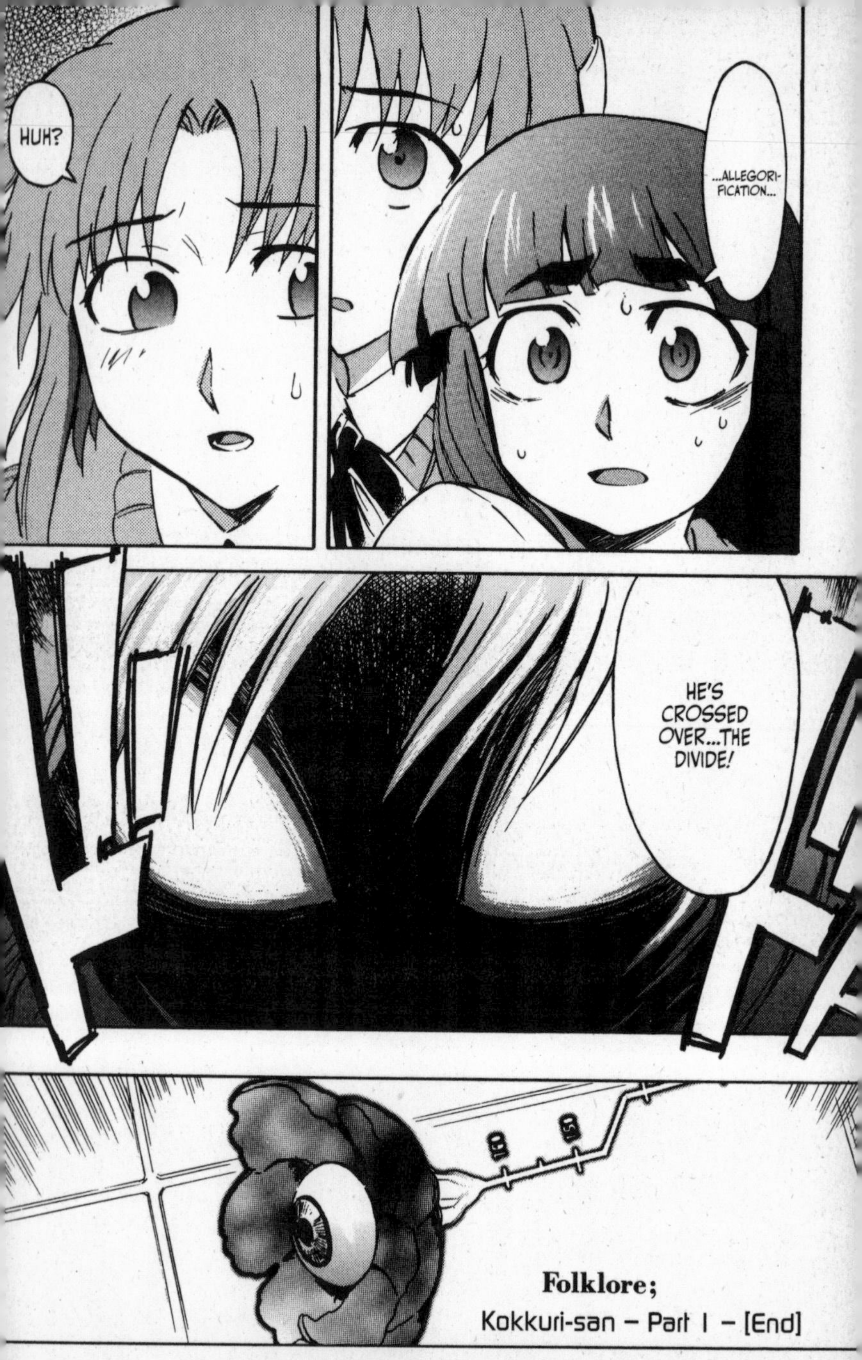
...ALLEGORIFICATION...
HUH?
HE'S CROSSED OVER...THE DIVIDE!
Folklore;
Kokkuri-san – Part 1 – [End]

to be continued... File;3

Commentary

The Demon in the Mirror

"If you face one mirror toward another at midnight, a Demon will appear."

A relatively well-known folklore. There are other variations, like it needing to be on Friday the thirteenth. Other twists include having your death mask reflect in the 13th mirror at 2 a.m., or if you face mirrors together at 4:44am you will die, and so on.

Facing Mirrors -- the sense of infinity and otherworldliness in reflecting a mirror's image in a mirror's image is fun to a childish mind, but the idea of seeing something else reflected in that image is an ancient fear.

THE DEMON WILL TAKE THE SOUL ...

Teke-Teke

Teke-Teke appears as the severed upper-torso of a woman, and "Teke-Teke" is the sound she makes as she uses her elbows to move. She is deceptively fast, able to chase her victims with terrifying speed before slicing them in two. The victim then becomes the next Teke-Teke.

Teke-Teke is often envisioned holding a sickle, an element also associated with the folklore of the Slit-Mouthed Woman. The motif of being lost is also similar to the folklore of Reiko Kashima, whose name is sometimes mistakenly attributed to Teke-Teke.

While folklore and urban legends usually propagate as rumors, they begin to take on specific characteristics and become more and more refined and unique, while still retaining certain common folklore tropes.

In addition to Teke-Teke, other fast-moving folklores include; Slit-Mouthed Woman, Jet Granny, Hanako of the Bathroom, Reiko Kashima, The Red-Caped Phantom, and many others.

The Piercing Hole and the White Thread

When a girl decides to get her first piercing she asks her friend to open the hole for her. When she does, a white thread comes out from the hole and, without thinking, the friend pulls it out. As soon as she does the girl's face becomes distorted.

"Hey, why did you turn off the lights?"

The white thread that her friend pulled was actually her optic nerve.

This is also a major folklore but subsequent to this, a strange offshoot version was born. If you walk through Shibuya, a girl, behind you, with her face looking down, will ask, "Hey, are you wearing earrings?" Never answer: "Yes, I am." If you do, she will hold you down with terrifying power and bite off your earlobes.

Actually, this girl is Kaori, the girl who lost her sight in the original white thread story.

Folklore based upon previous folklore is somewhat rare.

Kokkuri-san

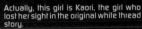

A form of spirit divination that is easy to attempt as long as you have paper and a ten yen coin. Consequently, many, many people have given it a try. There are times when it has also been called Cupid-san, Angel-san or Guardian Spirit-sama.

"Why does it move?"

There is a similar type of spirit divination called "table-turning," such as the Ouija board game. According to the physicist Michael Faraday, the movement of the coin, or playing piece, is caused by people unconsciously moving their muscles due to their intense anticipation or emotions. It is sometimes called "the ideometer effect."

...It appears that it has nothing to do with spirits or foxes.

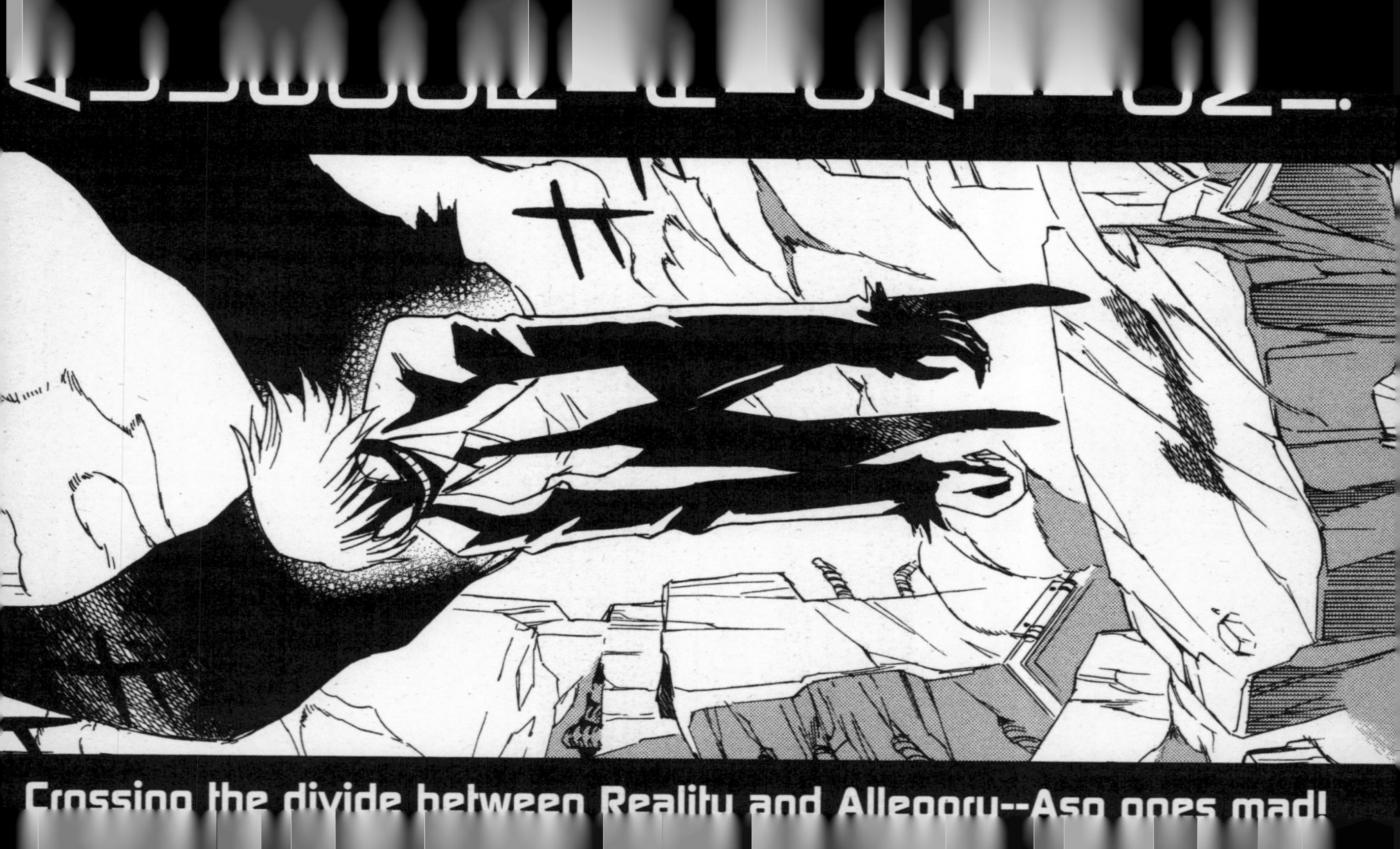

Crossing the divide between Reality and Allegory--Aso goes mad!

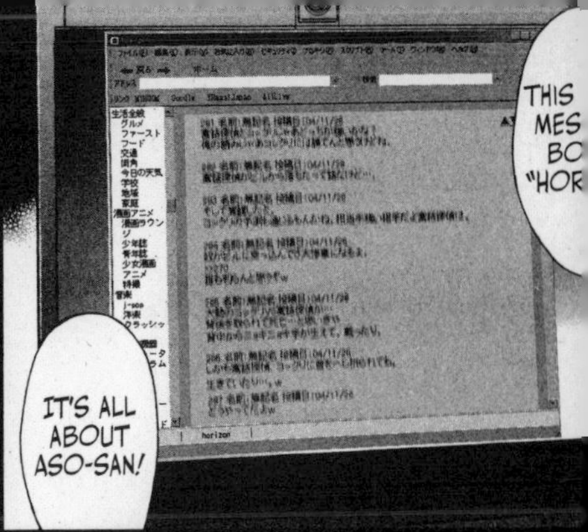
THIS
MES
BO
"HOR
IT'S ALL ABOUT ASO-SAN!

Kitou-Kokkuri is determined to eliminate the transmogrified Aso.

Who will survive in this battle of the Allegories?!

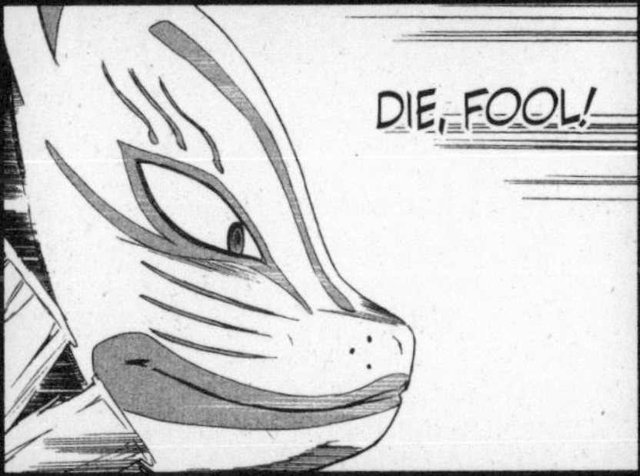
DIE, FOOL!

Can Hanako and Kanae return the Allegorification of Aso back to reality?!

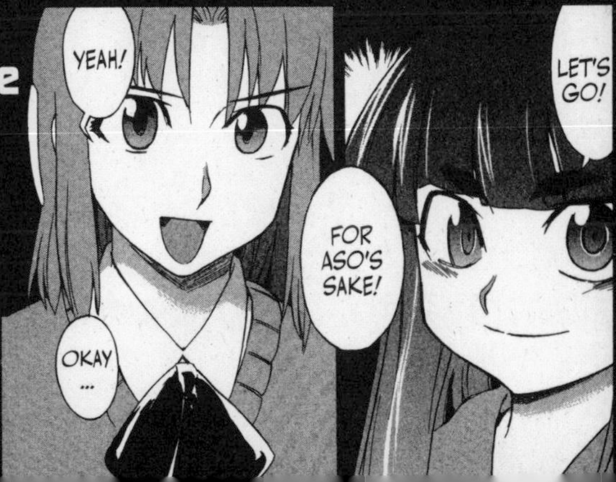
LET'S GO!
YEAH!
FOR ASO'S SAKE!
OKAY ...

Be here for the explosive 3rd volume!

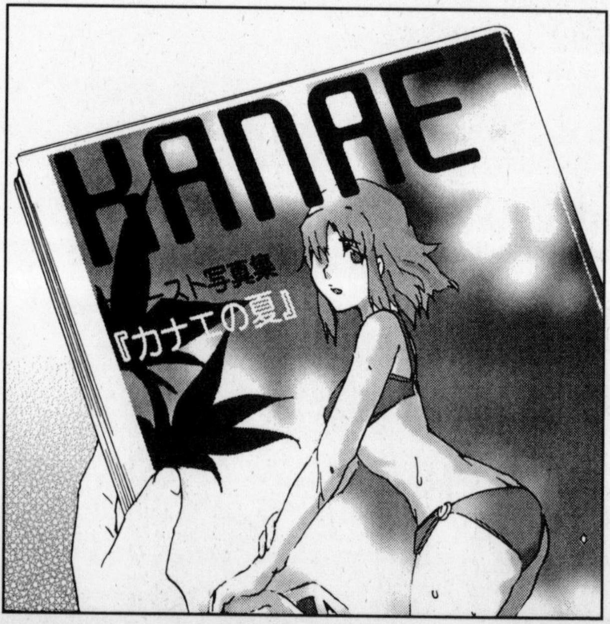
KANAE
ースト写真集
『カナエの夏』

カリ カリ カリ カリ

Editor's Notes

Cindy Suzuki

is month has been quite crazy! seems that everyone here in the ice is running around with new ojects and a ton more things ded to their to-do list. Crazy, azy…

Left to Right: Tida, Lily, Kate, Erinn, Dominique and Erin.

eaking of crazy, we just got unch of brand spankin' new erns that will be handling a huge tion of the logistics, market- and event planning for the KYOPOP Tour. Some will actually on the tour bus, and a few ers will be here in our L.A. office adquarters.

really cute seeing the new interns interact with each other and the rest of the TOKYOPOP family. get a fresh batch of bright-eyed and bushy-tailed interns every few months, and each group a unique personality of its own. This particular team has one intense mission, and I can feel ir energy as they stomp the halls and commandeer our normally quiet surfboard meeting table a manga and anime taskforce area of serious business.

at's also really interesting is that they're from all over the United States. We have some fellow elinos, a few from Colorado, a New Yorker, and there is even an intern from Alaska!! So I'd like ake this time to welcome our energized team…the very first group of talented, young individu- to join TOKYOPOP on an adventure of a lifetime.

you again next month!

ly Suzuki, Editor

exclusive updates, be sure to find us here:

v.TOKYOPOP.com
v.Facebook.com/TOKYOPOP
v.Twitter.com/TOKYOPOP

A TOKYOPOP® Manga
E-mail: info@TOKYOPOP.com
Come visit us online at www.TOKYOPOP.com

RightStuf.com asks...

"What kind of OTAKU are you?"

STOP!

This is the back of the book.
You wouldn't want to spoil a great ending!

This book is printed "manga-style," in the authentic Japanese right-to-left format. Since none of the artwork has been flipped or altered, readers get to experience the story just as the creator intended. You've been asking for it, so TOKYOPOP® delivered: authentic, hot-off-the-press, and far more fun!

DIRECTIONS

If this is your first time reading manga-style, here's a quick guide to help you understand how it works.

It's easy... just start in the top right panel and follow the numbers. Have fun, and look for more 100% authentic manga from TOKYOPOP®!